MINING WOMEN

Gender in the Development of a Global Industry, 1670 to the Present

Edited by

Jaclyn J. Gier

and

Laurie Mercier

palgrave
macmillan

MINING WOMEN

Copyright © Jaclyn J. Gier and Laurie Mercier, 2006.

All rights reserved.

First published in hardcover in 2006 by PALGRAVE MACMILLANÆ in the United States – a division of St. Martinís Press LLC, 175 Fifth Avenue, New York, NY 10010.

Where this book is distributed in the UK, Europe and the rest of the world, this is by Palgrave Macmillan, a division of Macmillan Publishers Limited, registered in England, company number 785998, of Houndmills, Basingstoke, Hampshire RG21 6XS.

Palgrave Macmillan is the global academic imprint of the above companies and has companies and representatives throughout the world.

Palgrave® and Macmillan® are registered trademarks in the United States, the United Kingdom, Europe and other countries.

ISBN: 978-0-230-62104-6

Library of Congress Cataloging-in-Publication Data is available from the Library of Congress.

A catalogue record of the book is available from the British Library.

Design by Newgen Imaging Systems (P) Ltd., Chennai, India.

First PALGRAVE MACMILLAN paperback edition: September 2009

10 9 8 7 6 5 4 3 2 1

Printed in the United States of America.

Transferred to Digital Printing in 2009

In Memory of Friends and Sisters

Reiko Miyauchi

Jennifer Keck

Jill Gier-Meyer

Jaclyn J. Gier

CONTENTS

PREFACE

We began this book project on mining women at the start of a new millennium with the joint hope that we might come to understand the role of women in relation to an industry that for nearly three hundred years of the previous one had little acknowledged their presence. The journey we began five years ago to study gender in the mining industry has taken us jointly and separately to many places—from Anchorage, Alaska to Istanbul, Turkey, from Akabira, Japan to New South Wales, Australia, from eastern Ukraine to Erfurt, East Germany, and from Montana, USA to Yorkshire, UK.

In our travels, we have benefited from the wise counsel of many scholars and organizations that have lent support and helpful criticism, most especially the Working-Class History Group at the University of Pittsburgh: Marcus Rediker, Maurine Greenwald, Wendy Goldman, and Joe White, among others, had many helpful suggestions. In Amsterdam, Lex Heerma Von Voss and Aad Blok at the International Institute for Social History have encouraged us to think globally, along with participants in the European Social Science History Conference in the Hague and in Berlin. Back in the United States, Chris Corey, Senior Program Officer for International Studies at the U.S. Department of Education and Professor Tony Judt at NYU's Remarque Center for Twentieth Century Studies, advanced our international education and reminded us of the European roots of the global mining industry. Palgrave's anonymous reviewers also pointed us in constructive directions. The International Oral History Association, Japan Oral History Association, and Oral History Association (USA) have reminded us that the voices of workers and indigenous peoples must be recorded to be heard. Harriet Jones at the Institute for Contemporary British History, Shani de Cruz and Meg Allen at the University of Manchester, Angela John at the University of Greenwich, and the Women's History Network in Great Britain have been there to remind us that women have been among the friends (and sometimes foes) of the mining industry. And Wyn Thomas and Dewi Gregory of the BBC confirmed the popular media appeal of our topic. Tom Sheridan and Graham Smith of the Australian Society for the Study of Labor History would provide friendship and a basis for understanding the Australian labor movement and the British Council a fellowship at University of Adelaide Center for British Studies and Center for Women's Studies. The University of Erfurt provided a Maria Sybilla Merian Fellowship, where colleagues Alf Luedtke, Theresa Wobbe, Jürgen Backhaus, and Dorthea Wierling, offered insights into the German mining tradition and gender history in eastern

Europe. Mercedes Steedman and Elizabeth Jameson shared their knowledge of Canadian and U.S. mining. Deirdre McCloskey in Europe and in the United States offered encouragement, enthusiasm, and friendship. Kayoko Yoshida of Sapporo, Japan, organized our travels to her country and provided us with hospitality beyond our wildest dreams. Washington State University Vancouver (WSUV) provided travel and collaboration assistance and the WSU College of Liberal Arts a completion grant. Candice Goucher, Barbara Campbell, and Linda Shopes provided astute guidance on many aspects of the book process, and Shari Clevenger and Marie Loudermilk at WSU helped maintain our sanity with technical assistance. Charlene Winslow, Chuck Zuzack, Bill McKinney, Adriane Martin, Peggy Denning, Eric Schreuers and the women of Gamma Sigma Sigma at SRU all supported, and gave advice when needed. Melissa Nosal at Palgrave Macmillan Press provided patiently logistical, technical, and moral support. Alex Viskovatoff helped greatly with editing, production processes, discussions of economic history, and intellectual support. John Hryciuk listened and loved. Friends Bill, Melissa, and Quinn Hulings lent support along the way, as did long-term British colleagues John Walton, Ritchie Ovendale, Rosemary Jones, and Phillip Ogden. Long over due thanks to Women Against Pit Closures and the South Wales Women's Support Group, especially Sian James, Kathe Jones, and Margaret Donavan. and to Abigail Porter for her wonderful photos and moral support. The strengths of this book are the result of collaboration and input from many colleagues and friends, not the least of which were our international contributors. We hope that our collaboration and work on this book is fruitful for our readers: we know that it has been for us.

Preface to the Paperback Edition

Shortly after the publication of this book, in October 2006, my co-editor Jaclyn J. Gier died of pancreatic cancer after fighting a year-long illness. Family, students, scholars and friends around the world have mourned her passing. Jaci would be very pleased to know of the enthusiastic reception of *Mining Women* and of continued efforts to investigate the intersections of mining work, gender roles, women's lives, and global capital.

Much of that work in recent years has reflected a heightened interest in addressing gender inequalities in mining. Women, especially in the developing world, bear disproportionate burdens associated with mining, including land and water pollution, HIV/AIDS, and sexual violence, without sharing the benefits of jobs that are typically reserved for men. Women have pressured governments, corporations, civil society groups, and NGOs to rectify these inequities. Many mining companies from Australia to Zimbabwe have begun to employ more women in their operations. The World Bank has supported projects to address gender bias in the mining sector, including its Women and Mining Action Plan in Papa New Guinea. NGOs such as Oxfam have assisted women in West Africa to seek legal redress from mining companies for environmental damage; other projects have advocated for the women who sometimes compose almost half of the labor force in artisanal and small-scale mining. The International Women and Mining Network, with members in over 30 countries, has led campaigns to protect human rights and sometimes to block mining where indigenous practices are threatened in India and the Philippines. Highlighting these changes, a contributor to this volume, Kuntala Lahiri-Dutt of the Australian National University, organized an international conference held in Canberra in November 2008 to assess the social, economic and political factors that affect the relationship between mining, gender and sustainable livelihoods. While we explore the ways that transnational corporations, governments, and international institutions can integrate women more fully in mining jobs, we might also ask whether mining—by its very nature socially and environmentally disruptive—can ultimately sustain women and men and their communities.

The past and the essays in this volume offer insights about the promises of mining sustainability and the realities of commodity production. Often invisible to the process are women, who, these essays demonstrate, histori-cally have been critical to mining work, communities, and protests. As a global industry, mining reveals how the seemingly rigid category of gender has been forged, resisted, and reshaped through time. In Jaci Gier's memory we continue the study and struggles of women in the mining world.

Introduction

Laurie Mercier and Jaclyn J. Gier

This is a book about women and mining history. This may seem a curiosity to many readers, given the apparent gender bias of the mining industry in favor of men, and at least historically, the marginal role played by women in miners' unions. But a focus on this most "masculine" of industries allows us to contribute to important discussions about the centrality of gender in shaping women's history, labor history, social history, and world history. The seminal work of Joan Scott and others articulated and shifted the parameters of women's history by identifying gender, or the sex roles for men and women, as not biologically fixed but socially constructed.[1] In so doing, many scholars have worked to interpret the relationship between social institutions, historical events, and culture-bound definitions of gender.

Women's historians now refer to gender relations rather than simply gender roles, and seek to discern gender identities as they emerge in particular social, cultural, and historical contexts. Then too, these scholars have begun to reassess the historical position of women relative to their productive and reproductive roles in the family, and their often undervalued roles as producers in the shadow economy of goods and unwaged services. But beyond this, women's historians have begun to examine the larger forces of a global history that have impacted upon and delineated definitions of gender difference historically and cross-culturally. For example, we cannot speak of the Industrial Revolution without some reference to "the division of labor," knowing full well that labor—whether in the household, on the farm, or in the factory—has always been divided in some way. Nevertheless, it invariably connotes a particular kind of division of labor between men and women based almost exclusively on gender, one that usually places men in the role of principal wage earner, and women in a secondary role as housewife and mother.

In both Europe and the United States, and wherever else colonial governments might prevail, the bourgeois model for the ideal family life of complementary roles for men and women was promoted through publications, legislation, schools, and from the pulpit.[2] The domestic ideology served as a political ideology for capitalists as well, for what better way to produce a stable and reliable workforce than to create "respectable" working-class families that reflected, albeit imperfectly, the middle-class ideal? As Eva Blomberg shows in chapter 6 of this book on Swedish mining communities, organized religion, the company, and in some instances even the state, all had a vested interest in promoting a cult of domesticity that would produce a "respectable" working class and a docile workforce. Sober, industrious fathers and good Christian mothers were the preemptive antidote to industrial strife and class conflict.

More often than not, the mirror image of middle-class respectability was shattered by the harsh realities of working-class life. In the nineteenth- and early-twentieth-century mining communities of Europe and North America, the grueling schedule of miners' wives meant that they might work around-the-clock preparing meals and hot baths for husbands, sons, and lodgers. And in places like Great Britain, where miners had the largest family size of any occupational group, young women were almost continuously pregnant, leading to rates of infant and maternal mortality in mining areas that were higher than any other region of the United Kingdom.[3] For miners' wives, the domestic ideology belied the real meaning of the division of labor in the mining household and the value of women's unwaged labor to the industry.

Given their heroic labors, it should come as no surprise that miners' wives and daughters are among the most legendary female figures in labor history and in working-class literature. The U.S. labor organizer Mother Jones is memorialized by the contemporary magazine that bears her name. In Britain, one of the youngest ever female members of Parliament, a Scottish coalminer's daughter, Jenny Lee, graced the coalfields and the Commons with remarkable oratorical skills and promoted education for adult students and the working classes by founding the Open University. In literature, the unforgettable Mrs. Morel of D.H. Lawrence's *Sons and Lovers,* and Mrs. Morgan, the indomitable Welsh Mining Mam of Richard Llewellyn's *How Green Was My Valley,* have contributed to the quasi-mythical stature of miners' wives. But the notoriety of these individual women is perhaps less spectacular when viewed in relation to the largely unwritten history of the organizations and protests of mining women around the world.

It was our mutual interest in labor union auxiliaries and women's militancy that first compelled us to issue a call for contributions to an anthology that would highlight new work on women's activism in the world's mining communities. Questions from prospective authors led us to alter our original focus. What constituted women's "protests?" In addition to examining formal and informal organizations that were often mobilized during major crises such as strikes, how could we interpret women's activities to improve their and their families' lives? Did their efforts to enter the mining workforce or gain more autonomy signify a protest against the rigid gender hierarchies that existed in most mining industries, unions, and families? And what of the preindustrial cultures where women mined or held customary rights over mineral wealth? How did such global historical forces as colonialism and capitalism alter customary gender roles in mining?

Historical assumptions about the thoroughly "masculine" nature of mining, moreover, provided an opportunity to explore what the "division of labor" actually meant in the mining industry in a variety of historical contexts. What were the particular cultural, political, and economic contexts for labor and domestic arrangements in mining communities, and how have women mounted challenges that at times destabilized existing inequalities? To what extent were gender roles in mining communities uniquely informed by the particularities of history and culture? How were gender identities constructed over time and to what extent were they emblematic of larger historical developments? How did industries, unions, and the state shape and reinforce gender ideologies? This anthology offers new perspectives on these questions. The fifteen essays presented here help advance our understanding of the historical process by which men and women came to be viewed as "different" and thus were assigned social, economic, political, and cultural roles within one global industry.

From glamorous gold to lowly coal, the tumultuous history of extracting the earth's resources has fascinated scholars and the general public for many years. Mining was a critical economic activity in human societies, shaping world history, and it fueled the colonial and capitalist empires of Europe and North America from the sixteenth through the twentieth centuries. Yet despite mining's importance in world history, its scholars have for the most part focused on technical, metallurgical, and capital developments and, more recently, on labor relations and environmental impacts, rather than on the social history of mining workers and communities, and the gender roles and relations that were primary to them.[4] A number of important case studies have appeared in the past two decades that examine gender relations in national, industrial, class, and community contexts.[5] No study to date has attempted to discuss the multidimensional aspects of women's work as miners and as miners' wives and the impact of gender differentiation in mining in a global/historical context.[6]

In the rush to monopolize the world's resources, capitalists followed new ore discoveries, often investing in, developing, abandoning, and redeveloping ferrous and nonferrous mines in Africa, Europe, the Americas, Asia, and the Pacific. One area abandoned in one century could be revitalized with new technology, political regimes, labor, and capital investments in the next. Western nations shipped minerals to their own industries, retaining most of the wealth extracted and leaving little for the producing regions. Engineers, managers, and miners followed capital from Cornwall to Brazil to Michigan to Australia to Mexico and to Japan.

They also carried with them firm ideas about appropriate roles for men and women, at times adjusted to accommodate prejudices based on class, ethnicity and/or race. Labor and capital did not work in concert to erect boundaries based upon gender difference in mining societies. Rather, the extent of inequality and the assignation of different roles emerged unevenly in these industries and communities. In some instances, the division of labor in the mining household and industry mirrored the vernacular culture of preindustrial societies. For example, women in precolonial Africa mined below and above ground, while in the precolonial Andes women were viewed as "bad luck" underground although they were central to mining work.

Attitudes toward women and mining were uneven in industrial societies as well. Officially, the British parliament prohibited women from underground works as early as 1842, although women miners continued to work in some regional pits such as those around Wigan into the early twentieth century. Elsewhere in the British Empire, Indian women slaved in British-owned mines for a fraction of the wages paid to their male counterparts in the United Kingdom. And even in societies such as Japan, where gender roles were rigidly enforced, surprisingly, women continued to mine underground until the mid-twentieth century.

For the most part, however, in the Americas and throughout Europe, societies and employers normalized women's exclusion from working underground through an elaborate set of superstitions, beliefs, traditions, sexual metaphors, and seemingly "rational" justifications. In industrialized North America and in Europe, the domestic ideology, generated during eighteenth-century debates on women's nature, was adapted to the particular circumstances of the Industrial Revolution and provided both a reasoned and moral justification for keeping women out of the mines and at home. No respectable Victorian woman could possibly work in close proximity to men hundreds of feet underground, and in any case why would she want to? No, women were to be good wives and mothers, they were to provide a civilizing influence on their husbands and raise children to be good Christians and respectable working-class citizens, or so the argument went.

In other parts of the world, the exclusion of women from the mines often came from the traditional beliefs of the indigenous population. In Latin America, as in Africa and Asia, archetypal myths of earth goddesses and women's special relationship to the underground world exist. In some regions, these older stories have become the basis for the superstitions about women in the mines that are held by male miners even to the present day. For example, in Peru, miners believe that for each woman who goes down a mine, a man will come up dead. In another legend, a mine stops producing when women go in to it. In the area of Huancavelica, the miners still sacrifice llamas as a tribute to Mother Earth in the belief that her blessing will keep them from harm and increase the yield of ore.[7] Chilean miners considered the mine "a feminized object on which they exercised their will" and also as a "punishing woman" who haunted the tunnels and could cause accidents if another woman entered the mine.[8] In chapter 3 of this book, Pascale Absi illustrates how Potosí miners eroticized their mining mountain, which, like a jealous lover, would not tolerate other women in the mines. In Brazil, it was unlucky for feminine skirts, even worn by priests, to appear underground.

Oral traditions perpetuated the notion of women's bad luck—whether they were priests, wives, or royalty. After the Empress of Brazil descended into a mine in 1881, many attributed the collapse of the mine a few years later to her visit.[9] A similar belief was held by Welsh miners, who considered even the sight of a woman en route to work as a sure sign of a pending fall in the mine and justification enough for taking a day off from work.[10] As late as the 1970s, women in Appalachia and Arizona confronted resentments to their entry into the profession, which was supported by the strong belief that women were bad luck underground.[11]

Miners built a combative work culture based on an exaggerated masculinity, which was required for the grueling work in the mine, taking on the company or state, and heading a household with wives and children. Men embraced masculinist ideals to support their own positions of privilege within the family and society, albeit within the confines of the capitalist economy. Assuming that women were "naturally" tied to the domestic world of reproduction, Alice Kessler-Harris explains, the "family" or male wage was constructed to supply a family's comfortable living. These practices, she argues, "affirmed existing values and integrated all the parties into a set of understandings that located the relationships of working men and women to each other."[12] Although economic realities may have contradicted the male breadwinner ideal, it nonetheless had powerful sway over men's and women's consciousness, engendering a psychological dynamic that sustained men's "sense of masculinity" and designated women's work as marginal.

When the breadwinner ideal was undermined, especially during an extended strike or mine closures, the role of the miner's wife to "stand by her man" acquired almost mythic cultural status. One of the most beloved novels of mining community life, Richard Llewellyn's *How Green Was My Valley*, portrays the Welsh Mining Mam as the center of the family. Her shrewd household managerial skills, physical stamina, and moral fortitude, make *her* the backbone of her family and community. This worldwide best seller, translated into forty-nine languages and made into a blockbuster 1940s Hollywood film, illustrated the enduring sentimental appeal of the domestic ideology, and the traditional ideals of mining community life—a place where men were still men and women were still women.[13]

The male breadwinner ideal and the reputed toughness of the work that disqualified women from mining often disintegrated when operations expanded or the supply of labor shrunk, when men required family assistance in the mines, or when these "masculine" jobs became seasonal and low-paid. In fact, as a number of essays in this anthology reveal, women often moved into the diggings and even dominated mining where enterprises were fairly marginal or provided sustenance when men were required or chose to work elsewhere. Sometimes women were allowed underground as independent wage earners, or to assist fathers and husbands. For the most part, however, mining became more exclusively associated with men as it became more capitalized and centralized.[14] Concentrated urban, industrial sites typically insisted on a rigid sexual division of labor, but more rural and subsidiary operations involved families or became the domain of women's work.[15]

For centuries, high fatalities in underground mining and deaths from silicosis have left women without husbands and sons. In the colonial Andes, silicosis combined with malnutrition claimed a high percentage of *mita* miners leaving parishes, as one priest noted, with "only women."[16] From the 1920s through the 1940s in the Minas Gerais district of Brazil, widows outnumbered widowers five to one.[17] Still, women in mining communities faced their own dangers above ground: domestic abuse, deaths from childbirth, and in places where environmental hazards were monitored, equally high rates of cancer. In Britain alone, where one out of every ten children was born to a mining family until 1927—and miners had the largest families of any occupational group before World War II—infant and maternal mortality rates far exceeded the male rate of death from accidents in mines.[18] Mining women were burdened by their own powerlessness and fears of losing the primary breadwinner in a mining accident or to death by disease. Perhaps more than men, miner's wives " 'carried the mine in them.' "[19] Mining, and sustaining mining families and communities, was hard physical and emotional work.

Although men came to dominate most mining, women's reproductive and domestic work increasingly became essential to the industry. As a U.S. Women's Bureau study concluded in the 1920s, miners' wives were of "peculiar industrial and economic importance" to keep miners in the region.[20] Moreover, women's waged and unwaged work played a critical role in the basic economy of the industry. Women created economic niches through direct relationships to mining in surface operations that admitted them and in the brothels, taverns and cafes, households, and businesses that maintained male miners.

Capital alternately viewed women as assets or liabilities in its efforts to control labor. Companies often encouraged marriage and constructed family housing in order to sustain a more docile workforce; at other times, they tried to limit the number of women in a mining camp. But despite company hopes that they would "settle" and make more complacent a male workforce, women often became the most militant community members in demanding better wages and living conditions. In the "General Strike" of 1926, for example, protesting miners' wives in the Rhondda Valley of south Wales assaulted police with rocks, served lengthy prison sentences, and in some instances, even lost custody of their children in support of their men. Halfway around the world in New South Wales, some miners' wives, as members of the Communist Party in Australia, entered into the vanguard of political militancy without ever belonging to a union.[21]

Miners around the world held reputations as strident proletarians or "labor elite" and were often considered the most significant sector of the working class in altering the political histories of countries such as Bolivia, Poland, and South Africa. Yet women's roles in labor protests also provided models of resistance to capital's claims on workers and communities. As U.S. labor historian David Montgomery has noted, "the solidarity of miners underground was reinforced powerfully by that of women above ground."[22] Women manipulated gender assumptions to more effectively and physically assert strike goals when men were enjoined from more public demonstrations through injunctions, or military and police violence. Women led pickets, attacked scabs, and employed the tools of their domestic work, beating on pots and pans, carrying children to demonstrations, and leading "broom brigades" to demand public attention to strike goals. They were commonly arrested for "unladylike" and "disorderly conduct."

Because these moments of protest often appeared as much about challenging patriarchy as capitalism, male miners and unions were not always supportive of women's independent militancy as they were when women performed more traditional support roles during strikes. Despite women's proven critical role in labor actions, male miners, as June Nash discovered in her study of Bolivian tin communities, often "ordered wives back to the kitchen."[23] But women and men repeatedly struggled over and renegotiated those gender roles. Popular culture—expressed in literature such as Emile Zola's *Germinal*, songs in Nigeria, or in films like *Salt of the Earth*—richly reveals contested discourse about women's resistance in mining communities. Several of the essays in this book examine how gender shaped forms of class identity and protest. At what times did men and women come together in their protest strategies, and over what issues did they divide? Did women's prominent roles in strikes and union auxiliaries, in acceptable roles interpreted as "domestic" in nature, provide them latitude for challenging traditional restrictions in the private sphere? Did women express desires to change power relations at home, or were they most concerned about improving the male breadwinner wage?

Mining communities around the world have shared many characteristics: they were usually isolated from the main centers of national trade, industry, and urban life; yet they were densely populated, industrial, and their residents worked for wages and sought the mutual associations and pleasures associated with urban life. Some of these communities were rigidly controlled company towns; others alternated loyalty to and independence from the employers who guaranteed or threatened their survival. They experienced booms and busts as companies responded to global market prices, the quality and quantity of ore reserves, and technological demands. Residents endured the harsh climates of high altitudes, industrial pollution, dangerous working conditions, mining-related diseases, and powerful corporations. Mining families faced formidable odds in fashioning their own communities. In fact, the enormous power of mining corporations, and their historic ability to align governments behind their interests, have challenged the most determined workers. Yet capital did not operate unchallenged—workers, their families and communities shaped productive relations and the histories of enterprises in different parts of the world.[24]

The essays that follow reveal how important the case study remains for illustrating the varieties of human experience and how comparisons can help us understand how gender ideologies, roles, and relations take shape. The anthology explores gender relations and women's work and activism in a variety of settings and from multiple national and disciplinary perspectives. Each essay is important for illuminating the ways in which gender is imagined, lived, inscribed, and contested in specific historical and material contexts; together, the essays reveal that despite the tremendous variation between industries, cultures, and national experiences, women have challenged the constraints of gender definitions on their lives, work, and militancy.

This collection does not attempt to cover all places or all times or even provide a general history of mining. Critical places in the mining world, such as China, the former Soviet Union, and Indonesia, are not represented here. The volume reflects the current strength and focus of scholarship in that most of the essays deal with the twentieth century, when the internationalization of capital accelerated the pace of change in mining communities and reshaped or reaffirmed the gendered division of labor. In the early twentieth century, 20 percent of the world's largest corporations were based in mining, revealing mining's significance to the world economy.[25] By the World War I era, working-class communities and their labor movements around the world embraced or accepted one kind of dominance, the ideal of households headed by a male breadwinner, even as they struggled against corporate dominance over their lives. A gender analysis of mining allows us to understand the importance of women so often obscured by the scholarly focus on male miners and unions or technological developments. A comparative global approach, moreover, allows us to see how gender conceptions are fluid and intersect with other identities such as class, race, culture, and nation. We hope this anthology stimulates additional research on and dialogue about the varieties of experiences of men and women in the mining communities of the world.

NOTES

1. Joan Wallach Scott, *Gender and the Politics of History* (New York: Columbia University Press, 1988), 1–11.
2. Marilyn Boxer and Jean Quataert, *Connecting Spheres: Women in the Western World, 1500 to the Present* (Oxford: Oxford University Press, 1987), 115, 214.
3. Report of Maternal Mortality, 1936–1937 XI, cmd.5423, 367.
4. See, e.g., the extensive literature on the history of the mining industry in the American West, and the few titles concerning women and gender, in Richard E. Lingenfelter, ed., *The Mining West: A Bibliography & Guide to the History & Literature of Mining in the American & Canadian West*, vols. 1 and 2 (Lanham, MD: Scarecrow Press, 2003). It is not unusual for even relatively recent publications to avoid mentioning women at all. See, e.g., Delphin A. Muise and Robert G. McIntosh, *Coal Mining in Canada: A Historical and Comparative Overview* (Ottawa: National Museum of Science & Technology, 1996).
5. See, e.g., Angela V. John, *By the Sweat of Their Brow: Women Workers at Victorian Coal Mines* (London: Routledge, 1984); Janet L. Finn, *Tracing the Veins: Of Copper, Culture, and Community from Butte to Chuquicamata* (Berkeley: University of California Press, 1998); Elizabeth Jameson, *All That Glitters: Class, Conflict and Community in Cripple Creek* (Urbana: University of Illinois Press, 1998); Thomas M. Klubock, *Contested Communities: Class, Gender, and Politics in Chile's El Teniente Copper Mine, 1904–1951* (Durham: Duke University Press, 1998).
6. In fact, there are too few global comparisons of working-class women in industrial communities, in contrast to the numerous comparative works on global

feminisms. See, e.g., Bonnie G. Smith, ed., *Global Feminisms since 1945* (London: Routledge, 2000); Amrita Basu, ed., *The Challenge of Local Feminisms: Women's Movements in Global Perspective* (Boulder: Westview Press, 1995); Janet Saltzman Chafetz and Anthony Gary Dworkin, *Female Revolt: Women's Movements in World and Historical Perspective* (Totowa, NJ: Rowman and Allanheld, 1986); Carole R. McCann and Seung-kyung Kim, eds., *Feminist Theory Reader: Local and Global Perspectives* (New York: Routledge, 2003).

7. Canadian International Development Agency. "No Longer a Man's World: Women of the Deeps." http://www.acdi-cida.gc.ca/cida_ind.nsf/0/5dc63c484463fcd685256a (April 2, 2005), 1.
8. Klubock, *Contested Communities*, 128, 141.
9. Marshall C. Eakin, email correspondence with Mercier, August 2004.
10. Trefor Owen, *Welsh Folk Customs* (Cardiff: National Museum of Wales, 1978).
11. Barbara Kingsolver, *Holding the Line: Women in the Great Arizona Mine Strike of 1983* (Ithaca, NY: Cornell University Press, 1989 and 1996), 3.
12. Alice Kessler-Harris, *A Woman's Wage: Historical Meanings and Social Consequences* (Lexington: University Press of Kentucky, 1990), 1–19. See also Kessler-Harris, "Gender and Work: Possibilities for a Global, Historical Overview," in *Women's History in Global Perspective*, ed. Bonnie G. Smith (Urbana: University of Illinois Press, 2004).
13. Richard Llewellyn, *How Green Was My Valley* (New York: Macmillan, 1940), 1–495.
14. Ruth Milkman has found that once an industry's labor force has been established as male, employers and workers resist any organizational change, reproducing the sexual division of labor and reinforcing ideas about gender differences to explain why women and men qualify for different jobs. Milkman, *Gender at Work: The Dynamics of Job Segregation by Sex During World War II* (Urbana: University of Illinois Press, 1987), 6, 124.
15. Women often play an important role in reviving mining on a small scale in various regions. For contrasting views on the benefits to women, see, Jeannette Graulau, "Peasant Mining Production as a Development Strategy: The Case of Women in Gold Mining in the Brazilian Amazon," *European Review of Latin American and Caribbean Studies* (Netherlands) 71 (2001): 71–106; Maurice Amutabi and Mary Lutta Mukhebi, "Women and Mining in Kenya: The Case of the Mukhibira Mines in Viliga District." *Jenda: A Journal of Culture and African Women's Studies* 1, No. 2 (2006): 1–26.
16. Enrique Tandeter, *Coercion & Market: Silver Mining in Colonial Potosí 1692–1826* (Albuquerque: University of New Mexico Press, 1993), 54.
17. Marshall C. Eakin, *British Enterprise in Brazil: The St. John d'el Rey Mining Company and the Morro Velho Gold Mine, 1830–1960* (Durham: Duke University Press, 1989), 188.
18. Report of the Ministry of Health and Investigation of South Wales Coalfield 1928–1929 VIII, cmd. 3272, 689.
19. Carol A.B. Giesen, *Coal Miners' Wives: Portraits of Endurance* (Lexington: University Press of Kentucky, 1995), 4.
20. Quoted in Mildred Allen Beik, *The Miners of Windber: The Struggles of New Immigrants for Unionization, 1890s–1930s* (University Park, PA: Pennsylvania State University Press, 1996), 94.

21. Jaclyn J. Gier, "Miners' Wives: Household, Family, and Community in the South Wales Coalfield," unpublished PhD Thesis, Northwestern University, 1993. See especially chapter six, "Household and Community on Strike."

22. David Montgomery, *Fall of the House of Labor: The Workplace, the State, and American Labor Activism, 1865–1925* (Cambridge: Cambridge University Press, 1987), 337.

23. June Nash, *We Eat the Mines and the Mines Eat Us: Dependency and Exploitation in Bolivian Tin Mines* (New York: Columbia University Press, 1979), 116.

24. On challenges to dependency theory, see, e.g., Elizabeth Dore, *The Peruvian Mining Industry: Growth, Stagnation, and Crisis* (Boulder: Westview Press, 1988).

25. Martin Lynch, *Mining in World History* (London: Reaktion Books, 2002), 213.

PART I

The Indigenous, Colonial, and Imperial Legacy

For thousands of years, peoples of the ancient world had sought, mined, smelted, and traded minerals such as gold, copper, bronze, tin, and iron. Imperial Rome and Imperial China depended on metals and coal for their industry, prosperity, and expansion. These early empires established a pattern of resource and labor exploitation that were shared by mining communities worldwide by the nineteenth century, as European and later North American nations and capital carved up the world. Industrialization fueled mining claims and operations, and tied to these ventures that succeeded or failed were the fates of men, women, and children who staked their futures on mining work. The essays presented in Part 1, focusing on Cuba, Ghana, Bolivia, and India, and covering the late seventeenth through the twentieth centuries, denote the indigenous, colonial and imperial legacy of mining. Whether through negotiating colonial or corporate control, or salvaging marginal enterprises after independence, the essays probe how at different times native and slave women became the center of, or were marginalized from, mining operations. Through these diverse experiences of mining women across time and space we learn how the sexual division of labor and gender meanings came to order the lives of many.

LATIN AMERICA

Improved sailing technology and desire for trade with the East drew Europeans into the Atlantic, where they established gold and slave trading centers on the African coast and soon conquered the indigenous peoples of the Caribbean, Mesoamerica, and the Andes for their gold and silver. The Spanish enslaved Indians to dig the riches of America, which by the mid-sixteenth century had become a main source for Spain's treasury. The silver camp at Potosí rivaled the largest cities of Europe in size. But fortunes were quickly realized and spent, and crown and capital chased new ore bodies, establishing the centuries-long practice of development, exhaustion, and flight. By 1600 the great mines of Potosí were exhausted, and production in

Mexico and Lower Peru increased over the next century, until Potosí was once again revived, revealing the changing fortunes of the industry.[1]

Despite sharing a common history that included Iberian and later British and North American dominance of mining, a period of nationalization in the mid-twentieth century, and widespread privatization in the late twentieth century, the mining communities of Latin America were as varied as the ore exploited. Some transformed historic indigenous communities and relied on peasant and slave labor, others were created in uninhabited areas that pulled migrants from all parts of the region. Mining dominated the export economies of some Latin American nations, and it was peripheral to others. Sex ratios, ore quantities, labor histories, capitalization, and national political movements all entered into shaping the productive lives and gender relations of community members.

Spanish colonial authorities considered both women and men critical to the mining workforce. Unable to depend on voluntary labor, colonists forced Andean peasant communities to contribute their labor to the mines. To meet this required *mita*, drafted workers brought their entire families to satisfy the work quotas. Population figures in Potosí reveal an equal number of men and women. Mine owners would often insist on using women in domestic service, but *mita* wages could not purchase adequate food, so women and children obtained work crushing ore in the refineries.[2] In the late sixteenth century, possibly because of mining expansion due to amalgamation, women took over from men the operation of the guayras, or furnaces that smelted ore. They found pieces of discarded ore in tailings to process, becoming keen collectors of higher quality ore.[3] Many Indians avoided labor coercion by "hispanizing" and adopting a wage labor relationship with their employers. Potosí soon attracted a sizeable male wage labor force, much like in the silver districts of Guadalajara and Zacatecas of New Spain.[4] Women continued working on the surface and engaged in agricultural and market activities to help families survive.

Gold strikes in the Minas Gerais area of Brazil in the eighteenth century drew thousands of new immigrants from across the Atlantic as well as colonizers and their slaves from the coastal regions. Portuguese colonists were committed to the idea of mining as male-defined work. Unlike their agricultural plantations, where the sex ratio was balanced, colonists bought and brought many more male slaves to mine; women were often less than 20 percent of the slave population. As Kathleen Higgins demonstrates in her study of the mining region, gender was a "critical determinant" in the ability of a slave to gain some autonomy over her labor, gain a master's patronage, and obtain freedom. Female slaves escaped grueling mine work and through their closer relations with masters, won manumission more often than male slaves, but gender ideologies, legal restrictions, and racial discrimination limited their freedom. Nonetheless, colonial authorities expressed concern for the "licentious liberty" that women slaves displayed.[5]

This anthology opens at the close of the seventeenth century, in the transitional period when Iberian mining investments in the Americas were in decline and before British and North American industrialization altered labor production and gender relations in new ways. In chapter 1, María Elena Díaz finds that in Cuba, the most important colonial Caribbean frontier, royal slaves revitalized copper mines abandoned by private contractors for their own subsistence. Although El Cobre village maintained a sexual division of labor, with men dominating agriculture and skilled aspects of metal production, women came to control the informal mining industry. Díaz suggests that the slaves may have revived precolonial African practices where men worked in underground mining but women and children did the surface gathering, washing, and sorting of ore. She helps us reconsider women in mining as an extension rather than departure from domestic responsibilities—women could mine near the village as they found time and trade ore for food and clothing for their families.

The story of El Cobre is important, too, for illustrating a central conclusion about women and mining: that women gained more importance in mining as the industry itself remained outside the industrial and export sector. Labor arrangements varied depending on the sophistication of the mining enterprise. After abolition in 1851 and colonial abandonment of commercial mining on Colombia's Pacific Coast, black families organized their gold mining through *troncos*, or family rights to mine a specific territory. The division of labor was sex-segregated, but both men and women could inherit *tronco* rights. Men broke up the slopes or terraces, men and women removed and washed sand and small stones, and women panned this mix for gold dust. Although fathers headed the work group, women could gain more authority as economic conditions of the community changed. When nearby oil and road construction opportunities offered cash wages in the 1970s, for example, men left the gold fields and women's control of the *troncos* increased.[6]

By the mid-eighteenth century, as ore sources became depleted in Europe, French and then British investors employed new technology to deepen Latin American mines and develop more extensive processing methods. After political independence in Latin America in the nineteenth century, British, and later, North American capital flowed into numerous new nation-states.

Traditional indigenous resistance to proletarianization and work in the mines, however, impeded the success of the new investments. The British company St. John d'el Rey developed and operated for over a century the largest gold mine in South America in Minas Gerais. The company recruited men, women, and children for its operations, but the local population was interested only in providing seasonal labor to supplement agricultural income. Until the late nineteenth century and the abolition of slavery in Brazil, the company depended on rented slaves for its workforce. Competing in the international market for mine labor, the company recruited workers from Cornwall, Portugal, Germany, the Brazilian coast, and China. But few immigrants remained, and, to the company's dismay, imported Spanish and Italian workers organized fellow Brazilian workers and led a series of strikes in the early twentieth century.[7]

Mechanization offered a partial solution to the perpetual labor crisis, but it also curtailed or eliminated work opportunities for women. Before the mid-nineteenth century and the mechanization of ore hauling, slave women had carried ore out of the mines to the reduction works. Women continued to carry out other tasks and comprised almost 69 percent of the reduction department and 17 percent of the total mining workforce at St. John d'el Rey. By 1924, women made up just 4 percent of the labor force. They were concentrated in breaking ore until mechanical crushers replaced them in the 1930s, and by the 1940s, social legislation had eliminated women from the mining process.[8]

In Bolivia, too, jobs for women diminished, although labor shortages could overcome rationalizations for their exclusion. In 1870, women comprised 43 percent of the workforce in the tin center of Siglo XX-Uncia-Catavi, albeit in sex-segregated, low-paying jobs. As machines replaced women workers, they had to create new sources of income. One creative and common enterprise was in trading commodities from the company store with rural clients.[9] The Chaco War in the 1930s pulled women back into mining, even underground, and in Potosí they remained 10 percent of the mining workforce until the national revolution of 1952 brought about nationalization and modernization of the mines, and the formal ban of women. Some women, particularly widows, remained in smaller numbers as *palliri*, picking ore-bearing rock from waste dumped by male miners in smaller mines.

Although women's mining options were reduced in the twentieth century and opposition to their presence in mines increased, Pascale Absi shows in chapter 3 of this book how this exclusion was socially constructed and at times unevenly enforced. Absi explores how Potosí miners maintained the belief that women were bad luck from the 1950s through the 1980s and developed forms of exclusion that kept women on the outside of the mines where their wages were much lower. In the process of naturalizing beliefs about gender, cultural barriers were sometimes broken, as in the case of women tourists or widows entering the mines, but miners constructed exceptions that did not consider them truly "women."

If women became less important to the mining production process by the twentieth century, companies increasingly saw them as critical to reproduction and throughout Latin America encouraged marriage and families as a way to maintain a stable workforce. As single men and single women migrated to the El Teniente copper communities in Chile, Kennecott Corporation viewed the regulation of sexuality as central to its efforts to control labor. It instituted a corporate welfare system to encourage family formation and settlement and sought to strengthen gender identities by instilling notions of "fatherhood" and "motherhood."[10] Farther north, in the 1920s the Anaconda Company established Chuquicamata as its main resource anchor for a far-flung copper empire. It crafted its communities by privileging married male workers and investing in housing and recreation. As its mines flourished in the 1950s, it sought an alliance with women to keep husbands working. The company accommodated miners' wives' demands for improved housing and offered *la compensacion de la mujer* or family allowance.[11]

Despite modernization and relatively high wages compared to other sectors, mining remained a precarious enterprise through the twentieth century, and women continued to bear the brunt of hardship due to accidents or work stoppages. Periodic economic crises pushed Bolivian mining women to revive peasant survival strategies, such as gardening, ore theft and trade, and the creation of games or lotteries to share scarce commodities. Mining wives, unlike their husbands, often retained connections to their peasant roots, turning to kin for mutual support, and capitalizing on their knowledge of ecosystem output to raise gardens on distant family plots for their own subsistence and trade.[12]

AFRICA

The first resources exploited in Africa by mercantilist capitalists were not minerals but rather the millions of human beings transported across the world during the centuries of the slave trade. Unlike Latin America, where early exploration and colonization was fixated on the discovery and acquisition of precious metals, namely gold and silver, the mining of mineral resources by the major imperial powers came relatively late to Africa. "The scramble for Africa" as it is sometimes called is associated with the last half of the nineteenth century, when major powers such as Great Britain and Germany were seeking to enhance their empires by carving up the African continent in a competition that fueled the second industrial revolution and ultimately led to World War I.[13]

Africa had a long tradition of mining and metallurgy that was unknown to the European venture capitalists of the nineteenth century. The world's oldest mine was uncovered at an iron site in Swaziland, where it operated more than 45,000 years ago. And Africans had used various types of iron in funeral ceremonies and in the production of cosmetics. In the great empires of Ancient Egypt, Ghana, and Mali, gold was used extensively in various types of ornamentation. The ancient Greek historian and geographer, Agatharchides, documented the extensive use of convict slave labor in the gold mines of Egypt and Ethiopia. Not only men, but often whole families including women and children, were made to work under the threat of beatings from overseers until they literally dropped dead from exhaustion.[14]

The centuries old exploitation of human "capital" in the extraction of precious minerals in Africa was later mirrored by the European venture capitalists in the late nineteenth and early twentieth centuries. The first diamond rush began in southern Africa around 1870 and gold was discovered in the Transvaal in the 1880s. Hundreds of thousands of black African laborers mined gold and diamonds of the region, their cheap labor helping quickly develop the mining industry. The Boer War began in 1899, when tensions between the Dutch Boer farmers and the British "Uitlanders" or "Outsiders," as they were called, led to an outbreak of hostilities. When the war ended in 1902, more than 50,000 Chinese laborers were imported to work in the gold mines to boost production hampered by the war. By 1910 these foreign workers were repatriated, but only after mounting protests over their living and working conditions.[15]

The main mining companies in the early years of the gold and diamond rush in southern Africa were Rio Tinto-Zinc, De Beers, and Consolidated Gold Fields. The infamous Cecil Rhodes, who owned both De Beers and Consolidated Gold Fields by the end of the nineteenth century, founded British South African Company (BSA). BSA would take the lead in colonizing central Africa and until the mid-1920s had truncated agreements with local chiefs granting mining concessions in all the territories it controlled. Essentially, private mining companies organized colonization on behalf of the empire, and this pattern of granting concessions was not limited to British Central and southern Africa. For example, in the Belgian Congo, The Katanga Mining Company ruled over the territory held by the Belgian state since the Berlin Conference of 1885 in exchange for exclusive mining rights.[16]

For the most part, mining activity in nineteenth-century Africa was located mainly in the southern part of the continent. One exception, however, was the Gold Coast of Ghana, which had a long and fabled tradition of gold mining that was centuries old. Indeed, the empire of ancient Ghana owed its fame to what Arab writers described as the richest gold mines on earth. In the ninth century, Arab writer Al Yaqubi described ancient Ghana as one of the three most organized states in the region. By the fifteenth century, the Portuguese had arrived in Ghana to trade for gold, ivory, and pepper, and by 1482 they established a permanent fortress there.[17] Eventually, the Dutch displaced the Portuguese as the main European presence, and by the eighteenth century both the Dutch and the British had established merchant companies in the region. The development of gold mining was overshadowed by the enormity of the West African slave trade with an estimated 4.5 million slaves sent to North America and South America between 1701 and 1810.[18]

By 1874 the British established a permanent Gold Coast colony and it is during this period, according to Kwabena Akurang-Parry in chapter 2 of this volume, that the anticolonial movement and the struggle over mineral rights begins. As Akurang-Parry's essay documents, the colonial authorities were willing to use any opportunity, including the acrimonious divorce of a king and his wife, to assert their control over the gold mines and other resources of the Wassa Fiase between 1876 and 1889. Nevertheless, the queen of the region, Adwoa Arduah, fought to secure the king's release from captivity when he was charged with and sentenced for illegally keeping slaves by the colonial government, and in so doing, she championed an anticolonial movement that helped to temporarily mitigate the impact of colonial gold mining.

In the long term, the triumph of Queen Adwoa Arduah, was short lived. By 1896 the Anglo-Asante war culminated in the deportation of the asantehene. The great kingdom of the Asante would henceforward be controlled by a British protectorate. Sir Francis Scott led the British troops into Kumasi in order to control the city and the Asante king was thus exiled, eventually finding permanent asylum in the Seycheles. By 1900, the British according to their own concept of dominion, appointed Arnold Hodgson as the chief representative of the British colonial government. He had the unprecedented audacity to ask for the "golden stool," the historic symbol of Asante royalty, and as a result the queen mother of Edwiso, Yaa Asantewaa, led an attack on the British fort in Kumasi. In 1902 the northern territories were proclaimed a British protectorate. It would not be until 1957 that the British colony of the Gold Coast would once again become an independent Ghana.[19]

Today the control of some smaller mining operations in Africa, mainly gemstone extraction, is in the hands of women, especially in some areas of southern Africa. But the women of the region face discrimination from men and resistance from traditional tribal chiefs who do not wish to have women owning mines in their regions or encroaching on their customary rights. The United Nations Development Fund for Women has assisted with the creation of the South African Development Community (SADC) and Women in Mining Trust in Zimbabwe. Elsewhere in that region, the Association of Zambian Women Miners (AZWM) was formed in 1996. In Tanzania, east Africa, the Tanzania Women Miners Association estimates that over one hundred thousand women are actively engaged in mining in that country alone.

Many women engage in mining for precious gemstones, copper, and other metals. The dangers they face as independent mine owners or as women operating in mines owned by others include attacks from wild animals in bush regions, rape, discriminatory government policies, and in some countries, such as Angola, an estimated 9 million land mines. In areas where small-scale mining provides women with a meager subsistence, prostitution or liaisons with several men may provide a strategy for survival, but as Maurice Amutabi and Mary Lutta Mukhebi have shown for gold mining in Kenya, there may be serious health consequences for women, who run the risk of acquiring HIV. Equally serious to their health is mercury poisoning associated with the gold mining industry.[20] Nevertheless, for many African women, mining is identified as an area of the economy where they can make money, more than in other occupations traditionally reserved for women—and with organizations like SADC and AZWM they have begun to organize to protect themselves and their segment of the mining market.[21]

SOUTH ASIA

The mining industry in South Asia has been dominated historically by the British presence in India during the period of colonial rule. As early as 1619, the first British outpost in South Asia was established by the English East India Company on the northwestern coast of India. By the end of the seventeenth century, the company opened trading stations in Calcutta, Bombay, and Madras. The trading stations in each of these locations was under the protection of the local princes, with whom the British cultivated hegemonic relations, gradually expanding their influence until, by 1850, they controlled most of present-day India.[22]

At the height of British imperialism during the rule of Queen Victoria a rebellion in the northern part of India started by Indian soldiers led the British government to take control of the situation by shifting political power from the East India Company to the Crown. As was the case in southern Africa, the government had allowed the private company to exercise colonial rule on its behalf for the benefit of its investors and the Crown. But when insurrection threatened British investments, the Crown and the military took control of the situation.[23]

As the British developed the infrastructure for the transportation of goods and raw materials across the Indian subcontinent, coal mining became one of the vital industries in which British agency houses invested. Although the coal mining industry began as early as 1774 in India, it was more than a century before production really took off. By the mid-1850s the East Indian Railway was built through the Bengali Ranigunji coalfields, thus facilitating the use of Indian rather than imported coal for the operation of both trains and steamers. But the development of the industry was slow at the outset, and it was not until the turn of the century that coal production exceeded 6 million tons per annum, in part as a response to the high cost of imported coal. When in 1894 the Jharia coalfields began production, this high quality coal was at last available for both domestic and overseas consumption. Much of this coal was sent via Calcutta, the capital of British South Asia until 1911.[24]

As Kuntala Lahiri-Dutt documents in chapter 4, coal mining expanded during the period of the British *raj* and became one area in which women played a substantive role in the production process as *kamins*, or manual laborers, in the mines. By the early twentieth century, Indian entrepreneurs held control over thirteen of seventeen companies.

The Bengal Coal Company produced 99 percent of Indian coal by 1860. Initially the techniques of mining were simple, and as Lahiri-Dutt argues, this allowed Indian landlords to enter the business with minimal capital investment. Women served as a cheap source of labor for these primitive mining operations, only to be displaced by male workers as the industry developed new technology for deep pit mining in response to demands to increase production.

Today the Indian coal mining industry is the third largest in the world and has been nationalized since 1972; in 1975 a public sector company, Coal India Limited, was created which has eight subsidiaries. One of the largest is Central Coalfields Limited or CCL, which has sixty-nine collieries and thirty mining projects and a host of non-mining projects. Significantly, none of the senior managerial posts is held by any individual from the local villages that surround the company's operations. And while women are excluded by law from work in the mines since 1935, they are often engaged in other productive activities that support the industry.[25]

Most mining in India today is open cast, rather than the deep pit mining of the late nineteenth century. In general, this has meant the disruption of larger areas of land, damage to the environment, and the displacement of adivasis (indigenous communities), leading to the destruction of their cultural histories and ways of life. A number of NGOs, such as Mines, Minerals, and People, have brought the plight of displaced indigenous women to the attention of the government. In Orissa, tribal women are fighting against displacement from bauxite mining and in Jharkhand, women are faced with the destruction and pollution of their lands and resources from coal mining.[26] The unfortunate legacy of colonial rule may be found in development projects that rarely consider the full impact of their programs on the very cultures and populations they seek to assist and that disregard the delicate balance between nature and indigenous populations, which have successfully lived off the land for generations.[27]

Notes

1. Enrique Tandeter, *Coercion & Market: Silver Mining in Colonial Potosí 1692–1826*. Albuquerque: University of Mexico Press, 1993.
2. Ibid., 42–43.
3. Peter Bakewell, *Miners of the Red Mountain: Indian Labor in Potosí, 1545–1650* (Albuquerque: University of New Mexico Press, 1984), 40–41, 104.
4. Ibid., 183, 188.
5. Kathleen J. Higgins, *"Licentious Liberty" in a Brazilian Gold-Mining Region: Slavery, Gender, and Social Control in Eighteenth-Century Sabara, Minas Gerais* (University Park, PN: Penn State University Press, 1999), 5, 11, 37.
6. Nina S. de Friedemann, " 'Troncos' Among Black Miners in Columbia," in *Miners and Mining in the Americas*, eds., Thomas Greaves and William Culver (Manchester, UK: Manchester University Press, 1985), 204–225.
7. Eakin, *British Empire in Brazil*, xiv, 8, 47–49.
8. Ibid., 134–135, 142, 170.
9. Guillermo Delgado P., "Industrial Stagnation and Women's Strategies for Survival at the Siglo XX and Uncia Mines," in *Miners and Mining in the Americas*, 163.
10. Klubock, *Contested Communities*.
11. Finn, *Tracing the Veins*, 95.
12. Delgado P., "Industrial Stagnation," 162–168.
13. H.L. Wesseling, *Imperialism and Colonialism: Essays on the History of European Expansion* (Westport, CT: Greenwood Press, 1997) 1–25; Susanne Zantop, *Colonial Fantasies: Conquest, Family, and Nation in Precolonial Germany, 1770–1870* (Durham, NC: Duke University Press, 1997).
14. For a fascinating discussion of mining in the ancient world, see especially John Temple, *Mining: An International History* (New York: Praeger, 1972), 5–21; and Wolfgang Paul, *Mining Lore* (Portland: Morris Printing Co., 1970).
15. Temple, *Mining*, 107–111; for a more analytical and detailed account of race, class, and gender, specifically representations of black male workers and masculinity, see Zine Magubane, "Mines, Minstrels, and Masculinity: Race, Class, Gender, and the Formation of the South African Working Class, 1870–1900," *The Journal of Men's Studies* 10, no. 3 (2002): 271; also, Francis Wilson "Minerals and Migrants: How the Mining Industry has Shaped South Africa," *Daedalus* 130, no. 1 (2001): 99.

16. Temple, *Mining*, 107–115.
17. For a general overview of Ghana and slave history in the region, see <http://www.ghanaweb.com/GhanaHomePage/history/slave-trade.php> (March 7, 2005). See also Steven Salm and Falola Toyin, *Culture and Customs of Ghana* (Westport, CT: Greenwood Press, 2002), chapters 1–3.
18. Ibid.
19. Kwabena O. Akurang-Parry, "Making a Difference in Colonial Interventionism in Wassa Fiase, Gold Coast (Ghana): The Activism of Two Women, 1874–1893," in this volume. For a general history/timeline on history of Ghana, see <http://www.ghanaweb.com/GhanaHomePage/history/timeline/php> (March 7, 2005).
20. Maurice Amutabi and Mary Lutta Mukhebi, "Women and Mining in Kenya: The Case of Mukibira Mines in Vihiga District," *Jenda: A Journal of Culture and African Women's Studies* 1, no. 2 (2000), 1–26.
21. Lewis Machipisa, "Rocky Path for Women Miners," Inter Press Services, December 8, 1997 <http://moles.org/Project Underground/mother-lode/gold/women.5.html> (April 1, 2005). For the situation of women miners and women in mining areas in relation to environment and health, see Janet Bujara and Carolyn Baylies, *AIDS, Sexuality and Gender in Africa: Collective Strategies and Struggles in Tanzania and Zambia* (London: Routledge, 2000), 14–17.
22. For a general overview history of India, see John Mcleod, *The History of India* (Westport, CT: Greewood Press, 2002); on the role of British East India Company, see P. J. Cain and A. G. Hopkins, *British Imperialism: Innovation and Expansion, 1688–1914* (London: Longman, 1993).
23. Kuntala Lahiri-Dutt, "Kamins Building the Empire: Class, Caste, and Gender Interface in Indian Collieries," in this volume.
24. Ibid.
25. Lahiri-Dutt, "Competing Histories: Voices of Indigenous Communities in the Coal Mining Region of Jharkhand, India," unpublished paper for Research School of Pacific and Asian Studies, The Australian National University, Canberra, Australia, 2003.
26. Ibid; see also Kavita Philips, *Civilizing Natures: Race, Resources, and Modernity in Colonial South India* (New Brunswick, NJ: Rutgers University Press, 2004), 1–10 and 87–89.
27. A number of NGOs and specifically women's organizations have dedicated themselves to addressing issues of environmental destruction by the mining industry and the impact of mining on indigenous peoples. These themes and groups are addressed in the epilogue to this volume; a useful Web site for learning about international mining protest groups has been created by "Mines and Communities" at <http://mines and communities.org/Links/women.html>; also "Project Underground" cited in note 21.

CHAPTER 1

Mining Women, Royal Slaves: Copper Mining in Colonial Cuba, 1670–1780

María Elena Díaz

The story of El Cobre is very uncertain, not to say fantastic, as it was populated exclusively by Indians [*sic*] and people of color until recently when the riches of its mines attracted more illustrious settlers and even foreign enterprises.

Gov. Cayetano de Urbina, February 1846

To the present, the greatest amount of copper that is gathered comes from the river that crosses the pueblo, some in grains, other in rock (which is the one that is smelted). . . . to this only the women are dedicated and are the ones who search in the deeper pools of the said river.

Don Joseph Palacios de Saldustum, July 31, 1739

El Cobre is a modest mining village of almost legendary character to many Cuban people. It lies in the mountains of the Sierra del Cobre, in the island's eastern region, in what used to be an important Caribbean frontier area in colonial days. In the imaginary of the Cuban people, El Cobre has long been identified as the abode of a miraculous image of the Virgin of Charity, protectress of this mining community and patroness of the Cuban nation. Yet, as its name suggests (*cobre* or copper), the village has also been connected with copper mining since its foundation in the sixteenth century. For generations, local families have worked in these copper mines under the aegis of the Spanish crown, private contractors, foreign companies, independent miners, or the socialist state. The centuries long cycles of rise and decline of mining production in El Cobre has constituted an important historical horizon for the development of social and political life in this village. As the crown official in the epigraph suggests, the story of El Cobre before the arrival of modern capitalist mining enterprises in the nineteenth century was quite unusual (not to say fantastic). This study constitutes an attempt to recover that fading memory and to elucidate the alleged fantastic character of that Afro Cuban mining community during an important century of its long colonial history.

Although throughout the first decades of the seventeenth century copper mining in El Cobre had constituted a large export-based enterprise worked with African derived slave labor, by mid-century mining production in the settlement had dramatically declined. Years of neglect and failure to comply with the terms of a contract led in 1670 to the Spanish crown's confiscation of the ruined mines from its former private contractor. At that time, some 270 private slaves became the king's slaves, a new category of slavery whose practical and ideological meaning would be negotiated in subsequent years. The mining settlement eventually became a pueblo (or village) of king's slaves and free people of color—the only such village in the island's history and to an extent in the Americas. I have narrated that remarkable (and perhaps "fantastic") multisided history elsewhere.[1] Suffice it to say here that El Cobre retained its character as a black pueblo of royal slaves until 1780, when an (ultimately unsuccessful) attempt was made to reprivatize the mining jurisdiction and reactivate intensive exploitation of its mines. By then, the small mining settlement had grown into a full-fledged village of some 1,320 inhabitants, of whom 64 percent were royal slaves, 34 percent free people of color (mostly manumitted descendants or relatives of royal slaves) and 2 percent private slaves of these villagers.[2] Specifically, I concentrate in this essay on the significant transformations in mining production and in the construction of social identity that took place in this local slave community after the Spanish crown's takeover of the mining jurisdiction in 1670.

To be sure, the Spanish crown's confiscation of the ruined mines of El Cobre did not bring back the prosperity of the earlier export-mining-based economy. For many years, the crown tried to find a private contractor willing to reactivate the mines, but could not find anyone interested in taking up the challenge. Yet, throughout those years copper mining did not come to a halt in El Cobre. As the former private slaves of the mining settlement began to reconstitute themselves as a "peasant" community of king's slaves, they also began to reshape the local mining industry by feminizing it, turning to surface mining, working informally on their own account, and producing mostly, but not exclusively, for a domestic market.

Paradoxically, despite the more pivotal role of agriculture in the village's internal subsistence economy, and the mostly male-based construction of that sphere, it was the mostly female-based copper mining activities that may have been most economically significant in the regional context of the time. Throughout the late seventeenth and most of the eighteenth century, the female royal slaves of El Cobre became not only the main, but with the exception of some short interruptions, also the sole producers of copper in Cuba. The sales of copper were not merely regional, but extended island wide to Havana and at times to other places in the Caribbean.[3] From 1670 to 1780, the royal slaves of El Cobre produced on their own account from thirty-one to ninety annual quintals (one quintal = one hundred pounds) of copper.[4] Although this level of production was modest, it was, until the last two decades of the eighteenth century, sufficient to supply domestic markets with a metal always in short supply in the Spanish empire. Thereafter, with the island's dramatic boom of sugar production, copper was increasingly imported from Mexico until the 1830s when mainly British foreign corporations took over mining and restructured production in El Cobre. The shift in the nineteenth century from a small and informal, rudimentary, mostly feminized local enterprise to a large export-based, foreign-owned capitalist industry employing sophisticated technology spelled once again major transformations in El Cobre, including re-gendering the production process. But those transformations remain beyond the scope of this study.

Thus, the wider context of this local history is not the more familiar story of an expansionist modern global capitalism. Nor is this history a variation of the related story of proletarianization—or even of gender inflected proletarianization—of mining workers of peasant or rural origin that has been studied elsewhere in Latin America.[5] (Although since modern capitalist mining production in El Cobre was based on slave labor well into the nineteenth century, the social history of this mining community would not exemplify the more typical story of peasant proletarianization applicable to other locations in Latin America.[6]) The contours of the history I examine here are somewhat different and the story unfolds further back in time. This is the history of a hybrid enslaved peasant-slave community and of the small informal mining industry that emerged in between two periods of large export-based mining production: an early colonial one operating during the first part of the seventeenth century and a modern late colonial capitalist one in the nineteenth century. The contours of the story are compounded by the ambiguous form of slavery (i.e., royal slavery) established in this village and by the central role of women in mining production during the time frame in question.

One way to understand the history of this mining community after the de-privatization of the mining jurisdiction in 1670 is to consider it in terms of the increasing autonomy both formally enslaved men and women took in the provisioning of their families. The emergence of a family-based peasant-mining economy among royal slaves in this community had far-reaching repercussions in terms of social identity and status formation. At stake was the appropriation of production, provisioning, and consumption practices that were construed as (de facto) forms of freedom in the context of colonial slave societies. Specifically in the case of copper mining, it meant the right to organize the extraction and sale of copper in ways that were at odds with the usual restrictions of slavery. Paradoxically, it also meant re-gendering mining production. Although the internal sexual division of labor in this village's informal mining industry would exclude women (and most men) from the more skilled aspects of production such as smelting and working the metal, (surface) mining became an inherently female sphere during the time in question. The development of a family-based mining economy—albeit, as we shall see, one still articulated to another (*corvée*) form of slave labor outside the village—gave way to historically specific gender formations during this forgotten century. These gender formations would again undergo change during the nineteenth century with the reorganization of production under capitalist foreign enterprises.

The politics I examine in this study were for the most part embedded in the everyday practices of working life in this community. As mentioned before, the negotiated laboring arrangements that became customary after 1670 and the (re)formulation of identity in which these arrangements implicitly and sometimes explicitly rested had enormous political significance in the context of a slave society. Yet, beyond their everyday forms of "laboring praxis," the royal slaves of El Cobre also mobilized collectively to defend a local and regional economy upon which their community—and their identities as quasi freemen and women—depended. To defend what they had come to understand as their rightful prerogatives and entitlements, the *cobreros* (people born in El Cobre) made full use of the limited forms of mobilization available to subordinate groups living under an absolutist regime. They accessed all levels of colonial courts to denounce abuses perpetrated by private citizens and crown officials, and they also staged local revolts and fled to the nearby mountains to pressure authorities to make concessions. These forms of mobilization, however, often covered a wide range of grievances and did not focus exclusively on mining related protest. Although males often appeared in records as the main agents of these actions, and it was mostly their voices that made their way into the records, females also participated in community-based mobilizations and protest.

Sources for this early period are limited in comparison with the documentation available to historians of mining communities in more recent periods. I work here with impressionistic accounts, letters, reports, memorials, as well as court depositions. Despite their limitations, these sources allow us to reconstruct the main transformations that took place in this community after the state's confiscation of the mines. At times the documentation even provides especially valued glimpses into the social and political significance these transformations had for contemporaries.

A NEW MINING ORDER

After the crown's confiscation of the mines in 1670, the only inhabitants left behind in the ruined mining settlement were some 270 royal slaves, perhaps a handful of free people of color, a parish priest, and a hermit overseeing a hermitage to an allegedly miraculous effigy of the Virgin of Charity. The confusion and neglect of those early years resulted in far-reaching transformations for the newly constituted royal slaves. The mining jurisdiction was put under the charge of the eastern region's governor then residing in the capital city of Santiago de Cuba, ten miles away from El Cobre. Lack of direct supervision by the private contractor or an administrator in the mines allowed the slaves to imagine community in bolder ways and opened the way to expedient solutions and arrangements that were later turned into customary entitlements. It took the state two decades to organize its new (male) slave labor force into a more or less efficient *corvée* system to work in the construction and maintenance of fortification projects in this region's Caribbean frontier. Male *cobreros* were also employed as militias with their own officers in the defense of the region from enemy attack. Thus, male royal slaves were forced to labor in the crown's military defense system—albeit only on a part-time basis. For the greater part of the year, royal slaves were left to labor and provide for themselves in their village. And married women were mostly exempt from forced labor requisitions. A communal land grant was made to the village where the *cobreros* established family farms to grow the staples of their diet and pasture grounds where they hunted animals to provide themselves with meat. The state neglected the mining sector and the *cobreros*, particularly the women and children, began to mine copper on their own account.

The transformations that took place in the mining sector, and the unusual arrangements they gave way to, were noted, criticized, and often contested by contemporaries during the early transitional years into crown rule. The political significance and controversial character of these changes were pithily depicted by a slave of El Cobre in the early 1670s: Nicholás Montenegro, a favored (and literate) slave of the former contractors became one of the main (and most critical) local chroniclers of the new order emerging in the mining jurisdiction. Montenegro looked after the private interests of his former owners and in this sense stood apart from most of his fellow slaves who welcomed their new ambiguous status as royal slaves and the new opportunities that had opened up to them. Thus, although a slave official, Montenegro's voice represents a defense of the status quo ante and the reigning strictures of the old private order in the mines.

Two years after the royal takeover of the mining jurisdiction, the mulatto slave Montenegro wrote to his former mistress Doña Paula de Eguiluz y Montenegro then residing in Havana: "As I tried to prevent [the slave blacksmith] Pedro Viojo from taking copper he said to me that he did not recognize these mines as belonging to [you] my Lady Doña Paula, but that they are the king's. All the others said the same."[7] The passage made reference to slaves' appropriation of resources in the mining jurisdiction and the sense of entitlement to them that most royal slaves had developed by then. The new principles implicit in the passage also suggest that these slaves had begun to consider those mineral resources as public, and that they were entitled to the property of their new master the king—a concise and practical reference to a change in the social and labor relations of the de-privatized mining jurisdiction.

In his real or assumed bewilderment regarding the transformations of private slaves into king's slaves, Montenegro tended to paint the world as upside down. He satirized the reorganization of relations of mining production and the productive activities of his fellow slaves. Wrote Montenegro: "they [the royal slaves] sit in the thrones with their cushions while their children engage in gathering copper and they give them tasks by the pounds of copper as if they were their own slaves."[8] Despite the negative significations with which he colored the scene of slaves mining on their own account, Montenegro succinctly delineated the major contours of this activity: the daily small-scale production measured by the pound; the active part of *muchachos* (adolescents) in the informal economy; the family-based (in his text unclearly gender marked) character of this activity that came to be dominated by women; and the independent basis of the production process with no master, overseer, or employer to supervise or oppress royal slaves engaging in this activity. On the contrary, Montenegro ironically distorted the scene by portraying the arduous labor of collecting nuggets and rocks by portraying royal slaves as comfortably laid back royalty assigning production quotas to their own slaves. To him, the appropriation of mining resources and the independent mining activity taking place among his fellow royal slaves symbolically put the former private slaves in the owner's or master's place. The parental authority over their own children (including the labor of their children) of which slaves were generally deprived due to the preeminence of the master's rights, was now reestablished by the children's incorporation into the family economy as in the case of free families.

Although Montenegro as representative of the private interests of his owners, and the previous mining order in the jurisdiction, opposed the transformations taking place with the de-privatization of the mines, crown authorities tolerated them, at least initially. Montenegro reported having informed the governor that royal slaves were mining copper on their own account without even paying taxes for the mineral extracted. He complained to his mistress Doña Paula that "I told the Señor governor [that they were extracting copper] and he asked me what kind of copper it was and I said that the tailings [*pedacitos*] and he hasn't responded a word to me yet. That is bound to be the situation of an estate without its owner."[9] Thus, according to him, the governor too had ignored his repeated efforts to preserve the older mining principles and strictures as well as his former private master's interests. But if in this case, the governor's neglect, indifference, or even approval of the slaves' mining activities effectively meant siding with the slaves against the former private concessionaires and not interfering with their mining activities, other governors in years to come would not be so compliant.

Other contemporaries described in greater specificity the mining activities the *cobreros* engaged in—and the gender character of these activities. One crown official reported that:

> The copper that is gathered in the village . . . proceeds from the river . . . and the experienced women . . . probe and find the small pieces of vein that they collect in the deposits that it leaves and when they have a portion of about 8 or 10 arrobas they smelt it. . . . They do the same probing the old terrain and a stream that runs behind the Sanctuary of Our Lady of Charity. . . .[10]

Thus, besides alluvial mining, surface mining also took place "probing the old terrain" of the mines. What this kind of surface mining operations entailed and the (new) labor and provisioning arrangements underlying them was tersely described by a parish priest in 1709:

> To subsist some of [the female royal slaves] search for copper grains among the tailing that remain from the time of the mines; and they also extract it industriously from the rocks that had been thrown away during the searches leading to the discovery of [new] veins of copper. Since [during the days of high mining] the main thing was to follow the vein of metal, the surrounding rock was not valued by the administrator, and in that way, with a lot of sweat and work they have reduced some *arrobas* [one @ = 25 lbs.] of copper to feed and clothe themselves.[11]

Royal slave women's petty mining activities, then, also consisted, in extracting value from the slagheaps left over from the more prosperous export mining days. In those former years, when underground mining had concentrated on working the veins, the metal content of the ores must have been very high, for even the tailings that the royal slaves still collected and recycled had between 10 and 30 percent copper content.[12] After collecting the small rocks from the river and the tailings surrounding the mines, women and their children had to grill, wash, and crush their booty into small pieces the size of a hazelnut in order to separate as much mineral from the rocks as possible. Sometimes they even made homemade kilns in holes on their patios to process their harvest.[13] The copper nuggets found by the river and the copper separated from the rocks became commodities that women usually sold or exchanged by the pound.

In his account, Father Pérez emphasized the self-subsistence character and exchange value of what he portrayed as arduous labor activities. And although he did not explicitly gender these mining activities, other witnesses did.[14] The priest took care, however, of highlighting the surface character of the mining and the recycling aspect of leftover mining operations from the past. In doing so he was suggesting that since no extraction of (royally owned) subsoil resources was taking place, there was no reason to tax these activities. Father Pérez's letter, written "on behalf of my [enslaved] parishioners," also underlined that the king's slaves appropriated resources in the mining jurisdiction to provision themselves and their families. The masters' obligation to subsist their slaves was here turned into the slaves' entitlement to resources in the royal jurisdiction to maintain themselves and their families. The underlying defensiveness of the priest's letter itself points to the contested character of the *cobreros'* surface mining activities and to the politicized character of what had turned into customary practice.

Contestation over the royal slaves' right to mine surface ores sometimes turned into dramatic confrontation, particularly when governors tried to persecute, criminalize, or at the very least tax the *cobreros'* copper mining activities. In 1708, for instance, Governor Joseph Canales prohibited mining activities in El Cobre and confiscated villagers' tools and smelting instruments, as well as a copper vat worth 200 pesos that a local coppersmith had made "with the intention of selling it to free himself."[15] These mining related measures and other abuses by Governor Canales prompted collective mobilization by the royal slaves. The latter fled to the mountains, and with the covert help of other prominent citizens in Santiago de Cuba sent a fellow royal slave representative to the colonial Council of the Indies in Madrid to denounce the governor's abuses.[16] The parish priest who wrote the above letter on behalf of his parishioners was one of the allies that the *cobreros* enlisted in defense of their perceived entitlements. Yet again in the 1730s, the royal slaves clashed with another governor over mining prohibitions and taxation among other issues. Thus, *cobrera* women's appropriation of the heap and their alluvial mining activities constituted contested customary rights that had to be repeatedly protected in this mining community. Royal slaves defended *cobrera* women's right to freely mine the slag piles and the streams and to freely sell their produce by the pound. Elsewhere in Latin America, working the slag piles and the streams could constitute a (private) right that had to be contracted and paid for. In fact, at times the right to work the slag piles had to be fought for in the first place, particularly in the case of women.[17]

It is unclear at what point in the seventeenth century did the feminization of surface mining begin to take place in El Cobre. Early chroniclers like Nicholás Montenegro or another parish priest did not explicitly gender their observations. By 1709, however, there were explicit statements of witnesses that dated back at least to the 1690s. Thus, it is difficult to determine whether surface mining had been regarded as women and minors' work all along or whether it was the result of a more gradual feminization of this sphere. An inventory of slaves and tools back from the old export-mining days suggests that slave women were involved in some mining production related activities such as washing and crushing ores.[18] Women, therefore, may have not only retained this activity after the de-privatization of the mines, but may have further extended their laboring sphere to the collection of the ores in the slagheaps and the nuggets carried by the river. It is even possible that female domination of surface mining activities in the riverbank was a practice whose origins among the royal slaves went even farther back in time: to practices brought back from West Africa by their ancestors earlier in the century. In many places in the precolonial African continent, including the Congo region, men worked in underground mining, but women and children did the surface gathering as well as the washing and sorting of ores.[19]

In any case, regardless of the specific origin of the gender division of labor in the mining sphere, by the end of the seventeenth century there seems to have been two main gendered sectors in the village's internal subsistence economy. Males were entrenched in the agricultural subsistence sector as peasants attached to family land. The masculinity of rural men was based on their identity as direct family providers through farming. That is, the role of paterfamilias among free rural sectors of Spanish society was strongly linked to the family plot. In working their *estancias* or small family farms, royal slaves were assuming the identity and status of free males and distancing themselves from that of dependent slaves.[20] Working the land may have also brought males a welcomed peasant status that put behind them memories of deep mining as slaves. Although women in El Cobre also worked as farmers particularly after they married, farming seems to have been in their case a more complementary occupational identity. Women's primary laboring sphere became mining and other (exclusively) female gendered activities such as sewing, spinning, and weaving performed within the domestic space or its extended space in the village's urban core.

However, aside from these independent self-provisioning activities that allowed the royal slaves of El Cobre to construe themselves as (quasi) "free" subjects, there was another sphere in which the *cobreros* had to labor as slaves, albeit in a part-time way, so to speak. Male royal slaves between the ages of sixteen and sixty were organized into a rotating labor draft system to work in the construction and maintenance of royal fortification projects around the city of Santiago de Cuba, some ten miles away from El Cobre. This *corvée* labor system called for male workers' absences from the village in two-week stints every two to three months. Women, particularly married women, stayed behind in the village and took charge of provisioning their families during the absences of spouses, fathers, and brothers. The narrowing down of the male labor sphere to agricultural activities and the exclusion of surface mining from that sphere may have also been affected by the forced labor requisitions imposed particularly on male royal slaves by the early 1690s. As males were systematically removed from the village for extended periods of time, they may have found less time to engage in activities other than farming and hunting, and women took over control of the mining sector of the village's internal economy. Thus, males in El Cobre did not migrate away from the village, as peasants elsewhere did, to employ themselves as wageworkers in the capitalist sector of the economy while leaving women behind in charge of the agricultural sector. In this precapitalist setting, males migrated "seasonally" to do forced slave labor for the state in the defense service sector, while females stayed home laboring as "free" in the village's mining subsistence economy.

Royal slaves defended women's right to mine the river and the slag piles without taxation precisely in terms of their family provisioning needs while the men worked in the state's fortification projects. During the conflicts of the 1730s, royal slaves protested the governor's refusal to heed their problems with land shortage, the increased forced labor requisitions he imposed on royal slaves, and the attempts he made to tax the copper produced in the community. According to the crown's attorney, the *cobreros* decried the governor's attempt to tax them with "a fifth of the copper that their wives and children washed from the leftovers of the river for their food and necessities . . . to sustain themselves while their husbands worked in the royal construction projects."[21] This constituted an explicit formulation of the discourse in which women's mining entitlements were cast, at least when trying to make a case to authorities. At stake was a family centered discourse (about "wives and children" and "husbands") that justified women's mining activities as complementary but necessary family provisioning activities during periods in which "husbands" could not fulfill their paterfamilias duties because they were away fulfilling their obligations to the state as royal slaves. (Note as well the portrayal of female alluvial mining almost as a scavenging activity to morally undermine the taxation injunction.) In any case, women in El Cobre did not have to construe their femininity through a discourse of complete subjection to a master or complete dependence on a paterfamilias. They could do so in a more autonomous and complementary way as co-providers in a family-based economy, albeit through a separate sphere of work. It was as if males as providers had the usufruct over the land resources in the community, while females as co-providers had claims over the mineral resources—particularly while their husbands were working for the crown. Females' provisioning role did not fully threaten males' control of land, their spheres of work, and their masculinity since it was for the most part grounded in a separate gendered sphere of mining activities.

A significant aspect of female royal slaves' informal mining production was the linkage to a market economy that it provided, if one still operating at a subsistence level. In fact, perhaps the main connection to a market economy that the royal slaves of El Cobre established was precisely through the mining activities of women and minors in the village. An early parish priest of El Cobre pointed to the exchange value of the mining activities of the royal slaves after the de-privatization of the mines. Father Pedro de Cerquera wrote in 1672:

> Today there is the best fair [or business] from the river's copper and from the tailings which are sold in exchange for the molasses, tobacco, clothes, soap, and other things that those who wish to buy want. A lot [of copper] has been extracted and until now it keeps on being smelted and it will be so until it is finished.[22]

Father Cerquera's early (nongendered) observations focused on the exchange value of copper that enabled royal slaves to insert themselves in a market economy and allowed them to buy what they could not directly produce themselves. These were supplementary goods to what were considered the fundamental staples of cassava and meat that in a subsistence economy were directly produced by the paterfamilias and other household members. Nicholás Montenegro concurred with the priest's observations regarding the royal slaves' connection to the market through their access to copper and its marketable power, noting in one of his letters that "indeed, my Lady, copper is the currency that nowadays moves around in the mines."[23] The liquidity of copper as a scarce commodity in the regional market must have given it an important place in this community's household economy.

Commodity production and access to the market, particularly in the case of slaves, were also activities often construed as forms of freedom. The royal slaves were sometimes portrayed as having the means to exchange goods in the market "as if they were free" and to select more or less freely what to buy in return for their productive activities. Montenegro, again with some ironic exaggeration noted the significance of access to the market and the possibilities it opened up. He wrote in 1672:

> There is no other occupation today in these mines nor other aspiration than to obtain more copper and to embellish their bodies. . . . They [the women] no longer take pride in adorning their skirts with [simple] laces, now they use silver ones. Before there was too much arrogance among these senores and senoras, as my Lady well knows, but today it is too much for they say publicly that they are free [horros].[24]

According to Montenegro, the slaves associated their release from private slavery and the new order in the mining jurisdiction under crown rule with freedom—or at least with a greater freedom than in former times. With the purchasing power of the copper they were mining on their own account they had gained access to purchasing power in the market. This concrete and practical freedom made possible the concomitant freedom of choosing clothing with which to publicly construct their social image. Access to the market enabled slaves control over their social body and to transcend their fixed place in the established social order. In this case, such dislocations were evidenced in breaches of sumptuary laws and dress codes such as the use of silver lace among enslaved women, in manifestations of "wealth" and empowerment that the conservative slave Montenegro considered inappropriate and "arrogant" in the case of slaves; and in provocatively explicit statements that articulated these changes as forms of freedom. Even if there was distortion and exaggeration in his account of a new local prosperity and the "luxuries" slaves were now able to afford, his understanding of the significance of these apparently minor expressions of social identity and status through dressing practices and commodities acquired in the market was to the point.

Yet the actual material value of women's mining activities does not seem to have been high. One crown official estimated in 1739 that for the collected copper nuggets the women "get one real of profit [or] two more or less to eat without having any other cost but their personal labor."[25] One real was considered the equivalent of a day's ration given to royal slaves while working in the fortification projects, whereas three reales was the ongoing wage for an unskilled male peon. Roughly speaking then, the women miners of El Cobre were earning the equivalent of (or slightly more) what was officially regarded the "bare subsistence" income to reproduce the labor force. Thus, although working as free independent producers, women miners were materially earning as slaves. The advantages of this productive activity for female royal slaves lay more in the social and symbolic aspects of production than in its low material benefit.

Women may have embraced copper mining for several reasons. It was an activity performed in the immediacy of the village houses—in the material and cultural space most strongly associated with females—and did not require long-distance displacements to outlying farms of the village. Women and children residing in the village could set themselves to work whenever they needed or wanted income or had time off from other obligations, and thereby they could regulate their own work rhythms. Surface mining near their village homes could have been construed as an extension of the household sphere. In addition, surface copper mining constituted a "low risk" activity not particularly subject to seasonal constraints, to the ravages of epidemics, or to the dangers of underground mining. Furthermore, copper provided guaranteed access to the market inside the village and in the nearby city and thus to obtain products—such as meat—that would have been difficult for women to obtain directly. Finally, there may not have been much choice left for women as males entrenched themselves in the agricultural sector and established control over land and farms in the village's surrounding area.

Beyond the portrayals of this economic activity as females' way of supporting a family particularly when males were away, copper mining would have constituted for many women (and youth) an important (if limited) independent source of income that could enable them to buy clothing, hair ribbons, handkerchiefs, small jewelry, ceramic and other petty commodities of the sort females in the village owned—and perhaps even, in some cases, the silver laces for Sunday-best skirts that Nicholás Montenegro deplored. Less likely these activities may have allowed women to acquire sufficient savings to purchase their own freedom or that of their children.[26]

Women, however, did not control all the sectors of the El Cobre's informal mining industry. There was another sexual division of labor within the mining sector of the local economy, one suggestive of possible internal tensions and exploitative relations. If women and adolescents dominated the labor surface mining and pre-smelting processing activities, it was a handful of men who were the skilled smelters and metal smiths in this community, and the local retailers to whom women sold their copper by the pound. If anyone in the village seems to have been able to profit or achieve some "prosperity" from the local copper mining industry, it was these few artisans and petty merchants. But any gender-based internal tension that may have existed between local female producers and male artisans and retailers did not make it to the records, despite the potential. The tensions that did find a way into the record were those between insiders and outsiders of the community. One such conflict took place in 1738 between crown officials involved in contraband trade who tried to block local retailers' access to the market. But if such complaints noted the operations of outside middlemen forcefully trying to monopolize the trade and to force down the local price of copper, they also suggested that such practices constituted breaches in custom and that indeed the *cobreros*, or some among them, were used to selling their copper directly at higher market prices in the nearby city of Santiago de Cuba. Such complaints, therefore, rested in these royal slaves' claims to operate freely as well in the regional market outside the village.

Women and Political Mobilization in El Cobre

Political mobilization took different forms in this early modern colonial milieu. Collective forms of protest and of defense of entitlements among the *cobreros* included flight and local revolt, but more surprisingly in the case of slaves, use of the courts as well. Although sometimes these forms of mobilization were autonomous, tactical (vertical) alliances with elite sectors of colonial society were necessary to navigate the courts. There were few forms of association possible for anyone in colonial society at this point in time, but particularly for slaves whose "socially dead" status excluded them from the body polity. There were no mining related guilds around which mine workers could have associated and trade unions did not exist at the time. Their ambiguous status as royal slaves living in their own village, however, allowed the *cobreros* to mobilize collectively as a corporate community. Since slaves had little or no legal persona whatsoever, taking on a corporate one constituted an unusual enough occurrence in a slave society of the Americas. The royal slaves of El Cobre were able to mobilize collectively through the judicial system, filing complaints and denouncing abuses against them.[27] Although women at times approached the courts individually, they were not able to officially act as representatives of the community since Spanish colonial law excluded them from public positions.

Although men were more visible and vocal in the records regarding acts of protest and resistance, women were by no means politically inactive in the community. One of the most acrimonious conflicts in this community took place during the long administration of hostile Governor Ximénez (1729–1738). Although the list of grievances included the governor's attempt to tax the copper mined in the village, it was by no means limited to mining related abuses. Protests over excessive labor requisitions and claims to land played a major role in the *cobreros'* protracted struggle of this decade. By 1737 the village was divided into two factions and one of them had initiated litigation in Havana. In that year there was a "tumult" in the village that resulted in the death of a local leader, the arrest of more than twenty men and eight women, and the confiscation of their property. The eight arrested women spoke little during the interrogations,[28] but the accusations brought against them by some local slave officials and by crown authorities may throw some light on the role of women during local collective mobilizations. The accusations also show how female roles were gendered and perceived as threatening. Particularly significant about these accusations were the kind of actions that royal officials—and some men in the community—construed as "subversive" transgressions.

The royal slave bailiff Patricio Cosme, declared that these eight women were "the ones who instigate and who incite men and make trouble, for in some of the disturbances that occur at any moment some of them attend and even bring a machete in their belts."[29] Another bailiff stated that the women in question were "bad and rebellious. . . ."[30] Another slave official, Joseph Cosme, said that he had heard that "the most unruly of all was the old hag

Maria de la Rosa who tells men to put on her skirts and let her put on their pants."[31] She was accused of using gender metaphors to provoke men and insult their virility. Francisca de los Reyes (age thirty-seven) was described as "a resolute woman who did not allow any soldier to enter her house to make embargoes . . . she has attended all the tumults with her brothers. . . . she is arrogant and has a talkative style."[32] The widow Isabel de Lugo (age sixty) and her unmarried daughter Andrea (age twenty-six) were accused of turning their house into a meeting place for the insurgents.[33] A recurring theme in the declarations of male villagers was the implicit double laden transgression for which these women were accountable: for their participation in public "disorders" and for gender transgressions that some of their acts allegedly constituted.

Yet other gender based accusations against these women were even more striking: Simona Vicente (age forty) was accused of dominating her husband by threatening not to sleep with him until he executed or performed what she wanted.[34] Magdalena Quiala's (age thirty-five) political transgressions also constituted articulations between domestic and public realms. Lieutenant Velasco Calderín informed the governor that she "is a very small woman but I gather she dominates her husband."[35] In ruling the house these dangerous women ruled the community and had the power to mobilize men—or so the power of these dangerous women was construed. Juana Chrisostoma (age fifty) was a more singular and complex case: although there were no gender transgressions on her part, as the wife of the leader Matías Moreno, she was presumably the main connection between him and the community. She may have even taken his place while he and other men went to file judicial complaints on behalf of the community in the courts of Havana. The crown official described her as "a virtuous woman, very devoted to the Sanctuary [of Our Lady of Charity], but with the defect that her husband Matías Moreno apparently left her power or orders to govern the pueblo [in his absence]."[36] She was reported as "one with voice and vote in the meetings and reunions that were held during the disturbances in the village."[37] It is unclear how unusual this role may have been for a female in unofficial political arenas, outside the rigid gendered strictures of the Spanish colonial state.

In short, although excluded from officials in municipal government or as community representatives in court, women participated in local disturbances, turned working tools such as machetes into weapons, held political opinions, made their voices heard, used their influence, agitated in public and private, offered their houses as alternative meeting places, stood up to soldiers, and at times enjoyed the right to vote in alternative assemblies.

CONCLUSIONS

The transformations that took place in this mining community after the Spanish crown's de-privatization of the mines were unusually noteworthy, to the point that they may have seemed fantastic to a nineteenth- or twentieth-century observer. A corporate pueblo of free people of African descent would have been rare enough in a New World slave society, but one constituted by royal slaves was almost anomalous. We know of no other such village in the Americas before the abolitions of slavery. The "miraculous" image of Our Lady of Charity that became patroness of the village during the last decades of the seventeenth century may have been emblematic of the quasi "fantastic" and unusual character of this community. More to the point for the purposes of this anthology is the remarkable spectacle of slaves mining on their own account and supplying a regional market with their own local production. Our case is particularly enthralling because of the central role women came to play in this local and regional copper mining economy. Although there is little memory today of a time when women played a central role in the mostly male construed sphere of copper mining in El Cobre, the story of this community shows how historically contingent gender roles can be. It shows as well how gender formations are articulated with other historically contingent identities such as status and class.

El Cobre presents us with a transition case from an export mining enterprise based on slave labor into a precapitalist family-based local and regional mining economy. In their transformation from slaves to royal slaves, *cobreros*—unlike regular slaves—took on a prominent role in the provisioning of themselves and their families. This provisioning role allowed males to construe their social identities as paterfamilias, a role not usually possible to enslaved dependent subjects in colonial slave societies. But since male *cobreros* were also subject to (part-time) forced labor requisitions as royal slaves, females played a particularly important provisioning role in the family economy. The royal slave women of El Cobre contributed to this family provisioning role with surface mining activities as well as with other "properly female" occupational activities such as sewing, weaving, and spinning common to free women in colonial society. In fact, mining became an integral part of the female occupational sphere in this community and a productive activity that construed their provisioning role in a separate but complementary way. Aside from their major (but complementary) provisioning role in the new local family economy, laboring in the mining sector entailed forms of freedom in other ways. It meant women and their children could work at their own rhythms, with no master or overseer to supervise them. And although at stake were subsistence level activities, mining production was linked to the market. Access to the market gave women access to a wide range of commodities of their choice and market exchanges were also construed as a form of freedom more proper to free men and women than to slaves. Yet, despite the claims of some early local chroniclers regarding the alleged prosperity reaped by slaves on account of their undue appropriation of the ores, it seems surface mining activities allowed *cobrera* women to barely scratch a living rather than draw much profit from them. The benefits royal slave women accrued from their mining activities were more social and symbolic than material.

Mining on their own account entailed laying claims on royal slave women's right to appropriate the slagheaps and the nuggets washed by the river and to do so without taxation. It entailed control of their own and their children's labor power, the organization of production in their own terms, and the right to access the market to freely exchange and sell their produce. There is, however, no record of women in El Cobre mobilizing exclusively on gender grounds in defense of their mining rights. When conflict and protest took place in this mining community, women mobilized with and against men around broader clusters of issues. Women's political mobilization both in the domestic and public domains, however, was often explicitly gendered by authorities and negatively rendered as "unfeminine" behavior.

Finally, the historicity of gender formations in the productive and laboring spheres of this community, particularly in the mining sector, become particularly clear if approached from a long-range perspective. Although under the first export mining period during the early seventeenth century female slaves had been involved in mining production, mining activities had been predominantly carried out with male slaves.[38] The gender marked character of mining would later shift again during the nineteenth century with the reactivation of deep mining under large foreign-owned capitalist enterprises. But the re-gendering of the mining sphere did not take place without some initial resistance from *cobrero* men who seemed to associate mining labor with female work, with the occupational sphere of their enslaved mining ancestors (and perhaps with that of the newly imported African slave labor force), and with proletarianization. In 1838, Intendant José de Aguilés reported that "the elder [male] *cobrero* miners do not have any inclination toward the profession of their fathers and it should be noted that women occupy themselves in separation of the minerals but the men say they are farmers [*labradores*]."[39] Full masculinization of the mining sector in this community may not have taken place until the twentieth century. Today it seems inconceivable to people in this mining community that once upon a time women engaged in—not to say dominated—mining production in this village, if only through their independent surface mining activities. There is little memory in present-day El Cobre of women working in the copper mines, even as surface miners. *Cobreros* recall one such woman and her children who picked over the rocks in the slag piles (one of these children is a mature woman today), but the fact that she is remembered as an extraordinary case in El Cobre suggests the extent to which the copper mining industry has been defeminized during the twentieth century, if not before.

NOTES

Epigraph. Report of Governor Cayetano de Urbina, Santiago de Cuba, Feb. 1846, Archivo Histórico Nacional, Ultramar 4638(2); Report of Don Joseph Palacios de Saldustum, Santiago de Cuba, July 31, 1739, fols. 13–15v, Archivo General de Indias, Santo Domingo 385.

Revised from *The Virgin, the King and the Royal Slaves of El Cobre: Negotiating Freedom in Colonial Cuba, 1670–1780* by María Elena Díaz © 2000 by the Board of Trustees of the Leland Stanford Jr. University. By permission of the publisher www.sup.org.

1. See María Elena Díaz, *The Virgin, the King and the Royal Slaves of El Cobre: Negotiating Freedom in Colonial Cuba, 1670–1780* (Stanford: Stanford University Press, 2000).
2. Inventory of slaves, 1670, fols.126–134/201–209, Archivo General de Indias (hereafter AGI), Santo Domingo (hereafter SD) 1631; Family census of 1773, AGI-SD 1628.
3. One such external market was the busy port of Cartagena de Indias in present-day Colombia; and some copper also ended up in nearby Jamaica through contraband trade. Nicholás Montenegro to Doña Paula de Eguiluz y Montenegro, El Cobre, July 7, 1672, AGI-SD 104; Report of Sánchez de Castel [ca. 1739] AGI-SD 380; Petition of the Pueblo of El Cobre to the king, Santiago del Prado, November 19, 1738, AGI-SD 426.
4. Díaz, *The Virgin*, 215, table 6.
5. A classic study is that by June Nash, *We Eat the Mines and the Mines Eat Us: Dependency and Exploitation in Bolivian Tin Mines* (New York: Columbia University Press, 1979). Other studies include Florencia Mallon, *In Defense of Community in Peru's Central Highlands: Peasant Struggle and Capitalist Transition, 1860–1940* (Princeton: Princeton University Press, 1984) and Thomas M. Klubock, *Contested Communities: Class, Gender, and Politics in Chile's El Teniente Copper Mine, 1904–1951* (Durham: Duke University Press, 1998).
6. There are no studies about how the transition from slavery to free labor took shape in mining communities in Latin America. El Cobre during the nineteenth century constitutes an ideal case study for the examination of that process. For histories of slave-based mining production in Latin America, see particularly Robert C. West, *Colonial Placer Mining in Colombia* (Baton Rouge: Louisiana State University, 1952); William F. Sharp, *Slavery on the Spanish Frontier: The Colombian Chocó* (Norman: University of Oklahoma Press, 1976); A.J.R. Russell-Wood, "Technology and Society: The Impact of Gold-Mining on the Institution of Slavery in Portuguese America," *Journal of Economic History* 37 (March 1977): 59–82. For a more social history with an explicit focus on gender, see Kathleen J. Higgins, *"Licentious Liberty" in a Brazilian Gold-Mining Region: Slavery, Gender, and Social Control in Eighteenth Century Sabará, Minas Gerais* (University Park, PN: Pennsylvania State University Press, 1999).
7. Nicholás Montenegro to Doña Paula de Eguiluz y Montenegro, El Cobre, July 7, 1672, AGI-SD 104.
8. Ibid.
9. Ibid.
10. Report of Don Isidro Limonta, October 4, 1779, fols. 1111–1113, AGI-Cuba 1231. Earlier reports similarly point to women mining the river. Report of Don Joseph Palacios de Saldustum, July 31, 1739, fols. 13–15v, AGI-SD 385; Testimony of Father Diego Duque de Estrada, Santiago de Cuba, April 24, 1711, C 23, fols. 77–79v, AGI-ESC 93A.
11. Father Juan Antonio Pérez, Santiago del Prado [El Cobre], April 14, 1709, Cuaderno (hereafter C) 23, fols. 7–11, AGI-Escribanía (hereafter ESC) 93A.
12. The estimate is based on the ratio of smelted ore to metal reported by royal slaves to crown officials. Report of Don Nicholás Velasco Calderín, July 31, 1739, fols. 19–20v, AGI-SD 385 and Don Bernardo Castillo, ca. November 1710–March 1711, C 23, fols. 33–36v, AGI-ESC 93A, and Report of Don Isidro Limonta, October 4, 1779, fols. 1111–1113, AGI-Cuba 1231. See Díaz, *The Virgin*, 203.

13. Reports of Don Nicholás Velasco Calderín, and of Joseph Palacios Salurstum, July 31, 1739, both in AGI-SD 385. Besides the holes in patios, more complicated smelting operations by skilled smelters also took place in the village, but these were carried out by men.
14. Testimony of Father Diego Duque de Estrada, Santiago de Cuba, April 24, 1711, C 23, fols. 77–79v, AGI-ESC 93A.
15. Letter of Father Juan Antonio Pérez, El Cobre, April 14, 1709, C 23, fols. 7–11, AGI-ESC 93A.
16. For a full account of this historical episode, see Díaz, *The Virgin*, 289–298.
17. June Nash, for instance, points to such a situation in the tin mines of Bolivia during the 1950s when indigenous men and women working for private contractors had to *buy* the rights to pan the metal from the streams or to pick over the rocks in the slag piles. Nash, *We Eat the Mines*,14, 116.
18. Slave Inventory of 1647, fols. 7–14, AGI-SD 104.
19. Eugenia W. Herbert, *Red Gold of Africa: Copper in Pre Colonial History and Culture* (Madison: University of Wisconsin, 1984) 19–23, 36, 44–45.
20. For a fuller discussion of the gendered occupational sphere of agriculture, see Diaz, *The Virgin*, 166–177.
21. Crown attorney's summary, Madrid, June 3, 1732, AGI-SD 493.
22. Father Don Pedro de Cerquera, El Cobre, June 10, 1672, AGI-SD 104.
23. Nicholás Montenegro to Doña Paula de Eguiluz y Montenegro, El Cobre, July 7, 1672, AGI-SD 104.
24. Ibid.
25. Report of Don Joseph Palacios de Saldustum, July 31, 1739, AGI-SD 385.
26. Until the 1730s there were few manumissions in the village and no major gender gaps can be detected in them. Thereafter for unclear reasons the number of manumissions dramatically rose and they became overwhelmingly male manumissions. See Díaz, *The Virgin*, 256–258.
27. For a discussion of the *cobreros'* use of colonial and metropolitan courts see Díaz, *The Virgin*, 285–313.
28. Of the eight women, three responded that their occupation was "copper gatherers," two others identified themselves each as a "seamstress" and a "spinner." The last three gave occupations related to farming: a sixty-year-old woman worked in her "garden plot," another construed her farming occupational identity in a complementary fashion as a "farmer [*estanciera*] with her husband" and only one identified herself fully as a "farmer." Interrogation of *cobrera* women, Autos of Governor Ximénez, Santiago de Cuba, 1737, fols. 350–364, AGI-SD 451.
29. Testimony of the bailiff Patricio Cosme, Autos of Governor Ximénez, 1737, fols. 100v–101, AGI-SD 451.
30. Ibid. Testimony of Felix Gerónimo Hernández, fols. 107v–108.
31. Ibid. Testimony of Joseph Cosme, fols. 133–133v.
32. Ibid., Report of Lieutenant Nicholás Velasco Calderín, fol. 162v, see also 177v.
33. Ibid., fol. 177.
34. Ibid., fol. 163.
35. Ibid., fol. 163.
36. Ibid., fols. 163–163v.
37. Ibid., fol. 177.

38. In the peak decades of mining production in El Cobre (1600–1620s) slave inventories listed a predominantly male African slave force. In 1620, for instance, females constituted only 34.9 percent of the mostly African slave force in the mining settlement. Elsewhere in colonial Latin America a mixed slave labor force was employed in gold mining in the Colombian Chocó, but in Minas Gerais gold mining constituted a male sphere strongly based on slave labor.

39. Report of José de Aguilés, Santiago de Cuba, Reino de Minería, August 31, 1838, Archivo Histórico Nacional, Ultramar 6(1). British companies dealt with shortages in the local male labor force by importing African slaves to work the mines in the nineteenth century, despite a British-Spanish international treaty prohibiting the slave trade in Cuba (1817) and right after the abolition of slavery in the British empire (1834).

CHAPTER 2

Making a Difference in Colonial Interventionism in Gold Mining in Wassa Fiase, Gold Coast (Ghana): The Activism of Two Women, 1874–1893

Kwabena O. Akurang-Parry

INTRODUCTION

This study deals with the history of two remarkable women whose respective activism impacted colonial rule and gold mining in Wassa Fiase in the Gold Coast (modern Ghana) during the last three decades of the nineteenth century. The two women were Amba N'kroma who was married to Enimil Kwao, the king of the gold-bearing state of Wassa Fiase, and the other was Adwoa Arduah, the queen[1] of Wassa Fiase. Apart from a brief review of women's activism and a historiographical rethinking of the looming presence of colonialism over the mining setting of Wassa Fiase, this chapter is divided into two major parts. The first portion examines the social activism of Amba N'kroma whose quest for divorce from King Enimil Kwao served as a catalyst for the maximization of colonial rule and the inception of corporate gold mining in Wassa Fiase. In 1876, Amba N'kroma traveled from Wassa Fiase, a backwater in the Western Province, to Cape Coast, the colonial capital in the Central Province, to seek divorce at the colonial courts. Among other things, she informed the colonial authorities that her husband, King Enimil Kwao, had engaged in slave dealing, a precolonial practice that had been abolished by the British in 1874–1875.[2] Consequently, Enimil Kwao was summoned to Cape Coast, tried, imprisoned, and exiled to Lagos, all spanning the period 1876–1889. His incarceration and subsequent exile created a political vacuum that enabled the colonial state to serve as an agency of corporate capitalist intervention in the local gold mining economy.

For its part, the second section discusses Queen Adwoa Arduah's unswerving determination to seek the freedom and reinstallation of Enimil Kwao as king of Wassa Fiase. I show that despite the colonial state's overwhelming interest in seeking the Wassa Fiases' acquiescence to colonial rule, Adwoa Arduah assiduously championed an anticolonial movement, effectively mitigating the impact of colonial rule and capitalist gold mining. In sum, through Amba N'kroma, the colonial state was able to remove King Enimil Kwao from the rich auriferous region of Wassa Fiase, enabling capitalist gold mining companies to operate there. For her part, Adwoa Arduah sought relentlessly to reassert the power of Enimil Kwao, thereby moderating the impact of colonial rule and capitalist gold mining.

LITERATURE REVIEW: WOMEN'S ACTIVISM

Indeed, the history of colonial rule and African responses in Wassa Fiase would not be complete without an assessment of the respective roles of Amba N'kroma and Adwoa Arduah. Unfortunately, the available data on these two women is not as comprehensive as could be wished. Their respective advocacy and activism, however, enhance our understanding of the nuances of gender, patriarchy—both indigenous and colonial—social change, and women's activism in the nineteenth-century Gold Coast and Wassa Fiase in particular. Furthermore, the actions of both women illustrate how women in backwater regions, like their counterparts in urban centers, used advocacy and activism in their efforts to build revolutionary pathways of adaptation to the political economy of colonialism. Above all, their respective activism and the consequent responses of the colonial state throw light on colonial rule, indigenous institutions, and capitalist gold mining, which was in flux in the late-nineteenth-century Gold Coast.

Scholarly work on women in the nineteenth-century Gold Coast has made great strides, but much of what we know deals with how women suffered the brunt of patriarchy and institutionalized economic exploitation, namely slavery, pawnship, and forced labor.[3] Very little is known about women who fought against gender inequality, patriarchal control, colonialism, and racism to better their lives and society in general.[4] However, a few studies have examined coastal and elite women's accumulation of wealth, power, and prestige.[5] The subject of the Asante queens' resistance to British imperialism has also been studied,[6] and the staple of the literature has centered on Queen Yaa Asantewa of Edweso. In fact, Yaa Asantewa has attained a folk heroine status, garnering considerable oral history.[7] In 1900–1901, the looming inevitability of British colonial rule in Asante intimidated Asante rulers to inaction and unspoken acquiescence. Unlike the other Asante rulers, Yaa Asantewa rose to the occasion and mobilized the demoralized Asante armies for the last military engagement with the British-led armies. As celebratory as the Yaa Asantewa historical epic has become, her heroic deeds sadly enough only punctuated the literature[8] until the centenary of the war in 2000, when the *Ghana Studies* journal came out with a special issue to memorialize her stellar achievements.[9]

With regard to women and gold mining, studies have concentrated on how women's labor, both unfree and free, sustained the mining industry in the precolonial period.[10] Several visitors to the mining region of Wassa Fiase reported seeing women engaged in different types of labor, including panning, porterage, placer mining, and other services.[11] According to Raymond E. Dumett, a large number of women were involved in mining and "women also participated with men in prospecting—both as a regular occupation and indirectly in the course of other tasks."[12] It would appear that capitalist mining companies that came into being during the gold rush in the late nineteenth century prejudicially employed male laborers, excluding female labor, with the hope of maximizing their capital output. Thus, very little is known about how women's role shaped the economic aspects of the gold mining industry during the last three decades of the nineteenth century.

BEFORE MAKING A DIFFERENCE: THE GOLD MINING SETTING

The arrival of the Portuguese in what later became the Gold Coast ca. 1471 popularized the availability of gold in the region, hence its name. From the mid-1870s, the gold-bearing region of Wassa Fiase received worldwide publicity[13] due to the unprecedented global commodification of gold.[14] Consequently, during the last three decades of the nineteenth century a gold rush occurred.[15] Luring both Africans in the Gold Coast and Europeans, the magnetic pull of the gold rush attracted corporate capitalists and cavalier prospectors alike.[16] From 1878 to 1895, about thirty-five gold mining and concession companies registered to operate in Wassa Fiase.[17]

The gold rush coincided with British colonial rule that was formally imposed in the Gold Coast in 1874–1875. Historians differ on whether the British authorities readily promoted capitalist gold mining or remained indifferent to the influx of gold mining companies to Wassa Fiase. Francis Agbodeka and Paul Rosenblum have argued that the colonial state provided congenial political and economic climates for the mining companies.[18] In contrast, Dumett asserts that until the late 1890s, when the British colonial economic development policy was inaugurated by Joseph Chamberlain, the colonial secretary,[19] the colonial state had very little to do with the capitalist exploitation of the Wassa goldfields.[20] Dumett's position is predicated on the fact that the colonial state failed to provide railways as a vent for gold mining despite the constant pressure from the mining companies. More recently, I have clarified that instead of railways, the colonial state provided roads to link the mining centers and the coastal ports.[21] In addition, the colonial state provided Wassa Fiase with social amenities, infrastructure, and constabulary authority, notwithstanding the fact that major parts of the coastal areas, the hub of colonial rule, lacked such colonial infrastructure and personnel.[22] Dumett recognizes these instruments of administration, but argues that they were woefully inadequate.[23] Indeed, that the colonial state developed structures in the backwater mining centers during the embryonic stage of colonial rule, and the fact that the coastal enclave, the axis of colonial rule, lacked such amenities, prove that the colonial state promoted capitalist development of the Wassa Fiase goldfields.[24]

There is no doubt that Britain, at the center stage of the phenomenal global commodification of gold, showed direct interest in the development of the Wassa Fiase resources. In order to gain control over the goldfields, the colonial government had to vigorously buttress colonial rule, but the resistance of the ruler of Wassa Fiase, King Enimil Kwao, posed impregnable barriers. Consequently, the colonial government capitalized on Amba N'kroma's allegation of Enimil Kwao's slave dealing to imprison, depose, and exile him, thereby paving the way for capitalist intervention in the Wassa Fiase goldfields.

Gold and Colonialism: Amba N'kroma's Social Activism and Its Effects

It would appear from the evidentiary standpoint that Amba N'kroma's social activism was individual-based: she was not influenced by anyone in her decisions and actions. Borrowing from Cheryl Johnson-Odim's biographical studies of Nigerian women, we may speculate that Amba N'kroma was a "feminist" because she sought to "challenge both the restriction of women's rights and women's marginalization from centers of power and decision making."[25] Amba N'kroma sought divorce from Enimil Kwao with the hope of transforming her social location. Hence her activism was an exemplification of gender consciousness rooted in the precincts of her oppression. But Amba N'kroma's case presents historical puzzles. For one thing, it is not clear whether her actions were indicative of indigenous practice. The complex social and structural spaces occupied by women among the Akans[26] make it difficult to pinpoint the political location of women's actions. For this reason, Johnson-Odim has aptly concluded that "we so often have contradictory pictures of women in 'traditional' West African societies."[27] For another, we are not certain about the influence exercised on her by the colonial state.

Amba N'kroma's story began in early 1876, a period of unceasing political crises between Enimil Kwao and his subordinate chiefs. She traveled from Wassa Fiase to Cape Coast to sue for divorce. The divorce action was undertaken on February 11, 1876, at the Judicial Assessor's Court, presided by Acting Judicial Assessor William Melton. It was when the arbitration panel was about to make its judgment known on February 15, 1876, that Amba N'kroma informed the colonial authorities that her husband, Enimil Kwao, had purchased seven slaves from an Asante man, named Yar Appia.[28] Anyway, using British laws, the Judicial Assessor's Court concluded that Amba N'kroma was not legally married to Enimil Kwao, but had only been cohabiting with him; consequently, she was granted her quest for divorce, but an anomalous one.

The outcome of Amba N'kroma's allegation of Enimil Kwao's slave dealing is important for understanding the early colonial history of Wassa Fiase and the incubation of corporate capitalist gold mining. In sum, in February 1875, Enimil Kwao was charged by Governor George Strahan's administration for allegedly buying seven slaves from Yar Appiah. Although Enimil Kwao denied Amba N'Kroma's allegation,[29] he was sentenced to three years imprisonment and fined £400 or 100 ounces of gold.[30] Apart from the sentence, Enimil Kwao was deprived of his kingly authority and "all [his] lands all was [sic] taken and properties by Governor Strahan."[31] The colonial government's actions paved the way for effective colonial rule and consequent corporate capitalist intervention in the goldfields.[32]

Overall, considering the indigenous normative order at the beginning of colonial rule, Amba N'kroma's actions appear to be unusual. It is doubtful whether the interior peoples traveled all the way to Cape Coast to seek divorce. Divorce was not only looked down upon, but it also stigmatized divorced women and their families. Most strangely, seeking divorce from a king was rare; even to this day it is uncommon. Certainly, the winds of social change and acculturation in the Gold Coast were transforming social institutions and structures, including customary marriage. But a clear distinction should be made between the coastal areas, the fertile centers of diffusion of innovation, and the backwater regions, the latter of which included Wassa Fiase, where normative practices remained largely unchanged. Additionally, Amba N'kroma was most likely illiterate; as a result, she was not informed like some coastal, urban women, whose education and changing social environment could raise their consciousness and radicalize them to use the colonial courts to seek divorce.

Given these equivocal explanatory perspectives, Amba N'kroma's ability to sue for divorce at Cape Coast may be assessed from other standpoints. Her husband, King Enimil Kwao, had problems with the colonial state. First, he had failed to appear before the Judicial Assessor's Court, the "highest tribunal open to those natives of the Gold Coast who claimed British protection before the formal proclamation of Gold Coast Colony" on July 24, 1874.[33] Also, he had had a number of hostile clashes with some of his subordinate chiefs, especially Kwabena Angoo, the chief of Tarkwa, the principal mining town. The antagonism between Enimil Kwao and Kwabena Angoo reached its peak in 1875, when the latter sued the former for his alleged unilateral control over the gold mines.[34] In that same year, Governor Strahan sent Cudjoe Sago, an African agent, to compel Enimil Kwao to free one Fawah, the wife of Gan Quow, who was being held in "forcible detention" due to Gan Quow's failure to pay a fine imposed on him by Enimil Kwao.[35] Enimil Kwao riled Cudjoe Sago by questioning his credentials, claiming that the case was "an old time palaver" and that if the colonial government had reasons to pursue it, Governor Strahan should summon him.[36] Due to the anticipated resistance to colonial rule, Governor Strahan sought to punish Enimil Kwao, hoping to use the punishment as a deterrent against African rulers who would want to disregard the authority emanating from the infant colonial state. Thus, Governor Strahan dispatched "a force of Houssas [constabulary force], under Captain [Alfred] Moloney," his private secretary, "to inquire into the matter of detention and to punish the King by the infliction of a fine."[37] Consequently, Enimil Kwao was fined thirty ounces of gold; in addition, he released Fawah to her husband and freed four Shama war captives.[38]

It is clear from all these incidents that the resistance of Enimil Kwao posed problems to colonial rule and capitalist exploitation of the goldfields. Hence, it is likely that the colonial authorities capitalized on Amba N'kroma's allegation of Enimil Kwao's engagement in slave dealing to remove him from the political scene to enable gold mining companies to have a field day in Wassa Fiase. The plausibility of this explanation stems from the fact that Amba N'kroma's quest for divorce at Cape Coast occurred immediately after the departure of the Moloney delegation from Wassa Fiase. Therefore, it is likely that she was influenced by either Captain Moloney or some agents of the colonial government.

Enimil Kwao's reasons for Amba N'Kroma's actions are also informative. He explained that when Yar Appiah brought the seven persons, that is, the alleged slaves, Amba N'kroma was absent; therefore, none of them was placed under her care.[39] Second, he claimed that Amba N'kroma may have reported him to the colonial authorities because her uncle owed him money. This meant that once Enimil Kwao's authority was weakened by the colonial authorities, her uncle could evade his debt payment.[40] All these, coming from Enimil Kwao, may be taken as speculative, self-serving explanations to exonerate himself. However, the chain of events suggests that the issue of slave dealing cropped up while Amba N'kroma was at Cape Coast and was seized upon by the colonial authorities.

Indeed, given the paucity of sources, the most plausible explanation for Amba N'kroma's journey to Cape Coast to seek divorce was her knowledge that the local community would not grant her divorce from Enimil Kwao. To understand this better, we may place Amba N'kroma's story in a comparative perspective. The encounters between Africans and Europeans have revealed that the effects of colonial rule, the Christian missionary enterprise, and social change on African institutions forced some Africans to abandon normative African practices in favor of European ones. Some Africans did so not because they perceived specific European practices to be superior to their own, but simply because specific European practices served their immediate needs.[41] One cogent example was the fact that a number of Enimil Kwao's subjects had sued him for various reasons at the Cape Coast colonial court, and in all cases, the colonial authorities had imposed fines on Enimil Kwao.[42] Thus, the colonial impact on chieftaincy, especially the erosion of the authority of Enimil Kwao, and the fact that his subjects now had a superior authority to seek redress, adequately explain why Amba N'kroma decided to sue for divorce at Cape Coast. The ability of the colonial state to exact punishment on African rulers, in this case, and the earlier punishments of Enimil Kwao, provide significant insights into Amba N'kroma's choices. This made her realize that despite Enimil Kwao's power and authority, the colonial state was more powerful than he. Hence, she gauged that her needs could be better met through the colonial authorities than through a direct request for divorce to Enimil Kwao and the local community.

Overall, Amba N'kroma's case shows how the colonial state used her unusual request for divorce as an instrument of colonial intervention in local affairs. The miscarriage of justice that burdened Enimil Kwao's slave dealing case, and which prepared the fertile grounds for capitalist gold mining, involved seven governors, and it attracted the attention of the Colonial Office, the Cape Coast-based *Western Echo*, and the London-based *African Times*.[43] Enimil Kwao's own assessment points to how the colonial state capitalized on his slave dealing trial:

> [A]lthough criminals had before then been tried by a Judge and a jury or a Judge and Assessor, as prisoner might elect, I was not given any option whatever, but was tried by the then Acting Assessor William Melton alone, and only the evidence of my said wife and accomplices was taken into consideration. . . . the Acting Assessor . . . stated openly in court that he would believe no other evidence in the face of my wife's evidence.[44]

Despite its relentless antislavery crusade, the *African Times* plaintively wrote about how the colonial state had twisted Enimil Kwao's slave dealing case to its own advantage. The *African Times* argued that there was the need to reconsider Enimil Kwao's case because he had readily submitted to the colonial authorities without any resistance. The *African Times* further explained that a new trial would be in order because of "the newness of the law which he was charged with having infringed . . . and the position with regard to himself of the person [Amba N'kroma] who denounced him to those authorities."[45] Also, claiming that the "present system of government is a farce," the Cape Coast-based *Western Echo* wrote:

> Without questioning the monstrosity of the proceedings . . . it may be fairly urged that the subsequent illegal action . . . can hardly be paralleled by the many iniquitous acts of our Government at various times and different occasions.[46]

Thus, it was not only Enimil Kwao who recognized the unusual injustice and motives that the colonial authorities brought to bear on the case, but his contemporaries also did. To conclude, Rosenblum's summary of the slave dealing trial and its effects on colonial rule and capitalist gold mining in Wassa Fiase is worth quoting at length:

> The destoolment [dethroning] and exile of King Enemil Quow of Wassa Fiasi and his replacement by a British-backed nonentity as paramount king was probably the most blatant example of the disruption of the traditional patterns of rule. . . . By enhancing the authority of these areas' traditionally subordinate stools [thrones], the British officials made it easier for the European newcomers to gain concessions to gold mines and other valuable properties. . . . in this way, the changed political conditions had profound influence on the subsequent European gold-mining activities in the Gold Coast.[47]

It is patently clear that the slave dealing trial was used by the colonial state to exile Enimil Kwao to Lagos from 1877 to 1889, allowing the colonial state to maximize political control and economic intervention in the auriferous state of Wassa Fiase.

Furthermore, Amba N'kroma's social activism indirectly created a political vacuum in Wassa Fiase. The complicity between the colonial state and some of Enimil Kwao's subordinate chiefs led to the installation of Kwamena Impira, Enimil Kwao's former slave, as king of Wassa Fiase.[48] By all accounts, Kwamena Impira lacked legitimacy and hence had to depend on the patronage of the colonial state and some of Enimil Kwao's subordinate chiefs for his authority and power. Consequently, he became a majestic pawn in the interventionist policy of the colonial state,[49] paving the way for the buttressing of colonial rule and the consequent capitalist intervention in the Wassa Fiase goldfields.

In the end, Amba N'kroma's quest for divorce was eclipsed by the more demanding issues of colonial rule, gold mining, antislavery, and the deposition of Enimil Kwao. Indeed, by the end of 1876, Amba N'kroma's personal goals had vanished from the records, but her case continued to serve as a prologue to a spate of correspondence between the colonial authorities and the Colonial Office, as well as the petitions served to the colonial government on behalf of Enimil Kwao. In fact, the coverage of the *African Times* and the *Western Echo* seemed to paint Amba N'Kroma with a diabolical brush of insouciance, questioning her allegations of Enimil Kwao's slave dealing, while negating her drive and motivation for divorce to an abysmal background.[50]

GOLD AND ANTICOLONIALISM: QUEEN
ADWOA ARDUAH TO THE RESCUE

As noted, the imprisonment and exile of Enimil Kwao created a political vacuum in Wassa Fiase[51]; the political vacuum was eventually filled by Queen Adwoa Arduah. Among the Akans, it was not unusual for queens to serve as regents or hold the reins of power during periods of interregna.[52] What was different about Adwoa Arduah's case was that it was not a period of interregnum, but rather a time of political crisis in Wassa Fiase, aggravated by the unwieldy weight of colonial rule. Kwamena Impira's feeble leadership created a conducive political climate for Enimil Kwao's detractors and subordinate chiefs, including Chief Kwabena Angoo. More importantly, as Agbodeka has demonstrated, throughout the 1880s, the colonial state was preoccupied with the rising tides of anticolonialism in Wassa Fiase,[53] consequently, the colonial authorities maintained a vigilant presence in the region. Lastly, problems of land concession granted to the mining companies and the struggle for power among chiefs intent on capitalizing on the wealth generated by the land concessions[54] also intensified political crisis in Wassa Fiase.

It was these concatenated political crises that Adwoa Arduah had to deal with. As Johnson-Odim has explained, "Much of West African women's anticolonial protest arose from a philosophical point of departure that was not anything they learned from the colonizers, and they employed tactics that were historically their own."[55] There is no doubt that Adwoa Arduah drew much needed experience from the wells of time-tested institutions, exemplified by her organizational abilities and reverential devotion to indigenous practices, despite the constraining burdens of colonial rule.

Adwoa Arduah's first task was to make sure that Enimil Kwao had a large retinue of servants and nobles to accompany him to Cape Coast to face the colonial authorities. An extrapolation from normative practice shows that this was not only a time-honored practice, but also a political strategy. First, it was meant to boost Enimil Kwao's sagging morale, and second, it was geared to convince the colonial authorities that Enimil Kwao had popular support on his side. It is probable, given the functions of a queen, that provisions and victuals for the journey to Cape Coast and the subsequent sojourn there in the course of the trial were provided by Adwoa Arduah, the matriarch of the royal family. It is also likely that through her efforts food and other items were supplied to Enimil Kwao to make up for the poor conditions in the colonial prison. In fact, the eventual imprisonment of Enimil Kwao forced Adwoa Arduah to relocate to Cape Coast not only to be nearer to where Enimil Kwao had been imprisoned, but also to seek his freedom. Overall, the paucity of data does not allow us to pinpoint the exact activities of Adwoa Arduah in Cape Coast. An extrapolation of the evidence shows that it was her activities at Cape Coast, which provided the political capital to buttress the popular quest for Enimil Kwao's freedom. In the end, Adwoa Arduah's formidable presence at Cape Coast, geared to seek Enimil Kwao's freedom, partly forced the colonial authorities to exile Enimil Kwao to Lagos.

Another major achievement of Adwoa Arduah was that in spite of the political maelstrom in Wassa Fiase, she was able to mobilize the chiefs, elders, and commoners of Wassa Fiase to champion a protracted protest and an anticolonial movement. For instance, during the peak of the crisis of colonial intervention in 1876, Adjuah Arduah mobilized seventeen chiefs of Wassa Fiase to send a petition to the colonial government appealing for the release of Enimil Kwao.[56] Adwoa Arduah's ability to mobilize Enimil Kwao's subordinate chiefs was a major achievement, considering the potent threat posed by the colonial state and the fact that some subordinate chiefs—for example, Kwabena Angoo—who were beneficiaries of Enimil Kwao's exile, continued to give their support to the colonial state. Overall, Adwoa Arduah's mobilization of the chiefs and the inauguration of anticolonial movement sought to do the following: reduce the effects of colonial rule and corporate capitalism, depose Kwamena Impira, and reinstate Enimil Kwao.

Adwoa Arduah sought the deposition of Kwamena Impira because he did not belong to the royal family, and there were several members of the royal family who could have succeeded Enimil Kwao.[57]

But as Rosenblum has cogently argued, despite Kwamena Impira's lack of leadership, the colonial authorities blocked his replacement, preferring his weak leadership or an interregnum that allowed the colonial state to have a free hand in the affairs of Wassa Fiase.[58] Adwoa Arduah's quest to destool Kwamena Impira reveals the conflict between the traditional state and the colonial state, and also underscores her persistence in reversing the percolation of unwholesome colonial policies into the core of customary laws and indigenous institutions. In the end the pressures mounted by Adwoa Arduah and her supporters forced the usurper, Kwamena Impira, to abdicate.

Once the Wassa Fiases realized that the exiled Enimil Kwao was in the legal grips of the colonial state, his supporters hired legal advocates to seek his freedom. One of the legal advocates who emerges in the records was John Hutton Brew, the editor of the *Gold Coast Times* and later the *Western Echo*.[59] Although the records are silent on how he was hired and who paid him, in all probability that credit should go to Adwoa Arduah.[60] Through her efforts, Brew wrote several petitions[61] to the colonial government, some of which were sent to the Colonial Office and also published by newspapers in the Gold Coast and England.[62] The content of the petitions explained Enimil Kwao's version of the slave dealing case, the travesty of justice that underpinned the case, the overbearing attitudes of the colonial authorities, the reasons why he should be given his freedom, and his poor living conditions in exile.[63] Remarkably, it was the spate of petitions that brought popular attention to be focused on the case.

Thus, throughout the duration of the case, Adwoa Arduah was instrumental in mobilizing public opinion, not only in the Gold Coast but also in England to focus on the incarceration and exile of Enimil Kwao. Her mobilization of public opinion in favor of Enimil Kwao through the use of petitions did not lead to the immediate release of Enimil Kwao from jail or exile. Nevertheless, her relentless efforts had the desired effects of drawing the attention of the Colonial Office. For instance, in 1877 Lord Carnarvon, the secretary of state for Colonies, responding to Acting Governor E.E. Lees' report on Enimil Kwao's exile to Lagos, pinpointed the legal implications of the Gold Coast Prisons Ordinance of 1876, asserting that the exile of Enimil Kwao in Lagos was *ultra vires*.[64] Thus, Carnarvon later advised Governor Sanford Freeling to "invite the opinion of Sir David Chalmers[65] or another competent legal authority on the question."[66] In addition, Carnarvon stated that he "could not however consent to any measure which would incidentally have the effect of making it a more severe one if Ennemil Quow is removed to Lagos."[67] Also, in 1879, Lees wrote to the Colonial Office, stating that he and the acting chief justice believed that if Enimil Kwao was allowed to return to his kingdom, "serious commotion" would occur.[68]

In response to Lees, another Secretary of State for Colonies, Sir Michael Hicks-Beach, called for a vigorous colonial policy:

I . . . acknowledge the receipt of your Despatch, No. 20 of the 7 of February last [1879] requesting authority for the detention of [Enimil Kwao], within the Settlement of Lagos. . . . I concur with your . . . thinking that it would be very undesirable, at all events for the present, to permit the return of Enemil Quow to Wassaw. . . . In order, therefore, to prevent any disturbance which his appearance at Wassaw might cause, I authorize you to detain Enemil Quow at Lagos until such time as it may be deemed expedient to allow him to leave the Settlement.[69]

Hicks-Beach further explained that if the colonial authorities realized that Enimil Kwao had paid the fine and served his prison term, they would have to furnish the Colonial Office with "strong reasons in proof of the danger that he would cause."[70] Additionally, in September 1882, Acting Governor Alfred Moloney wrote about the tangled political state of Wassa Fiase to the Colonial Office:

The influence of the present King Quamin Enimil [the former slave] is little and a strong party it would appear yet exists in Wassaw in favor of the former [Enimil Kwao]. The adoption of this recommendation might admit of the withdrawal of restraint on the liberty of a subject and dispose of a political difficulty that has been felt and admit the restoration to his country but not to power of Enimil Quow now at Lagos.[71]

Yet, another secretary of state, the Earl of Derby, responded as follows:

With respect to Enimil Quow, I have to request that you will consider and report to me whether he should be allowed to return to the Gold Coast, and if so under what if any restrictions.[72]

These differing policy prescriptions, however, show how Adwoa Arduah's efforts to publicize the case attracted the attention of the Colonial Office, partly accounting for the eventual freedom of Enimil Kwao.

Furthermore, Adwoa Arduah bore the financial responsibility of Enimil Kwao's trial and exile. The evidence does not indicate whether it was her subjects who contributed the funds or whether it was her own money that was used in pursuing Enimil Kwao's case. What the records do make clear, in any case, is that she paid the fine of 400 ounces of gold,[73] which the colonial government imposed on Enimil Kwao.[74] The payment of the fine became a controversial issue: supporters of Enimil Kwao claimed that they had paid the fine, but successive colonial governments denied that the fine was ever paid.[75] In fact, the colonial authorities insisted that they had no records to show that the fine had been paid despite the overwhelming evidence to the contrary.[76] It was this assertion that contributed to the detaining of Enimil Kwao in Lagos after he had finished serving his prison sentence there.[77] Also, when the colonial authorities requested that Enimil Kwao should come up with a sum of £3,000 as a security for his good behavior upon his release, it was through the instrumentality of the Adwoa Arduah that the sum was paid.[78]

The unyielding efforts of Adwoa Arduah eventually led to Enimil Kwao's freedom and reinstatement as king of Wassa Fiase in 1889. Enimil Kwao ruled until his death in 1895. The records are silent on the immediate circumstances leading to the release of Enimil Kwao. What is certain is that Enimil Kwao was set free when the Wassa Fiases paid the £3,000 security demanded by the colonial authorities. Following the release of Enimil Kwao, he resorted to his anticolonial stance by trying to halt timber cutting and land concessions that sustained the gold mining industry, which had occurred during his imprisonment, deposition, and exile. Timber cutting was creating environmental dilapidation and land concessions were having divisive effects on his subjects.[79] Given the anticolonial fervor of Adwoa Arduah, it is fair to add that Enimil Kwao, who had been away from Wassa Fiase for almost fourteen years, benefited from the prudent, vibrant cumulative anticolonialism of Adwoa Arduah.

CONCLUSION

The case of Amba N'kroma is unique and it certainly appears to be uncommon in the backwater enclave of Wassa Fiase. We cannot but admire her courage and tenacity. Apart from throwing light on how women in the Gold Coast sought divorce, even from potentates like Enimil Kwao, her case also reveals how the colonial state responded to women's issues. In the end, the colonial state, using British laws, granted her an anomalous divorce on the grounds that she was not legally married to Enimil Kwao. Lack of sources do not allow us to fathom whether the outcome of a complete divorce would have, apart from its emotional victory, benefited her materially. By rejecting her divorce and latching onto a grand scheme of using her allegations of Enimil Kwao's slave dealing to intervene in Wassa Fiase's gold mining political economy, the colonial state demonstrated its patriarchy, economic exploitation, and cultural hegemony and domination. For her part, Adwoa Arduah is lesser known than Yaa Asantewa, the queen of Edweso, who mobilized the Asante armies for the last onslaught against British imperialism. But there is no doubt that Adwoa Arduah was tenacious, enterprising, and unflinching in her anticolonial stance. That she resisted colonial rule, mitigated the effects of corporate gold mining, mobilized her subjects, and ceaselessly sought the freedom of Enimil Kwao, should win her an exceptional place among the eminent heroes and heroines of anticolonialism in the Gold Coast.

Certainly the data on Amba N'kroma and Adwoa Arduah lacks the details to help us reconstruct comprehensive biographical accounts. Amba N'kroma was apparently from a modest background, whereas Adwoa Arduah was a queen in her own right. Both pursued interests that sought to better their lives and society at large. While both women were constrained by patriarchy, Queen Adwoa Arduah's anticolonial role, her ability to mobilize the resources of Wassa Fiase, and her persistence, despite the overwhelming colonial presence, indicate that aristocratic women, to a considerable extent, played significant political roles in the Gold Coast. Both women appear larger than life in the various roles entrusted to them either through their own choices or by fate. In sum, both women enhance our understanding of the dialectics of the late-nineteenth-century African institutions, the gold rush, and the colonial state's role in corporate capitalist gold mining.

NOTES

1. Popular usage in the extant literature is "queen-mother." The use of "queen-mother" however does not adequately capture the institution that it purports to describe. Obviously, a colonial construct that tended to mean the mother of the queen instead of a queen in her own right. Throughout this study, I follow Kwame Arhin's usage of *ohemma* or queen instead of queen-mother. See Kwame Arhin, "The Political and Military Roles of Akan Women," in *Female and Male in West Africa*, ed. Christine Oppong (London, 1983), 93–97.

2. For the processes of abolition in the Gold Coast, see e.g., Gerald M. McSheffrey, "Slavery, Indentured Servitude, Legitimate Trade and the Impact of Abolition in the Gold Coast, 1874–1901." *Journal of African History* 24 (1983): 349–268; Raymond Dumett and Marion Johnson, "Britain and the Suppression of Slavery in the Gold Coast Colony, Ashanti and the Northern Territories," in *The End of Slavery in Africa* ed. Suzanne Miers and Richard Roberts (Madison 1988), 71–116; Kwabena Opare-Akurang [Akurang-Parry], "The Administration of the Abolition Laws, African Responses, and Post-Proclamation Slavery in Colonial Southern Ghana, 1874–1940," *Slavery and Abolition* 19 (1998): 149–166. Kwabena O. Akurang-Parry, "Slavery and Abolition in the Gold Coast: Colonial Modes of Emancipation and African Initiatives." *Ghana Studies* 1 (1998): 11–34; Kwabena O. Akurang-Parry, " 'A Smattering of Education' and Petitions as Sources: A Study of African Slave-Holders' Responses to Abolition in the Gold Coast, 1874–1875," *History in Africa* 27 (2000): 39–60; Kwabena O. Akurang-Parry, "Rethinking the 'Slaves of Salaga': Post-Proclamation Slavery in the Gold Coast (Colonial Southern Ghana), 1874–1899," *Left History* 8, no. 1 (2002): 33–60; and Peter Haenger, *Slaves and Slave Holders on the Gold Coast* (Basel, 2000).

3. See, e.g., Claire C. Robertson, "Post-Proclamation Slavery in Accra," in *Women and Slavery in Africa* ed. Martin Klein and Claire C. Robertson (Madison, 1983), 220–245; Beverly Grier, "Pawns, Porters, and Petty Traders: Women in the Transition to Cash Crop Agriculture in Colonial Ghana," in *Pawnship in Africa: Debt Bondage in Historical Perspective* ed. Toyin Falola and Paul E. Lovejoy (Boulder, 1994), 178–182; Gareth Austin, "Human Pawning in Asante, 1800–1950: Markets and Coercion, Gender and Cocoa," in *Pawnship in Africa*, ed. Falola and Lovejoy, 119–159; Kwabena O. Akurang-Parry, "Colonial Forced Labor Policies for Road-Building in Southern Ghana and International Anti-Forced Labor Pressures, 1900–1940," *African Economic History* 28 (2001): 1–25; Kwabena O. Akurang-Parry, " 'What is and What is not the Law:' Imprisonment for Debt and the Institution of Pawnship in the Gold Coast, 1821–1899," in *Pawnship, Slavery, and Colonialism in Africa* ed. Paul E. Lovejoy and Toyin Falola (Trenton, NJ, 2003), 427–447; Kwabena O. Akurang-Parry, "Labor Mobilization and African Responses to the Compulsory Labor Ordinance in the Gold Coast, 1875–1899," *Transactions of the Historical Society of Ghana*, forthcoming; and Kwabena O. Akurang-Parry, " 'The Loads Are Heavier than Usual': Forced Labor by Women and Children in the Central Province of the Gold Coast (Colonial Ghana), 1900–1940," *African Economic History*, forthcoming.

4. Claire Robertson, "Ga Women and Socioeconomic Change," in *Women in Africa: Studies in Social and Economic Change* ed. Nancy J. Hafkin and Edna G. Bay (Stanford, 1976), 111–117; Agnes Akosua Aidoo, "Women in the History

and Culture of Ghana," in *Women's Studies with a Focus on Ghana* ed. Mansa Prah (Schriesheim, 1995), 206–217; Haenger, *Slaves and Holders*, 32–48; Kwabena O. Akurang-Parry, "These are Matters . . . The Most Refreshing': Aspects of Elite Women's Agency and Activism in the Gold Coast (Colonial Ghana), 1874–1890," *International Journal of African Historical Studies*, forthcoming.

5. See, e.g., Aidoo, "Women in the History and Culture of Ghana," 216–217; and Robertson, "Ga Women and Socioeconomic Change," 111–117.

6. See, e.g., Ivor Wilks, "She Who Blazed the Trail: Akyaawa Yikwan of Asante," in *Life Histories of African Women*, ed. Patricia W. Romero (Atlantic Highlands, NJ, 1988), 113–139; Aidoo, "Asante Queen Mothers," in *Life Histories of African Women* ed. Patricia W. Romero 65–77; and Arhin, "The Political and Military Roles of Akan Women," 95–97.

7. See, e.g., Aidoo, "Women in the History and Culture of Ghana," 206–226.

8. See, e.g., W.W. Claridge, *A History of the Gold Coast and Ashanti* Vol. 2 (New York, [1915] 1964), 547, 553, and 565; and David Kimble, *A Political History of Ghana* (London, 1963), 319–321.

9. *Ghana Studies* 3 (2000).

10. See, e.g., Emmanuel Terray, "Long Distance Exchange and the Formation of the State: The Case of the Abron State of Gyaman," *Economy and Society* 3 (1974): 315–345; Emmanuel Terray, "Gold Production, Slave Labor, and State Intervention in Precolonial Akan Societies: A Reply to Raymond Dumett," *Research in Economic Anthropology* 5 (1983): 95–192; Raymond Dumett, "Precolonial Gold Mining and the State in the Akan Region with a Critique of the Terray Hypothesis," in George Dalton (ed.), *Research in Economic Anthropology* 2 (1979): 37–68; and Raymond E. Dumett, "Precolonial Gold Mining in Wassa: Innovation, Specialization, Linkages to the Economy and to the State," in *The Golden Stool: Studies of the Asante Center and Periphery*, ed., Enid Schildkrout (New York, 1987), 209–224.

11. For a summary, see Raymond E. Dumett, *El Dorado in West Africa: The Gold-Mining Frontier, African Labor, and Colonial Capitalism in the Gold Coast, 1875–1900* (Athens, OH: Ohio University Press, 1998), 72–73.

12. Ibid., 72.

13. See, e.g., the spate of reports on the potential of the Wassa goldfields in *The African Times* (London), between 1862 and ca. 1899; Richard F. Burton and Verney L. Cameron, *To the Gold Coast for Gold*, 2 Vols., (London, 1883); Gold Coast Reports on Gold Mines, Parliamentary Papers, 1889, C. 5620–5624 (hereafter C. 5620–5624); Kwabena O. Akurang-Parry, " 'We cast about for a remedy': The Opposition of the Gold Coast Press to the Chinese Mine Labor Experiment in the Gold Coast, ca. 1874–1914," *International Journal of African Historical Studies* 34, no. 2 (2001): 365–384.

14. Dumett, *El Dorado in West Africa*, 8–11 and 20.

15. See, e.g., ibid., 85–123; Francis Agbodeka, *African Politics and British Policy in the Gold Coast 1868–1900* (London, 1971), 104–106; and Paul Rosenblum, "Gold Mining in Ghana 1874–1900" (PhD thesis, Columbia University, 1972), 1; 72–76; and 149–161.

16. See, e.g., information on the activities of three Europeans and an American adventurous gold prospectors in Wassa, Akyem Abuakwa and Twifo Denkyera, and Kumasi, see, e.g., Strahan to Carnarvon, August 2, 1875, No. 65, in

Papers Relating to Her Majesty's Possessions in West Africa, Parliamentary Papers, 1876, C. 1402 (hereafter C. 1402); and C. 1402, Strahan to Carnarvon, June 11, 1875, Encl. 2 in 70.

17. Dumett, *El Dorado in West Africa*, 120–123. See also Rosenblum, "Gold Mining in Ghana," 1–2 and 149–167.

18. Agbodeka, *African Politics* 104–106; and Rosenblum, "Gold Mining in Ghana," 72–117.

19. Dumett, *El Dorado in West Africa*, 277–278. For Joseph Chamberlain's policies, see e.g., Raymond E. Dumett, "Joseph Chamberlain, Imperial Finance and Railway Policy in British West Africa in the Late Nineteenth Century," *The English Historical Review* 90 (1975): 287–321; and G.T.Z. Chada, "Labor Protests, Group Consciousness and Trade Unionism in West Africa: The Radical Railway Workers of Colonial Ghana" (PhD thesis, University of Toronto, 1981), 1–37.

20. Dumett, *El Dorado in West Africa*, 86–88; 163–172; and 277–278.

21. Kwabena O. Akurang-Parry, "To Wassa Fiase for Gold: Rethinking Colonial Rule, El Dorado, Antislavery, and Chieftaincy in the Gold Coast (Ghana), 1874–1895," *History in Africa* 30 (2003): 11–36.

22. Ibid.

23. Dumett, *El Dorado in West Africa*, 156–157 and 184–186.

24. Akurang-Parry, "To Wassa Fiase for Gold."

25. Cheryl Johnson-Odim, "Actions Louder than Words: The Historical Task of Defining Feminist Consciousness in Colonial West Africa," in *Nation, Empire, Colony: Historicizing Gender and Race* ed. Ruth Roach Pierson and Nupur Chaudhuri (Bloomington, 1998), 82.

26. Arhin, "The Political and Military Roles of Akan Women."

27. Johnson-Odim, "Actions Louder than Words," 80.

28. Rosenblum, "Gold Mining in Ghana," 107–108.

29. *The African Times*, November 1, 1879, 122.

30. Ibid., 123 and 128; Gold Coast Despatches from Governor to Secretary of State, 1875–1876, March 4, 1876, No. 48, National Archives of Ghana, Accra (hereafter NAGA), ADM, 1/2/20; and Gold Coast Despatches from Governor to Secretary of State, 1877–1879, February 7, 1879, No. 20, NAGA, ADM 1/1/22.

31. Gold Coast Despatches from Secretary of State to Governor, 1878, Pt. 2, April 24, 1878, No. 53, NAGA, ADM 1/1/45.

32. *African Times*, November 1, 1879, 123.

33. Rosenblum, "Gold Mining in Ghana," 83–85. Enimil Kwao was summoned to appear before the court because a suit had been brought against him by Quacoe Buafoo. Enimil Kwao had imposed a heavy fine on Buafoo for failing to attend his enstoolment ceremony as the king of Wassa Fiase. Buafoo was imprisoned pending the payment of the fine and was only released by Enimil Kwao through the intervention of the chiefs of Wassa Fiase. After his release, Buafoo moved to Cape Coast and sued Enimil Kwao in the Judicial Assessor's Court.

34. Ibid., 100–107. The suit resulted from confrontations between the supporters of Enimil Kwao and Kwabena Angoo between March and August of 1875. Eventually, in August 1875, Kwabena Angoo was forced to flee from Tarkwa to Axim. Kwabena Angoo's suit included the allegation that Enimil Kwao had threatened to "kill [him] and causing five people to pursue him until he was compelled to take refuge in the bush."

35. Strahan to Carnarvon, March 18, 1875, Encl. 1 in No. 47, in Papers Relating to Her Majesty's Possessions in West Africa, Parliamentary Papers, 1875, C. 1343 (hereafter C. 1343). For this type of imprisonment for debt in the Gold Coast, see Akurang-Parry, " 'What is and What is not the Law.' "
36. C. 1343, Strahan to Carnarvon, March 18, 1875, Encl. 1 in No. 47.
37. C. 1343, Strahan to Carnarvon, March 18, 1875, No. 47.
38. C. 1343, Strahan to Carnarvon, March 18, 1875, Encl. in No. 47.
39. *African Times*, November 1, 1879, 123.
40. Ibid.
41. For this type of explanation, see, e.g., Kwabena O. Akurang-Parry, "A Campaign to Get Fetishes Destroyed": The Basel Mission's Pupil Recruitment and Missionization in the Gold Coast 1850–1877," *Groniek Historisch Tijdschrift* 151 (2001): 163–165.
42. For the number of suits against Enimil Kwao, see Rosenblum, "Gold Mining in Ghana," 82–107.
43. See, e.g., Akurang-Parry, "To Wassa Fiase for Gold."
44. *African Times*, November 1, 1879, 123.
45. Ibid. See also *African Times*, July 1, 1876, 7; and *African Times*, November 1, 1879, 128.
46. *Western Echo* (Cape Coast), August 17–31, 1887.
47. Rosenblum, "Gold Mining in Ghana," 116. See also 83–117.
48. Gold Coast Despatches from Governor to Secretary of State, 1875–1876, April 22, 1876, No. 101, NAGA, ADM 1/2/21; Gold Coast Despatches from Governor to Secretary of State, 1877, January 15, 1877, No. 26, NAGA, ADM 1/2/21; Gold Coast Despatches from Governor to Secretary of State, 1876–1877, April 5, 1877, No. 89, NAGA, ADM 1/2/21; and Gold Coast Despatches from Governor to Secretary of State, 1876–1877, June 20, 1877, No. 163, NAGA, ADM 1/2/21.
49. Rosenblum, "Gold Mining in Ghana," 83–117.
50. See Akurang-Parry, "To Wassa Fiase for Gold."
51. *African Times*, July 1, 1876, 7. For a fuller account, see Rosenblum, "Gold Mining," 104–115 and 122. The goldfields were located in the area ruled by Kwabena Angoo, but traditionally, Enimil Kwao, the king, exercised greater control over the mines.
52. See, e.g., Arhin, "The Political and Military Roles of Akan Women," 93–95.
53. Agbodeka, *African Politics*, 104–106.
54. See, e.g., Akurang-Parry, "To Wassa Fiase for Gold."
55. Odim-Johnson, "Actions Louder than Words," 81.
56. *African Times*, July 1, 1876, 7.
57. Gold Coast Despatches from Secretary of State to Governor, 1878, Pt. 2, April 24, 1878, No. 53, NAGA, ADM 1/1/45. In the petition to the secretary of state, the Wassa Fiases noted that Enimil Kwao was the hundredth king, a direct descendant of Geythuya Mansu, the first king of Wassa. See *African Times*, January 28, 1873, 76–77; and *African Times*, July 1, 1876, 7.
58. Rosenblum, "Gold Mining in Ghana," 114–115.
59. *African Times*, July 1, 1876, 7. Brew also wrote the Gold Coast anti-abolition petitions. For an account of the anti-abolition petitions, see Akurang-Parry, " 'A Smattering of Education.' " For a fuller account of Brew, see Margaret Priestley, *West African Trade and Coast Society: A Family Study* (London, 1969).

60. Rosenblum, "Gold Mining in Ghana," 110–111, has detailed the problems that arose, as court clerks and others tried to capitalize on the case to make some money.

61. For the petitions, see e.g., *African Times*, July 1, 1876, 7. The use of petitions should not come as a surprise. I have argued that the Africans in the Gold Coast, especially from the second half of the nineteenth century, resorted to the use of petitions as an instrument of policy to address whatever problems they had with the British authorities. The use of petitions was a diffusion of innovation stemming from the fact the African intelligentsia were aware of British constitutional and quasi-legal methods. See Akurang-Parry, " 'A Smattering of Education.' "

62. See, e.g., *African Times*, July 1, 1876, 7; and *African Times*, November 1, 1879, 123.

63. See, e.g., Akurang-Parry, "To Wassa Fiase for Gold."

64. Gold Coast Despatches from Secretary of State to Governor, 1877, March 9, 1877, No. 407, NAGA, ADM 1/1/43.

65. Sir David Chalmers wrote the slave emancipation ordinance and was instrumental in the abolition of slavery in the Gold Coast. During the early phase of colonial rule, he was considered the most competent legal authority in the Gold Coast. See Strahan to Carnarvon, September 19, 1874, No. 5, in Further Correspondence Relating to the Abolition of Slavery on the Gold Coast, Parliamentary Papers, 1875, C. 1139 (hereafter 1139). Also, he wrote a report on the effects of abolition on the Gold Coast. See C. 2148.

66. Gold Coast Despatches from Secretary of State to Governor, 1877, March 9, 1877, No. 407, NAGA, ADM 1/1/43.

67. Ibid.; and Gold Coast Despatches from Secretary of State to Governor, 1879 Pt. 2, April 4, 1879, No. 246, NAGA, ADM 1/1/47.

68. Gold Coast Despatches from Governor to Secretary of State, 1877–1879, February 7, 1879, No. 20, NAGA, ADM 1/1/22.

69. Gold Coast Despatches from Secretary of State to Governor 1879, April 4, 1879, No. 246, NAGA, ADM 1/1/47.

70. Ibid.

71. Gold Coast Despatches from Governor to Secretary, 1882, September 4, 1882, No. 415, NAGA, ADM 1/2/27.

72. Gold Coast Despatches from Secretary of State to Governor, 1882, Pt. 4, December 23, 1882, No. 8, NAGA, ADM 1/1/58.

73. The fine of £400 was the heaviest in any slave dealing case in the Gold Coast. In fact, prior to the fine of £400, the biggest fine had been £108 imposed on King Akwasi Baidoo of Denkyira in 1874 for refusing on two occasions to hand over war captives and slaves to the colonial government. For King Akwasi Baidoo's case, see, e.g., Strahan to Carnarvon, September 24, 1874, No. 115 in Correspondence Relating to the Affairs of the Gold Coast, Parliamentary Papers, 1875, C. 1140 (hereafter C. 1140).

74. *African Times*, November 1, 1879, 123.

75. Gold Coast Despatches from Secretary of State to Governor, 1878, Pt. 2, April 24, 1878, No. 53, NAGA, ADM 1/1/45; Gold Coast Despatches from Secretary of State to Governor, 1879 Pt. 2, April 4, 1879, No. 246, NAGA ADM 1/1/47; Gold Coast Despatches from Governor to Secretary of State, 1880–1881, November 9, 1880, No. 287, NAGA ADM 1/2/24; *African Times*, November 1, 1879, 123 and 126; *Western Echo*, February 14–28, 1887; and *Western Echo*, August 17, 1887.

76. *African Times*, November 1, 1879, 123–124 and 126; *Western Echo*, August 17, 1887 Gold Coast Despatches from Secretary of State to Governor, 1879 Pt. 2, April 4, 1879, No. 246, NAGA, ADM 1/1/47; and Gold Coast Despatches from Governor to Secretary of State, 1880–1881, November 9, 1880, No. 287, NAGA, ADM 1/2/24.

77. See, e.g., *African Times*, November 1, 1879, 123 and 126; and Gold Coast Despatches from Secretary of State to Governor, 1879 Pt. 2, April 4, 1879, No. 246, NAGA, ADM 1/1/47.

78. For his release, see Agbodeka, *African Politics*, 106; and Rosenblum, "Gold Mining in Ghana," 114–115.

79. Report (Tarkwa) for the Quarter Ended May 31, 1893, May 26, 1893, NAGA, ADM 27/1/5.

CHAPTER 3

Lifting the Layers of the Mountain's Petticoats: Mining and Gender in Potosí's Pachamama

Pascale Absi

Translated by Michele A. May

In Potosí, as with most Andean mining sites, it is understood that women should not enter the interiors of mines due to the fear that they will cause the lodes to vanish.[1] After examining the symbolic representations that manifest this belief, this essay turns to demonstrating the social, economic, and ideological factors that define this exclusion of women. In turn each justification, whether accepted or rejected, depending on the historical moment, and either becoming mandatory or modified, the belief in the bad luck of women also provides an opportunity to interrogate the nature of this cultural norm and the way in which the actors appropriate and employ it.

In Potosí, both men and women agree that women should not go into the mines and this ban organizes their work—men inside the mine, women outside—and the ways labor is characterized. Nevertheless, in the mining cooperatives that excavate the mountain of Potosí, no statute precludes women from entering the underground galleries or prevents them from working there. Their exclusion lies in tradition, which brings to the forefront various explanations—economic, social, and religious.

The first explanation seems self-evident: underground exploitation is dangerous and grueling work, above all a manly activity. "How can a woman do the same thing we do?" male workers ask themselves. They also talk of wanting to protect women from the frequent accidents as well as from their own disrespectful behavior. But it is the entirety of this belief that provides the most explicit argument for the ban. In the mine, women's presence will make the lode disappear. It is therefore because they cause bad luck that women should not go near the metallic veins.

However, it was not always this way. Several old workers recall that during the 1950s, women worked inside the mines. Some even carried hammers and rods to the mine. In this case, no one said they made the veins disappear. Even today, a handful of women venture into the galleries to extract ore and every day female tourists visit individual mining operations. Thus, this exclusion, although explained and justified as stemming from tradition, is nevertheless a social construction and can occasionally become obligatory or violated. The issue of whether women truly are bad luck is secondary to the social role of the ban itself. What concerns us here then is an analysis of the ways in which this exclusion is mobilized with respect to circumstances and what is at stake, rather than to try to understand whether those who express this conviction truly believe that women bring bad luck to the mines.

THE HISTORY OF FEMALE LABOR IN BOLIVIAN MINES

In spite of the apparent masculine nature of mining, since the era of the Incas, and perhaps even before, women represented a significant portion of mining labor, both within the mines and from the exterior. During the age of the Incas, peoples subject to the empire were assigned, in pairs, to gold and silver mining sites.[2] Later, during the sixteenth century, the Spanish conquerors established a system of forced work by Indians in the Potosí silver mines. This mandatory conscription only affected men, but wives and children moved with them to Potosí where they assisted by sorting and transporting the ore.[3]

Little is known about the evolution of female labor during the early years of the republic. But we do know that by the end of the nineteenth century, international demand for tin increased, contributing to the massive forceful incorporation of women to work the mines. As in the colonial era, their involvement basically consisted in sorting and treating the ore, both in and outside the mines. It is probable that among these women, some also participated in drilling. In the mid-1930s, the departure of men for the war between Bolivia and Paraguay augmented the involvement of female labor to include underground extraction. On the eve of the National Revolution of 1952, there were officially 4,000 women working in mining, or 10 percent of all workers.[4] Following their armed victory over the dominant oligarchy, the National Revolutionary Movement (MNR) declared the nationalization of all mines. In these modern national mining operations, women's underground work was banned from this point on. Nevertheless, from outside the mines, women continued to sort the mineral and lease the right to recycle slag from the state. As for minor mining operations, women were granted the right to work in restructured cooperatives. Distinct from salaried state workers, these independent miners were compensated by the sale of what they personally produced. For them, the issue of luck—to discover a good metallic vein—was crucial. However, as previously stated, until recently, women participated in cooperatives' underground exploitation where the work continued to be physical and rudimentary.

After the decline in ore flow and the closure of state mines during the mid-1980s, all Potosí mining operations were subsequently in the hands of cooperatives. Following this crisis, the number of female cooperative members declined significantly, but women still represent around 100 for every 6,000 workers. Except for four women who work inside the mines, the rest work with the ore outside. Most recycle slag; others sweep up ore that falls as it is being moved. These workers are called *palliris*.[5] They are miners' widows who as their full retirement have been granted, on behalf of the cooperative, the legal right to a place of work.

Women's Bellies, the "Evil Eye," and Jealousy

In Potosí, women's bad luck has a name: it is because they are *banco ñawi* that women should not enter the mines. For miners, *banco ñawi* is synonymous with *mal agüero* (evil omen) or *mala sombra* (evil shadow). The word *banco* can signify a change in the metallic vein's state, a change in its direction or its attenuation.[6] As for *ñawi*, Quechuan for "eye," the notion is that of the "evil eye" in the sense of desire. But to be *banco ñawi* does not necessarily mean a conscious willingness for malice, this kind of bad luck is more commonly understood as the nature of misfortune.

Anyone known to be able to make the metallic vein disappear by coming near it is labeled *banco ñawi*. Thus, not only women are affected. If, as a stroke of bad luck, the vein being exploited dries up in the days immediately following his starting to work, a male menial worker could just as easily be fired immediately for *banco ñawi*. It would then be difficult for him to find a new job. Because it is impossible to know—except as the result of an unlucky experience—whether a person is *banco ñawi*, or not, miners avoid exposing their lode to others, including their fellow workers. However, unlike men, women are not even given the opportunity to prove themselves; they are immediately considered *banco ñawi*. As Doña Paulina explains, it is enough for a woman, any woman, to just look at a vein in order to make it disappear; thus woman's very nature justifies her exclusion from the mining beds:

> Us, we want to work in the mine. Why shouldn't we penetrate the rock like men? Is it difficult? No, it's not difficult. But there is this story that woman is, as we say, *banco ñawi*. I don't know what this means, but it is what makes the veins dry up. How can I explain it, a woman enters, looks, and, two days or twenty-four hours later, the veins disappear. So, we know what's happened and we don't insist on going into the mine. Paulina Fernandez, 48, *palliri*, Ckacchas Libres Cooperative[7]

While some miners dare to put their faith to the test, many, like Don Macario, today regret doing so. He states, "Once, I had been working hard, I let my wife in to my worksite and goodbye ore! Ever since, I have never let another woman enter the place where I am working." These declarations occur frequently and reinforce the legitimacy of women's exclusion.

The basis for the disappearance of veins in light of women's presence can be summed up as a tale of female jealousy between the mine and women. Potosí miners think of their mountain as a woman they deflower through their work, who is fertilized by their offerings and thus bears them minerals everyday. This image of the mountain as female is fused with that of *Pachamama*, the Andean deity of earthly fertility and the symbol of mining activity, which is deeply steeped in agricultural rationale. Inside the belly of the mountain, Pachamama, ores combine and ripen; this is why, according to miners, the mountain of Potosí continues to offer new veins in spite of nearly 500 years of uninterrupted exploitation. Within this context, to expose her wealth is equivalent to lifting the layers of the mountain's petticoats one by one. *Chunkaiskayniyoq polleras*, twelve skirts, is in fact the traditional name for Pachamama of Potosí, whose petticoats are mixed with the mountain's insides and mineral beds. The mountain Pachamama is also linked to the Virgin Mary whom Spanish missionaries tried to use to replace the pre-Hispanic cult of the mountain god. But miners are simply the mountain's birthing coach due to their role in appropriating her wealth and rendering her a sexual possession.

Simultaneously tender and brutally demanding, the passion that emerges when workers talk about the mine charges their discourse with a sense of eroticism. They hope to seduce the mountain in order to be desired by her, so that she will offer herself up and accept their caresses or refuse them right there: they must have believed at one time that miners' entreaties were meant for a woman in order to appreciate the mine's sensuality and her identity as a mistress of minerals:

> In the mine we say, "Give me one of your skirts, you of 12 skirts, Virgin Pachamama, Madame, give me one of your skirts." This means we are asking her for a mineral vein. This is the rational version. But when someone is a bit drunk, he gets down on his knees with particular devotion, takes off his hat and recites these words: "Little Mother, now I'm going to open you up like this, Pachamama, now give it to me, if you don't give it to me, I'm not going to give it to you either." Those who are less well educated [say]: "lift your skirt, I'm going to place the dynamite, show me your vagina." Or the miner when he is a bit wound up: "show me your ass." Don Elias, 44, retired miner

The mountain gives herself to men with her metal, but in exchange she takes their offerings, their desire, and the eroticism of their bodies. The nourishment offered to mountain Pachamama—alcoholic drink, coca leaves, sacrificial llamas—serves to satisfy her sizeable appetite, precludes any accidents, and encourages her goodwill; the workers' foul language and the insults they use are thought to excite her. To make the mountain give up her treasure, the miner must therefore know how to seduce her. David's testimony clearly demonstrates this: simply longing for the mountain is not enough to attain her ore, she must also make her choice. The successful discovery of ore depends on this consent, and good fortune in mining is entirely shaped by the random nature of attraction:

> We say that when a man enters the mine, the woman [the mine] gives herself up. Some men go in lucky and come out winners, others no, the woman doesn't want to give herself up. I think that the mine chooses the man she wants. Often the metal chooses who will cultivate it. As I just told you, sometimes when someone touches it, and truly wants it, the metal disappears, because it wasn't intended for him; another miner then comes along and it appears. That's how it happens. It's the same with a young woman: you truly love her, but if she doesn't love you, what can you do? Then all of a sudden, another guy comes along and he's ugly, goofy, and he doesn't deserve her, but the young woman loves him and gives herself to him. It's the same thing with metal. It's just like that, finicky, it's got it in for us. David Cruz, 36, miner, Unificada Cooperative

The emergence of metallic veins in the mine is therefore the result of a sexual coming together between men and the mountain in which they replicate their romantic disposition. Life giving, jealous and impulsive, the lode may disappear at any moment. To be sure, this disappearance is seen as a betrayal on the part of Pachamama. "Just as you have total faith in your wife," explains David with respect to the ore, "when you least expect it she cheats on you. The ore is the same, it can leave you for someone else."

The admission of women to the mine thus disrupts the romantic relationship between men and the mountain Pachamama. Jealous, the miners' mistress of minerals keeps herself from them and due to her longing, her ore beds become exhausted. Doña Paulina states:

> How can I explain it? Pachamama could be men's proprietor and the men her husbands or something similar. And when, we, the women, enter, wouldn't Pachamama become jealous? She thinks we might steal her men or her ore from her. That's what I think, I don't know. It's only for men that Pachamama makes the ore show up, right? That's what makes you believe.

This romantic facet and strongly held belief renders underground extraction a decidedly masculine activity. Even fatal accidents are part of this seduction-possession relationship. Thus, when a worker dies in the mine, it is sometimes said that Pachamama fell in love with him.[8] Whether a crime of passion or the fatal embrace of a man-eater, all too often in any case, the mountain demands exclusive rights to her lovers' lives. And the miners' wives' jealousy toward this mountain-woman who steals their husbands rivals Pachamama's:

> We always say of the miner: "Where is he going again? He must have a mistress somewhere." But no, it's the mine that takes up all of our time and the women are totally jealous of the mountain. Because the workers leave their house at 7 o'clock in the morning and sometimes at 10 o'clock at night they still aren't back. Women would like it if the mine didn't even exist. Or perhaps just sometimes, of course, so they could have some money. When miners come down with mining sickness, women curse the mine. And even more so when men die.

"The mine took my husband from me, that's why I'm in agony." Victor Alcaraz, 47, miner, Unificada Cooperative

SYMBOLIC MOTIVES AND PRACTICAL STAKES

Expressed as emotional jealousy, the enmity between women and the mine is surely related to a rivalry over fertility. Woman's fertile womb is suspected of stealing the mountain's fruitfulness. In certain mining operations, it is said that the vein will disappear during the woman's next period of menstruation following her admission to the mine.[9] In order to avoid any ill-fated involvement, some miners even prohibit women from coming near the tools used to pierce the mountain and that are part of men's sexual union with the mountain.

As with many other images of mining, the idea of women's fertility interfering with that of the mine is a legacy inherited from the agricultural community from which most miners originate. Thus, in the Quechuaphone countryside in the Potosí region, women who are menstruating are not allowed near the fields out of fear of losing the harvest. For the Andean people, menstruation is considered the most fertile moment of the female cycle; it is when the competition between women's fertility and that of the earth is at its height. Sometimes, peasants also bring up the repulsive aspects of menstruation, its assault on the sense of smell that also calls to mind particular mining interpretations pertaining to the misfortune of women in the mine.[10] But how, then, do we explain that women's exclusion, which is only temporary in agricultural production, becomes permanent in the mines?

The sexual facet of mining extraction is no doubt related to the fact that the work takes place underground. As in open-pit mining, the relationship between peasants and Pachamama does not have the same erotic charge as underground production that requires miners to deeply penetrate the goddess's body. Elsewhere, where fieldwork necessitates the participation of both men and women of peasant families, mining extraction is customarily a rather masculine activity. The physical effort required explains why female labor has primarily been dedicated to tasks other than perforation, with the exception of periods when labor was scarce as was the case during the war against Paraguay. In this circumstance, women were kept away from the metallic veins but were not completely absent from the mine's interior where they worked loading, sorting, and selecting metal.

The gradual departure of women from the mine's underground galleries during the last several decades is related to several factors. First is the modernization and mechanization of production. We must keep in mind that female labor in state mines had been prohibited since the early 1950s, for both social and work-related reasons. The progressive ideology behind this ban also influenced miners' practices in the cooperatives. During the mining crisis of the mid-1980s, stopping production of tin in favor of commercialized silver eliminated the need for sorting the metal, the primary use of female labor both in and outside the mines. The *palliris* stay on and are able to fall back on outdoor activities, particularly the recycling of slag and sweeping up residue. Today, the mine no longer attracts young women, who prefer to migrate elsewhere. Therefore, during the past several decades the number of *palliris* on the mountain has declined significantly, and at the same time women have left the mines' interiors. The need to keep women at a distance from the ore inside the mines is thus a *fait accompli*. Due to their presence no longer being necessary, women's ill-fated involvement with underground production takes on its contemporary meaning. Thus, we understand that, in the Potosí mines, peasant belief in the rivalry between women's fertility and that of the earth could either expand or diminish in response to the randomness of labor demands and the history of mining production.

Today, the exclusion of women from the mines allows male cooperative workers to assert their authority and protects them from the threat of female interference resulting in exhausting the underground ore beds. In theory, from a legal point of view, nothing prevents widows from inheriting their late husband's underground worksite and exploiting it. However, due to male pressure, women prefer to look for work outdoors. The symbolic motive thus legitimates the economic domination by those men who maintain their underground exploitation themselves; it is much more lucrative. A *palliri* earns six to ten times less than an underground worker.

In this context, the distinction between underground and open-pit mining is understood in terms of basic sexual differences that reinforce the apparatus that governs domestic life. The exclusion of women reinforces the urban ideology of a sexual division of labor—man at work, woman at home—that prevails in mining families. For men, starting work in the mine can take on the connotation of a male rite of passage. Often following marriage, the hiring of a miner as regular worker confirms his standing as an adult male, capable of supporting a family. For women, on the other hand, marriage marks the end of their *palliri* activity, which is reserved for single women and widows. Being an underground miner becomes synonymous with being a man. Workers who are not as tough, who do not fit the formula where masculinity is equated with physical strength and underground mining, are given the nicknames *señorita, doña, chola* (miss, ma'am . . .). And the few men who work in open-pit mining are certainly considered *q'ewa* (effeminate) or *maricón* (gay). "Only stonemasons work out of doors, men, miners, they're in the mine. Those who work outside are girly-men because we, men, we prefer to work in the mine," banters David. Women too, like Doña Paulina, do not hesitate to make fun of these men:

> In the mine there are men who sweep [the ore]. They do the same thing I do. They aren't embarrassed; how is a man going to sweep? It's embarrassing. It's only for women. Men have the right to work in the mine and only women have the right to sweep here, outside. That's why we criticize them. Those who sweep should wear a skirt or a dress.

Paradoxically, although the domain of mining has borrowed peasant symbolic representations, women's status in the mines draws upon traditional urban and industrial definitions of status in which the sexual division of labor and the role of masculine authority are even more pronounced than in the countryside. Notably, within the small artisan country cooperatives on the outskirts of Potosí, where workers are at the same time miners and peasants, mining has remained quite familial and women participate in their husband's underground work.

The Demon of the Mine, the Personification of Masculine Space Prohibited to Women

The masculine aspect of mining activity comes alive in a very real way in the masculine virile figure of Tio, the evil deity of the mine, whose troublesome presence contributes to the exclusion of women from the mine's galleries. Made out of clay, underground figurines of Tio acquired their horns and their cloven hooves from the Spanish missionaries who believed they witnessed the devil in pre-Hispanic miners' native gods. The miner's god has been restored today as a type of life force, fertile but savage, from the netherworld, that contemporary preachers link with hell.[11] But, even though they nicknamed him *diablo*, mine workers think of Tio by and large as the owner of the metallic veins that he shows them in exchange for offerings: alcohol, coca leaves, and cigarettes. A tireless worker, he moves the ore from place to place within the mines and helps men produce. In the stillness of the galleries, from time to time one hears rock being pierced or the cart being emptied. Neither good nor bad, the demon worker knows how to show generosity to his supporters but he can also mercilessly admonish those who neglect him. It is said that miners who died at work have been eaten by Tio. Ruler of the mine, a taskmaster, his powers complement Pachamama's generative powers.

Meeting Tio in person can drive men and women insane and the latter are more susceptible to his powers and his sizeable sexual appetite. Too weak to confront Tio's strength, women are the preferred victims of his unbridled libido as is borne out by the underground figurines' inordinate penises. This sexuality is not without reference to that of the miners who explain, with irony, that women have too many children with laborers, which plays a role in their exclusion from entering the mines. An archetype of the underground worker, Tio personifies the miner's virile traits, his staying power and his sexuality: the working society he oversees is, in essence, a male society. The mutual identification of the miner and Tio includes a notion of possession: through his work, man is possessed by the deity's virile power and himself becomes a demon.[12] This is why the miner is able to sexually possess and impregnate Pachamama, Tio's spouse. In this way, his character embodies the nature of the underground world—masculine and off-limits to women.

Exclusion of women from the galleries also assures a certain balance between these worlds. The openness of their vaginas is particularly vulnerable to the netherworld's active forces. The meeting of women's fertility with these forces produces monstrous beings. Even so, a woman's rape by Tio can lead to an ill-fated pregnancy. This is why the women who keep watch over the mine's entrance avoid sleeping alone at night, at the behest of the underground demon:

It's dangerous for us women to sleep here near the mine. Once, on the mountain, there was a young girl about 20 or 25 years old. She was the daughter of the mine's guard. They say that her mother went into town. That night, while her mother was out, I don't know what holiday it was, a man entered the guard's house. According to the girl's tearful account, he had taken advantage of her. As a result, the girl became pregnant. She kept repeating, "I dreamed it, I dreamed it." They say she woke herself up screaming, but no one was there. Since that day, she can't eat. Everything disgusts her. People say, "Whose child is it?" When the baby was born, he wasn't normal; he had the head of a monster. Fortunately, he died. His ear, it wasn't a human being's ear; it was long like a horn. Who was this man? Even the girl didn't know. Perhaps it was the demon, Tio, who had escaped from the mine. This is why they no longer hire women with young daughters. They accept older women, because otherwise Tio takes advantage of them. Filomena Fernandez, 48, guardian, November 10th Cooperative

Half man, half demon, the result of a union between a woman and Tio challenges the division between the world of man and the brutal and wicked netherworld. This is why it is important to protect women from the demon. Keeping women out of Tio's grip also prevents society as a whole from slipping into his realm. This demonic possession that accompanies underground work gradually disconnects men from human society. The domestic abilities of women, guarantors of social reproduction, assure a counterbalance to the demon's domination of their husbands. The woman assures the bridge between the brutal netherworld in which her husband ends up and civil society. But if women were to work inside the mines and if they too became demons, then who would guarantee the continuation of the domestic and social world?

The exclusion of women from the mine incorporates all the social and ideological structures that constitute mining society. Nevertheless, this prohibition can be breached.

TRANSGRESSIONS AND MODIFICATIONS

Discouraged by the poor yields resulting from open-pit mining, Doña Isabel and Doña Julia, miners' widows, decided, about ten years ago, to go into the mine to work like men. Ever since, every morning, they trade their large traditional skirts for work pants. Because workers from other mining operations would not accept them, they renewed an abandoned mine. There are no men with them; only Julia's brother comes, from time to time, to provide some muscle. Doña Julia and Doña Isabel are not working for women's rights. They did not make their choice out of feminist convictions, but consider their work a last chance to do something they know. For them, one thing is certain: the misfortune attributed to women disguises men's basic desire to dominate. For male workers, on the other hand, things are much less obvious. How can the work of these two women be reconciled with the various explanations that serve to legitimate their exclusion and construct a masculine identity?

The first question to ask workers is, yes or no, do these two women produce ore. How could they considering the mountain's jealousy? Where do they get the strength and the manly courage to attack the rock? Generally speaking, miners suppose, but they do not know for certain, that the women's production is minor. Ultimately, their work is a triumph over the male ego. Thus, men needed some type of rationalization: because they work in the mine, Doña Julia and Doña Isabel are not really women. They are thought of as a homosexual couple and dubbed *qharimachu* (lesbians). By declaring the ambiguity of the women's sexual identity, male workers avoid challenging the social and symbolic representations of mining perforation currently reserved for men. Don Victor states:

They're strange those two women who go into the mine, they even work at night. It's as if one is the husband and reassures the other as a husband would his wife. . . . They say that one of them is a half-man, half-woman and that there could be [sexual] relations between Isabel and Julia, Julia and Isabel.

In fact, only Julia's work, to pierce the rock and handle dynamite, poses any real problem. Isabel's work is much less subversive. Responsible for evacuating the barren rock and ore, she stays out of the actual extraction process. Her activity is similar to the mining work women did until the 1950s. In the Isabel-Julia couple, the first therefore has the status of a woman who backs up her husband in the mine and it is Doña Julia who is targeted personally by Don Victor's comments since he implies that one of the women is a half-man, half-woman. Possibly, the status of widowhood, which serves as a sort of social menopause, plays a role in this interpretation. In this way male honor remains unscathed: only men and those like them, never women in any case, exploit the underground veins.

Doña Julia's and Doña Isabel's experience clearly demonstrates that women are not passive participants in their exclusion. Might it be in order to avoid work that is all too demanding that women are not more interested in working inside the mines? Herein lies the ambiguity of Doña Paulina's feminist discourse in which she affirms women's desire to work inside the mine while at the same time, under the veil of attacking male domination, appropriates their arguments. Why, having affirmed her desire to work in the mine, does she hold on to the idea that women make the ore beds dry up? Why does Paulina accept as valid, what she knows to be false, that Isabel and Julia's work is less fruitful than her own? In fact, why is she the first to challenge the masculinity of her mine's male guardian who, like her, sweeps up ore and who, teasingly, she regularly proposes to lend her skirt to?

Doña Julia and Doña Isabel are not the only women to look at the veins of ore everyday. Among the handful of international visitors who visit the mines everyday since the late 1980s, nearly half are women. Of course, these visitors do not come to work in the mine and do not pose a threat to the male workers' ego. However, the presence of these women must be reconciled with the belief that women cause the metallic veins to dry up. This emphasizes first of all that miners have a vested interest in allowing these women access to their mining operations. Other than their desire to make their work—largely undervalued within Bolivia—known beyond their local borders, the miners are motivated by tourists' gifts (coca, dynamite . . .) and the admission fees they shell out, which help the mine. The discourse underlying this practice must now be explored.

At first glance, the workers of mining operations open to the public seem to have reconsidered the existence of a malevolent interference between women and the ore. Since these women began visiting their mines, male miners confirm that they have not mourned the loss of a single vein. However, the admission of women visitors was not unproblematic. At the beginning, guides were confronted with the miners' refusal to allow female visitors into their place of work. Even today, not everyone accepts their presence and many keep an eye out to be sure no one comes either too close, or stays for too long, near their veins. Even those who accept these visitors outright have not forsaken their belief. But, like Julia and Isabel, because female tourists are not considered real women, they can be permitted to enter the mine without changing the structure of the miners' convictions:

> "Our women do not want to go in, for fear of making the veins dry up. What then, what will they live on?"
> "But then, why can *gringas* go in?"
> "There, that's different, *gringas* come to visit, not to work."
> "But, they're women?"
> "It's different . . . here in Potosí, women usually wear skirts, and hardly any of them wear pants." Conversation with Marcos Rejas, 43, miner, Candelaria mine, Unificada cooperative

In the mining world where, from puberty, young girls abandon their childhood skirt or pants in order to take up the large traditional skirt, outsiders' pants are understood as a sign of their sexual immaturity. Child-women, not yet sexually grown-up, are perceived neither as real women, nor as Pachamama's rivals.

The warm welcome reserved for female tourists can also be explained by the supposed existence of their special involvement with the gods of prosperity. The *gringos*'[13] wealth feeds the miners' fantasies; one must surely be somewhat of a millionaire to spend his life on vacation! Perhaps international visitors even have especially good secrets that allow them to obtain the favors from the masters of the world's riches, and therefore *Tios*'! The fact that Tio becomes visible in the mine as a blond man with blue eyes—a *gringo*—reinforces his empathy with international tourists. The coca, cigarettes, alcohol, and dynamite given to workers are seen as signs that tourists bring good luck. So, as Eliana says, the *gringo*, whether man or woman, has money, therefore he is lucky:

> They have their beliefs, "My wife is going to bring me bad luck, but her, she's a tourist." Whether man or woman, the *gringo*, he has money, therefore he is lucky. That's why they allow them [in the mine]." Eliana Garnica, 29, miner's daughter, handicraft saleswoman

Tourism's stimulus has in this way led workers of mining operations open to the public to modify their discourse. In this instance, women's bad luck has lost its unwavering character in order to concentrate on miners' wives, simultaneously rivals of Pachamama and the men themselves. But for the workers in other mines, the relationship between *gringos'* good luck and that of the mineral beds is not so obvious. Asked about this, David specifies that the mining operations open to the public had a good yield so that the negative impact of female tourists went unnoticed.

My anthropological research connects the experiences of female tourists and miners' wives. Not all miners let me accompany them underground. Some were opposed due to the remoteness and inaccessibility of their place of work. But my status as an outsider in pants is often enough to get them to agree. In fact, it took me a while before I understood that, underneath their carefree appearance, the miners paid serious attention to hints indicating my good or bad luck. It is self-evident that the disappearance of a vein, following one of my visits, would jeopardize the evolution of my research and the possibility of such an unfortunate incident compels me to space out my underground visits. In order to limit my personal responsibility, after a first visit, I preferred to wait for the miners to take the initiative. In fact, sometimes, out of a sense of foreboding, I put off the invitation. I also respected the need to keep women away from the veins. Regardless of the reasons, it is this self-restraint that makes women true actors in their own exclusion.

In conclusion, unexpected modifications within the productive context of Cerro Rico, which occurred during the past century, have allowed for the establishment or the reestablishment of a base peasant belief in an ill-fated interference between women's fertility and the earth's. Because their contribution was not as essential as in the countryside, and because women competed with men for work, the exclusion of women has taken on a much more systematic quality in mining. At the same time, transgressions of the rule and the resulting reconstruction of the discourse confirm that this belief is a social construction, in opposition to the frozen and dogmatic character that is often attributed to it. Is it not, moreover, this ability to accept and resolve contradictions that guarantees the perpetuation of this belief in the bad luck of women?

NOTES

1. The town of Potosí is located south of the Bolivian Andes. Its mountain, appropriately named Cerro Rico (Rich Mountain), which reaches an altitude of nearly 4,800 meters, has been excavated since 1545, the year of discovery by Spanish Conquistadores. In addition to silver, the mines produce tin, lead, and zinc.

2. Jean Berthelot, "L'exploitation des métaux précieux au temps des Incas," *Annales ESC* 5–6 (1978): 948–966.
3. Enrique Tandeter, ed., *L'argent du Potosi: Coercition et marché dans l'Amérique coloniale* (Paris: Ecole des Hautes Etudes en Sciences Sociales, 1997), Centro de Promoción Minera (CEPROMIN), *El trabajo invisible de la mujer minera boliviana* (La Paz, 1996).
4. Cepromin, *El trabajo*, 16.
5. From the Quechuan *pallar:* to collect, gather. The word *palliri*, which during the colonial period ranked workers, men and women, who worked in mineral selection, today refers exclusively to women who work in open-pit mining.
6. Frédérique Langue and Carmen Salazar-Soler, *Dictionnaire des termes miniers en usage en Amérique espagnole, XVIe-XIXe siècle* (Paris: ERC ed.,1993), 64.
7. All interviews conducted by author and in her possession.
8. René Poppe, *Cuentos Mineros* (La Paz: Ed. Hisla, 1985), 73.
9. Ibid., 101.
10. Some of my interview subjects blame the aroma of women's makeup and perfume.
11. Thérèse Bouysse-Cassagne and Olivia Harris, "Pacha: En torno al pensamiento Aymara," in *Tres reflexiones sobre el pensamiento andino* (La Paz: Hisbol), 11–59.
12. Pascale Absi, "Le diable au corps. Organisation sociale et symbolique de la production minière dans les coopératives de Potosi, Bolivie" (PhD dissertation, Ecole des Hautes Etudes en Sciences Sociales, Paris, 2001).
13. Miners consider all whites *gringos*.

CHAPTER 4

Kamins Building the Empire: Class, Caste, and Gender Interface in Indian Collieries

Kuntala Lahiri-Dutt

INTRODUCTION

Contrary to popular notions of "Indian women" representing weak and tradition-bound vulnerable victims of patriarchy is the image of a female mineworker sweating in Indian collieries. It is an image that is hidden from the direct gaze of social scientists looking for "labor" or the "working class" in the mines. Conventional Western stereotypes of labor and industrial relations are characterized by hard management, wage and capital and the archetypal proletariat,[1] the coal miner also tends to dominate and hides from view women in nontraditional roles such as those in mining. When women and the mines are indeed written about, women are seen as members of mining communities and their roles as miners' wives tend to shadow the various productive roles they played and still play in and around the mines.[2]

Women have participated in mining in Asian countries for a long time.[3] The mines are not isolated from the societal context in which they belong, however much an "enclave" character they may have assumed in the colonial time. Simple questions such as who were these women and where do they belong in the social and gender hierarchies of the mines are raised when one looks at women mineworkers either on surface or underground. Was the experience of women miners the same as those of Europe? If not, can we lead from there toward a gendered mining history of the "Asian" or even "Indian" kind?

This essay examines the caste-class interface in the collieries of India by examining the participation of women miners, commonly called *kamins*[4] in collieries. Written accounts of Indian mining history itself is sparse and dominated by colonial sources, which put overwhelming stress on male miners.

Indian *kamins* are barely visible outside of the mines as the proletarian miner becomes the hero and shrouds his female counterpart who can give us a better understanding of a gendered mining history. The *kamins* of India tell us about the way the British colonial empire brought modernity in India and gendered the resource extraction process. The essay enriches itself from the past work on Asian women miners by Burke[5] and uses the marking theory to understand how specific roles and jobs become assigned to women and men in the context of the mine.

Marking theory is used widely in linguistics; markedness stands for the linguistic phenomena consisting of polar opposed pairs.[6] Since mining is generally constructed as a "masculine" world, where the codification of women and mens lives as separate is seen as complete and total, marking theory provides us with a suitable theoretical tool to understand the ways mining jobs become gendered. Marking is closely linked with hierarchy that suits our purpose since role and status are two inseparable terms that are bound to appear in any discussion of role-fixing. Are *kamins* the opposites of coolies? In traditional Sanskrit the connotations are described as *laksya* (marked) and miners as having *laksanas* (markers). Such application of marking theory in explaining social roles has been attempted before. The American anthropologist Hage's work was a fundamental application of the theory to social contexts such as kinship analysis in a cross-cultural and historical manner.[7] In my analysis, the gender markedness in mining arises from two *laksanas*, the job being perceived as risky and dirty, thus requiring "protection" for the weaker and fairer sex, and the job itself attributing a male solidarity among its workers, leading to a strong sense of male bonding and labor militancy. Here one may recollect the early work of Kerr and Seigal who suggested that the isolation of miners from the wider community (both in their work and their lives outside the mine) makes them a particularly cohesive group who tend to be characterized as the quintessential "other". The manifestations of these *laksanas* are in space as well as in time, in the collieries—underground and on the surface—and in the present and in the past. Burke compared this bipolarity in terms of Yin and Yang. According to her, "The lack of visibility of women miners, both in public perceptions and scholarly work, raises questions familiar enough in other, better explored, areas of women's history. In modern mining history, however, it takes on a particular quality due to the contrasting high profile of male miners. The Ying of invisible women is matched by the Yang of only too visible men."[8] My essay examines the gender roles and notes how the markedness had been applied in popular conscience in the coalmines of eastern India.

MARKING GENDER IN THE COLLIERIES

Coal mining, like the plantations in *raj* times, fully manifested almost all the symptoms of colonial modernity that descended on feudal economic relations and production systems of India—private investment and the involvement of indigenous capital, import of labor from other parts of the country to build up a reserve of "captive labor," and a low level of technology. Coal mines were essentially the secondary "enclaves" meant to serve the primary metropolitan enclaves located in Calcutta within a vast sea of subsistence agriculture. Coal mining in India until the independence of the country in 1947 took place almost entirely in the eastern part. The Raniganj-Jharia-Bokaro region had collieries that began in colonial times, and the history of coal mining is synonymous with the way modern development has unfolded its trajectory in India whether in colonial or in postcolonial times. Coalmines are an important part of the colonial modernity where race and gender are constructed or invented in ways that are quite different than in urban India. In collieries, *kamins* played a role in building the empire whereas in cities, "native" women came out of homes under British patronage to learn English and the ways of the outside world. However, *kamins* played an insignificant role in the colonial discursive practices[9] that constructed gender ideologies by selectively focusing on certain aspects and ignoring other aspects. Colonial modernity in India highlighted fragmented aspects of an imagined reality, in urban-based education, and thereby invented gender paradigms.

Thus, the inclusion of local, poor, *adivasi* (original inhabitants) and lower-caste women in coal mining is in no way comparable to the way women in urban India were exposed to colonial modernity. In Bengal, where the British influence was felt earliest and was strongest, urban women of upper caste or elite families were beginning to form new social subjectivities or forms of representation. Bannerji in 2001 has shown how the colonial ruling class invented moral identities in which one can encounter constructive and interpretative attempts where Bengali/Indian women are subject-objects of both colonial and indigenous hegemonic exercises. In the primary enclave of Calcutta metropolis, a category of *bhadramahila* or the gentlewoman was being created under the patronage of social reformers, both English and Indian. They were teaching urban Indian women how to read and write, and how to interact with men in spaces other than domestic.[10] What happened in the mines is a different process from the metropolis. In Calcutta, according to Bannerji, "The woman here, unlike in 'Age of Consent,' is an upper-class/caste woman with more than a physical function. Thus she is not just a tropical body, a combination of animal sex and fecundity but rather the object-subject of a moral constellation which signifies transcendence. . . . As such, Bengali/Indian women end up as the agents and subjects of their own invention."[11]

The women miners in colonial collieries were quite different from the more monolithic colonial stereotypes of middle-class women. As we see, they transcended the markedness of gender roles by virtue of the manual nature of their work and by their ethnic origins. Bengali women, Standing noted in 1991, have conventionally taken little part in waged work with the exception of a small professional group from the upper class. The separation of *ghar* and *bahir*, the home and the outside world, was so complete by the emerging nationalist ideology in colonial India that there were only a few instances where women worked shoulder to shoulder with men as in the collieries.[12] Hence it is important to examine the *kamins* who did and see what they tell us about the colonial modernity in India. The gendered history of coalmines leads us to a rediscovery of Indian women and helps us to identify the reasons for the Indian women miners' invisibility.

COAL MINING AND MINERS IN INDIA

The necessities of fueling the industrial-urban engine during the British *Raj* encouraged coal mining in Raniganj in Bengal and its counterpart Jharia in Bihar. Here coal was first struck by Suetonius Grant Heatly and John Summer, two employees of the East India Company in 1774. Coal mining in India continued to be sporadic in nature as long as it did not become economical to extract. The British emerged as the main investors when by the second part of the nineteenth century coal mining picked up in the region in spite of immense difficulties. Transport of coal to the main market in Calcutta was the main problem as the Damodar and Ajoy rivers were not navigable in dry season and were flood prone during the monsoons, and often upset transport schedules. Koilaghat (coal point) on the Hooghly river in Calcutta strand still bears the old memory of riverine coal transport. Three factors provided the initial stimuli for growth of the coal mining industry—the abolition of East India Company's trading monopoly in 1813; opening of the Raniganj mine under European supervision; and the introduction of railways in 1855 to facilitate coal transport to the market in Calcutta, which was the capital of the British empire in South Asia until 1911.[13]

Indian entrepreneurs, mainly landlords, eventually came to dominate coal production; as many as thirteen of the seventeen companies were owned by Indian operators in the early part of the twentieth century.[14] Prince Dwarkanath Tagore's Carr, Tagore and Co. merged with Gilmore Humfrey and Co. to form the Bengal Coal Company that soon became the largest operator. In 1860, the fifty collieries of Bengal Coal Company produced 99 percent of Indian coal. The low levels of technology and capital investment ensured that Indian landowners could make an easy entry into the industry.[15] They were little different from the local landlords in their style of operation. Techniques of mining and mining tools were simple. Shafts were sunk every few hundred feet and quarries were often opened below the high water mark whenever an outcrop was found near a waterway. Coal was brought from the face to pit bottom in head baskets, usually by women. There it was put into larger baskets (6–7 maund or about 250 kg) and taken to the surface by a winding engine, called a "gin" (an abbreviation also used in other industries such as cotton). The gin was worked by women, perhaps by more than twenty. Small "beam" engines were occasionally employed to do the combined work of pumping and winding and were operated by three women. Steel-tipped curved pieces of iron were used as picks with shapeless wedges and hammers and one-inch round crowbars. This type of mining continued until about the 1920s, when the technology of coal production in India began to change in response to greater demands. Deeper shafts replaced open cast and inclined mines.

Around the same time various measures were adopted to "protect" women from heavy mining work. The measures and their resultant exclusion of women workers took place on several scales. At the international level, several ILO measures—the 1919 Convention on Night Work (Women), and the 1935 Convention on Underground Work (Women)—restricted women workers from working in both shifts and from working in underground mines.[16] At the national level, the Indian Mines Act, initiated first in 1901, restricted the age of employment of children in mines. In 1929 and finally in 1935 the Mines Act entirely prohibited company owners to employ women in underground work. Such orders were issued again in 1946, and then a complete ban was imposed in 1952, which stated that women miners will be employed only in surface work during the day shifts.[17] These acts restricted the period of work from sixteen to twelve to ten hours and eventually eight for underground workers and nine hours for surface workers. The acts/measures were presented as a means of protecting women from an unsafe job such as mining. The Indian state assumed its traditional benevolent role through its commitment to the protection of women. The legislations tell us that women miners were perceived by the state as one group that needs to be "protected" from the hazardous mining work.

In the period after independence, the "company" raj, non-Bengali business entrepreneurs, the "company" owners, replaced local *zamindar*[18]—owners of many Raniganj collieries. The feudal relationship between labor and colliery owners had been replaced by a more cash-oriented relationship, and the mining companies' main objective was to increase production to fuel the industrial dreams of planned development.

The land laws of India changed during the 1930s to give both surface and sub surface rights of the land to mining companies.[19] As long as coal mining was "extensive" in nature, technology did not undergo any decisive changes, the units of production did not grow in size, and mines of similar size were added to each other to increase production, women miners continued to take a significant role in the industry. With more intensive, technology-oriented production, and higher capital investments, women's role in coal mining began to decline. In 1901 women formed about 48 percent of total mineworkers in India. Of these women, 65 percent worked in underground collieries. The proportion remained more or less the same until 1921 (61 and 60 percents, respectively). The data in table 4.1 show that the participation of women was significant till the 1930s. The proportion of women miners decreased from such high levels to about 20 percent in postcolonial India and now has fallen to only about 6 percent. Most substantial declines, however, have taken place in recent decades under state ownership of the mining industry.

The Indian coal mining industry was "nationalized" or brought under state ownership in several phases during 1971–1973. Nationalization of coal mining was in tune with the socialistic rationale of the Indian National Congress party representing the modernizing bourgeois elite and ruling the country from Delhi at that time since 1947.[20] All minerals were classified into two categories,

Table **4.1** Proportion of women workers in eastern Indian collieries 1901–1996[i]

Year	Female	Male	% of Female to total
1901	26520	55682	47.6
1921	70831	115982	61.1
1973	15181	60620	20.0
1980	16094	169136	9.7
1990	12875	165829	7.2
1996	9879	151855	6.1

[i] Compiled from Seth (1940), Census, CIL and Eastern Coalfields Limited Reports.

"major" and "minor", and all major minerals including coal were brought under state control. India is now the third largest coal producer of the world with an annual production of about 299 million tons, which is about 68 percent of total energy resources of the country.[21] In eastern India, the individual colliery owners were given compensation at the time of nationalization, but the labor relationship they had instituted continued in the collieries. Women's role in the mining industry has declined at a significant rate during the last two and a half decades under state ownership. Women now occupy a marginal position in the Indian coal industry (around 5 percent of the labor force) because they were made redundant in the labor process.[22]

ETHNIC IDENTITIES, GENDER AND THE WORKING CLASS

Cultural identities such as ethnicity, caste, and religion have powerful influence on social and gender relationships within the formal industrial labor force in India. Class is inextricably intertwined with identities such as gender and ethnicity, a situation which necessitates that the assumption of a singular, monolithic working class be reconsidered. The relationship between the politics of class and community has been noted by subaltern historians who opposed the Marxist notion of a working class having universal validity in India.[23] The political economy of coal mining in India has traditionally been characterized by three hierarchies—caste,[24] class, and gender. In coal mining, a specific cultural group of women participated traditionally; exclusion means these women are being denied of their subsistence. Everett simply called them "lower-class" women but that brings us to the debate of the relationship between caste and class in India, whether they can coexist or are mutually exclusive. The *adivasi*s or the indigenous peoples and the lower castes together form that vast amorphous mass whom the Indian officialdom calls "weaker sections of the society." In the Indian collieries, women from lower castes and *adivasi* groups formed the initial labor force. Here, caste has been a useful tool in examining gender identities. This transcendental role of caste has at one level helped build allegiances; but at another level it has also provided the means to exclude and subjugate some sections of the society.

Was the definition of a "working class" valid in such cases? Chakrabarty has shown that in India such universal categories of Marxist thought as "capital" and "labor" are not valid in defining the industrial working class. In Indian collieries, the labor process or the choice of technology is rooted in the culture of the "company" owners as well as the laborers. The deeply entrenched mercantilist outlook and the cultural milieu of the British *raj* in India was not discontinued after the independence of the country,[25] and have played significant roles in selective exclusions—whether of *adivasi*s or women—in Indian coal mining.

In India, caste divisions played a part both in actual social interactions and in the ideal scheme of values. Members of different castes are, up to a point, expected to behave differently and ascribed different status according to their castes. Formerly birth in a particular caste fixed not only one's ritual status, but by and large also one's economic and political positions. Today it is possible to achieve a variety of economic and political positions in spite of one's birth in a specific caste, although caste still sets limits within which choice is restricted.

Other subaltern groupings of indigenous populations of India include tribals, untouchables, *adivasi*s, *dalit*s (the oppressed), and *Harijan*s (children of God, called by Gandhi). Of them, "Tribal" is a colonial construction and has fallen into disrepute whereas the term *dalit* is often used generically to include (in the words of the Dalit Panther Manifesto of 1973–1975) "members of the scheduled castes and tribes, neo-Buddhists, the working people, the landless and poor peasants, women and all those who are being exploited politically, economically and in the name of religion."[26] Recently, Mendelsohn and Vicziany have retained the original term, "untouchables," in their study arguing that both *harijan* and *dalit* are political names for a creature whose identity continues to be rooted in the concept of ritual pollution that is itself a part of a very elaborate theology of the pure and the impure.[27] To call them "unntouchable" is to stress the fact that the destiny of these people is crucial to the social order—the caste society—which excluded them in a way such that their exclusion sustains the symbolic architecture on which this order is founded. Clearly, the terms *dalit* or *harijan* are far more wide ranging for my purposes of this chapter.

An understanding of the ethnic division of labor in Indian collieries is important in examining the problem of the decline of women workers in nontraditional roles outside the home such as in the organized coal mining sector. I emphasize that the increasing marginalization of women miners in the postcolonial or the post-nationalization period has to be seen beyond the economic changes taking place within the country or the industry. It has to be put in the specific regional perspective and examined in terms of the overall transformations occurring in that context. The exclusion of women miners and the transformation of the labor force into a predominantly immigrant male working class represent a gender politics in the Indian collieries.

When Heatley opened his first mine in 1774, he had brought in some experts from England besides employing the local labor. William Jones, one of the early British entrepreneurs to invest in coal mining, was the first to employ local *adivasi* and lower-caste labor around the middle of nineteenth century. The British administrator of Burdwan district, Paterson reported in the Imperial Gazetteer that two-thirds of the total workforce in the mining industry was "locally born."[28] Of the different local *adivasi* and lower caste groups, the Bauris were the first to bring their women into the collieries and their contribution in the early development of Indian coal mining industry was quite significant. As a result, they came to be known as "traditional coal cutters" though the traditional occupation of these peoples has been agriculture-related work. The Santhals, Kols, Koras, and Bhuinyas also joined the mining workforce along with their women. Other low-caste populations such as Beldars, Mallahs, and Jolahs worked in the mines with their women. Upper-caste women usually stayed away from the dirty, heavy work of collieries. Women of different local castes and communities participated in varying proportions in coal mining, as evident from table 4.2.

Around the 1930s, women miners were employed in a variety of operations in collieries. As steam engines "phased out" gin girls, and collieries came to be owned by Indian entrepreneurs, women found themselves working as *kamins* on the surface as well as doing underground work. However, eventually women workers came to specialize in jobs as "loaders"—lifters and transporters of coal cut by their male partners—father, brother, or husband.[29] This "family labor" system was suitable in view of the primitive techniques used in the shallow open cast mines, locally called *pukuriya khads* as well as the inclines.

To British visitors A.A. Purcell and J. Hollsworth such a family system of labor appeared entirely "different" from that "in our collieries" where miners as an industrial working class had already been formed.[30] Indian coal miners collectively were not yet an industrial class and their traditional rural roots and occupations were still strong. The family system of labor operated well for several social reasons too—the adivasi sentiments of family attachment, and the unwillingness of women to carry coal for men of another caste. Above all, the dominant economic reason was that it provided uninterrupted maintenance of work schedule.

Table 4.2 Ethnic division of women miners in eastern India, between the wars

Castes	Women/100 men of their caste	Castes	Women/100 men of their caste
Doms	111.0	Kurmis	67.5
Jolahs	59.4	Bauris	55.8
Telis	45.5	Rajputs	27.2
Goalas	24.5	Beldars	102.0
Santhals	87.9		
Bhuinyas	80.1		
Mallahs	79.5		

Source: Seth (1940), p. 129.

An account of coal mining in Raniganj in the early twentieth century was written by Col. Frank J. Agabeg, the general manager of Apcar and Co., the pioneering coal mining concern. He described how Asansol, now a major urban center, had then just started to develop and Raniganj was the most important mining town. Barakar was the western terminus for the East Indian Railway, whereas Ondal had a large railway siding. These towns have now grown into major urban centers with populations of over two hundred thousand. Collieries located at a distance from the railway transported their coal by bullock carts across dirt tracks. Only those adjacent to the railway lines had sidings for loading and unloading of coal. The cost of such infrastructure construction was borne by the companies using them. However, the Bengal-Nagpur Railway eventually extended the subsidiary lines to the less accessible collieries after the 1930s and an intricate network of "company roads" grew up around the collieries.

What was the view from below? Paku Mejhen, whose Santhal adivasi ancestors came originally from nearby Dumka four generations ago, describes the hierarchical colliery life, which placed women workers like her great grandmother at the bottom:

In the colliery, Managershaheb was the boss. Borobabu ["babu" denotes the educated Bengali middle-class men, the Bhadralok] was under him, translated his instructions and in case of any trouble controlled the situation. The managershaheb would shout, "borobabuko bulao" (call the borobabu) if any problem arose! Gomostababu managed the coolies and kamins, Gudambabu looked after the store, Hazribabu took attendance, Loadingbabu supervised coal loading, and Batibabu distributed the lights. We Santhals did all the dirty and heavy jobs—our men cut the coal and women loaded it in baskets. We grew up on collieries; my great grandmother first went into the khadan (mine) with my great-grandfather. She had to work very hard even on days she wasn't well.

Clearly, women were at the bottom of the pits" gender hierarchy. More *babus* (clerks) from upper-caste Hindu families gradually came to occupy middle positions between the *malkata* (coal cutters) and the manager in collieries after the 1930s. The Bijlibabu for instance appeared with the advent of electricity in collieries around World War II. So came Compassbabu (surveyor), Miningbabu, and inchajbabu (in-charge). This structure has remained more or less unchanged till now.

The social fabric of colliery communities went through a process of transformation as coal began to be mined. The physical and social isolation of the *adivasi* lands of *jungle mahal* was more or less complete before mining began in the region and cultivating castes had claimed much of the more accessible land. Since the local adivasi and semi-adivasi labor left the collieries during cropping season to work in the agricultural fields, and this interfered with maintaining mining operations, collieries were interested in creating a captive labor force. They began to employ "upcountry labor" from north India around the early twentieth century. *Thekadars* (contractors) brought hardworking able-bodied males from eastern Uttar Pradesh, Bihar, and even

Madhya Pradesh. Intrastate voluntary migration was initially comparatively smaller in volume, possibly due to the ravages left by frequent *bargi* (Maratha raiders) attacks from the western states of India.[31] A statutory body called the Coalfield Recruiting Organisation was formed to maintain, often forcibly, the supply of labor to the mines.[32]

Tales of how laborers were kept in chains in the coolie barracks have now become part of the folklore in Raniganj. Workers labored at least twelve hours and cash wages could never compensate for a kind of work that these agricultural people could not even visualize. Many of the upcountry labor left the mines after their eleven-month contract period never to come back. Collieries are known to have maintained *lethel* (armed guards) to regulate and control the new recruits.[33] Paku Mejhen remembers how "Bilaspuris" and "Gorakhpuris" (labor from Bilaspur in Central Province and Gorakhpur in north India) were brought in to work in collieries and kept in "labor depots." The manager used to send the *sardar* (leader of workers, a foreman) to a depot to get a few additional hands as soon as there was a labor shortage. The organization received commission from the companies in return.

Bilaspuris and Gorakhpuris, of course, began to permanently live in Raniganj-Jharia-Bokaro collieries as working conditions began to improve in postcolonial times when trade unions began to wield their full weight. Paku still names each *coolie dhaora* (residential quarters of miners) by its cultural origin; to her it is always a Santhal *basti* (settlement), Kora, Nu nia, Madesiya Gorakhpuri or a C.P. (Central Province) *dhaora*. As mining brought in a large number of male laborers from adjoining parts of the country, the *adivasis* and lower-caste workers, in order to maintain their family units of production, opted for work in plantations or in construction of roads or railways where both women and men could again "join hands together." The *adivasi* labor, had exchanged "the plough for the pick" and still continued to prefer the plough from which they were displaced by the first wave of colonization.[34] Gradually a large segment of the workers in the collieries was typically immigrant and male, caste Hindus from north or central India. Women like Paku's grandmother still carried on, although their contribution in the resource extraction process increasingly began to be devalued in more ways than one.

During the years from 1891 to 1931, the outbound migration was almost double in size of the inbound migration in the colliery tracts of eastern India. However, the high rates of outflow of local laborers subsided over the years and inbound migration grew rapidly as more collieries were opened. In a heterogeneous local labor market of the collieries, an abundance of unskilled local workers was certainly available. Still, the majority were drawn from outside areas. Moreover, the colliery workers, like other rural-based workers in Indian industries,[35] neither economically nor ethnically belonged to the same class. The withdrawal of *adivasi* labor from Indian collieries during late nineteenth and early twentieth centuries proves this. It also indicates how changing production relations changed the social-ethnic composition of labor, and eventually affected its gender composition.

Women still participate in mining, including coal mining in India and elsewhere in the world,[36] but their roles remain marginal. In India, women miners in the collieries show how changes in the economic organization of resource extraction in colonial and postcolonial India have interacted to produce rigidly hierarchical and marked roles for women and men.

GENDER AND THE WORKING CLASS IN INDIAN COLLIERIES

The trade unions have come a long way in the Indian collieries from the old days of long working hours, lack of security, and frightful conditions as described by the leading Marxist leader Dange in 1945. The formalization of the coal mining industry and successful bargaining have now put the trade unions in a place to have representations in each management decision and discuss issues like pollution in the region. The unions have indeed earned for the workers many of the benefits they enjoy now, and have in turn made getting a job in collieries a highly attractive proposition—far better than what was described by the Government of India in its 1967 survey report on labor conditions in the coal mining industry. It is true that instead of treating "family" as a unit of production, trade unions fought for equal wages and have thus helped to achieve a better valuation of women's work in mining. Ensuring that a widow gets the job of her deceased husband was also the achievement of these unions.

The trade unions have remained insensitive to the declining numbers of women workers in collieries. As institutions they are male dominated in that neither the leaders are women, nor have the number of women members registered a significant increase. But above all, although some trade unions have added women-related issues to their "list of workers' demands" their policies have not placed them at the forefront of these agendas. Women workers are excluded at the level of leadership and policy, and even if women are members they are discouraged to participate in union meetings. The belief in a monolithic working class is shared by all trade unions whether leftist or not, thus subsuming gender issues within the class issues.

Union activity seems to be shaped by a gendered discourse that looks at women as a "special" category externalized from the general interests of workers.[37] The *colliery majdoor sabha* (labor congress) takes pride in their mass movements and in how women "participate" in these movements, but most often these are dominated by upper-caste men. Mining is such an overwhelmingly male world in terms of power and domination; men are perceived to be risking their lives to earn the bread for their families. The notion is that women belonged in the home and were only working to earn "the butter," claiming equal wages where it is clear that their frail bodies cannot put in the kind of hard labor demanded by coal mining.

The recently introduced Voluntary Retirement Scheme (VRS) is a good example of how women workers are made redundant. Pholumoni Kora, an indigenous woman, told me how she has been identified as "surplus labor" by the mining company and will be retired soon in spite of her repeated requests for jobs that she is skilled to do, such as sorting coal or making *guli* (mud-containers for explosives) or baskets. These are skills that *adivasi* and lower-caste women workers have acquired over generations of participation in coal mining work. It may not be impossible to train Pholumoni to do other kinds of machine work toward the creation of "womanpower" in the collieries. In postcolonial India the exclusion of women from the industrial workforce and the subsequent construction of a male working class have not been limited to the coal mining sector alone.[38] But in coal mining, trade unions are less responsive to women workers than their male members' interests.

The lack of activism among the women coal miners is partly due to political silencing and partly because of the organizational strength of the *majdoor* unions.[39] The militancy of the trade unions has a long history that is outside the purview of this paper. The Hindi term *majdoor* itself denotes a male worker and the trade unions usually perceive themselves as male organizations. They prefer to avoid the responsibility of ensuring jobs for the widows of deceased mineworkers, a right that was historically granted by the companies. For example, Dulali lost her husband in a wall-collapse accident in late 1980s, and applied to the company for a job. During our conversation, she noted: "I made rounds of colliery offices for two years. Finally I went to the union leaders who insisted that I accept to my elder son being given the job. Following their advice, I decided in favor of my son and now I hardly get two square meals a day." Her son has now deserted her and she lives by what she describes as "collecting coal" from an abandoned local mine. She remained quiet for a long time when I asked why mine widows like her do not protest about the union's reluctance to entertain them. She then said, "We are always ready for action, but first think before shouting. If the leaders are enraged, we will be in big trouble. So we keep quiet." When I probed further, she said, "Look at Prakashbabu (the local trade union leader)—he is just like other babus in colliery. How can we talk to him as an equal?" What we have here is a double dose of exclusion, where ethnic or caste identity along with gender creates a position of double minority for *kamin*s in the Indian collieries.

CONCLUSION

Mining is an area where women had at once interfaced with men, with overlapping spheres of activities. It is a sector that has geographical ramifications from the local economy and sociocultural levels of the regional, national, as well as international levels. Indian collieries made the country part of the large global enterprise, a network created through the British empire that brought the remote, isolated, jungle tracts into the contact of European modernity. As we see, women played a major role in this aspect of empire building, and thus, *kamin*s in Indian collieries provide a fascinating way to trace these connections conceptually and visibly. Here we see how the male coal miners' "markedness" as manifest by the masculine conceptualization of their work derives from the fundamental inconsistency of their position and the effects these have upon gender identities. In Indian collieries, coolies have come to occupy the position of the archetypal mineworkers whereas *kamin*s have been relegated to the background. However, as we have seen in this essay, the opposite of "coolie," the *kamin*, does not necessarily imply the wives of miners located in homes. The *kamin*s have their special places alongside men, as partners in the production process in the Indian collieries. They played equally important roles in empire building in the Indian subcontinent, and in quite different ways than urban women in the metropolitan city of Calcutta educated themselves to turn into that idealized feminine who is equally at home with outside men and family members.

The state measures reflect a compartmentalization of the issue of women workers. The various protective legislations developed for women miners, though probably designed to improve their working conditions, have acted as instruments to exclude them from the formal mining sector. The nationalized company has been unwilling to recruit women because of their special and protected status on the one hand, and on the other hand the legislation has not included any means for the protection of employment opportunities and job security. Thus the special biological attributes of women have been at the center of concern by the "protectors" rather than against discrimination due to cultural, social, and economic factors.[40] As a result, the *kamin*s, women of lower castes and indigenous ethnic groups that traditionally did mining jobs have been more affected than white-collar workers. The exclusion of women miners brings out how the real exigencies of power struggles between genders in party politics are downplayed successfully and an ideology of "protection" dominates women's active role in natural resource management. The separation of "home" and the "workplace" becomes complete, and women become "protected" within the family and the home; "work" in the mines becoming a mode of access to the public space, the mines. Mining becomes constructed as a "masculine" world, where the jobs are gendered and codified as women's and men's. Here marking theory provides us with a suitable theoretical tool to understand the ways mining jobs become gendered and stratified according to gender divisions. Role and status are two inseparable concepts that we have noted to operate in this process of role-fixing. Are *kamin*s the opposites of coolies? In this analysis, the gender markedness in mining arises from two markers, the job being perceived as risky and dirty, thus requiring "protection" for the weaker and fairer sex, and the job itself attributing a male solidarity among its workers, leading to a strong sense of male bonding and labor militancy. The manifestations of these markers appeared in the collieries—underground and on the surface—turning into special and gendered places as well as in time, in the past and in the present. The markedness of gender roles eventually becomes set in concrete in popular conscience.

Notes

1. Campbell, Alan B. and Reid, Fred. 'The Independent Collier in Scotland,' *Independent Collier: The Coal Miner as Archetypal Proletarian Reconsidered*. ed. Royden, Harrison, Sussex (England: Harvester Press, 1978), pp. 54–74. Harrison's 1978 book on the tensions an "independent collier" as archetypal proletariat faces between existences as "honorable men or degraded slaves".

2. Eriko Furumura, "The Heritage that the organization of Miner's Wives Left in Their Community: Especially about 'Tanpukyou.' " Paper presented to the "International Mining History Conference," Akabira, Hokkaido, Japan, September 2003. Kathy Robinson, "Love and Sex in an Indonesian Mining Town," in *Gender and Power in Affluent Asia*, ed., Krishna Sen and Maila Stevens (London & New York: Routledge, 1998). Also see Gibson-Graham's work on how women's organizations in Australian coal mining towns gained legitimacy by supporting men's struggles. J.K. Gibson-Graham, " 'Stuffed if I Know!': Reflections on Post-modern Feminist Social Research," *Gender, Place and Culture* 1, no. 2 (1994): 205–224.

3. Amarjit Kour, "Labour Dynamics in Plantations and Mining: An Historical Perspective" in *Changing labour Relations in South East Asia* ed. Rebecca Elmhirst and Ratna Saptari (London: Curzon, 2001). Kayoko Yoshida and Reiko Miyauchi, "Invisible Labour: Comparative Oral History of Women in Coal Mining Communities of Hokkaido, Japan, and Montana, USA, 1890–1940." Paper presented to the "International Mining History Conference," Akabira, Hokkaido, Japan, September 2003.

4. "*Kamin* is the common name of Indian women mineworkers working at manual jobs in the mines. The term is a feminine opposite of "coolie," the physical laborer in almost all contexts in India. *Kamin*s can be found also in the quarries such as stone.

5. Gill Burke, "Asian Women Miners: Recovering Some History and Unpacking Some Myths." Paper presented to the "Women in Asia Conference," University of Melbourne, October 1–3, 1993; "Miners, Labour Militancy, Gender and Other Deconstructions." Paper presented to the "Third International Mining History Conference and Symposium on the Preservation of Historic Mining Sites," Colorado School of Mines, Golden, June 6–10, 1994; "The Confucian Collier? Labour Relations in Mining in the Asia-Pacific Region." Paper presented to the AIRAANZ Conference, Melbourne, February 1995.

6. For example, the phonological feature unvoiced-voiced, the antonyms long-short, the grammatical relations singular-plural and active-passive. In such binary oppositions (contrasts) the poles also represent asymmetry such that one pole may be more special or specialized, more focused or constrained, less general and more complex than the other. In such cases, the specialized element is said to be marked and the more general one unmarked. The first discussion of markedness in modern linguistics originated in 1930s in the writings of the Prague school of structural phenologists Nicolai S. Trubetzkoy and Roman Jakobson. For more details on the development of markedness in linguistics, see R. Asher, and J. Simpson (eds.), *Encyclopaedia of Language and Linguistics* (Oxford: Pergamon Press, 1994).

7. P. Hage, "Marking Theory and Kinship Analysis: Cross-Cultural and Historical Applications," *Anthropological Theory* 1, no. 2 (June 2001): 197–211 (15).

8. Burke, "Miners, Labour Militancy, Gender and Other Deconstructions," 2.

9. I am aware that the concept of colonial discourse is a highly complex one and a contested terrain. In this chapter, I use the term in the sense of a domain in which social practices and institutions pertaining to the colonial enterprise—such as the collieries—created marked identities for women and men. For a deeper analysis, see Gayatri Spivak, *In Other Worlds: Essays in Cultural Politics* (NY and London: Methuen, 1998); or Homi Bhabha, *The Location of Culture* (London: Routledge, 1994).

10. Malavika Karlekar, "Kadambini and Bhadralok: Early Debates over Women's Education in Bengal," *Economic and Political Weekly: Review of Women's Studies* 21 (1986): WS 25–31; *Voices from Within: Early Personal Narratives of Bengali Women* (Delhi: Oxford University Press, 1991).

11. Himani Bannerji, *Inventing Subjects: Studies in Hegemony, Patriarchy and Colonialism.* (New Delhi: Tulika Books, 2001), 4.

12. Partha Chatterjee, *The Nation and Its Fragments: Colonial and Postcolonial Histories* (Princeton, NJ: Princeton University Press, 1993).

13. Kuntala Lahiri-Dutt, *Mining and Urbanization in the Raniganj Coalbelt* (Calcutta: The World Press, 2002); Sunil Kumar Munsi, *Geography of Transportation in Eastern India under the British Raj.* CSSSC Monograph 1 (Calcutta: K.P. Bagchi & Co, 1980).

14. Harasankar Bhattacharyya, *Zamindars and Patnidars: A Study of Subinfeudation under the Burdwan Raj* (Burdwan: Burdwan University Publication Unit, 1985).

15. Detmar Rothermund and D.C. Wadhwa (eds.), *Zamindars, Mines and Peasants: Studies in the History of an Indian Coalfield and Its Rural Hinterland* (New Delhi: Manohar Publications, 1978).

16. International Labour Organization, Coal Mines Committee, Twelfth Session: Manpower Planning, Training and Retraining for Coal Mining in the Light of Technological Changes, Report II. Geneva: International Labour Office, 1988; Women Workers: Selected ILO Documents, Second Edition. Geneva: International Labour Office, 1988; International Labour Conventions and Recommendations 1919–1951, Vol. 1, Geneva: International Labour Office, 1996; Sectoral Activities: Mining. Geneva: International Labour Office, 1997.

17. *Coal Handbook* 1997. Office of the District Magistrate, Burdwan: Government of West Bengal.

18. A *zamindar* (spelt often as *zeminder* or *zamindaar*) is a landlord who does not cultivate his own land. The *zamindars* emerged primarily as a result of Permanent Settlement and became an intermediary between the *raj* and the *ryot* or the peasant. For more discussion on the sub-infeudation process in Burdwan/Raniganj region, see Bhattacharyya, Zamindars and Patnidars.

19. K.C. Mahindra, *Indian Coalfields Committee Report* (New Delhi: Manager of Publications, 1946).

20. S.M. Kumarmangalam, *Coal industry in India: Nationalisation and Tasks Ahead* (New Delhi: Oxford and IBH Publishing Co., 1973).

21. *World Hard Coal Production*, 1989–1998 (Mt) (London: BP Statistical Review, 1999).

22. Anjan Ghosh, "Escalating Redundance: Dispensability of Women Labour in the Coal Mines of Eastern India." Paper presented in the Conference on Women Technology and Forms of Production, Madras, October 30–31, 1984.

23. Ranajit Guha, (ed.), *Subaltern Studies: Writings on South Asian History and Society*, Various Volumes (Delhi: Oxford University Press, 1982–1997).

24. Caste has been famously described by Risley as the smallest endogamous group of people in Indian society. H.H. Risley, *The Tribes and Castes of Bengal, Volumes I & II* (Calcutta: Firma KLM (P) Ltd., 1998) [original edition 1891]. Beteille has given the simplest definition of caste as "a system of enduring groups whose mutual relations are governed by certain broad principles." Andre Beteille, *Caste, Class and Power: Changing Patterns of Stratification in a Tanjore Village* (Delhi: Oxford University Press, 1996).

   Louis Dumont declared the uniqueness of caste-bound Indians as "Homo Hierarchicus." (L. Dumont, *Homo Hierarchicus: The Caste System and Its Implications* [London: Weidenfeld & Nicolson, 1966].) This has been severely criticized by Dipankar Gupta, "Continuous Hierarchies and Discreet Castes." *Economic and Political Weekly* XIX nos. 46–48 (1984): 1955–1958, 2003–2005, 2049–2053. Though "caste" is predominantly a Hindu phenomenon, similar groupings are also found among Muslims and Christians in India. The caste division of Indian society is in the realm of "cultural" relations, and Marx's formulation of caste for class is opposed to this cultural interpretation. Bayly dates the making of modern day caste to the eighteenth century and colonial intervention, which increased the stake that Indians had in their "traditional" caste order. See Susan Bayly, *The New Cambridge History of India: Caste, Society and Politics from the Eighteenth Century to the Modern Age* (Cambridge: Cambridge University Press, 1999).

25. The government of India sees the presence of "lower caste" called the Scheduled Castes population as a criterion of backwardness in a region. However, Rudd has recently shown that in some rural areas of Bengal, being of a "lower caste" attributes greater political empowerment. See Arild Engelsen Rudd, "The Indian Hierarchy: Culture, Ideology and Consciousness in Bengali Village Politics." *Modern Asian Studies* 33, no. 3 (1999): 689–732. Mukherjee noted that today caste is denoted more and more as identification within the class-stratum its constituents belong to. See Ramakrishna Mukherjee, "Caste in Itself, Caste and Class, or Caste in Class." *Economic and Political Weekly* 34, no. 27 (1999): 1759–1761.

26. Barbara Joshi, ed., *Untouchables! Voices of the Dalit Liberation Movement* (London: Zed Books, 1986).

27. Oliver Mendelsohn and Marika Vicziany, *The Untouchables: Subordination, Poverty and the State in Modern India* (Cambridge: Cambridge University Press, 1998).

28. J.C.K. Paterson, *Bengal District Gazetteers: Burdwan* (Calcutta: Bengal Secretariat Book Depot, 1910).

29. Rakhi Ray Chaudhury, *Gender and Labour in India: The Kamins of Eastern Coalmines, 1900–1940* (Calcutta: Minerva, 1996).

30. Pabitrabhaskar Sinha, *Development of the Mineral Industries of Bihar-Muzaffarpur* (Calcutta: Calcutta Book House, 1975).

31. R. Guha, *Bengal District Records: Burdwan* (Calcutta: Bengal Secretariat Press, 1955).

32. Mahindra, *Indian Coalfields*.

33. Priyabrata Dasgupta, "Lathial Theke Mafia," *Natun Chithi*, Sarad Sankhya, 25, Burdwan, 1997, 270–274.

34. Margaret Read, *The Indian Peasant Uprooted* (London: 1931).

35. For more discussions on the cultural rootedness of industrial labor force in Bengal. See Dipesh Chakrabarty, *Rethinking Working-Class History: Bengal 1890–1940* (Delhi: Oxford University Press, 1989) and Arjan de Haan and Samita Sen, *A Case for Labour History: The Jute Industry in Eastern India* (Calcutta: KP Bagchi & Company, 1999).

36. See, e.g., Yameema Mitha, Nigat Said Khan, Masood Anwar, and Asmaa Javed Pal, *Patterns of Female Employment in Mining and Construction Industries* (Islamabad: Ministry of Women Development, Government of Pakistan, 1988).

37. Amrita Basu, *Two Faces of Protest: Contrasting Modes of Women's Activism* (Berkeley: University of California Press, 1992).

38. Jhabvala first showed how retrenched women workers from cotton mills of Ahmedabad in west India were pushed into lower-paying and insecure jobs. (Renana Jhabvala, "From the Mill to the Streets: A Study of Retrenchment of Women from Ahmedabad Textile Mills," *Manushi* 26, no. 2 [1985]: 2–5.) Banerjee (*Inventing Subjects*) noted the lack of political protection of women workers by unions in the unorganized sector. Basu (*Two Faces*) demonstrated that in the textile industry in South India, gender segregation is most marked in the mills where regulation and trade union activity is more evident. Fernandes showed how the politics of gender, class, and culture produces notions about the spheres of work of women and men. (Leela Fernandes, "Beyond Public Spaces and Private Spheres: The Politics of Gender, Family and Community in the Calcutta Jute Mills," *Feminist Studies* 23, no. 3.)

39. Lindsay Barnes, "Women, Work and Struggle: Bhowra Colliery, 1900–1985," unpublished PhD thesis, Centre for the Study of Social Systems, Jawaharlal Nehru University, New Delhi, 1989.

40. Zakia Pathak and Rajeswari Sunder Rajan, "Shahbano," in *Feminists Theorize the Political*, ed., Judith Butler and Joan W. Scott (New York: Routledge, 1992).

PART II

Engendered Bodies and the Masculinization of the Mining Industry: Separate Spheres and the Role of Women in Mining, the Mining Household, and Community, 1800–1940

The transition from pre-industrial to industrialized societies transformed the role of men and women and their relationship to nature and the natural world. Although the development of new technology made it possible for humans to do work that might have been impossible before industrialization, the human body and human strength were still essential to the work of the miner, whether the body was male or female. The fact that Britain ushered in the first industrial revolution and by the late nineteenth century had an empire that covered much of the globe had a profound impact on the course that industrialization would take in other nations. "Victorianism," and Victorian values broadly defined would be adapted and adopted around the globe and would set a standard for the "civilized" world, just as the debates during the Enlightenment about the nature of man and woman had shaped the discourse on gender a century before and gave rise to the domestic ideology.

"Gentlemanly capitalism," as it was called by Cain and Hopkins in their monumental study of British imperialism, was neither particularly gentlemanly nor purely capitalist given the degree of government involvement, nevertheless it set the tone for other European nations and much of the colonialized world, which sought to impose or emulate these values.[1] Middleclass men and women were to be transformed into "gentlemen" and "ladies," roles that members of the working class might aspire for, but had little hope of achieving. Nevertheless, under certain circumstances this ideal became the justification for employers, governments, and male trade unionists to exclude women from underground work in the mining industry, usually under the guise of "protective" legislation. That women miners were being deprived of the independence afforded by work, however ill paid, was rarely a consideration.

In Europe, women miners were prevalent in areas where women had worked in shallow pits that had previously been part of preindustrial family operations, which included children. Their smaller, lighter bodies made it possible for them to be lowered by ropes into manually dug pits, where they could pick coal, mainly for household consumption. As industrialization progressed in Britain and elsewhere, the demand for coal, copper, and other minerals essential to industry increased and with it capital investment in mining. Mines were often located in areas far from population centers, and the first miners under the new regime of the industrialized nations were often an itinerant workforce of single men who moved from place to place as mines were opened and then closed when no longer productive.

But as technology and mining techniques developed, deeper and more expensive mines led to a professionalization of the mining industry and the role of miner. In parts of Germany, the emergence of the Cameralist tradition in the eighteenth century epitomized the view that the future of the mining industry should be tied to trained, loyal, servants of the state.[2] Whereas in the rest of Europe the mining industry remained largely in the hands of capitalists until the twentieth century, trade unionists and social reformers mounted campaigns to exclude women from work underground. In countries that industrialized earlier, women's exclusion from work underground usually followed sooner than in lesser developed nations where women's work in mines was part of the tradition of the indigenous population. This exclusion of women was perhaps also indicative of the extent to which industrialization relied upon women's unpaid work in the home once the site of most waged work was removed from the household to the factory or mine.

In both Britain and Sweden, women were excluded from underground work in the 1840s, although some female miners continued to work underground long after legislation was passed forbidding it. In Japan, where thousands of women worked underground through the 1920s, the government lobbied for international exclusions, obtaining International Labour Office resolutions in the early 1930s that banned women from mining.[3] Nonetheless, the exclusion of women from work in the mines came as late as 1954 in Japan, in India by 1935, and in Russia, the Bolsheviks excluded women from mine work as early as 1917, although in some regions women continued to mine through World War II. Elsewhere in Asia and Africa, the pattern of exclusion varied; in areas where white male workers and their unions dominated the industry, such as the gold mines of South Africa, indigenous women workers were excluded before the end of the nineteenth century. In Latin America, exclusion was also varied and determined by particular historical circumstances, depending on the profitability of the mining enterprise, the demand for labor, or the customary beliefs held by male mine workers. As Latin American mines "modernized," women became increasingly marginalized from all phases of minerals production.

In North America, the need for women to provide domestic labor and the shift away from family production led provincial and state governments to pass legislation restricting or prohibiting women and children from mining.

Although British Canada did not formally restrict women until decades after British legislation, culture and tradition effectively prohibited them from mining, except for native indigenous women who worked in and around the pitheads through the nineteenth century. Where white women were in demand on the mining frontier for their assumed reproductive roles, native women's racialized bodies made them acceptable miners. On Vancouver Island in the 1850s and 1860s, native men and women provided the back-breaking work of coal hauling and loading before white boys and Chinese men came to dominate this work.[4] North American demands for labor allowed racial minorities and male children to work in mining until white miners organized to exclude them.[5] In the United States, too, traditions carried by immigrant miners made it unnecessary to pass laws prohibiting female labor, and young boys worked with fathers to maintain the family system of production. States began passing laws preventing child labor in the late nineteenth century, and several Western states passed legislation to forbid the employment of women underground.[6]

But perhaps more important than the formal exclusion of women from mine work were the exigencies of the industry itself. As Eva Blomberg argues in chapter 6 of this volume, many mine owners in Sweden encouraged miners to marry and bring their wives and families with them, believing that married men were less likely to strike and that family life created an environment of stability, social order, and productivity. In spite of that, women's unwaged household labor was given minimal recognition, despite the fact that their work preparing meals and baths and managing the household was critical to the support of the miner and thus, the industry itself. And as Rosemary Jones argues in chapter 5, the almost iconic status of the Welsh "Mining Mam" was more than mere myth, for women *were* the dominant figures in many Welsh mining households.

New scholarship on the North American mining frontier reveals that who provided this essential domestic labor involves a more complicated construction of "woman." In the multiethnic mid-nineteenth-century California gold rush, the skewed sex ratio of ten times as many men as women created a homosocial world, where ideas about gender became malleable and race became more inscribed. Susan Johnson illustrates how "race could be mapped onto constructions of gender in the diggings," as non-Anglo-American men came to be associated with such "womanly" tasks as cooking and washing. Productive roles could be reframed, too, as groups of men might together work a placer and also alternate domestic duties. Men sometimes embraced womanly tasks and the companionship they offered, such as rainy-day sewing circles.[7]

If miners and employers viewed women's domestic and reproductive roles as essential, women found economic opportunities serving and sustaining the male labor force. These enterprises expanded on women's domestic work, taking in boarders or laundry, or selling eggs or sex, and allowed women to bring in income while tending to husbands and children. Many single women migrated to booming mine camps to seize chances to earn wages, and many miners' wives' subsistence activities made the difference in a family's ability to endure.

As the four essays in part II argue, women did not always respond passively to exclusion from mine work, nor were bourgeois prescriptions for separate spheres for men and women uniformly accepted by miners' wives. Rosemary Jones's chapter argues that although separate spheres for men and women were part of the isolated coalfields of Wales, the Welsh tradition of female popular protest that predated industrialization continued to be expressed by women who exercised their influence through neighborhood networks, and through customary forms of protest during strikes and other community crises. Although the public sphere of community life was dominated by men and their organizations that excluded women, miners' wives had their own forms of public redress to shame men who had violated the community and family values.

But the pattern of exclusion of women from underground mine work, however varied according to historical circumstances, generally resulted in the creation of circumstances that left the miner's wife vulnerable to the forces of capitalism. Miners' wives were first and foremost dependent upon their spouses' wages for survival in the nineteenth and early twentieth centuries. Few countries before World War II protected workers from the dangers of the industry with occupational health and safety laws, and even where they existed in fledgling form, governments were reluctant to enforce them against the interests of mining companies. The dangers of the mining industry made it inevitable that many miners' wives would become young widows, or, if their husbands were seriously injured, be left to support their families. Both Sachiko Sone's essay on Japanese mining women in chapter 8 and Eva Blomberg's chapter on "gender relations in Swedish iron mining communities," discuss the impact upon the miner's wife of the untimely death or serious injury of a spouse.

Compensation for injuries or death was often grudgingly given, even when the union fought on behalf of the miner's widow. In British coalfields, pre-World War II compensation for injury was paid according to the part of the body that was injured or lost, and the claimant had to prove that the loss was not through his own negligence. With a similar absence of compassion, widows would usually receive lump sum payments for the death of a spouse that clearly favored the company in that no consideration was given to cost-of-living increases or whether or not the money provided could support a young family with children to adulthood. And for those widows whose husbands had died outside of the mines, but clearly from diseases related to work in the mine, there was little chance of any kind of compensation in Britain or Japan, and in Sweden, only in accordance with the bureaucratic benevolence of the mine owners. Where the local authorities stepped in, as was sometimes the case in Britain, judges most often sided with the mine owners and awarded little compensation to the miners' wives, often noting that generosity to working-class widows would encourage a lack of frugality.[8]

Physically strong, healthy bodies were a necessary prerequisite for both male and female miners, and as Sone notes in her essay, social historians of the postwar period idealized these women for their physical prowess in the mines, while Japanese feminists of the early twentieth century regarded female miners as little more than women reduced to an animal-like state, crude and defeminized. Kayoko Yoshida and Reiko Miyauchi note in chapter 7 that Japanese patriarchal family demands and an expanding mining industry from the 1910s through the 1920s pulled thousands of women into the mines. Despite enduring the same grueling labor as men, women's bodies earned less and were expected to award sexual favors to men who wanted a "wife in the pit." Yet some women who excelled in their work developed a sense of pride and became known as "goddesses of the pit" by both male and female miners. Clearly, women miners were an object of fascination if not revulsion for middle-class observers of either sex in the late nineteenth century. Stripped of every outward symbol of femininity, the female miner was thus the embodiment of the deepest fears of Victorian era and the middle-class observers of the working-class world, the masculinized female.

But the miner's wife did not fare much better in the public arena than the female miner. As John Benson notes in his book, *A Social History of British Miners in the Nineteenth Century*, miners, their wives, and their families were generally perceived as dirty, immoral, and inclined to produce too many children. If they were the "aristocracy" of labor, they wore a crown raised from the gutter, so-to-speak, for their culture and their habits were as alien to most middle-class city dwellers as if they were visitors from another world. And yet, ironically, in mining areas such as South Wales, women and men struggled to achieve the status of "respectable working class." The schedule and discipline of the household and the miner's wife was as dictated by the rhythms of the industry as her husband's work and was at least as rigid. It has been argued by some historians that miners' wives had so little control over their lives outside the home, that many developed a near compulsion for cleanliness and order. And in general women were valued in the community according to their reputations as housekeepers and household managers. In union newspapers and socialist publications, the figure of the miner's wife was alternately portrayed as the starving, exhausted victim of capitalism, or the plump and powerful heroine of the household, fending off greedy capitalists while supporting her husband on strike.[9]

If women's labors, whether in the mines, household, or community, remained largely invisible and unrecognized by male observers, employers, and family members, women's community building efforts, so critical for family survival and labor solidarity, have also gone unacknowledged. In chapter 7, Kayoko Yoshida and Reiko Miyauchi compare the coal mining towns of Red Lodge, Montana, and Yubari, Hokkaido and find that in addition to women's paid and unpaid labor, women in both communities created support networks and institutions to survive the hardships of the mining economy and derive some pleasure from women's solidarity. Yubari miners' wives developed the custom of *ochanomi*, or visiting one another while husbands slept off shift, which provided the basis for friendship, mutual support during accidents, and union organizing. Because of their socialist outlooks and more companionate marriages, the Finnish women who immigrated to Montana developed more public spaces to merge community and domestic work, including the Finnish Workers Hall, where they organized and performed in plays, and created children's programs.

As the mining industry became increasingly masculinized in the nineteenth century, mining community women would serve as a counterpoint to that process. With few exceptions women's exclusion from mine work around the world signaled the beginnings of a division of labor based principally on gender, not on physical ability, that would further erode preindustrial concepts of the value of women's work. Ideas about the female body were also transformed—women were no longer workers capable of arduous physical labor—but working-class housewives and mothers, dependent upon a male wage earner for support. In the century that followed, the miner's wife would become the foundation upon which the capitalists, the mining family, and mining society would rest, but the value of her work would remain as subterranean and as unacknowledged as that of the female miner.[10]

NOTES

1. P.J. Cain and A.G. Hopkins, *British Imperialism: Innovation and Expansion, 1688–1914* (London: Longman, 1993).
2. David F. Lindenfeld, *The Practical Imagination: The German Sciences of State in the Nineteenth Century* (Chicago: University of Chicago Press, 1997), 81–101.
3. Marat Moore, *Women in the Mines: Stories of Life and Work* (New York: Twayne Pulishers, 1996), xxvii.
4. John Douglas Belshaw, *Colonization and Community: The Vancouver Island Coalfield and the Making of the British Columbian Working Class* (Montreal: McGill-Queens University Press, 2002), 87–88.
5. In 1873, organized coal miners in Nova Scotia successfully passed legislation that limited the employment of boys in the mines, but did not formally exclude women until 1951. In 1877 the British Columbia assembly prohibited women from working underground collieries and restricted their presence on the surface. Alberta enacted legislation in 1906 that prohibited women as well as boys under 12 from working in the mines. Allen Seager and Adele Perry, "Mining the Connections: Class, Ethnicity, and Gender in Nanaimo, British Columbia, 1891," *Histoire Sociale/Social History* 30, no. 59 (1997): 74.
6. Many coal families evaded the child labor laws out of economic necessity. Priscilla Long, *Where the Sun Never Shines: A History of America's Bloody Coal Industry* (New York: Paragon House, 1989), 71–72. In the case of Colorado, it was not until the early 1970s that women mining engineers formally challenged and overturned the law prohibiting their work underground. Sally Zanjani, *A Mine of Her Own: Women Prospectors in the American West, 1850–1950* (Lincoln: University of Nebraska Press, 1997), 303–304.
7. Susan Lee Johnson, *Roaring Camp: The Social World of the California Gold Rush* (New York: W.W. Norton, 2000).
8. John Benson, "Non-Fatal Coalmining Accidents," *Of the Society for the Study of Labor History* 32 (1976): 20–22.

9. Images of miners' wives were used regularly in *The Miner*, the official publication of the Miners' Federation of Great Britain prior to nationalization of the industry. Every issue from 1926–1931 contains some references to mining community women and many articles specifically mention the importance of their role in supporting the union and their husbands. *The Miner*, July 1926–December 1931.

10. For accounts of the work of female miners, see Angela V. John, *By the Sweat of Their Brow: Women Workers at Victorian Coal Mines* (London: Routledge, 1984). For a social history of miners' wives in the nineteenth century see John Benson, *British Coal Miners in the Nineteenth Century: A Social History* (New York: Holmes and Meier, 1980), 119–130.

CHAPTER 5

Sociability, Solidarity, and Social Exclusion: Women's Activism in the South Wales Coalfield, ca. 1830 to 1939

Rosemary Jones

INTRODUCTION

The history of women in the South Wales Coalfield is largely one of omission.[1] As was the case in so many other mining districts throughout the British Isles and beyond, the coalfield communities of South Wales were characterized by a rigid gender segregation based on the prevailing mid-nineteenth century notion of "separate spheres" for men and women.[2] Male breadwinners occupied the "public" sphere of workplace and formal politics, while women acted as custodians of the "private" sphere of home and family, a role that condemned them to a life of domestic drudgery and political, as well as physical, "isolation." Due to the economic preponderance of coal mining, these communities offered few employment prospects for women outside the home. From the 1840s onward, the employment of women underground was prohibited by law and, although a small number of women continued to work on the surface, considerable social prejudice against such work—coupled with the relentless physical demands of running a household—ensured that most women opted to remain at home.[3] This sexual division of labor was particularly apparent in those communities, such as the Rhondda Valleys, which had developed in response to the series of "coal rushes" that transformed the demographic structure of the coalfield during the second half the nineteenth century. In the Rhondda district, for instance, by the beginning of the twentieth century, only 14.4 percent of women over the age of ten were recorded as being "gainfully employed."[4]

The concept of "separate spheres" for men and women was an integral component of these "frontier" communities from the outset, although the dependence on the male wage packet has tended to obscure the importance of women's unpaid domestic labor within the local economy. Despite being confined to the domestic sphere, women exerted considerable influence within that domain. The prevailing image of female domesticity was the iconic "Welsh Mam," a paragon of virtue who reigned supreme within the domestic sphere and struggled to make ends meet against a backdrop of hard physical drudgery.[5] Eulogised as "the backbone of her family, the peace-keeper, the self-sacrificer, the tower of strength,"[6] the "Welsh Mam" was the embodiment of female virtue and power, the linchpin of home and neighborhood. But she also, paradoxically, exemplified the subordinate position of women in general, being totally dependent on the male wage earner and exerting little or no influence over the political decision-making process. The women of the South Wales Coalfield were effectively excluded from the formal world of workplace politics—to such an extent that a Rhondda newspaper could assert, in 1912, that a "smile will arise at the notion of a collier's wife attending a lodge meeting."[7]

This was in stark contrast to the early nineteenth century, when women were often in the vanguard of popular protest.[8] Mining women had played a conspicuous role in the sporadic food riots, which characterized the popular political activism of the period, often drawing upon long-established notions of "female privilege" and the license of the "disorderly woman" to advance the interests of the wider community.[9] Women had also been instrumental in the furtherance of Chartist principles during the 1830s and 1840s.[10] During the post-Chartist era, however, the emphasis shifted toward formal male-dominated political organizations such as trade unions and other pressure groups that severely curtailed the opportunities for female engagement in formal political activism and led to the effective marginalization or "withdrawal" of women in formal political terms.[11] The political "invisibility" of women during the second half of the nineteenth and early part of the twentieth centuries has been further compounded by the preoccupation of labor historians with formal trade unionism and, most especially, with the formation and "hegemonic" preeminence of the South Wales Miners' Federation ("The Fed"), founded in 1898.[12] Women barely feature in the historiography of the trade union movement, most of which has a strong masculine bias.[13]

It needs to be emphasized, however, that although most women exercised no formal power within the "public" arena, this did not preclude participation within wider neighborhood affairs. Despite the constraints of "separate spheres," there was considerable scope for female agency, both in shaping their own lives and those of immediate family and neighbors. Many women negotiated the boundaries between the "public" and the "private" with considerable resilience and resourcefulness, using, in particular, their shared neighborhood networks as a means of negotiating a degree of power and autonomy. By forging alliances with female neighbors, and participating in a range of exclusionary tactics—such as gossip and social ostracism as well as more direct verbal or physical attacks—against individuals who contravened the community's social and political norms, women were able to gain considerable social status and authority as the community's self-proclaimed "moral guardians."

There were also significant continuities in the organizational structure of industrial protest that facilitated a degree of female agency within the "public" arena of popular political activism. During the second half of the nineteenth century, working-class politics was marked as much by continuity as by change, but a preoccupation on the part of social historians with formal political institutions has tended to distract attention from the resilience of earlier, preindustrial patterns of protest and, therefore, the continued importance of women. Despite the increasing preponderance of more formal, institutionalized methods of collective action at a grassroots level, formal political strategies fused with more "primitive" direct-action tactics. Even in communities where the sexual division of labor was most pronounced, working-class activists—both male and female—continued to draw upon earlier strategies and alliances that predated the "public"/"private" dichotomy of the Victorian era, thus facilitating cooperation between the sexes in defense of the wider community.

As in earlier decades, the local community remained the focal point of women's political activism, and their role within industrial disputes was usually an extension of their everyday roles within family and neighborhood. In particular, the neighborhood networks and alliances associated with female sociability provided a firm basis for women's spontaneous mobilization during periods of acute political tension. Women often spearheaded the various repressive sanctions that were commonly deployed against the community's perceived "enemies" during periods of industrial upheaval and, in the process, played a pivotal role both in the structuring of popular political values and the maintenance of communal discipline at a grassroots, neighborhood level. In this respect, the roots of working-class activism and political expression remained firmly embedded within the "traditional" domains of home and neighborhood as well as in the more institutionalized, male-dominated domains of workplace and trade union activity.

Although in recent years, Welsh labor historians have emphasized the need to develop a "social history of labor" that encompasses "the history of everyday life as well as that of institutional and workplace concerns," the work of recovering and illuminating the lives of women in the South Wales Coalfield—particularly in relation to industrial protest—has barely commenced.[14] This chapter seeks to contribute to this process of historical "recovery" by examining the role of women in the day-to-day affairs of their immediate neighborhoods as well as in more overtly political expressions of communal solidarity. The central, integrating theme is the role of women within the community's informal rituals of social "inclusion" and "exclusion." Attention is focused on two main spheres of activity: first, the everyday networks of female sociability (in which the brokering of "gossip" was crucial) and, secondly, the role of women within a popular shaming ritual known as the *ceffyl pren*—a Welsh variant of the "rough music" or *charivari* tradition identified by historians of other European countries.[15]

These activities formed the basis of women's involvement in wider community affairs and are central to our understanding of how women mobilized during periods of social or political dislocation. For instance, the *ceffyl pren*—a punishment normally reserved for sexual or moral transgressors—could also, during industrial disputes, provide a focal point for the expression of communal solidarity, being zealously deployed against "blacklegs," nonunionist miners, colliery officials, and other "political" transgressors. Particular emphasis is placed on the notorious "white shirting" processions of the early twentieth century, in which women played a prominent role. During these highly theatrical displays of political unity, "blackleg" miners were forced to don a white shirt before being frog-marched through the streets, or paraded in a wheelbarrow, in true *ceffyl pren* fashion. Initially, however, some attempt must be made to illuminate the everyday networks, strategies, and alliances forged by women, in recognition of their centrality to the gender dynamics of industrial protest.[16]

FEMALE SOCIABILITY AND COMMUNITY SANCTIONS

The communities of the South Wales Coalfield were characterized by a rigid gender segregation, with men and women developing separate, mutually exclusive social networks. Whereas male culture, identity, and camaraderie were based upon workplace and pub, women developed their own networks and allegiances, based on daily interactions in home and neighborhood, which acted as a counter to the "public" world of men. In particular, the mutual dependency of working miners was mirrored above ground in the strong attachments and mutual-aid mechanisms brokered by their wives. It was the women who, quite literally, held these communities together; it was they who cemented relationships within their own extended families and also maintained links with other families in the immediate neighborhood. Indeed, it is possible to identify a distinctive female culture of mutual assistance and dependency, with female kin and neighbors providing various types of moral, emotional, and practical support during times of hardship, poverty, illness, or childbirth.

In addition to the practical benefits of neighborhood sharing, considerable emphasis was placed on the emotional benefits of female companionship and sociability. Since the social horizons of most women were confined to the domestic sphere, friendships were forged primarily through daily exchanges on the hearth and in the street. During the eighteenth and early nineteenth centuries, the desire for female companionship was sometimes channeled through quasi-institutionalized networks such as the *Clwb Te* ("Tea Club"), a "gossip" circle of married women that gained particular popularity in the industrialized valleys of southeast Wales.[17] But, as the nineteenth century progressed, women came to rely almost exclusively on impromptu "chats" with friends and neighbors, who often felt at liberty to "pop" in and out of each other's homes for an informal cup of tea and a "gossip." The "etiquette" of colliery communities—where front doors were routinely left open all day and "private" homes were often viewed as property held in common—ensured that most women maintained an "open house" for female neighbors in search of company or support.[18]

The networks of female sociability, though spontaneous and informal, were constrained by the demands of women's shared domestic routine, which bound them in a "straightjacket of hard physical drudgery."[19] Outdoor chores—such as hanging the washing on the line or "donkeystoning" (i.e., polishing) the front step—encouraged female gatherings, as did household errands to the local shop, well, or bakehouse. Women often congregated for hours at village wells and taps—which were said to be "great places for gossip"[20]—and, once their essential domestic tasks were complete, customarily "posted" themselves on their front doorsteps to converse with passersby.[21]

In view of these dense social networks it is hardly surprising that women were, in most instances, the first to hear and disseminate news and gossip.[22] It was they who coordinated an immediate response to current rumors by investigating their authenticity and, where necessary, taking prompt remedial action. When, in 1904, it was rumored that all the children of Senghen(n)ydd were to be forcibly vaccinated, it was the women of the community who immediately protested at the school gates with such intensity that the "police were asked to assist in keeping the peace."[23] From the shared vantage point of doorstep and street, women were also to observe the comings and goings of neighbors and scrutinize "strangers" who ventured into the locality.

They were also well placed to "watch out" for incursions by bailiffs, police officers, and other representatives of officialdom and were usually the first to organize resistance.[24] When, in 1894, an attendance officer attempted to apprehend a young truant at Llwynhendy, the boy's "hysterical" screams immediately summoned "a group of angry women [who] surrounded the hapless officer and after a wild scene forced him to give up his charge."[25] Since women were the ones who were already effectively in possession of the streets, particularly during daylight hours, it was their informal networks that could be mobilized quickly in the face of immediate external threats.

But women also scrutinized and passed judgement on the behavior of immediate neighbors and kin. Under the relentless gaze of female neighbors, who "took an interest in everyone and everything,"[26] privacy was difficult to maintain and "private" indiscretions could easily become the subject of "public" discourse. Gossip was an important method of social regulation in these communities and, in their self-appointed role as "moral custodians," women played a pivotal role in the identification and policing of aberrant social behavior.[27] Far from being a vehicle for "idle talk," gossip could serve important social and communal functions. It helped to delineate the boundaries between "respectable" and "deviant" behavior and, as such, was central to the structuring and maintenance of collective values at a grassroots, neighborhood level. Through these gossip networks, women became central actors in the daily rituals of social inclusion and exclusion, which marked the boundaries of "community" and determined who belonged. In this sense, participation in the local "grapevine" conferred upon women a considerable degree of informal influence and power over their immediate neighborhoods. Despite being confined to the "private" sphere of home and street, gossip about "domestic" indiscretions could make or break the "public" reputations of its victims and could be used to particularly devastating effect against those who valued their economic or professional status within the community.[28] In 1867, for instance, the brisk trade previously enjoyed by one Mrs. Forsdyke, landlady of the Northumberland Hotel at Llanelli, was found to have plummeted after her effigy was burnt by disaffected neighbors who accused her of adultery.[29]

Gossip networks therefore empowered women, affording them a significant "voice" within the affairs of the wider community. But, paradoxically, it was also women who were often most susceptible to the social consequences of public scandal, particularly when emanating from an alleged sexual misdemeanor. Female reputation was dependent on sexual conduct, and women dreaded losing their "good name." Women who wished to avoid being the object of gossip took great care to adhere to agreed social norms.

Moreover, this code of sexual honor was internalized and rigorously enforced by female neighbors and kin, who were particularly harsh on other women who had "fallen by the wayside." As D. Lleufer Thomas, stipendiary magistrate for the Rhondda, stated in 1919, women were generally "a great deal harder on women than others were, particularly when one woman had been in trouble."[30] At a time when the reputation of a particular neighborhood could stand or fall by the reputation of its womenfolk, women often felt they had a duty to collectively protect their sexual "honor" by taking swift remedial action against female offenders—such as adulteresses or prostitutes—who, by their flagrant disregard for shared standards of public decency, were deemed to have brought the entire neighborhood into disrepute. "Immoral" women were often subjected to repeated verbal or physical attack—as well as social ostracism—over an extended period. During the summer of 1918, for instance, Stanleytown in the Rhondda witnessed a series of heated disturbances against a certain Margaret Gilgrass, a soldier's wife who "it was alleged did not conduct herself as she should. Consequently her presence was resented by the neighbors" who hurled buckets of water as well as verbal abuse when she ventured into the street.[31]

Apart from providing a strong inducement to social and moral conformity, participation in gossip and other collective sanctions also helped to forge strong social bonds between women, which, in turn, facilitated the development of shared identities, values and allegiances. Being part of a network of female friends and neighbors had immense emotional as well as practical benefits, and most women derived considerable comfort, entertainment, and mutual support from the communal friendships that were nurtured on doorstep and street. In this respect, gossip networks underpinned a sense of belonging and served as an important marker of social acceptance within the community. However, the networks of female sociability could also be used to actively exclude individuals who did not conform. Although on the whole, women were remarkably supportive of each other, those who failed to adhere to agreed standards of behavior could find themselves ostracized by their female neighbors or persecuted by rather more overt tactics of social exclusion. Neighbors often adopted a particularly aggressive stance toward "outsiders," who often found it difficult to integrate and gain acceptance, particularly if their demeanor or values deviated markedly from those of their neighbors. Faced with ostracism or ridicule, it is hardly surprising that most women were reluctant to openly engage in behavior that could cause potential offence or set them apart from the wider community of female neighbors.

Gossip networks, therefore, were a vital component of women's shared culture, which not only cemented strong bonds of mutual attachment between individual women, but also helped induce conformity to a shared moral code. Women used these informal alliances to exert considerable collective pressure against social and political "deviants." As arbiters of the community's unwritten laws, women played a vital role in the molding and mobilization of public opinion against a range of transgressors. Women often identified violations of customary morality and ensured that these "crimes" were proclaimed through the public thoroughfares. But, apart from identifying aberrant behavior, women's "gossip" could also trigger wider disciplinary action against the offending individuals. The public denunciation of antisocial behavior often rendered the victim a "marked" man or woman, thus ensuring his or her vulnerability to further attack or victimization by the wider community at a later date.

In addition, women assumed a leading role in the public humiliation and punishment of offenders. A variety of punitive sanctions could be adopted for this purpose, ranging from covert strategies—such as "gossip," social ostracism, and exclusive dealing—to more violent and openly confrontational tactics, such as physical or verbal abuse and the destruction of property. Reference has already been made to the treatment of erring female neighbors, but the safety of numbers also empowered women to intervene directly against violent or abusive men, and those who neglected their paternal responsibilities. At Morriston, for example, in 1893, around seventy women stoned the house of a man who had refused to work and support his daughter.[32] Similarly, at Cwmparc in 1910, "hordes of angry Amazons" attacked a local collier accused of cruelty toward his stepchild and, in the opinion of one eyewitness, "the affair would have looked ugly" but for the timely intervention of the police.[33]

However, there are also innumerable cases of women working in consort with men—and not necessarily in a secondary or supporting role—particularly where there was agreement as to the gravity of the alleged offence. In 1887, for instance, a Llanelli man charged with assaulting and beating his servant girl was "besieged by an excited crowd, in which women took an active part."[34] Gender cooperation was an integral feature of many community sanctions and—as proved to be the case with the *ceffyl pren*, to which our attention now turns—one that helped to ensure the adaptation and survival of these traditions during periods of acute social and political change.

The *CEFFYL PREN* Tradition

The *ceffyl pren*, as already stated, forms part of a broader European, if not worldwide, tradition of popular shaming customs, of which the French *charivari* is probably the best-known variant.[35] Most communities sanctioned some form of informal collective denunciation of aberrant social behavior and the closely knit neighborhoods of both rural and industrial Wales were no exception. Such rituals may be loosely referred to as the *ceffyl pren* tradition, although the phrase *ceffyl pren* (or "wooden horse," to use the literal English translation) is here deployed as a generic term to describe a range of related rituals and sanctions.[36] Strictly speaking, as its name implies, the central motif of the *ceffyl pren* procession was an actual or symbolic "riding," although the exact configuration of the "horse" and "rider" motif could vary considerably from place to place. In most instances, the offending individual was paraded through the neighborhood on a makeshift "horse"— such as a pole, ladder, or hand-drawn cart—from which he or she was subjected to a barrage of verbal invective and physical abuse. However, regional variations were legion: in rural southwest Wales, for instance, a life-size effigy of a horse was often carefully constructed from wood and straw, whereas in parts of the Rhondda Valley, prior to industrialization, offenders were paraded on an actual horse—albeit the most bedraggled and unimposing specimen that could be found—seated backwards with their faces toward the tail.[37] Although the miscreant was usually paraded in person, effigies were often carried in the intended victim's place and ritually "executed," amid loud applause, by burning, hanging, or shooting. Mock courts, which apportioned guilt and afforded popular legitimacy to the prescribed punishment, invariably formed an integral part of the proceedings and were often conducted "with all the pomp and ceremony of a real assize."[38]

Other recurring features included the "rough music" serenade—a cacophony of discordant sounds, produced on a variety of improvized "instruments," such as frying pans, kettles, and tins—the discharging of guns and fireworks, the blowing of horns, the singing of mocking rhymes, and the adoption of various forms of ritual disguise, such as blackened faces, the wearing of masks, and, in the case of many male participants, the donning of women's clothing or reversed jackets. Although victims were frequently subjected to repeated and often brutal assaults, the overriding air was usually one of festive hilarity and theatrical licence, with participants seeking to capitalize on the long-established imagery of ritual inversion and social burlesque commonly associated with the "carnivalesque."[39]

The *ceffyl pren* has been most commonly associated with the predominantly rural districts of southwest Wales, particularly during the period of heightened political tension, which spawned the so-called Rebecca Riots of 1839 and 1843–1844.[40] However, most parts of rural Wales adopted similar communal shaming rituals. The rural districts of Glamorgan and Breconshire—including those communities that, with the onset of industrialization, were later to fall within the perimeters of the South Wales Coalfield—nurtured a particularly vibrant tradition during the eighteenth and early nineteenth centuries. Contemporary accounts of the Glamorgan *cwlstrin* ("coolstrin") or *cwltrin* ("cooltrin") provide an interesting case in point.[41] Although the localized term *cwlstrin* appears to have been used generically to describe a variety of related shaming tactics, most observers emphasize the primacy of the elaborate "mock court," which invariably formed a central plank in the proceedings, followed by a highly ritualized "rough music" procession through the immediate neighborhood. During the early decades of the nineteenth century, for instance, when the custom was directed primarily against hen-pecked husbands and their "shrewish" wives, the *cwlstrin* procession often featured two surrogates who parodied the behavior of the couple in question. As stated by one contemporary observer at Llangynwyd (Maesteg), the *cwlstrin* "court" and its "officers" commonly formed:

> [A] solemn procession, a great feature of which was a car drawn by horses, perched in [which] . . . was a huge wooden horse, on which were placed two men, disguised, sitting face to face and fighting. This procession was made to pass, and most likely to pause, by the house where the quarrelsome couple lived.[42]

Although increasingly on the wane during the second quarter of the nineteenth century, village "courts" such as these continued to hold sway in parts of Glamorgan until at least the 1850s.[43]

Highly-ritualized popular shaming rituals such as the *cwlstrin* and the *ceffyl pren* were therefore deeply rooted in the largely rural districts of southeast Wales prior to the onset of industrialization and, not surprisingly, quickly took root in the earliest "frontier" settlements of the South Wales Coalfield. Contemporary newspaper reports attest to the vitality of these customs in the early iron town of Merthyr Tydfil, where coal miners lived in close proximity to those engaged in iron manufacturing, during the 1830s and 1840s. In 1836, for example, a collier who had lost a fight with his wife was paraded through the town before "at least two thousand pitmen" and, in 1845, a workman was similarly punished following a prolonged drinking spree in the infamous "Cellars" region of the town.[44]

Early colliery towns such as Aberdare and Gelligaer witnessed similar scenes during the 1840s and 1850s, when they were the fulcrum of coal production in the South Wales Coalfield. For instance, at Aberdare in 1856, a collier accused of adultery was paraded on a ladder and pelted with "every kind of filth."[45] These early settlements not only had a high percentage of first-generation migrants from the adjacent rural hinterland but also acted as a magnet for workers from other parts of Wales—particularly, in the earliest stages of industrialization, from the rural and largely Welsh-speaking districts of southwest Wales, where the *ceffyl pren* tradition was also firmly entrenched.[46]

Under such circumstances, indigenous "folk" traditions fused with those of migrant workers, creating a vitality and sense of common purpose, which was to endure for at least a generation. The survival of such rituals in the middle and eastern valleys during the latter half of the nineteenth century has yet to be examined by historians but, although seemingly losing much of their earlier momentum, the available evidence suggests that remnants of the tradition persisted in many communities until at least the eve of the twentieth century. The "rough music" serenade was still being deployed at Risca during the 1860s and, as late as 1875, moral deviants in the Aberdare district continued to be threatened, on occasions, with a "ride on the cheap" by their fellow townsmen.[47] Furthermore, at Gelli in the Rhondda, at the exceptionally late date of 1900, a young woman who had allegedly "misconducted herself with a married man" was burned in effigy by local youths.[48] In the western districts of the South Wales Coalfield, however, the *ceffyl pren* continued with remarkable tenacity throughout the second half of the nineteenth century and was particularly robust in and around the town of Llanelli, with numerous incidents being reported in the local press during the period ca.1840–1900.[49] Here, as occurred in November 1864, the common practice was to parade effigies of the offending individuals to the accompaniment of a "rough music" serenade; as the local press reported:

> [S]everal hundreds of men, women, and children, congregated together and paraded the Sea Side, shouting, yelling, and singing, and accompanied by a tin kettle band, and two effigies, and when they came opposite a certain house the effigies were burnt amidst a most hideous noise.[50]

Similar scenes were witnessed with surprising regularity in the surrounding colliery villages and, in some districts, remained a relatively familiar phenomenon until the eve of World War II.[51] For instance, the village of Pont-henri was disturbed by a series of dramatic incidents in 1909, when the local postmistress, a married woman, was accused of "immoral relations" with her lodger.[52] These largely anthracite-producing districts on the western side of the coalfield developed relatively late and, during the late nineteenth and early twentieth centuries, comprised a large proportion of first-generation migrants from the adjacent agricultural districts, who retained a strong adherence to the customs and traditions of their rural past.

Despite considerable regional variation in the popular sanctions deployed, there appears to have been broad agreement throughout the South Wales Coalfield—and beyond—as to the type of "aberrant" behavior that warranted punishment. During periods of relative political calm, the majority of offenders were punished for displays of moral laxness or domestic strife— "offences" that were not contrary to the law of the land and could not, therefore, be remedied via official legal channels. Adulterous liaisons were high on the *ceffyl pren* agenda and were subjected to relentless scrutiny throughout the nineteenth century. When, in 1872, a married Aberavon women attempted to elope with her lover, who was younger than her, both parties were burned in effigy by their outraged neighbors.[53] Similarly, in the town of Llanelli, the vast majority of recorded *ceffyl pren* incidents were inspired by cases of proven or suspected adultery. For instance, in 1867, around 200–300 townspeople were reported to have "mobbed" the house of a suspected adulteress, burning effigies of the woman "and her alleged paramour . . . before her own door step."[54]

Blatant cases of domestic violence or discord also incurred the wrath of neighbors, although the targets of such attacks changed considerably over time. Up until around the second quarter of the nineteenth century, popular sanctions were directed primarily against wives who beat their husbands and the "hen-pecked" spouses who submitted to such treatment. At that time, the patriarchal domination of the husband over his wife was perceived as the cornerstone of wider social and political stability and "scolding" wives who sought to invert the "natural" order of things by dominating their husbands were therefore viewed as a threat to the wider patriarchal establishment.[55] During its heyday, the Glamorgan *cwlstrin* sought to buttress the patriarchal ideal by publicly chastizing domineering wives and those weak, compliant husbands who, having failed to regulate their households, represented "a disgrace to manhood."[56] It did so by routinely deploying the imagery and symbolism associated with the so-called battle for the breeches, which epitomized gender conflict at this time.[57] For instance, the procession often featured two standard bearers—one of whom carried a petticoat mounted on a pole, the other a pair of breeches, which were turned upside-down to symbolize the subversion of male authority by "petticoat government." Outside the home of the quarrelsome couple, the petticoat was pelted with mud, stones, and addled eggs, until it fell to the ground in tatters, while the breeches were elevated in its place "as the standard of masculine government." The procession also featured two surrogates dressed to represent the couple in question and, since one was invariably a man dressed in women's clothing, this served to further throw the husband's masculinity into question.[58]

However, by the middle decades of the nineteenth century, the wife beater had, to all intents and purposes, replaced the husband beater as the main victim of community sanctions, the use of public shaming rituals against scolding wives being a relatively rare phenomenon by that time.[59] This reflects the wider shift in gender relations, which occurred during the Victorian period and was linked to a diffusion of beliefs about the innate passivity and vulnerability of women, with wives increasingly being portrayed as fragile, submissive creatures, in need of chivalrous compassion and protection, rather than as the scheming "viragos" of previous generations. Abusive husbands could experience immediate retribution at the hands of their neighbors, by either being paraded in effigy—as occurred at Ystalyfera in 1860—or, as was more commonly the case, by being placed in person on a makeshift "wooden horse."[60] At Aberdare in 1855, for instance, a notorious wife beater known as "Dai Dumpin" was paraded through the town by his fellow colliers.[61]

On occasions, as had formerly been the case with "hen-pecked" husbands, the symbolism deployed sought to undermine the masculinity of the equally "cowardly" wife beater. In particular, as was witnessed at Pontypridd during the 1850s, wife beaters were often forced to don a white shirt—a common form of improvized female "disguise"—before being subjected to the jibes and jeers of their neighbors.[62] As with later "white shirting" rituals, the use of a makeshift white shirt to represent women's apparel could prove especially useful when the offender was carried in person and was therefore disinclined to cooperate with his tormentors.

A central and unifying component of many of these early "ridings" was their inherent *maleness*. The Glamorgan *cwlstrin* court was dominated by men, the proceedings at Pontypridd, for instance, being monopolized by a small cadre of village poets (all of them men) known as "Clic y Bont."[63] The avowed aim, until at least the second quarter of the nineteenth century, was to endorse and enforce the patriarchal domination of husbands over their wives. Women appear to have been entirely excluded from the proceedings—except as the unwilling butt—and, on occasions, vociferously taunted those men who participated in these ritualized public displays of male supremacy.[64] Even when the focus of such proceedings shifted from the punishment of husband beaters to that of wife beaters, the collective public expression of masculine values and identity remained a central feature. Men may have exerted authority over women but they also felt a duty to protect them and violence against women increasingly came to be condemned as both cowardly and "unmanly." Those colliers who punished "Dai Dumpin," the notorious Aberdare wife beater, in 1855, were not only protecting his hapless wife from further abuse: they were also engaging in a very public expression of male unity and camaraderie by endorsing shared standards of "respectable manhood." Having

> administered to "Dai" this specimen of Aberdare justice, [they] spent the remainder of the day at the several public-houses, regaling themselves with a few extra glasses, after the performance of what they considered their bounden duty in the way of protecting the weaker sex.[65]

The main emphasis was now on the perceived fragility and *inferiority* of women, rather than on their enforced subordination. However, the increasing shift toward the vilification of wife—as opposed to husband—beaters nevertheless encouraged greater female participation in communal shaming rituals of this type. Despite their former reluctance to denounce "scolds," women often figured prominently in *ceffyl pren* demonstrations against abusive husbands and were occasionally prosecuted as a result. At Cwmaman, for example, in 1856, two women were among seven people who were apprehended by the police for an attack on a local collier suspected of beating his wife: It appears that the accused, with a great mob of persons, entered complainant's house and dragged him off the bed to the road, then placed him on a ladder and carried him about till the ladder broke, after which they carried him by the arms and legs for about 2 hours, when they let him free.[66]

In addition, not only did the shift in targets render these sanctions more inclusive and representative of wider community interests, it also encouraged more women to act independently in defense of downtrodden wives. Such was the case at Pontarddulais, in 1843, when around forty women, led by a woman blowing a horn, gathered outside the home of a neighbor "who was in the habit of rather ill using his better half" and threatened to duck him in a river unless he reformed his ways.[67] There are numerous instances of women acting alone—rather than in consort with men—to defend the weakest members of the community, who often viewed their female kin and neighbors as their first line of defense. Women were especially repulsed by the abuse or neglect of young children, frequently intervening on their behalf.

Women were also outraged by cases of sexual impropriety, particularly adultery, and encouraged the use of popular shaming rituals against offending individuals. For instance, the victim of a *ceffyl pren* attack at Aberdare in 1856 was a collier from Mountain Ash "who had incurred the displeasure of the women, in seducing a fair demoiselle of Aberdare, concealing the fact that he was a married man with three children."[68] Although male adulterers were treated with contempt, women were particularly brutal in their treatment of female adulteresses. At Merthyr Tydfil, in 1834, three women were among five people prosecuted for an "outrageous assault" on an alleged adulteress who was "called from her work, forced upon a ladder . . . carried in a violent and tumultuous manner . . . [and] pelted with stones and mud"; as a result of which she "was four days in a succession of fits, and so injured as to be unable to turn in her bed."[69]

Female outrage against adulteresses was often underpinned by a desire to defend the sexual honor and reputation of women in general and, as a result, the most vociferous critics were often the victim's immediate female kin. When, in 1849, a suspected adulteress was burned in effigy by the people of Llanelli, "one of the most vigilant of the crowd was the woman's own and only daughter, who plied the fire with all the energy possible."[70] Less agregious cases of sexual or moral impropriety could also be greeted by a "rough music" serenade—a form of popular ridicule which, in many communities, women adopted as their own. When, in 1861, a fifty-year-old widow from Risca eloped with a man many years her junior—who was also, most damningly, betrothed to her daughter—the younger women of the community, including the jilted daughter, "endeavoured to get up a demonstration, with tin pans and kettles, to welcome the return of the deceitful pair."[71] Cases such as these underpinned the role of women as self-proclaimed "moral guardians" within their respective communities. Although the division of labor was firmly in place in Welsh mining communities, along with a domestic ideology that encouraged women to focus their attention on the private sphere of household and family, local custom and the particular vernacular culture of the mining regions allowed women to act as moral guardians of the community, asserting their gender identity in the public domain. Such public expressions of disdain for those who violated community standards were within the purview of women's role and expected. Women as individuals as well as in groups took responsibility for the public expression of disapproval or dissent, and thus upheld a centuries-old Welsh and European tradition of female activism.

NOTES

1. Although mineral and metal mining was undertaken in various parts of Wales from an early date, the South Wales Coalfield was by far the most important of all the Welsh mining districts. It witnessed unprecedented demographic change during the nineteenth and early twentieth centuries, as thousands of rural migrants gravitated toward the coalfield areas, creating a series of "frontier" communities reminiscent of the American West. The population of the Rhondda Valleys increased at a phenomenal rate, from under 2,000 in 1851 to 152,000 in 1911. By the beginning of the twentieth century, more than half the entire population of Wales resided within the South Wales Coalfield. The period prior to World War I was one of particularly rapid change, when (as a result of the large-scale export of steam coal from the 1870s) the coalfield became one of the most rapidly expanding industrial centers of the world. For an introduction to the pace and scale of these developments—and the attendant social, political, and cultural consequences—see, e.g., Chris Williams, *Capitalism, Community and Conflict. The South Wales Coalfield 1898–1947* (Cardiff: University of Wales Press, 1998); David Egan, *Coal Society. A History of the South Wales Mining Valleys 1840–1980* (Llandysul: Gomer Press, 1987); John Williams, *Was Wales Industrialised? Essays in Modern Welsh History* (Llandysul: Gomer Press, 1995); E.D. Lewis, *The Rhondda Valleys* (Cardiff: University College Cardiff Press, 1984 edition); Arthur H. John and Glanmor Williams, eds., *Glamorgan County History, vol. V: Industrial Glamorgan* (Cardiff: Glamorgan County History Trust Ltd., 1980); Prys Morgan, ed., *Glamorgan County History, vol. VI: Glamorgan Society 1780–1980* (Cardiff: Glamorgan County History Trust Ltd., 1988); J.H. Morris and L.J. Williams, *The South Wales Coal Industry 1841–1875* (Cardiff: University of Wales Press, 1958); Ieuan Gwynedd Jones, *Communities: Essays in the Social History of Victorian Wales* (Llandysul: Gomer Press, 1987); Geraint H. Jenkins, ed., *Language and Community in the Nineteenth Century* (Cardiff: University of Wales Press, 1998), chapters 4, 5, and 7; Gwenfair Parry and Mari A. Williams, eds., *The Welsh Language and the 1891 Census* (Cardiff: University of Wales Press, 1999), esp. chapters 2 and 4–10.

Until relatively recently, women have been conspicuous by their absence in the historiography of the South Wales Coalfield. For the role of women in the coalfield districts (although the emphasis of recent research has usually been upon their indispensable role within the domestic sphere rather than their networks or strategies within the wider "public" world of political activism) see, in particular, Dot Jones, "Counting the Cost of Coal: Women's Lives in the Rhondda, 1881–1911" in *Our Mothers' Land: Chapters in Welsh Women's History, 1830–1939*, ed., Angela V. John (Cardiff: University of Wales Press, 1991), 109–133; Angela V. John, "A Miner Struggle? Women's Protests in Welsh Mining History," *Llafur*, 4, no. 1 (1984): 72–90; Carol White and Sian Rhiannon Williams, eds., *Struggle or Starve. Women's Lives in the South Wales Valleys between the Two World Wars* (Honno: Dinas Powys, 1998); Michael Lieven, *Senghenydd: The Universal Pit Village, 1890–1930* (Llandysul: Gomer Press, 1994), chapter 6; Rosemary Crook, " 'Tidy Women': Women in the Rhondda between the Wars," *Oral History*, 10, no. 2 (1982), 40–46; Mari A. Williams, "Women and the Welsh Language in the Industrial Valleys of South Wales 1914–1945" in *"Let's Do Our Best for the Ancient Tongue": The Welsh*

Language in the Twentieth Century, ed., Geraint H. Jenkins and Mari A. Williams (Cardiff: University of Wales Press, 2000), 137–180; Mari A. Williams, "Aspects of Women's Working Lives in the Mining Communities of South Wales, *c.* 1891–1939," *Folk Life*, 38 (1999–2000), 56–70. On the lives of Welsh women generally during the nineteenth and twentieth centuries, see John (ed.), *Our Mothers' Land* and Deirdre Beddoe, *Out of the Shadows: A History of Women in* Twentieth-Century Wales (Cardiff: University of Wales Press, 2000).

2. The literature on "separate spheres" is extensive but see, e.g., Sonya O. Rose, *Limited Livelihoods: Gender and Class in Nineteenth-Century England* (Berkeley and Los Angeles: University of California Press, 1992); Sonya O. Rose, "Gender and Labor History: The Nineteenth-Century Legacy," *International Review of Social History*, 38 (1993), 145–162; Anna Clark, *The Struggle for the Breeches: Gender and the Making of the British Working Class* (London: Rivers Oram Press, 1995); Theodore Koditschek, "The Gendering of the British Working Class," *Gender and History* 9, no. 2 (August 1997), 333–363; Catherine Hall, *White, Male and Middle-Class: Explorations in Feminism and History* (Cambridge: Polity Press, 1992); and Leonore Davidoff, *Worlds Between: Historical Perspectives on Gender and Class* (Cambridge: Polity Press, 1995). For a Welsh perspective on "separate spheres" and the mid-Victorian cult of domesticity see Sian Rhiannon Williams, "The True 'Cymraes': Images of Women in Women's Nineteenth-Century Welsh Periodicals," in *Our Mothers' Land: Chapters in Welsh Women's History, 1830–1939* ed. Angela V. John (Cardiff: University of Wales Press, 1991), 69–91 and Rosemary Jones, " 'Separate Spheres'?: Women, Language and Respectability in Victorian Wales," in *The Welsh Language and Its Social Domains* ed. Geraint H. Jenkins (Cardiff: University of Wales Press, 2000), 177–213.

3. On women's work see, L.J. Williams and Dot Jones, "Women at Work in the Nineteenth Century," *Llafur* 3, no. 3 (1982): 20–41 and Dot Jones, "Serfdom and Slavery: Women's Work in Wales, 1890–1930" in *Class, Community and the Labour Movement: Wales and Canada 1850–1930*, ed., Deian R. Hopkin and Gregory S. Kealey (Society for Welsh Labour History/Canadian Committee on Labour History, 1989), 86–100. On the employment of women in the coal industry, and the impact of the legislation (1842) that prevented women from working underground, see Angela John, *By the Sweat of Their Brow. Women Workers at Victorian Coal Mines* (London, Boston, Melbourne, and Henley: Routledge and Kegan Paul, 1984). The proportion of women working on the surface declined steadily during the nineteenth century and was negligible by 1881 (Dot Jones, "Counting the Cost of Coal," 131 n10). For the working lives of coalfield women as unpaid "domestic laborers" see Jones, "Counting the Cost of Coal" and Williams, "Aspects of Women's Working Lives," 56–58.

4. L.J. Williams and Dot Jones, "Women at Work in the Nineteenth Century," 28. In England, one in every three women were employed, compared to only one in seven in the Rhondda. By 1931 the proportion had fallen to 11.4%. The vast majority of the occupied female workforce comprised young single women.

5. For the "Welsh Mam" see Deirdre Beddoe, "Munitionettes, Maids and Mams: Women in Wales, 1914–1939" in, *Our Mothers' Land. Chapters in Welsh Women's History, 1830–1939*, ed., Angela V. John (Cardiff: University of Wales Press, 1991), 206–207 and Angela John, "Women between the Wars" in *Wales between the Wars*, ed., Trevor Herbert and Gareth Elwyn Jones (Cardiff: University of Wales Press, 1988), 137–138.

6. Elaine Morgan (born Pontypridd 1920); quoted in Carol White and Sian Rhiannon Williams, eds., *Struggle or Starve. Women's Lives in the South Wales Valleys between the Two World Wars* (Honno: Dinas Powys, 1998), 5.

7. *Rhondda Socialist Newspaper*, December 21, 1912. Quoted in Chris Williams, *Capitalism, Community and Conflict. The South Wales Coalfield 1898–1947* (Cardiff: University of Wales Press, 1998), 113.

8. For the role of women in popular protest during the eighteenth and early nineteenth centuries, see David J.V. Jones, *Before Rebecca: Popular Protest in Wales 1793–1835* (London: Allen Lane, 1973), esp. chapter 1; and David W. Howell, "Riots and Public Disorder in Eighteenth-Century Wales" in *Crime, Protest and Police in Modern British Society: Essays in Memory of David J. V. Jones* ed., David W. Howell and Kenneth O. Morgan (Cardiff University of Wales Press, 1999), 42–72.

9. On "female privilege" and the license of the "disorderly woman" see, in particular, Natalie Zemon Davis, *Society and Culture in Early Modern France* (Oxford: Basil Blackwell, 1987 edition) chapter 5; E.P. Thompson, *Customs in Common* (London: Merlin Press, 1991), 325–331; and Rudolf M. Dekker, "Popular Protest and Its Social Basis in Holland in the Seventeenth and Eighteenth Centuries," *Theory and Society* 16 (1987), 342–344.

10. See David J.V. Jones, "Women and Chartism," *History* 68, no. 222 (February 1983), 1–21. On Chartism in the South Wales Coalfield see David J. V. Jones, *The Last Rising: The Newport Insurrection of 1839* (Oxford: Clarendon Press, 1985) and Ivor Wilks, *South Wales and the Rising of 1839: Class Struggle as Armed Struggle* (London and Sydney: Croom Helm, 1984).

11. On the "marginalization" of women within working-class politics during the early and mid-nineteenth century, see Dorothy Thompson, "Women and Nineteenth-Century Radical Politics: A Lost Dimension" in *The Rights and Wrongs of Women* ed., Juliet Mitchell and Ann Oakley (Harmondsworth: Penguin Books, 1976), 112–138; Catherine Hall, *White, Male and Middle-Class: Explorations in Feminism and History* (Cambridge: Polity Press, 1992), esp. chapters 6 and 7; and Anna Clark, *The Struggle for the Breeches: Gender and the Making of the British Working Class* (London: Rivers Oram Press, 1995).

12. There is a rich tradition of historical writing on trade unionism and the labor movement in the South Wales Coalfield. In addition to the works cited in footnote 1, see, e.g., Hywel Francis and David Smith, *The Fed: A History of the South Wales Miners in the Twentieth Century* (London: Lawrence and Wishart, 1980; reprinted Cardiff: University of Wales Press, 1998); David Smith, "Tonypandy 1910: Definitions of Community," *Past and Present* 87 (1980), 158–184; Chris Williams, "The South Wales Miners' Federation," *Llafur* 5, no. 3 (1990), 45–56; Chris Williams, " 'The Hope of the British Proletariat': the South Wales miners, 1910–1947" in *Miners, Unions and Politics, 1910–47*, ed., Alan Campbell, Nina Fishman and David Howell (Aldershot: Scolar Press and Brookfield: Ashgate, 1996), 121–144; Deian Hopkin, "The Great Unrest in Wales 1910–1913: Questions of Evidence" in *Class, Community and the Labor Movement: Wales and Canada 1850–1930*, ed., Deian R. Hopkin and Gregory S. Kealey (Society for Welsh Labor History/Canadian Committee on Labor History, 1989), 249–275; Jane Morgan, *Conflict and Order: The Police and Labor Disputes in England and Wales, 1900–1939* (Oxford: Oxford University Press, 1987); David Gilbert, *Class, Community, and Collective*

Action: Social Change in Two British Coalfields, 1850–1926 (Oxford: Oxford University Press, 1992). See also the important series of articles, by various authors, published annually in *Llafur: The Journal of the Welsh People's History Society* (formerly the Society for Welsh Labor History). Useful comparisons with other coalfields include Roy Church and Quentin Outram, *Strikes and Solidarity. Coalfield Conflict in Britain 1889–1966* (Cambridge: Cambridge University Press, 1998); Roger Fagge, *Power, Culture and Conflict: The Coalfields of West Virginia and South Wales, 1900–1922* (Manchester: Manchester University Press, 1996); and Stefan Berger, "Working-Class Culture and the Labor Movement in the South Wales and the Ruhr Coalfields, 1850–2000: A Comparison," *Llafur* 8, no. 2 (2001), 5–40. For specific reference to women within the labor movement, see Neil Evans and Dot Jones, " 'To Help Forward the Great Work of Humanity': Women in the Labor Party in Wales" in *The Labor Party in Wales 1900–2000*, ed., Duncan Tanner, Chris Williams, and Deian Hopkin (Cardiff: University of Wales Press, 2000), 215–240.

13. For instance, women are largely absent from David Gilbert's study of Ynysybwl (see Gilbert, *Class, Community, and Collective Action*). For a community study that is unusually good on gender relations, see Michael Lieven's "Senghenydd and the Historiography of the South Wales Coalfield," *Morgannwg*, XLIII (1999).

14. Chris Williams, " 'Going Underground'? The Future of Coalfield History Revisited," *Morgannwg*, XLII (1998), 54. See also Michael Lieven, "Senghenydd," 8–35 and Michael Lieven, "A 'New History' of the South Wales Coalfield?" *Llafur* 8, no. 3 (2002), 89–106.

15. For the *ceffyl pren*, see Rosemary A.N. Jones, "Women, Community and Collective Action: The *Ceffyl Pren* Tradition" in *Our Mothers' Land. Chapters in Welsh Women's History, 1830–1939*, ed., Angela V. John (Cardiff: University of Wales Press, 1991), 17–41; Angela John, "Popular Culture, Policing and the 'Disappearance' of the *Ceffyl Pren* in Cardigan, c. 1837–1850," *Ceredigion* XI, no. 1 (1988–1989), 19–39; David J.V. Jones, *Rebecca's Children: A Study of Rural Society, Crime and Protest* (Oxford: Clarendon Press, 1989), 196–198; and David J.V. Jones, *Crime in Nineteenth-Century Wales* (Cardiff: University of Wales Press, 1992), 11–13. For similar traditions in other countries, see footnote 50.

16. For general background information on women's networks in working-class neighborhoods, see Elizabeth Roberts, *A Woman's Place. An Oral History of Working-Class Women 1890–1940* (Oxford and New York: Blackwell, 1984), especially chapter 5; Ellen Ross, "Survival Networks: Women's Neighborhood Sharing in London Before World War I," *History Workshop Journal* 15 (Spring 1983), 4–27; Carl Chinn, *They Worked all their Lives: Women of the Urban Poor in England, 1880–1939* (Manchester: Welsh Press, 1988); and, for early modern precursors, Bernard Capp, *When Gossips Meet. Women, Family, and Neighborhood in Early Modern England* (Oxford: Oxford University Press, 2003). For the Welsh dimension see Rosemary Crook, " 'Tidy Women': Women in the Rhondda Between the Wars," *Oral History*, 10, no. 2 (1982), 40–46; Mari A. Williams, "Women and the Welsh Language in the Industrial Valleys of South Wales 1914–1945" in *"Let's Do Our Best for the Ancient Tongue". The Welsh Language in the Twentieth Century*, ed., Geraint H. Jenkins and Mari A. Williams (Cardiff: University of Wales Press, 2000), esp.

155–162; and the autobiographical material that appears in Carol White and Sian Rhiannon Williams (eds.), *Struggle or Starve.*

17. For the activities of the *Clwb Te*, see Isaac Foulkes, *"Cymru Fu," yn Cynwys Hanesion, Traddodiadau, yn nghyda Chwedlau a Damhegion Cymreig (oddiar lafar gwlad a gweithiau y prif awduron . . .)* (Liverpool: Isaac Foulkes, 1864 edition), 90–91; and Edward Matthews, *Hanes Bywyd Siencyn Penhydd* (Wrexham: Hughes a'i Fab, 1867), 43–44. Membership was restricted to married women, with new recruits often being invited to join on the eve of their wedding. Men were entirely excluded from the proceedings and, since meetings of the *Clwb Te* were often a guise for the clandestine "tippling" of rum or brandy as well as the exchange of gossip, members were sworn to secrecy.

18. For example, Philip Massey, "Portrait of a Mining Town," *Fact*, no. 8 (November 1937), 49; B.L. Coombes, *These Poor Hands. The Autobiography of a Miner Working in South Wales* (London: Victor Gollancz Ltd., 1939), 22–23; Katie Olwen Pritchard, *Gilfach Goch in Cameo. Volume One* (Risca: Starling Press, 1974), 20 and 62; Ivor Howells, *A Rhondda Boy 1906–1914* (Pontypridd: J & P Davison, 2001), 46.

19. Dot Jones, "Serfdom and Slavery" in *Class, Community and the Labor Movement*, ed. Hopkin and Kealey, 93. For details of this shared domestic routine, see Deirdre Beddoe, "Munitionettes, Maids and Mams: Women in Wales, 1914–1939," 200–207; Mari A. Williams, "Aspects of Women's Working Lives in the Mining Communities of South Wales, c. 1891–1939," *Folk Life* 38 (1999–2000), 56–70; White and Williams, eds., *Struggle or Starve*, esp. 15–17; Rosemary Crook, "Tidy Women"; Bill Jones and Beth Thomas, *Teyrnas y Glo/Coal's Domain: Historical Glimpses of Life in the Welsh Coalfields* (Cardiff: National Museums and Galleries of Wales, 1993), 21–24; S. Minwel Tibbott and Beth Thomas, *O'r Gwaith i'r Gwely/A Woman's Work. Housework 1890–1960* (Cardiff: National Museums and Galleries of Wales, 1994).

20. Coombes, *These Poor Hands*, 41.

21. This custom of "sitting out" on the doorstep was common throughout the South Wales Coalfield. See, e.g., James Hanley, *Grey Children. A Study in Humbug and Misery* (Local Study in Rhonda Valleys, London, 1937), 51, 54–55, and 160. In one particular street at Blaenllechau in the Rhondda Fach (Long Row), so many chairs were reputedly positioned on the pavements that pedestrians were forced to walk down the center of the road. See Dei Treanor et al., eds., *Green Black and Back. The Story of Blaenllechau* (Treorchy: Rhondda Community Arts, 1993), 44 [evidence of Olwen Eddy].

22. For a vivid literary representation of this local "grapevine," see Menna Gallie, *Strike for a Kingdom* (Honno: Dinas Powys, 2003), 32–36. The author was born in Ystradgynlais in 1920.

23. J. Basil Phillips, *Senghenydd. A Brave Community* (Abertillery: Old Bakehouse Publications, 2002), 92–93.

24. There are innumerable references in the local press to the prosecution of women for attacks on bailiffs and other officials. See, e.g., the case of two Merthyr Tydfil women who, in 1849, were each fined £1 for attacking a county court bailiff "with pokers, frying-pans, and stones . . ." (reported *Cardiff and Merthyr Guardian*, November 3, 1849).

25. *South Wales Press*, February, 1894.

26. Mary Davies Parnell, *Block Salt and Candles. A Rhondda Childhood* (Bridgend: Seren Books, 1993 edition), 54.

27. The literature on women's "gossip" is extensive but see, in particular, Melanie Tebbutt, *Women's Talk? A Social History of "Gossip" in Working-class Neighborhoods, 1880–1960* (London: Aldershot, 1995); Melanie Tebbutt, "Women's Talk? Gossip and "Women's Words" in Working-Class Communities, 1880–1939" in *Workers' Worlds: Cultures and Communities in Manchester and Salford, 1880–1939* ed. Andrew Davies and Steven Fielding (Manchester: University of Manchester Press, 1992), 49–73; and Ellen Ross, " 'Not the Sort that would Sit on the Doorstep": Respectability in Pre-World War I London Neighborhoods," *International Labor and Working Class History*, no. 27 (1985), 51–52. For an earlier period, see Bernard Capp, *When Gossips Meet. Women, Family, and Neighborhood in Early Modern England* (Oxford: Oxford University Press, 2003).

28. For an interesting case study that underlines this point, see Kirsten McKenzie, "Women's Talk and the Colonial State: The Wylde Scandal, 1831–1833," in *Gender and History* 11, no. 1 (April 1999), 30–53.

29. *Welshman*, March 6, 1868. Mrs. Forsdyke claimed that since September 19, 1867 (the night her effigy was burnt) "there has been a great decline in the takings of my house. I used to take from £8, £10, and £15, now I don't take £3, sometimes not 6s a day. The decline in the receipts began next day."

30. *Glamorgan Free Press*, January 30, 1919; cited in Mari Williams, "Welsh Language," 159.

31. *Rhondda Leader*, July 20, 1918. When Mrs. Gilgrass's attackers were taken before the local police court in July 1918, it was reported to be "the tenth case arising out of similar circumstances."

32. *Cambrian*, March 24, 1893; cited in David J.V. Jones, *Crime in Nineteeth Century Wales* (Cardiff: University of Wales Press, 1992), 73.

33. *Rhondda Leader*, October 29, 1910.

34. *South Wales Press*, April 28, 1887. See also May 5, 1887, when it was reported that hundreds of people had demonstrated outside the the man's home for two successive evenings.

35. For the French *charivari*, see Eugen Weber, *Peasants into Frenchmen: The Modernization of Rural France, 1870–1914* (London: Chatto and Windus, 1977), chapter 22 and Natalie Zemon Davis, *Society and Culture in Early Modern France* (Oxford: Basil Blackwell, 1987 edition), chapter 4. For similar rituals in England (often referred to variously as "rough music," "riding the stang," or "skimmington") see E.P. Thompson, *Customs in Common* (London: Merlin Press, 1991), chapter VIII; E.P. Thompson, "Rough Music Reconsidered," *Folklore* 103 (1992), 3–26; A. James Hammerton, "The Targets of 'Rough Music': Respectability and Domestic Violence in Victorian England," *Gender and History* 3, no. 1 (Spring 1991), 23–44; Martin Ingram, "Ridings, Rough Music and the 'Reform of Popular Culture' in Early Modern England," *Past and Present* 105 (1984), 79–113; Martin Ingram, "Ridings, Rough Music and Mocking Rhymes in Early Modern England" in *Popular Culture in Seventeenth-Century England*, ed., Barry Reay (London: Croom Helm, 1985), 166–197; Martin Ingram, "Juridicial Folklore in England Illustrated by Rough Music" in *Communities and Courts in Britain 1150–1900*, ed. Christopher Brooks and Michael Lobban (London and Rio Grande: Hambledon Press, 1997), 61–82; and David Underdown, "The

Taming of the Scold: The Enforcement of Patriarchal Authority in Early Modern England," in *Order and Disorder in Early Modern England* ed. Anthony Fletcher and John Stevenson (Cambridge: Cambridge University Press, 1985), 116–136. For North America, see Bryan Palmer, "Discordant Music: Charivaris and Whitecapping in Nineteenth-Century North America," *Labor/Le Travailleur*, iii (1978) and William Pencak, Matthew Dennis and Simon P. Newman, eds., *Riot and Revelry in Early America* (Pennsylvania: Pennsylvania State University Press, 2002).

36. The phrase "rough music" has been similarly used by E.P. Thompson and others to describe a range of related ritualized forms in England.

37. See Rosemary Jones, "The 'Disappearance' of the *ceffyl pren*," 23; Cardiff Central/County Library MS 4.939: William Jones ("Erwllwyn"), "Tomos ap Gwilym Cilfynydd. Prydydd enwog y ganrif ddiwetha." For the custom of "riding backward," a persistent theme in the "folk" traditions of most European countries, see Ruth Mellinkoff, "Riding Backwards: Theme of Humiliation and Symbol of Evil," *Viator* 4 (1973): 153–176.

38. Marie Trevelyan, *Glimpses of Welsh Life and Character* (London: Unknown, 1893), 76.

39. For the "carnivalesque" see, e.g., B.A. Babcock, ed., *The Reversible World: Symbolic Inversion in Art and Society* (Ithaca: Cornell University Press, 1978); Peter Burke, *Popular Culture in Early Modern Europe*, chapter 7; Natalie Zemon Davis, *Society and Culture in Early Modern France* (Cambridge: Polity Press, 1987 edition), chapters 4 and 5.

40. For example, David Jones and Rosemary Jones, *Ceredigion: A Journal of Welsh History*.

41. For descriptions of the Glamorgan *cwlstrin*, see Charles Redwood, *The Vale of Glamorgan: Scenes and Tales among the Welsh* (London: Saunders and Otley, 1839), 271–295; Marie Trevelyan, *Folk-Lore and Folk-Stories of Wales* 258–260; Marie Trevelyan, *Glimpses of Welsh Life and Character* (London: Unknown, 1893), 76–77; T.C. Evans (Cadrawd), *History of Llangynwyd Parish* (Llanelly, Printed at Offices of Llanelli and County Guardian, 1887), 162–163; and Wirt Sikes, *British Goblins: Welsh Folk-lore, Fairy Mythology, Legends and Traditions* (Unknown: London, 1880), 317–320. For Breconshire, see "Breconshire Traditions, &c.," *Archaeologia Cambrensis* (1858), 159. The term *cwlstrin* was probably derived from the English "cowlstringing" or "cowlstaffing" (i.e., to parade on a cowl/coul-staff or pole); indeed, the term "coul stringing" was used to describe an incident at Aberdare in 1856, when a man was paraded on a ladder (see *Cardiff and Merthyr Guardian*, May 3, 1856). However, some contemporary observers claimed a derivation from the Welsh words *cwl* ("sin") and *trin* ("to deal with")—i.e., "to purge sin." See Cardiff Central Library (David Jones of Wallington MSS), Vol. 18, MS 2.1111 (3/11) [I am indebted to Richard Suggett for this latter reference].

42. T.C. Evans (Cadrawd), *History of Llangynwyd Parish* (Llanelly, Printed at Offices of Llanelli and County Guardian, 1887), 162–163.

43. A *cwlstrin* court was said to have been held on the "Tymbl" at Pontypridd, in the Rhondda Valley, as late as 1856. See Huw Walters, "Beirdd a Phrydyddion Pontypridd a'r Cylch yn y Bedwaredd Ganrif ar Bymtheg: Arolwg" in Hywel Teifi Edwards (ed.), *Cyfres y Cymoedd. Merthyr a Thaf* (Llandysul: Gomer, 2001), 255. However, by the 1880s, such courts were described as "apparently

obsolete, unless in occasional rural communities remote from railroads." See Wirt Sikes, *British Goblins: Welsh Folk-Lore, Fairy Mythology, Legends and Traditions* (London, 1880), 317.

44. *Merthyr Guardian*, April 23, 1836 and *Cardiff and Merthyr Guardian*, June 14, 1845. For similar examples see *Merthyr Guardian*, March 1, 1834 and *Cardiff and Merthyr Guardian*, September 19, 1846. The *ceffyl pren* was also reported to have been deployed in the eastern districts of the coalfield, such as Tredegar and Blaenafon. See, e.g., Evan Powell, *History of Tredegar: Subject of Competition at Tredegar "Chair Eisteddfod" held February the 25th, 1884* (Newport: Unknown, 1902) 117 and *Seren Cymru* (Star of Wales) 21 Mawrth 1857.

45. *Cardiff and Merthyr Guardian*, May 3, 1856. For an earlier incident in the same town see *Chester Chronicle*, September 29, 1855.

46. Welsh-born migrants predominated in the South Wales Coalfield prior to the 1850s—most of them drawn from the adjacent counties of Carmarthenshire, Pembrokeshire and Cardiganshire—and continued to comprise a significant share of migrants during the second half of nineteenth century. For example, during the period 1861–1871, the Welsh share of migrants into the county of Glamorgan stood at 59.1%, and still amounted to 44.4% of new migrants during the period 1891–1901. See Philip N. Jones, "Population Migration into Glamorgan 1861–1911: A Reassessment" in Morgan (ed.), *Glamorgan County History (VI)*, 182–183.

47. *Pembrokeshire Herald*, February 6, 1861 (reprinted from *Monmouthshire Merlin*) and *Tarian y Gweithiwr*, 3 Medi 1875.

48. *Rhondda Leader*, April 7, 1900.

49. For example, *Welshman*, November 4, 1864 and March 6, 1868; *South Wales Press*, April 18, and June 13, 1895; and Gareth Hughes, *A Llanelli Chronicle* (Llanelli Borough Council, 1984), 41–42.

50. *Welshman*, November 4, 1864. The custom appears to have experienced a resurgence at this time, the newspaper reporting that the "burning the effigies of living personages, who have scandalised themselves and others, is becoming very popular."

51. This was the case in the Amman Valley. See, e.g., D. Myrddin Davies, "Testun Cân a Llosgi Lun. Rhai o Hen Arferion Dyffryn Aman" in *Western Mail*, May 24, 1938. The author (born 1895) was a native of Garnant and had himself witnessed two such incidents.

52. *South Wales Press*, December 8 and 15, 1909.

53. *Cambrian*, September 6, 1872.

54. *Welshman*, March 6, 1868.

55. This was also the case in early modern England, where it has been argued that an increasing preoccupation with "scolding" woman was expressive of a wider "crisis" in gender relations. See David Underdown, "The Taming of the Scold: The Enforcement of Patriarchal Authority in Early Modern England," in *Order and Disorder in Early Modern England*, ed., Anthony Fletcher and John Stevenson (Cambridge: Cambridge University Press, 1985), 116–136. For a critique of Underdown's work, which argues that this perceived "crisis" has been overstated, see Martin Ingram, " 'Scolding Women Cucked or Washed': A Crisis in Gender Relations in Early Modern England?" in *Women, Crime and the Courts in Early Modern England*, ed. Jenny Kermode and Garthine Walker (London: University College London Press, 1994), 48–80.

56. This point is best illustrated by Charles Redwood, *The Vale of Glamorgan: Scenes* and *Tales among the Welsh* (London: Saunders and Otley, 1839), 271–95.

57. For the symbolism associated with the "battle for the breeches" see, e.g., Kathryn Gleadle and Sarah Richardson (eds.), *Women in British Politics, 1760–1860: The Power of the Petticoat* (Basingstoke and New York: Macmillan Press and St. Martin's Press, 2000), 1–18 and Anna Clark, *Struggle for the Breeches*. Petticoats were often mounted on poles as a means of ridiculing the inversion of accepted gender roles and, in particular, to act as counterpoint to the male "breeches," which symbolized the husband's patriarchal authority within the home.

58. Charles Redwood, *The Vale of Glamorgan: Scenes and Tales among the Welsh* (London: Saunders and Otley, 1839), 271–295.

59. A similar shift in targets may be observed in England at this time. See E.P. Thompson, *Customs in Common*, 510–513.

60. *Seren Cymru*, 3 Awst, 1860.

61. *Chester Chronicle*, September 29, 1855. See also Rosemary Jones, "Women, Community and Collective Action," 29–30.

62. For the use of a white shirt at Pontypridd see Cardiff Central Library MS 4.939, 3. The makeshift use of a white shirt, smock, nightdress, or chemise to simulate ritual of female disguise was a common device in many countries during the early modern period and was popular with the Rebecca rioters. A white night cap often completed the "disguise." See, e.g., Natalie Zemon Davis, *Society and Culture in Early Modern France* (Oxford: Basil Blackwell, 1987 edition), 148–149; E.P. Thompson, *Customs in Common*, 476; *Quarterly Review*, 74 (June and October 1844), 129; and Evan D. Jones, "A File of 'Rebecca' Papers," *Carmarthen Antiquary*, 1 (1943–1944), 24 and 50. However, it may also have been influenced by the custom known as "white sheeting." This was a punishment once imposed by the ecclesiastical courts, which entailed forcing offenders to stand before the congregation, during divine service, dressed in a white sheet. See, e.g., E.P. Thompson, *Customs in Common*, 502–503; Laura Gowing, "Language, Power, and the Law: Women's Slander Litigation in Early Modern London" in *Women, Crime and the Courts in Early Modern England*, ed., Jenny Kermode and Garthine Walker (London: University College London Press, 1994), 33; "Breconshire Traditions," *Archaeologia Cambrensis* (1858), 159; and David James, "Gleanings from Consistory Court Records," *Carmarthenshire Antiquary*, XXVIII (1992), 106.

63. These poets were recognized moral leaders within the community. They invariably composed mocking rhymes to accompany the proceedings and the "testimony" of witnesses was also given in verse form. See Huw Walters, "Beirdd a Phrydyddion Pontypridd a'r Cylch yn y Bedwaredd Ganrif ar Bymtheg: Arolwg" in *Cyfres y Cymoedd. Merthyr a Thaf*, ed., Hywel Teifi Edwards (Llandysul: Gomer, 2001), 254–255. For further information on the bardic circle known as "Clic y Bont" ("The Bridge Clique") see Meic Stephens, ed., *The New Companion to the Literature of Wales* (Cardiff: University of Wales Press, 1998 edition), 114 and J. Dyfnallt Owen, *Rhamant a Rhyddid* (Llandysul: Y Clwb Llyfrau Cymraeg/Gwasg Gomer, 1952), 57–63.

64. Redwood, *The Vale of Glamorgan*, 293–294.

65. *Chester Chronicle*, September 29, 1855.

66. *Carmarthen Journal*, October 3, 1856.

67. *Ibid.* December 1, 1843.

68. *Cardiff and Merthyr Guardian*, May 3, 1856.

69. *Merthyr Guardian*, March 1, 1834.

70. Gareth Hughes, *A Llanelli Chronicle* (Llanelli Borough Council, 1984), Llanelli Chronicle, September 14, 1849, 42.

71. *Pembrokeshire Herald*, February 6, 1861 (reprinted from *Monmouthshire Merlin*).

CHAPTER 6

Gender Relations in Iron Mining Communities in Sweden, 1900–1940

Eva Blomberg

For some time gender historians in Sweden have discussed the extent to which the theory on gender systems and gender contracts launched by the Swedish historian, Yvonne Hirdman, with its focus on segregation and subservience, is fruitful as an analytical tool for a historically variable process.[1] Included in these discussions is the extent to which gender contracts may be used in historical analyses. In many respects, Hirdman's work parallels that of Joan Scott by asking how gender operates and works in social contexts. How does gender create meaning—in an organization, a social context, in the world of concepts, as a representation?[2] In contrast to Scott, Hirdman has systematized and formalized the structural and general patterns of subservience and segregation that appear to arise and be reproduced time after time, in spite of constant changes in historical development. Both authors stress the gender forming process in historical context, in the interplay between discourse and social practice. This essay focuses on an analysis of gender relations in the Swedish mining industry during the period 1900–1940 using Scott's and Hirdman's different levels of analysis: in organizations and work processes, in the local social context, and on an ideological/conceptual level.

The central argument of this study is that it was not the structural conditions within the mining industry that made women's work unnecessary as the work became more mechanized. Rather, it was the main participants involved, the employers and trade union organizations, which restricted women's opportunities for supporting themselves in the mines and made women's influence in the unions impossible, and this in turn made it more difficult for women to protect their rights. Thus, women were separated out from men and turned into a special category. Women developed different and new means of support among themselves and were assigned gender specific duties, but always in a subservient role vis-à-vis the men in the mining communities.[3]

TRADE CONDITIONS

Since the end of the nineteenth century, mining production has been divided into two industries: export mining and the ironworks mining industry. Industrialization entailed increased demand for iron and steel while at the same time new steel processes made it possible to start mining ore rich in phosphorus, as in the ore fields of northern and central Sweden. The great demand also meant that the old ironworks companies in central Sweden were subjected to strong pressure and increased competition from the new companies. The domestic market increased in importance.[4]

After the boom period of World War I the state of the market swung rapidly within the industry. The speculative companies disappeared, while at the same time the remaining ones on the one hand reduced their operations, and on the other took the opportunity to increase their holdings of mines. A large number of companies vanished from the scene, whereas others changed owners or were bought up. This restructuring of the whole iron, steel, and ironworks industry reached a climax during the 1920s.[5] After the crisis of the 1930s the two sides of the industry became even more polarized. One effect of the restructuring and changing trade conditions was that the demand for miners fluctuated powerfully during the period.

GENDERED DIVISION OF LABOR

Just as in other countries, women in Sweden have worked in the mining industry both above and below ground.[6] Several researchers have examined mining work in the past and report that, up to 1840, it was not specific to any particular sex. Approximately 50 percent of the labor force consisted of "mining lasses" (*gruvpigor*), who worked both above and below ground, doing different kinds of work. After 1842, however, the proportion of women went down considerably.[7]

What, then, is the explanation for this masculinization of the industry? Some researchers think that the falling numbers of women in the industry was an effect of the rise in population during the nineteenth century. A larger available male workforce replaced women in the mines. The women were driven out and now became a reserve labor force. Increased production and longer hours at the mine-face also indicate that mining work was no longer a seasonal phenomenon, but a full-time occupation. The result was an increase in production. Mining work also became differentially and better paid. Before restructuring men and women had the same wages, at least in some of the mines, and the wages were paid out collectively, that is, to the household. With the introduction of piecework, however, the women began to be paid less. "Men's day work" and "women's day work" were brought in (1840s–1850s), where the women's day work formed approximately 80 percent of a man's. This suggests that the household was initially the primary income unit, and the question of who did the work was not important.[8]

Other researchers think that division into genders was a result of capitalist restructuring, whereby women were relegated to unpaid housework and men to the full-time work of earning the wages. The situation of the household worsened: from having been an economic productive unit it was now dependent on paid work and work in the home. The proletarianization of the household created different situations for the sexes: the male wageworker was dependent on female household work, and vice versa.[9] This is not to say that the dependence was equally divided. On the contrary, a power relation was created in which women were subservient to the men. They ended up in a subordinate work relation to the men, if they were not completely pushed out to the "sphere of the home," so that women's collective powers became significantly reduced in relation both to men and to employers.

One should also analyze the role of the state in this process, particularly during the nineteenth century. In Sweden the state controlled the mines through the local mine inspectors and the assembling of statistics. The mine inspectors often seem to have made proclamations far and wide as to the place of mining women in society: moral collapse was at hand if women worked in the mine.[10] This moral discussion on the theme of women and mining was constantly reiterated, not only in Sweden, but in much of industrialized Europe. The policies of the mine inspectors can be analyzed as offshoots of an attitude to the female labor force, which developed during the nineteenth century. Women's work and the nature of women were a part of the social discourse, which eventually resulted in discriminatory legislation in Sweden as well as in other countries.[11] In 1900 women in Sweden were forbidden to work underground. This law, then, was not only an expression of the fact that the boundaries between masculinity and femininity were debated but also that it was regarded as necessary to regulate these boundaries via legislation.[12]

Another consequence of this negative attitude to women's work was that the mining inspectors failed to report back fully on the mining girls in their statistical returns. They themselves also had difficulty in getting information from the companies as to the number of mining girls employed:

> To the extent that the administration of the mines and the work therein is ordered after the use of women in the mines themselves, so that now for instance at Dalkarlsberget alone 4, and in the Striberg field proper 8, women were used for mine working, instead of as previously when half the number of mining hands belonged to the female sex—as is still the case at the smaller mines—no specific information thereon could be obtained.[13]

Although the historical records are scant it is clear that mining work in Sweden had not previously been an exclusively male sphere, but became so in the middle of the nineteenth century. This change took place parallel with capitalist developments that began to make their way into the industry while at the same time intense debates on female gainful employment and "the eternally feminine" were being carried out by the middle classes.[14]

At the beginning of the twentieth century women were only used in the Swedish mining industry for work above ground. During World War I the female labor was reduced, and after 1918 only a quarter of them remained.

Rationalization during the 1920s and 1930s increased the laying off of male workers. An aging work force was transferred to more suitable placements as needed. In general, older men were moved to work above ground, and consequently women were pushed out of the work force, which became almost entirely male. By and large the women formed 1 percent of the work force during the period 1910–1940, that is, some 60–80 people. It was mostly chance and market forces that accounted for the women remaining in the industry. There were still women left in the smaller mines throughout the 1930s and even later.[15]

It was not the actual mechanization that made women lose their jobs, but masculinization, which was mainly about men and women being separated from one another in the work process. The gendered labor division meant that women were no longer allowed to work underground and eventually also shut out from work above ground.

The Mining Industry in Sweden

The ironworks mines had had an internal labor market for many centuries. Recruitment took place within the community exclusively. In spite of this, however, there were occasionally opportunities for the skills of those who were outsiders to the local community.

The new export industry, on the other hand, which was established after 1890, had entirely different problems. It had to look for labor from outside in competition with other companies and industries. Compared with other industries these mining companies could not, in the beginning, attract labor through orderly conditions. It was therefore extremely important to create stable communities since there was a constant threat of disorder from the outside labor force. The great problem of the export mines from the second decade of the twentieth century on was to create new communities where none had existed before and build up a stable and permanently settled core of workers, at least if the companies were farsighted in their interests. The shortsighted interests of speculative companies created other types of conditions for the workers. In addition, fluctuations in market forces sometimes produced great demands for labor and at other times vast unemployment.

Ironworks miners had different expectations of their employers as compared with the export mineworkers. Social relations had been established long ago and norms existed as to how workers and employers should conduct themselves. The employer was to look after certain rights. Not so the export companies, however. There the workers learnt early on to trust their own resources and take care of their own problems. They had to fight for their rights. It is symptomatic that the first trade union in industry was created in one of the new export mines in Central Sweden, Grängesberg, in 1893, two years before the founding of the Swedish Miners' Union. Trade unions were a means of acquiring rights and respect.

If one looks at the way the employers treated the workers there is a clear pattern. The male workers were divided into two categories: the variables and the constants, as the employers termed them in the twentieth century. The constants were the ones kept by the employers even during times of depression and it was they who knew all the different stages in the work process. The variables, on the other hand, were a category used as reserve labor.[16] From now on, I shall call these two groups mobile and stationary. The young men who were taken on were seen as mobile, until they had been put to the test by the employers as well as their workmates. They could thus qualify for the stationary group depending on their age, civil status, and reliability.

There is much to suggest that the situation of women was different. They were mentioned only as "women" and their conditions were not like those of the men. Rather, their situation was ambiguous: they were seen as a mobile group in terms of work, but treated as a stationary category in the community, depending on their collective and individual merits: work experience, kinship, age, and civil status.[17] Most of those who worked in the industry were girls or widows, but it was not unusual for them to be married.[18] Even if the employers wished, for ideological reasons, to rid themselves of female labor, they were hindered by their own need for low cost labor. Despite that, there was a sense of social responsibility to assist women who had been abandoned by the male breadwinner. Many women were the sole supporters of their families, since it was not unusual for men to disappear, often to the United States, Canada, or to other mining communities in Sweden.[19]

Male and female workers experienced different power relations with employers. The classifications to which the male workers were subjected created partially conflicting interests and attitudes as well as special power relations between different male groups in relation to the employer. Also, the male working collective and the employer together created a power relation vis-à-vis the group known as "women." These power relations were both structurally and traditionally determined and were a result of the staff policies pursued by the company management.[20]

Several researchers emphasize the different conditions experienced by the male groups.[21] The stationary group, in general, comprised those who were married and living in company houses. The mobile group was to a great extent unmarried and living in lodgings or bachelors' barracks. They lived the life of bachelors, even if they were not always so. The employer had a strong interest in having a labor force that was reliable, and the employers regarded married men as more stable.[22]

When the workers sought loans for their own homes, the employer scrutinized them. Those who were considered for loans were the ones whom the company judged to be reliable. The central Swedish mining company Vulcanus's management did not think the company should be dependent on unmarried and younger workers, since they were regarded as "particularly mobile," and it was therefore important to grant land to those building their own homes. For the company it was of importance to verify which people were married or unmarried, the number of children they had, and the family circumstances. It was also a matter of the company's housing policy, since they had to know what types of houses to build—accommodation in which several families could be housed, or bachelor barracks.[23]

Employment policies and housing policies provide evidence of links between the labor market and the marriage market. The exchangeability of the male workers was a matter of their position in the work process and their total social situation. This policy made it more difficult for the mobile workers to influence their own situation, in particular until 1933, since market conditions varied so greatly. But what was it like for the women?

ANOMALIES

What, actually, was a mineworker? During the second decade of the twentieth century, the employers and the male employees arranged themselves into different organizations. They finalized collective nationwide agreements for the whole mining branch and for each of these a criterion was formulated as to what a mineworker was:

> A satisfactory worker is understood in the agreement as someone who can carry out every sort of work, for which no direct expert knowledge is required, or those who can carry out every work process within their field of expertise.[24]

According to this paragraph a woman could not be regarded as a mineworker with regulated minimum wages. She could not, for example, carry out every sort of work, since she was forbidden to work underground. This disqualified her from receiving a regulated hourly wage and from the status of being a mineworker.[25] It was understood that the nationwide agreement did not regulate hourly wages for women's work because of the above-mentioned paragraph. Instead their wages were regulated informally, as other researchers have also maintained. Thus, women were shut out from the minimum wage regulations in the agreements.[26]

In a memorandum from 1939 the employers' organization, of the central Swedish Mining Council agreed on rules that were to apply to women and minors:

> As far as contracts are concerned certain workshops apply the rule that adult male workers' [so-called temporary workers, my observation] contracts are reduced to 3/4 when handed over to male workers of 18–20 years of age, and to 2/3 for male workers of 16–18 years of age, and to 1/2 for those who are even younger. Others see to it that minors and women may never carry out the work of adult male workers. The contracts for minors and women are fixed according to other premises than those for adult males.
>
> The contracts for women are generally issued proportionately to the contracts for adult males, for example at a rate of 2/3 for women who are 18 years of age and 1/2 for women under 18 years of age. During normal periods attempts are obviously made to arrange as far as possible that the work is not moved from one to another of the above-named categories, but it cannot even then be entirely avoided. Even at the present time the above-mentioned differentiation must be observed.[27]

The employers' memorandum suggests that the wages were gender coded. Women were not to compete with the men and they were not to replace them even in times of war, a practice common in other types of work. The employers' opposition to women's labor is also evident in the memorandum; all the way through the document has an apologetic tone, which becomes hostile in attitude when referring to the female labor force. What is not apparent is why this opposition existed. It is therefore important to analyze the values that were fundamental to the wage structure and attitude to women.[28] If the women felt themselves at a disadvantage it could be difficult for them to change unspoken premises and rules. In John Gaventa's discussion on power and participation, the consequences of the payment system were that women ended up in a particular category, "women", with very little chance of changing the system, since it was not codified. There were no formal rules to which women could refer in order to bring about change. It was a system that created powerlessness and nonparticipation.[29] One can only conclude that the formal structures favored the men and were unfair to the women. Noncodified rules were more difficult to recodify, and established practice changed slowly.

The differentiation of workers, then, was based on different systems that strengthened each other. The fundamental point was that the companies needed (1) different sorts of labor force: mobile, stationary, and women, and (2) separate spheres for production and reproduction. The gendered labor-division hierarchy strengthened the differences between the categories and the masculinization process created a power relation where women were subservient to men, both economically and socially. They became an anomaly in the mining industry.

But how did conditions look at a local level? Sweden is an oblong country with long distances between communities and villages and it may therefore be of importance to analyze how the various mining communities differ, and what they have in common.

STAFF POLICIES

The most northerly mining community in Sweden, Kiruna, became segregated to a greater extent than any other community. Kiruna was Sweden's Klondike and first became a town in 1900. The company, LKAB—the most important mining company in Sweden—was forced to create both a totally new community and a new place of work.

Labor policies were, from the beginning, the great problem in Kiruna. The company wanted stable, married men and women as inhabitants. They therefore tried to avoid prostitution and slums, by checking the trains from the south: unmarried women without male protection were not allowed to come to Kiruna.[30] But evidence suggests this was not how it really was.[31] They had no success either in controlling the recruitment of women or in limiting entry to married men. But they did succeed in staving off slums and prostitution, though in a completely different way from Malmberget, the other large mining community in the north, not far from Kiruna. The statistics kept by the company show the importance of keeping an eye on the labor force. The company calculated the probability of the workforce staying, taking into consideration such factors as where the workers came from, their civil status, and number of children, number of children at home, and other family circumstances. Between 1921 and 1928 the unmarried workers were in the majority: out of 1,454 workers 935 were unmarried, 498 married, and 21 widowed.[32]

Conditions for women were especially difficult. They came to the mining communities as housewives or housekeepers and were expected to take responsibility for everything that had to do with reproduction. That meant that they were gainfully employed as landladies, or ran cafés, or were cooks, cleaners, and washerwomen for all the unmarried men.[33] LKAB was extremely male dominated and women were simply not employed.

The mining work took place above ground and in extremely difficult circumstances, above the polar circle. It was therefore especially important that the company built washhouses, drying rooms, and bathhouses and tried in all possible ways to make this tough life, with its extra stresses and strains, easier. Another problem in Kiruna was the acquisition of provisions. During some periods it was simpler to get hold of beer than milk, and it was necessary to go hunting and fishing to obtain additional fare. There were also several types of temporary work for women connected with the pioneering phase in Kiruna: driving planks and timber, making tiles and bricks, working in cafés and serving food. But at the same time the company made it difficult to support oneself since other firms were forbidden to establish themselves! The company dictated conditions totally. The fact that Kiruna became an expansive community in spite of all this was soon evident, however, since the new working groups arriving in the town were those of midwives and women teachers.[34]

LKAB's family policies and bureaucratic management strategy in relation to women were evident in their "widows' policy". The company distinguished between three sorts of widows: (1) widows with sons employed in LKAB and living in company accommodation; (2) widows who did not have sons employed in the company, but were living in company accommodation; (3) various, living in company accommodation. From the company's statistics it is apparent that there was a systematic attempt to treat the widows equally. It is not apparent, though, whether the company tried to find work for the widows and their grown-up children or whether these people did so themselves. In any case, the company went in as "protector" if the widow did not have any work and if she did not have any grown-up sons who could shoulder responsibility for supporting the family. In so doing the company took on itself some sort of patriarchal responsibility, or rather, bureaucratic responsibility, since it was steered by formal routines and calculability, in Max Weber's sense of the expression.[35]

The actual point of the company's policy toward widows was to handle them bureaucratically and formally, and not out of patriarchal benevolence.

It was mainly a question of money, and therefore also important for the company to sort out which widows were in need of help and which could manage on their own.[36] It was not the actual status of widowhood that was decisive in the protection given by the company, but the widow's chances of supporting herself and her family. This break with earlier conditions in the mining industry was a modern development.

The mining communities in central Sweden were not really as single sex as those in the north. Here both large and small mines were fairly close to each other. The mining industry had been in existence in the area since the Middle Ages, and when the new mining settlements grew up there was already an older settlement close at hand. A gender structure existed with different levels of work for men and women, but women were also employed in mining work—even if only to a very small extent during the twentieth century. The women also had different opportunities from those in the north when it came to supporting themselves—the traditional cottage industry of handcrafts and other small-scale activities.[37] Sometimes cottage industry work was combined with other small business activities. The most significant aspect was that a new labor market also opened for women with the establishment of new mining companies: they might own, and work in, cafés and other places serving refreshments, which were well frequented by unmarried men.

The biggest export mining company in central Sweden was the Grängesberg Company. Its policy toward widows was quite different from that of LKAB in the north. The newly widowed were provided with compensation, depending on the number of fatherless children they had.[38] There were plenty of opportunities, too, for them to support themselves in Grängesberg and the surrounding area, and a dynamite factory provided a large place of work for women, where only such widows and young girls might be employed.

In general the export companies pursued a gender-structured policy, which changed and worsened conditions for women. In 1892, however, the head of Stora Kopparberg (now Stora Enso) started mobile courses in cooking for the daughters of mine workers. By 1900 this course activity had expanded into a full-blown course for housewives. The aim was to "train workers' wives-to-be" so that they could create a good home atmosphere—in order that the workers could achieve more."[39] It was not, then, a question of creating a labor market for women, but of steering the women toward work in the home. The training policy of the company was imbued with middle-class values and notions: the woman's place was in the home or the washhouse, and the man's in the mine. The deliberate family policies of the company were part of a larger pattern. They could pay the stationary men relatively well and encouraged them to be steady and conscientious: these men got family-support wages and also obtained advantageous conditions for homes of their own if they behaved well. The whole point of the policy was to create a gender-structured system with separate places for the two sexes.

The idea was to create calm and stable communities. During the second decade of the twentieth century hordes of young men, particularly young and revolutionary syndicalists, had been attracted to the mines. They opposed the company management, picketed places of work, and went on strike. The company's remedy for this was to concentrate on married men. It was for this reason that the women—as wives—became important for them, since they were seen to have a calming influence on the men.

One might argue that the export companies' gender policies can be seen as a model with roots in the nineteenth century. At that time it was the mine inspectors who argued for women being taken away from mining work, and during the twentieth century one can say that the social engineers turned these ideas into reality. The only difference was that the twentieth-century engineers tried to create model communities where people had their own homes, collective washing facilities, and gardens. They tried to create more tolerable conditions for married women.

However, the ironworks mines in central Sweden had a completely different standpoint. They had an internal labor market, and since time immemorial new generations of mine workers, including women, had grown up in close proximity to the mine and been socialized into the myths and conceptual values of the place, and the actual work itself. When the children were small they were already helping to pick up ore from the slagheaps. Large numbers of youngsters as well as young girls under eighteen years of age were employed. It was not until after 1920, in connection with the shortening of working hours, that jobs for youngsters disappeared.[40] As is apparent, a number of women were employed in the ironworks mines.[41] The low-wage policies in existence were a consequence of uncertain operative conditions and internal market yields. But they can also be interpreted from a gender perspective. Here mineworkers' wives were supporters of the household to a greater extent than in other minefields.[42] Many were farming wives, smallholders and agricultural workers on their own farms. Others worked in sanatoriums and cottage hospitals. The effect of low-wage policies was that women's gainful employment was necessary for the support of the family, while at the same time the system upheld low-wage policies. This should also be seen as an effect of the benefits in kind that existed. The company management could rely on this model in their low-wage policies. The low-wage system of the iron miners therefore implied another system, which had consequences for the family policies of the company.[43]

Like the other companies, there were reduced rates for accommodation, light, fuel, and provisions.[44] And in the ironworks mines there were many more benefits: free potato planting, free cow houses, plowing for nothing, Christmas presents, and clothing for those in need. The company defrayed the cost of funerals and the elderly had no rent to pay.[45]

The companies' policies toward widows were combined with benefits in kind, and the company contributed free lodgings and a certain number of cubic meters of firewood per annum. It was the status of widowhood that entitled one to the benefits and not, in the first place, the support aspect. There were, besides, always opportunities for creating work above ground or elsewhere.[46]

The family policies of the companies to a certain extent favored marriage despite the fact that they passively supported non legalized partnerships; cost of living allowances (bonuses) were also paid out to housekeepers who had children, that is, to those who lived with a man without being married. If a worker married and became the supporter of a family there was also a good chance of him getting a home from the company.[47] His chances of remaining in work also increased considerably during times of depression. By contrast with the export mines the family policies of these companies were not orientated toward creating family households to the same extent. The policies were inconsistent and passive, and meant in practice that different forms of household could exist side by side. In the small ironworks mine of Stripa there was, for example, barracks accommodation only for such widowed households.[48]

In Sweden labor market and family policies came to control developments in mining communities. But there were great differences between companies. The export companies created more single-sex communities, where the labor market for women was gradually reduced. The companies' family policies built up places for the different sexes in a tangible way and women were made dependent on men—and their incomes.

ORGANIZATION

Within the mining industry there were two competing trade unions. One was the *Swedish Miners' Union*, which was reformist, and the other was the *Revolutionary Syndicalist Organization*.

There was a great difference between the two, and this is particularly important as far as female organization is concerned. The development of the Syndicalist organization was based on the idea that *all* who lived in a particular place should be systematized into local joint organizations irrespective of work. The development of the Swedish Miners' Union was based on the idea that all *mineworkers* should be organized into a chapter in a particular place. It was the Swedish Miners' Union that reached an agreement with the employers, and this organization linked itself with the definition of a mineworker, as formulated in the agreements. Here we have an explanation as to why women did not organize themselves under the auspices of the Swedish Miners' Union, since the association only organized mineworkers (= men). Women were shut out by definition, right from the beginning.

The Revolutionary Syndicalist Organization, on the other hand, drew up the boundaries in another way. It was built up differently and in theory should have had a lively interest in organizing women as a means of increasing its strength, in particular when the organization lost more and more of its power in the 1930s. And in fact during the second decade of the twentieth century the Syndicalist men were not wholly dismissive toward female organization. There were, at least, some male voices taking the view that women should be organized, at least in some communities. In a number of places separate female organizations were set up as subchapters of the Syndicalist organization. But organizing of women was limited and the associations were short-lived.

The democratic breakthrough of 1921, with universal suffrage, came to have great consequences for the organizing of women. They got themselves together in sewing circles, temperance lodges, consumers' associations, the Women's Economic Associations, Women's Cooperative Guilds, and many others.[49] There does not seem to have been any difficulty for the women to organize themselves, but it was not the Syndicalist organization they chose. It is therefore difficult to maintain that women in general took no interest in organizing; it was rather a question of what type of organization was interesting as far as they were concerned, and which could look after their needs and concerns.[50]

The 1920s also meant that women began to make new and different demands. In 1920 the Women's left-wing Socialist Club in Grängesberg announced that they wished to rebuild their club as a women's Syndicalist club, and now wanted to be linked with the local Syndicalist organization. The matter was brushed aside with the remark that the local Syndicalist organization was ". . . purely a union organization. . . ." and that ". . . such a women's club had no chance of doing anything in this field."[51] The women were referred to the youth club. Instead of being discouraged, however, they seem to have developed an organization of their own: the Grängesberg Women's Economic Association. When the local Syndicalist organization later had the opportunity of hearing a famous Syndicalist agitator they felt that this was not something for them but for the Women's Economic Association, because the agitator was female. The Women's Economic Association, however, returned time and again to the local Syndicalist organization and requested that someone from that group come and enlighten them about the trade union movement. It seems that the local Syndicalist organization was not willing to share its knowledge. However, the contacts gradually became better and they invited each other to meetings and festive occasions until an internal controversy within the local Syndicalist organization led to the breaking off of joint cooperation.[52]

During the 1920s the women developed their own network and pursued political questions of both a local and more national character, often in conjunction with other women's organizations and sometimes with the director's wife. When men's organizations became closed it meant that the women could not pursue union matters, and because of this they did not obtain any union training in the political apparatus either, as the men did. The union and political organizations have long been intimately bound up with each other in Sweden and many members of the Swedish parliament have, after 1932, been recruited from trade union organizations. This route, though, was in principle closed to women and the consequences of female exclusion have been long term.

It was not until the 1930s that the Revolutionary Syndicalist Organization took up the question of female membership at the top level and encouraged all local units to organize women. The most visible result, however, was the establishment in 1937 of a separate women's organization, The Women's Syndicalist Association.[53] The negativity that developed when some members of the local Syndicalist organizations discussed the organizing of women, was connected with views of relations between the sexes, and the particular view of women held by the male members. There is no evidence in the minutes that members considered consulting the women themselves as to what they needed or would like. It was the men who decided whether the women were to belong to the organization or not, despite the fact that in principle it was open to *all* who subscribed to Syndicalist ideas.

Yvonne Hirdman treats power as a spatial phenomenon, a matter of hindering women's ability to move about.[54] In the Syndicalist organization one can see how this process took shape, since the men decided for the women where their place was to be, and hindered them from joining the association on the same terms as the men—thereby creating a power relation of inequality.[55]

What interest, then, had the women in preserving these relations and not challenging the men in their own domains? Was it perhaps an advantage for them that the men were the ones who reacted outwardly and confronted the company management, or made political careers in the local districts? Women thereby escaped the relation of dependence on the company but at the same time were dependent on individual men, not least economically speaking. Those who were dissatisfied with things as they were had really only one choice, and that was to leave the area and seek out some large town with better opportunities.

And that was precisely what many women did during the 1930s when they left the countryside and moved into the towns, where shop and service work tempted them with better wages and working conditions, and where they were welcomed into the trade union organizations.[56]

The women who chose to try and change things in Swedish mining communities were able to do so through different women's organizations and individual men. But their position in the mining communities was limited because they had no direct channels of communication to the company management or district politics. But they could obtain influence and power via political parties, particularly if they showed an interest in family and social policies, but in other areas of political discourse their presence was not welcome.[57]

SUMMARY

Ideas of masculinity and femininity influenced the gendered division of labor and the development of communities. Women's opportunities for supporting themselves within the mining industry were increasingly reduced, but at the same time their chances of participating in surrounding industries were extended, at least in central Sweden. Conditions for women varied enormously in the different communities, depending on the staff policies of the companies and whether the mine was an export-based place of work or not.

The specific order in the mining industry made the man the norm: in work, organization and the public arena. Everything revolved round men and their work: wet clothes, wear and tear on the body, building a home of one's own, union meetings, drinking, work, and unemployment. Women, on the other hand, were made subservient to men: women's associations, sewing bees and bazaar work became part of what supported men in their work or in their organizations. In the beginning it was as if men and women had their different and appointed places in society, and supported different activities needed by everyone. However, both the male norm and the subservience of women were questioned, albeit indirectly when women demanded membership in male organizations or created their own. The work of women's organizations gradually bore fruit: the organizations became a nursery for political activity and an important element in the general welfare policy.[58]

Joan W. Scott has pointed out that paradoxically when women organized, they did so as a special category—women.[59] And it was made clear that they were different from men in all respects, despite their political and union efforts. When Swedish women became more visible as subjects it is obvious that the organized men were provoked. For male mine workers manliness was built upon their prerogative as men and as political subjects, both in the mine and in the union, and women's activism posed a special challenge to their privileged position.

NOTES

1. Yvonne Hirdman, "Genussystemet," in *Maktutredningen, SOU 1990:44*, ed. Olof Petterson (Stockholm: Carlsson, 1990), 74. Yvonne Hirdman, "Om genuskontrakt." *Häften för Kritiska Studier* 2 (2000): 28–39.

2. Joan Scott, *Gender and the Politics of History* (New York & Oxford: Columbia University Press, 1988), 28–31; Lena Sommestad, *Från mejerska till mejerist. En studie av mejeriyrkets maskuliniseringsprocess* (Lund: Arkiv förlag, 1992), 22; Lena Sommestad, "Genuskontrakt och försörjning. Gemensam problemlösning på ojämlika villkor." *Häften för Kritiska Studier* 2 (2000): 45–48;Gro Hagemann, *Kjønn og industrialisering* (Oslo: Universitetsforlaget, 1994), 330; Renée Frangeur, *Yrkeskvinna eller makens tjänarinna? Striden om yrkesrätten för gifta kvinnor i mellankrigstidens Sverige* (Lund: Arkiv förlag, 1998); Yvonne Hirdman, "Om genuskontrakt," *Häften för Kritiska Studier* 2 (2000): 28–39; Eva Blomberg & Inger Humlesjö, "Inledning," in *Häften för Kritiska Studier* 2 (2000): 2–3; Gro Hagemann & Klas Åmark, "Från 'husmorskontrakt' till 'jämställdhetskontrakt'." "Yvonne Hirdmans genusteori." in *Häften för Kritiska Studier* 2 (2000): 4–27; Maria Sjöberg, "Från husbondekontrakt till jämställdhetskontrakt?" in *Häften för Kritiska Studier 2 (2000)*: 39–44; Kjell Östberg, "Kvinnlig klass och manligt kön?" *Häften för Kritiska Studier* 2 (2000): 49–52.

3. This article is based on my PhD thesis, *Män i mörker. Arbetsgivare, reformister och syndikalister. Politik och identitet i svensk gruvindustri 1910–1940* (Stockholm: Almqvist & Wiksell International, 1995) [Men in Darkness. Employers, Reformists and Revolutionary Syndicalists. Politics and Identity in the Swedish Mining Industry 1910–1940].

4. Artur Attman, *Svenskt järn och stål 1800–1914* (Stockholm: Jernkontorets Bergshistoriska skriftserie, 1986), 151; Nils Meinander, *Gränges. En krönika om svensk järnmalm* (Stockholm: Grängesbergsbolaget, 1968), 22.

5. Jan-Erik Pettersen, *Från kris till kris. Den svenska stålindustrins omvandling under 1920–och 1970–talen* (Stockholm: Handelahogskolan, 1988), 66; Jan Glete, *Ägande och industriell omvandling. Ägargrupper, skogsindustri, verkstadsindustri 1850–1950* (Stockholm: SNS, 1987), 124.

6. Angela V. John, *By the Sweat of Their Brow. Women Workers at Victorian Coal Mines* (London: Croom Helm, 1980) passim; Michael Lewis, *Rioters and Citizens. Mass Protest in Imperial Japan* (Berkeley:University of California, 1990) chapter 5.

7. Henrik Henriksson, Kvinnor i gruvarbete. Exemplet Dalkarlsbergs gruvfält 1814–1860, Historia FSK 21–40 Högskolan i Örebro, Institutionen för humaniora, 1992, 16–22; Bertil Boëthius, *Gruvorna, hyttorna och hamrarnas folk* (Stockholm: Tidens forlag, 1951).

8. Henrik P. Henriksson, Kvinnor i gruvarbete. Exemplet Dalkarlsbergs gruvfält 1814–1860, Historia FSK 21–40, Högskolan i Örebro, Institutionen för humaniora, 1992, 19, 29, 35.

9. Anders Florén, *Genus och producentroll. Kvinnoarbete inom svensk bergshantering, exemplet Jäders bruk 1640–1840* (Uppsala: Opuscula Historica Upsaliensia 7, 1991) 102.

10. Anders Florén, *Genus och producentroll. Kvinnoarbete inom svensk bergshantering, exemplet Jäders bruk 1640–1840* (Uppsala:Opuscula Historica Upsaliensia, 1991) 23; Kerstin Berglund, Kvinnor i gruvhantering åren 1870–1913, 60. Historiska institutionen, Stockholms universitet, fall 1983; Henrik P. Henriksson, Kvinnor i gruvarbete. Exemplet Dalkarlsbergs gruvfält 1814–1860, Historia FSK 21–40; Högskolan i Örebro, Institutionen för humaniora, 1992.

11. See Joan B. Landes "Republiken förkroppsligande," in *Häften för Kritiska Studier* 2/1991: 39; Christina Carlsson, *Kvinnosyn och kvinnopolitik. En studie av svensk socialdemokrati 1880–1910* (Lund: Arkiv forlag, 1986) 77; Ulla Wikander "Kvinnorna i den tidiga industrialiseringen," in *Kvinnohistoria. Om kvinnors villkor från antiken till våra dagar* (Stockholm: Utbildningsradion, 1992) 131; Ulla Wikander, "Delat arbete, delad makt: om kvinnors underordning i och genom arbetet." En historisk essä, in *Kontrakt i kris. Om kvinnors plats i välfärdsstaten*, ed., G. Åström, Gertrud & Y. Hirdman (Stockholm: Carlsson, 1992) 25.

12. Ulla, Wikander, *Kvinnoarbete i Europa 1789–1950. Genus, makt och arbetsdelning* (Stockholm: Atlas Akademi, 1999) 29–39.

13. Henrik P. Henriksson, Kvinnor i gruvarbete. Exemplet Dalkarlsbergs gruvfält 1814–1860, Historia FSK 21–40, Högskolan i Örebro, Institutionen för humaniora, 1992, 17–39. Quotation from page 20.

14. L. Karlsson and U. Wikander, "Om teknik, arbetsdelning och ideologi som formare av kvinnors—och mäns—arbetsvillkor." in *Historisk Tidskrift* 1/1987: 59.

15. W. Petersson, J. Leffler, and A. Johansson, eds., *De tekniska vetenskaperna*. Avdelning Bergsvetenskap. Band I Gruvvetenskap (Stockholm: Gruvventenskap, 1931) 525; *Statens Offentliga Statistik, Bergshantering* 1910–1950.

16. Stripa Grufvebolag [Stripa Mining Company], Board meeting 16/12–17.

17. Joan Scott, *Only Paradoxes to Offer. French Feminists and the Rights of Man* (Cambridge: Harvard University Press, 1996); Joan Scott, "Kvinnor har bara paradoxer att erbjuda: fransk feminism 1789–1945," in *Häften för Kritiska Studier* 4/1993.

18. Interview with Karl Nilsson, a miner of Stripa Mining Company.

19. Interview with Hilding Hagberg, a miner of LKAB Mining Company.
20. John Gaventa, "Makt och deltagande," in *Maktbegreppet*, ed., Olof Petterson (Stockholm: Carlsson, 1987), 31.
21. See Bo Stråth, *Varvsarbetare i två varvsstäder. En historisk studie av verkstadsklubbarna vid varven i Göteborg och Malmö* (Göteborg: Svenska varv, 1982) Tommy Svensson, *Från ackord till månadslön. En studie av lönepolitiken, fackföreningarna och rationaliseringarna inom svensk varvsindustri under 1900–talet* (Göteborg: Svenska varv, 1983).
22. Mellansvenska Gruvförbundet (the Central Swedish Mining Council), Envelope 38 Sabotage, correspondence AB Mellansvenska Malmfälten (Central Swedish Orefield, a mining company) Minutes of board meeting 25/2–20.
23. Bergverksaktiebolaget Vulcanus [Vulcanus Mining Company], Minutes of board meeting 19/6–13, LKAB, Vol. Sociala förhållanden [Social Conditions], Grufaktiebolaget Dalarne [Dalarna Mining Company], Minutes of board meeting 2/10–16.
24. Mellansvenska Gruvförbundet [the Central Swedish Mining Council], Minutes of negotiations 8–9/11–32, appendix B. See also Mellansvenska Gruvförbundet, Envelope 65. Price lists and agreements, price list between Mellansvenska Gruvförbundet and Svenska Gruvindustriarbetareförbundet [the Swedish Miners' Union] dept. 44 Dannemora 6/11–23.
25. This came out very clearly in the interviews, where the men did not regard the women as mineworkers.
26. Johansson, *Arbetarrörelsen och taylorismen: Olofström 1895–1925. En studie av verkstadsindustrin och arbetets organisering* (Lund: Arkiv, 1990), 43.
27. Mellansvenska Gruvförbundet [the Central Swedish Mining Council], circular 21/12–39.
28. Alice Kessler-Harris, *A Women's Wage. Historical Meaning and Social Consequences* (Lexington: University Press of Kentucky, 1990), 7.
29. John Gaventa, "Makt och deltagande," in *Maktbegreppet*, ed., Olof Petterson (Stockholm: Carlsson, 1987), 39.
30. K. Hägg, *Kvinnor och män i Kiruna. Om kön och vardag i förändring i ett modernt gruvsamhälle 1900–1990* (Umea: Umeå universitet, 1993), 44.
31. LKAB, Vol. 88 Personalförhållanden [Staff Conditions] II. Statistics.
32. LKAB, Vol. 88 Personalförhållanden [Staff Conditions] II. Statistics, Number of workers employed each year from 1921 onward, divided up according to date of birth and civil status, Kiruna 18/6–29.
33. K. Hägg, *Kvinnor och män i Kiruna. Om kön och vardag i förändring i ett modernt gruvsamhälle 1900–1990* (Umea: Umeå universitet, 1993), 55.
34. K. Hägg, *Kvinnor och män i Kiruna. Om kön och vardag i förändring i ett modernt gruvsamhälle 1900–1990* (Umea: Umeå universitet, 1993), 50–59.
35. Max Weber, *Kapitalismens uppkomst* (Stockholm: Ratio, 1986).
36. *LKAB*, Vol. 88 Personalförhållanden [Staff Conditions] II, Statistics. Information on widows living in company houses and widows living in the community, widowed 1921–1927.
37. Sten Rydberg, *Dalarnas industrihistoria 1800–1980.*(*Några huvudlinjer*, 1992: 147).
38. TGO [The Mining Company in Grängesberg], Minutes of board meeting 27/9–13.
39. Sten Rydberg, *Dalarnas industrihistoria 1800–1980.* (*Några huvudlinjer*, 1992: 169).

40. Stripa Grufvebolag [Stripa Mining Company], Annual reports 1911–1925; Interview with Harald Jansson, no. 134, in Lindesbergs Historical Archive; Interview with Karl Nilsson.
41. Persbergs Grufveaktiebolag [Persberg Mining Company], Minutes of board meeting 3/6–14, 5/6–23, 12/6–34.
42. Interview with Karl Nilsson.
43. Interview with Karl Nilsson, Göte Andersson, and Harald Jansson, all miners, interviews no. 134, 100 in Lindesbergs Historical Archive.
44. Stripa Grufvebolag [Stripa Mining Company], Minutes of board meeting 1919.
45. Persbergs Grufveaktiebolag [Persberg Mining Company], Minutes of board meeting 20/12–28, 27/12–29, 22/12–30. 3/3–31; Eva Blomberg, *Samhällets fiender. Stripakonflikten 1925–1927* (Stockholm: Federativs förlag, 1993), 63.
46. Interview with Karl Nilsson and Göte Andersson.
47. Stripa Grufvebolag [Stripa Mining Company], Minutes of board meeting 30/11–15; Interview with Karl Nilsson and Harald Jansson, no. 134 in Lindesbergs Historical Archive; Persbergs Grufveaktiebolag [Persberg Mining Company], Minutes of board meeting 5/10–16.
48. Interview with Karl Nilsson.
49. Hägg, *Kvinnor och, Ett och annat från Pershyttan. Några glimtar från Pershyttans hembygdscirkel* (Nora 1983), 26.
50. G. Björk, *Att förhandla sitt medborgarskap. Kvinnor som kollektiva politiska aktörer i Örebro 1900–1950* (Lund: Arkiv förlag, 1999); Kjell Östberg, *Efter rösträtten. Kvinnors utrymme efter det demokratiska genombrottet* (Stockholm/Stehag: Brutus Östlings bokförlag, 1997).
51. Grängesberg LS [the local Revolutionary Syndicalist Organization], Minutes of board meeting 29/8–20.
52. Grängesberg LS, Minutes of board meeting 10 or 16/2–24, 9/3–24, 11/5–24, 12/10–24, 25/10–24, 9/11–24, 14/12–24, 22/9–25.
53. Pershyttans LS [the local Revolutionary Syndicalist Organization], Minutes of board meeting 7/6–36, 1/11–36.
54. Y. Hirdman, "Genussystemet," in *Maktutredningen, SOU 1990: 44,* ed. Olof Petterson (Stockholm:Carlsson, 1990), 79.
55. John Gaventa, "Makt och deltagande," in *Maktbegreppet,* ed. Olof Petterson (Stockholm: Carlsson, 1987).
56. K. Hägg, *Kvinnor och,* 99.
57. G. Björk, *Att förhandla sitt medborgarskap. Kvinnor som kollektiva politiska aktörer i Örebro 1900–1950* (Lund: Arkiv förlag, 1999); K. Östberg, *Efter rösträtten. Kvinnors utrymme efter det demokratiska genombrottet* (Stockholm/Stehag: Brutus Östlings bokförlag, 1997) Karin Nordberg, "De skötsamma fruarna i Holmsund," in *Häften för Kritiska Studier* 2/1990.
58. K. Nordberg, "De skötsamma fruarna i Holmsund," in *Häften för Kritiska Studier* 2/1990; Gunnela Björk, *Att förhandla sitt medborgarskap. Kvinnor som kollektiva politiska aktörer i Örebro 1900–1950* (Lund: Arkiv förlag, 1999); R. Frangeur, *Yrkeskvinna eller makens tjänarinna? Striden om yrkesrätten för gifta kvinnor i mellankrigstidens Sverige* (Lund: Arkiv förlag, 1998).
59. See Scott 1996 and 1993.

CHAPTER 7

Invisible Labor: A Comparative Oral History of Women in Coal Mining Communities of Hokkaido, Japan, and Montana, USA, 1890–1940

Kayoko Yoshida and Reiko Miyauchi

This essay presents a comparison of working-class women in two coal mining communities of Hokkaido, Japan, and Montana, USA. These two seemingly different areas have actually been linked through similar frontier development policies and patterns since the late nineteenth century. When the government of Japan looked to develop agricultural and mineral resources in its northern frontier of Hokkaido after the Meiji Restoration in 1867, it introduced many of the same policies employed by the United States in developing its vast western lands, including forced removal and assimilation of the indigenous inhabitants. Japanese officials deepened the connection to the American West by inviting American development specialists to advise them on how to integrate the region as a vital part of the new modern nation. The development of resources and the formation of resource-based communities happened in similar ways in both Hokkaido and Montana.

There are only a few works that examine the labor and social history of women who lived in the mining communities of Hokkaido during the late nineteenth and early twentieth centuries.[1] Moreover, there has been no substantive research comparing women's experiences in mining communities on both sides of the Pacific. In this study, we attempt to close this historical gap by focusing on the women who lived in the booming coal towns of Red Lodge, Montana, and Yubari, Hokkaido. Because these women did not leave much written documentation about their lives, we have relied on oral history interviews with women who worked and lived in these mining centers.

Mine workers in Hokkaido—both men and women—were tied to the fate of the company they worked for, under the motto of *Ichizan Ikka*

(One mine, One family). When they began in the 1890s, coal operations were often under *zaibatsu* (a handful of giant corporations) control. Mining companies, part of a *zaibatsu*, were heavily subsidized by the national government in the name of achieving national industrialization goals. It was a unique corporate world, where people totally depended upon the company and lived like one family with a strong sense of solidarity to one another and to their employer. Geographical isolation helped strengthen the sense of extended quasi-family bonds. Additionally, patterns of work, that is, around-the-clock operations with three eight-hour shifts daily, often cut off contact with the outside world and contributed to building a sentiment of the whole community as one extended industrial family, which was especially apparent when mine accidents happened.

If *Ichizan Ikka* was the ultimate form of Japanese company paternalism, patriarchy at home greatly affected women's lives in the mining town, as was true everywhere in Japan before World War II. Fathers had a great amount of power as *kacho* (head of the household) over family members, whereas a woman's role was to serve the family. Women were, by law, placed in a subordinate position in society with little say in family matters, limited rights of inheritance, and few choices available in charting their own course of life.[2] Thus, under the "dual lock" of paternalism and patriarchy, some hard-working women nonetheless engaged in the perilous work in pitch-dark underground mines to help support their families. They received little acknowledgment or credit from the strongly male-dominated Japanese society, which until recently rendered their labor invisible. In these remote mining communities, women's lives could not escape thick layers of economic and social constraints.

Coal mining in the American West began contemporaneously in the late 1880s, but there, women rarely worked in the underground mines. How, then, did women live and work in those isolated mining communities? Did they share the same goals and domestic lives with their Japanese counterparts? In order to explore these questions, we chose to study Finnish-American women in the mining town of Red Lodge, Montana. There were several factors contributing to this decision. Montana shared a similar development history with Hokkaido, and it had the largest coal reserve of 120 billion tons in the United States. There was a notable concentration of Finnish immigrants in Red Lodge, when the coal mining company began its operation in 1887, one year earlier than the opening of the Yubari coal mines. By 1910, Red Lodge had become the coal kingdom of Montana, and Finnish immigrants and their children constituted over one third of the town's population. They lived in their own ethnic enclave and preserved much of their social and cultural heritage, including language, foodways, the sauna ritual, and music. Immigrant women with little command over English inevitably had to work at unskilled jobs and labored as laundresses, domestics, and boarding-house workers.[3] Just like Japanese women in Yubari, the labor of these working-class women remained largely invisible and unacknowledged in regional histories of mining.

Geographical isolation and the vulnerability of one-industry mining towns, which bound together the women who lived there, presented women in the Japanese North and in the American West with similar challenges. Frontier life in Hokkaido and Montana imposed harsh conditions upon migrants and immigrants new to the area, challenging survival skills and traditional cultural practices. The burdens and opportunities of mining community life contributed to the necessary fierce independence of women in both regions. But despite characterizations of both places as "frontier," industrial residents tried to create the informal and formal community institutions and practices that fostered a collective sense of solidarity amid the dangers and vagaries of the mining economy. It is our objective, therefore, to explore work, family life, and leisure activities of women in Yubari and Red Lodge through oral history records, highlighting how different socioeconomic as well as cultural constraints affected gender relations in these early-twentieth-century communities of the Pacific Rim.

Yubari Coal Development and Women Miners

In 1888, American geologist Benjamin Smith Lyman discovered a large coal deposit in Yubari, located in the Ishikari Coal Field in Hokkaido. After 1889, when the first mine opened in Yubari, new mines rapidly opened one after another. Like Red Lodge, which attracted many immigrants, mining opportunities in Yubari pulled migrants from all over Japan, especially poorer farm families from Tohoku, the northern part of Honshu. In its heyday, twenty-four coal mines operated, and the population peaked at 110,000 in 1959. In the 1960s Yubari's coal industry gradually declined, and in 1990 the last mine in town closed.

It is not widely known that many women worked as miners in these coal mines from the 1910s through the 1930s. Initially, *tsuchi-kumi* (a work group based on family labor) was the work unit of coal mining. The father or husband ordered women to work underground in order to make up the absence of another family member who was part of the *kumi*. Japanese society was still under a feudal and discriminatory old family system, called *ie*, and if the order came from the head of the household, women were usually not allowed to refuse that order. They started working underground, not necessarily voluntarily, in order to supplement the family income.

By the late nineteenth century, there was a universal ban on women working in the mines among industrialized nations in Europe, but Japanese women performed strenuous physical labor under ghastly working conditions.[4] Since they had started working to fill in for absent family members, they had not been considered as miners or counted as such in official statistics until 1916. In that year, 2,382 women were recorded as miners in Hokkaido for the first time. The number increased during World War I, and in 1920, 5,127 women worked in Hokkaido coal mines, including the Yubari mines, when Yubari coal supported the booming Japanese economy after

Figure 7.1 Natsuyo Kanno (80 at the time of photo), one of the underground miners interviewed. Photographer: Reiko Miyauchi; reproduced by permission of Noriko Riyauchi

World War I.[5] It was a time when "women miners worked side by side with men. It was not a rare sight to see teenage girls work everywhere inside the mine," according to a record of the Yubari Municipal History.[6]

Natsuyo Kanno (figure 7.1) started working underground in 1921 when she was thirteen years old, right after finishing elementary school.[7] She worked as an *atoyama* (a miner who collected coal with a shovel and put it in the coal-box to transport it out of the pit) for six years. She described her difficult work in the underground mine:

> Oh, it was so dark. I couldn't think of any place darker than that. It was the bottom of this world. We didn't get to see the sunlight, of course. Only a narrow space where a safety lamp reached was vaguely light. It was hot and humid and a thin underwear would just do right. There was no ventilation and you felt you were closed in. The smell of the coal and the smell of rotten timber in the tunnel filled your nostrils. In a closed space, I was always scared, wondering if the ceiling would fall on me. When the powder was set, I lay on the ground. The blasting sound would shake the whole pit. In the coal dust, I shoveled the coal, which *sakiyama* (head miner) extracted, and put it in a coal-box. I carried the coal-box up to the cart. The box with full of coal weighed more than 90 pounds. Through the narrow and low tunnel, I had to pull the box with my knees, or carried it on my shoulders, or pulled it with a rope and pulled with both hands and legs. The skin on my back was always peeling and sharp edges of coal always hurt my skin. When the box was full, I pushed the cart with my wooden name tag on through the tunnel up to the ground. Sometimes the cart could not make the curb and fell over the side of the track. While collecting the coal and putting it back in the box, you blocked other people and they always yelled at me.

Inside the pitch-dark pit, special relationships often formed between men and women. A skillful *sakiyama* miner often recruited a capable woman *atoyama* and she sometimes served as "wife in the pit." However, the relationship was strictly contained inside the pit and "wife in the pit" had nothing to do with a male miner's real wife outside the mines. Other women resisted men's advances. Natsuyo recalled her experience with men in the pit: "When you were working among men, you just could not afford to look too friendly. In the dark pit, you may get seduced by men, who would approach you and say, 'I'll give you an extra scoop of coal in the box.' They thought you would be tempted because you could get out of the darkness sooner that way. I wasn't fooled by these men."

Yasu Nakayama worked underground for three years from 1919 until she had her first child. Her husband talked her into going underground as *atoyama*. Her husband put her to work in a different *kumi* from his, insisting that if the wife works with the husband, she tends to be too spoiled and dependent on him. He was not a considerate type and he teamed up with another woman. He was often absent from work, while sending Yasu to work. Life was never easy. Yet she reflected on the pride she and other women felt by achieving respect and good wages as a miner.

We worked and made money. It was a competition. Women who were good miners were called the "goddesses of the pit." They were well respected by both men and women. They served as leaders and took good care of other women working in the mines. When I was working, there were women who even worked as *sakiyama*, and there was one woman, *sakiyama no Osaku* (Osaku the head miner) who was looked up to as a real super woman. Women worked everywhere in the mines and competed against men. It was such a booming time.

Besides these *atoyama* miners, women worked as *toban* (door-keepers) who were at the door to the pit and were in charge of the ventilation, *senpuuki* (fanners) who pumped the ventilator, and *zatsueki* (lunch and tool carriers) in the mines, and as coal sorters, safety lamp maintenance workers, and telephone operators outside the mines. *Sentanfu* (coal sorters) became women's major field of work in the mining communities. However, after the 1950s the coal sorting process became largely mechanized, and large-scale machines replaced most of manual female *sentanfu* work.

The most peculiar work practice at Yubari mines was that of the twenty-four-hour work shift. The work hours were extended when the economy was booming and were cut short at the time of recession. Hours were determined according to the convenience of the company. When demand for coal increased, the company announced an "extra-mining day" and on those days, miners were not able to leave the mines unless they extracted enough to meet the quota, often spending eighteen to twenty hours underground. Natsuyo recalled the grueling physical demands of a typical extra-mining day.

Women did not work in the third (night) shift, but whenever extra-mining day came around every two weeks, the second shift continued to work through the third, working for sixteen hours a day. In the evening, rice balls were provided to feed the miners, but nobody sat down to eat it. We competed fiercely to meet the quota and everybody was anxious to get out as soon as possible. It was very hard. I sometimes mixed clay and rotten timber with coal and put them all in the coal-box. I was jealous to see people who finished early and left the mine. When it was finally over, it was very painful to climb up out of the pit. Somebody grabbed the tale of a horse, and everybody went up hand in hand, pulled by the horse. We all rushed to the public bath to wash ourselves. By the time we got home, dawn was breaking. It was merciless labor.

Despite the fact that women worked in the same place for the same hours, the wage disparity between women and men never narrowed. Although they played an integral part at the workplace as coal-box carriers, transporting extracted coal outside of the mine, they were treated as if they were invisible. In 1926, men working as *sakiyama* made 2.78 yen per day, while female *atoyama* earned 1.67 yen, or 60 percent of their male counterparts. Nonetheless, women miners earned a lot more than their contemporaries in urban centers. For example, in the same year, a department store sales lady in Sapporo earned an average of 0.80 yen.[8] It is clear that working in the mines was economically more rewarding than most of the jobs available for women, even if more physically demanding. Some women like Natsuyo voluntarily started mining for that very reason.

From the mid-1920s, modern machines began to replace the old pick and shovel down in the pit, and mechanization eventually eliminated women's work underground. Skills with tools and traditional mining methods eventually became obsolete. Large-scale operations involving more than a dozen workers had replaced family mining. The company had total control over labor management and work plans inside the mines. Miners were no longer considered skilled wage labor, but became salaried workers.

Pressure to ban women's underground work also mounted. In 1933, women's underground work was officially prohibited in the Yubari mines. Prior to this official ban on women working inside the mines, a series of protective regulations had existed. The protective regulations of 1916 delineated the right to maternal leave, limited working hours at night for women, and excluded women from some physical labor such as managing explosives and lumber work.[9]

During World War II, women temporarily returned to work inside the mines because of the male labor shortage and growing demand for coal. Two hundred women worked underground in the Yubari mines for three years beginning in 1943, under an exception to the 1933 law banning women's underground work. The era of women miners formally came to an end during the postwar occupation of Japan.

FAMILY LIFE AND GENDER RELATIONS IN THE COAL TOWN

Many women worked inside or outside of the mine to supplement family incomes, but they also faced a "double day" at home, responsible for household duties and caring for children and husbands. Many other women had few alternatives to remain in the household to work full-time caring for families. Birthrates were high, and many women cared for seven to eight children in crowded houses as well as feed husbands on erratic mining shift schedules.[10] In these private spaces miners' wives carved out some social autonomy as well as contributed to the efficient economic functioning of the mining community.

Recognizing their essential labor in homes and in the mines, women expected some reciprocity from the coal company. The company dominated life in a mining town, and families depended on it to provide for many basic needs. Min Abe recalled that as a housewife in Yubari company provisions alleviated many worries that working-class women in other places had to endure:

> A coal-mining town was a place you could live without any cash. That's why they said it's a good place to live. Our company housing was nothing but a shack, but the rent was almost nothing. We had electricity much earlier than the rest of Hokkaido and it was cheap, too. Water was free from the communal tap

water. You took the pay card with you to the company general store and you could buy anything in the store, up to 70 percent of the salary with credit.

These amenities, however, were minimal, and poorly built housing offered little privacy for individual families. Miners and their families all lived in the company housing. Although Yubari is a cold and snowy area, the plywood houses were not insulated. One long harmonica-shaped building accommodated twenty-four households. Each apartment consisted of a living room, a bedroom, and a small kitchen. Without insulation, sounds carried straight through the neighbors' walls. Opening the entrance door exposed the entire interior of the house, providing little privacy for residents.[11] In fact, in the coal town, every place where you wanted privacy was shared and public: water, bath, and toilet. The physical layout of the housing naturally brought people closer and increased the sense of belonging to *Ichizan Ikka*. It fostered strong solidarity, and at the same time created a closed community atmosphere.

The mining company expression, "injury and lunch are their own responsibilities," revealed how central women were to the enterprise and to what extent they bore the burden for crippling accidents that could threaten family survival. Lunch preparation was a serious part of women's work, since a miner could not come out of the mine once he was down there and depended on adequate nourishment to labor successfully. Housewives had to cater to their husbands' needs and cope with irregular hours. They had to prepare meals or pack lunches for their husbands who would leave early in the morning, in the afternoon, or late at night. Mining was dangerous work, and company compensation was never enough. Min revealed the sentiment of a miner's wife: "You never know when the news of an accident comes. I will be sorry if I am not home when the news arrives." Irregularity and anxiety tied housewives to their homes. Essentially wives worked around-the-clock for the company as their husbands' work partners.

Amid busy daily chores, women found time for one pastime. They gathered in a house where the husband went to work on the day shift, and enjoyed *ochanomi* (having tea together) (see figure 7.2). After finishing lunch at home, they brought tea, sweets, and pickles and spent the afternoons chatting about all sorts of matters until it was time to prepare supper. Sometimes such gatherings became a place to teach sewing and embroidery. The custom of *ochanomi* started when women wanted to leave their husbands sleeping quietly after a night shift. Because of the cramped space in the house, women had to leave and go somewhere in the neighborhood to kill time. Eventually, however, *ochanomi* became an excellent support system, where necessary information and help were often provided for women in need in the community. *Ochanomi* served as an instrument to build women's networks and solidarity within the limited scope of housekeeping and childrearing responsibilities. At the end of World War II, women built on this practice to fully organize themselves into a formal mutual aid system when the mine workers finally unionized.[12] The tightness of the community environment both in

Figure 7.2 Women socializing over *ochanomi*—tea drinking—in one of the miner's row houses. Photographer: Reiko Miyauchi; reproduced by permission of Noriko Riyauchi

terms of physical layout and the abundant spirit of good neighborliness aided women's efforts to support union organization, which they believed helped enforce company responsibilities to families and community.

LIFE IN FINN TOWN: FATHERS WORK IN THE MINES, MOTHERS WORK AT HOME

In 1887, the Rocky Fork Coal Company began mining coal deposits at the foot of the Beartooth Mountains on the east bench of the Red Lodge valley, feeding ongoing railroad construction and the silver and copper smelters in the region. Immigrant miners—Finns, Italians, Serbs, and Austrians—quickly moved in, seeking new economic opportunities. By 1890, the population of Red Lodge was over 1,000 and that number climbed to 5,000 by 1911, when Carbon County had become the largest coal producing county in Montana. Almost half of all miners were Finnish immigrants, and 87 percent of the Finnish males worked in the mines, revealing how committed to mining this immigrant group was. The lives of most Finnish immigrants and their families depended on Rocky Fork coal production.[13]

The Finns in Red Lodge were committed to work and community: they built institutions familiar in other Finnish American communities, including boarding houses, saunas, and cooperatives. Until the mines closed in the 1930s, they had built around these institutions their own ethnic enclave, called Finn Town, and developed their rich social and cultural heritage. Here,

Sigrid and Clara Timonen, Taimi Peltola, and Leona Lampi were born and spent their childhoods in the 1910s through the 1930s.[14] Maria Timonen, mother of Sigrid Timonen and Clara Timonen Jarvi, came to Red Lodge from Finland in 1904 with her daughter Tyyne. Maria joined her husband Isaac, who had obtained work in the Red Lodge coal mine one year earlier. Sigrid was born as the seventh child in 1912 and Clara was born in 1918 as the fourteenth and the last child of the family. Both of them still live in Red Lodge.

Isaac Timonen worked for the Northwest Improvement Company (NWIC), the former Rocky Fork Coal Company that was taken over and renamed by the Northern Pacific Railroad in 1900, and then for the new Westside Mine when it opened in 1907. Mining work was a family affair. The company designed shifts with the male family breadwinner in mind, putting single men on night shift, and wife and children prepared lunch buckets and retrieved the weekly paycheck. Both Sigrid and Clara agreed that their parents considered work in the mines as simply a source of income. "Mom said to Dad '*Terve*' everyday when he left for work. It simply means—have a good day." Sigrid recalled her work roles as a child and her observations of her father's work:

> In 1918, Dad worked eight hours a day and was paid eight dollars a day. I remember he got this much because I was sent to the Main Office to get Dad's weekly pay check when I was six. . . . There was a night shift in the mine, but dad only worked during the day. Single men who lived in boarding houses worked the night shift. Dad worked eight hours a day, five days a week. He left home in the morning with a lunch pail. The lunch pail had water at the bottom and a sandwich, biscuits, always biscuits, and a piece of fruit on top. I always opened it to check for leftovers when he came home from work. I don't remember that he said anything about the work as a miner. He did not talk about it. It was work, you know. He worked at the mines until the mines closed in 1933. He was about fifty-one or fifty-two when he quit. Not many Finns in Finland work until that age.

Although excluded from mining, Red Lodge women maintained families through demanding routines and contributed to family incomes through various home-based enterprises. Maria Timonen cared for fourteen children and also kept cows to help feed the family and to earn extra income by selling milk. She rose at six each morning to milk the cows and dedicate herself to various chores, such as washing and ironing, depending on the day of the week. The single industry community that limited income opportunities for women also presented special industrial challenges. When Timonen did the wash, she always had to watch which way the wind was blowing so that the clothes did not get dirty from the smoke and soot from the mine. Despite her busy schedule and demanding family, Maria still found time to have coffee in mid-morning and socialize with neighbors. If tea-drinking was often the only leisure activity for women in Yubari, women in Red Lodge also found time to get together over coffee. Sigrid and Clara remembered that "the door was always open and the coffee pot was on at any time of day." In her daughters' memory, "Mom was always gracious and jolly."

Lillian Mattson met John Lampi at her family farm in British Columbia while he was there as a director of dramatics. They married in Red Lodge in 1917, and Lillian gave birth to daughter Leona in 1924. John joined Bloom and Company, a grocery and dry goods enterprise that catered to Finnish miners and their families. Leona vividly recollected the community's gender division of labor that applied not only to her mother's routine of weekly work:

> Of course, there was a division of labor between Dad and Mom. He did work outside and she did all the housework. Like the men whose lives were regimented by their jobs, the women, who were homemakers, gave themselves strict schedules to follow in the household. Monday was washday. Tuesday was ironing day. Wednesday was something else day. Thursday was baking day. Friday was the day that everybody went around and had coffee with everybody. Saturday was cleaning day. Everybody did the same thing. Everybody competed to get their sheets on the lines faster than anybody else on the block on Monday. There were undoubtedly some Finnish housewives who were not what we consider a stereotype Finnish housewife, who was ultra, ultra-clean and follows everything perfectly. But almost everybody I remember followed that routine.

Interviews with Red Lodge women reveal that although domestic and work roles were sex-segregated, and fathers had ultimate authority, Finnish women and men approached marriage as a partnership. In having some say in family matters, life for Finnish women in Red Lodge seemed to differ from the women in Yubari, even if miners' wives in both communities labored under similar domestic and industrial demands. Sigrid and Clara Timonen commented on how decisions were made in their family: "Dad made all the decisions but it was a democratic house. Dad always told Mom and older children about important matters. And we talked about it openly."

WOMEN AS COMMUNITY BUILDERS

One of the striking differences of Red Lodge households from their Yubari counterparts was the distinctive use of private and public spaces. Yubari miners spent their time at home mostly drinking *sake* (rice wine) as soon as the shift work was over. As long as father was home, it meant he was drinking, even in the early hours of the morning. Irregularity of working hours and the fact that husbands spent much of their free time drinking at home left little time for wives to have any public life. On the contrary, Red Lodge Finns, at least the married men, kept regular working hours with weekends off, and family life was not disturbed by the odd hours of the work shift. When men took to drinking, it was often in the public spaces outside the home, in one of the many saloons in town. Although women might worry about husbands drinking away their paycheck, they retained some control over use of space in the home.

Finnish miners did not earn stable work hours without organizing themselves. By 1899, the United Mine Workers of America had a union local in Red Lodge. In 1903, miners earned five legal holidays and a forty-eight-hours-a-week work contract with management. Therefore, by the time Isaac Timonen was settled and worked for NWIC, workers had already earned the right to forty-eight hours (or less) a week. However, in the early twentieth century, miners in Red Lodge had no workers' compensation available in case of accidents. The Finnish Temperance Society extended assistance to its members in the event of an illness or an accident.[15] Even after the Workmen's Compensation Act became effective in 1915 and after the company provided limited health care to miners and their families, the Temperance Society's illness and accident insurance program was taken over by the Finnish Illness and Accident Assurance Company. The association functioned into the early 1930s when the last mine in town closed.[16]

Unlike Japanese women in Yubari, Finnish women in Red Lodge actively engaged themselves in ethnic fraternal, religious, and cultural organizations such as the Temperance Society, Lutheran Church, and the Finnish Workers Hall. They were ardent community builders, developing or joining the Temperance Hall Girls' Choir, church choirs, music bands, and athletic clubs. They organized and performed plays at the Workers Hall. They organized and executed children's programs.

Both Lillian and John Lampi were active in directing and acting in performances at the Finnish Workers Hall, the heart of cultural activities in Finn Town.[17] Lillian Lampi remembered her involvement in the hall in a 1982 interview:

> The acting part seemed to be the main center of our work. Once a month we would put on a big play, three- and four-act plays, and every second week we would put on the two-act plays. . . . and then we had quite a few visits from [companies from] other towns like Butte.[18] Plays and our programs always contained ordinarily the chorus group. We always had three-four songs prepared for them and then the children's programs. We had Sunday schools, you know. We taught the children. The children's program, we gave them one evening and it was performed at the Workers Hall. Every evening we were busy. After work, we'd always go to the Hall. No wonder Leona was always left alone.

Leona was the only child in the family, and so Lillian had more freedom to spend time in community activities. She worked as actress, costume mistress and makeup artist, and stage manager of the Finnish performances, which Finns in Red Lodge came to enjoy on weekends at the Workers Hall. Leona recalled how her mother juggled parenting and performing: "Since my parents were involved in a lot of activities in the Workers Hall, many Saturday evenings were spent for practices. Ever since I was a baby, I was left home alone and Mother ran back between scenes to check on me. Our life was pretty much centered around the Workers Hall activities."

The Workers Hall provided space for Finnish women's public participation, but churches also competed for women's time and affiliations. Lillian

Lampi explained the three philosophical divisions among the town's Finnish residents:

> An awful lot of people who went to church wouldn't come to the Workers Hall. The Finnish church, the Lutheran church. See, they thought it was sinful to go. I mean when the Finnish were religious, they were really religious. . . . We never felt that . . . it was anything wrong to put on a play, because you were playing with the story. . . . Then we had two different groups of workers. We were with the American—although we weren't members of it—the IWW— the In[dustri]al Workers of the World. . . . Three different types of people in town. One that were churchgoers who didn't believe in any of this movement improving workingmen's conditions. And then the IWW's and the other one was—the United Mine Workers.

Maria Timonen had little time for leisure and cultural activities, but as a devout Christian, she devoted much of her limited free time to church functions. She always told her children that they were able to have daily meals by the Lord's blessing. She always attended the Suomi Synod, the most lay-centered and widespread Lutheran Church, established in Red Lodge in 1891. At dedication ceremonies in 1902, Reverend Erland Wikkuri outlined the role of the Finnish American Christian. He encouraged his parishioners to acquire American citizenship, proclaiming it their duty to lead a Christian life and provide an example for other immigrants to follow.[19] Maria closely followed his proclamation to be a good Christian and often went to Bible study classes. For her, religion was the basis of running a family.

Women who preferred the Workers Hall as the center of their social world found they could merge their domestic responsibilities with community-building activities. Lillian Lampi and other women organized children's programs at the hall to provide cultural education as well as childcare. For Taimi Peltola, born in 1917 and the eldest daughter of Kasper Peltola and Olga Nikula, the fondest memory of her childhood was not from school or home but in her Workers Hall activities. She went there with her brother and sister almost every day after school to play and practice for performances held on weekends. All Finnish children around her were involved in the plays. Taimi recalled Christmas at the hall: "They had a big Christmas tree, Santa Claus would come and hand packages to the kids. They got candy and I remember I got a doll. My sister got a dress. She would have loved that doll. We had so much fun."

Because children were included in Workers Hall activities, women could participate in the shaping of their ethnic community. Finns in Red Lodge routinely brought children to weekend activities—Saturday night dances, performances both musical and dramatic, weddings and funerals. Although the hall itself was a contested place between the middle-of-the-road socialist camp and the more radical IWW supporters, it did not matter for the children like Taimi, who spent many happy childhood days right in the hall. Finnish women always included their children in their social activities, and children were embraced warmly in their ethnic enclave. Until the 1930s when the last mine closed, women played a pivotal role in cultural activities and entertainment in Finn Town, despite political divisions.

Conclusion: Comparing the Worlds of *Ryosai Kenbo* and *Oma Tupa, Oma Lupa*

The coal communities of Yubari and Red Lodge shared much: they were originally set up as company towns, located on isolated mountainsides with rich coal deposits, and they each became known as "the coal kingdom" from the 1910s through the 1930s. Migrants and immigrants came to the mines for economic opportunities and established homes and cultures of solidarity. Although women in the two communities shared similar survival strategies, particular industrial circumstances and political/cultural orientations shaped women's lives differently. Many Yubari women worked in the underground mines as subordinate labor. They were wage earners but they had little say about their working conditions as their work was often considered temporary and managed by husbands. Housewives planned their housework according to their husbands' around-the-clock work schedules. They built a well-functioning support system in the community, but it did not become a social or a political movement until after World War II. After all, miners and their families were totally controlled by the omnipresent company in every facet of their lives. Company housing and weekly entertainment may have been perceived as benefits, but they also curtailed the development of other public gathering spaces and associations. The combination of corporate paternalism and patriarchy oppressed not only women's but also men's spirit for independence and self-help and often conditioned them only to seek the pleasure of the moment.

The traditional Japanese family code taught women to pursue the ideal of *ryosai kenbo* (good wife and wise mother), who devotes herself to her husband and sons. Even in the remote coal town, women often sacrificed themselves to fulfill this ideal. By totally devoting themselves to serve their spouses, these women served the company and the nation as well. However, these women's stories tell us that even within such cultural constraints, they were able to gain some economic independence and pride through the work in the mines as men's equals and built strong mutual support through *ochanomi* in the neighborhood. While outside the chronological scope of this essay, these early networks invariably fostered the strong, militant union culture that emerged in mining communities after World War II. The National Miners' Wives Association, created in 1946, assisted miners and launched their own independent campaigns to address issues important to women.

The situation in Red Lodge at the outset of the community's formation was not that different from Yubari. However, the union and ethnic associations, instead of the company, eventually took over the community-building responsibilities. For many Finns, the spirit of self-help provided momentum to build their own closely knit community, just like their proverb goes—*Oma tupa, oma lupa*, your own cottage, your own independence.

Finnish men and women occupied separate economic worlds in Red Lodge. While men worked in and around the mines, many immigrant wives without English-language skills worked at home with occasional income-generating activities in their own ethnic neighborhood. Unlike Yubari women, however, they lead active public lives. Some were ardent churchgoers, and others developed cultural activities in the community. There were also women who were aware of the strong women's movement in Finland and organized clubs to promote the cause in Red Lodge.[20] Finnish socialist traditions and leanings lead many Red Lodge families to practice greater gender equity within families.

Oral interviews with women miners, wives, and daughters allowed us to discover how closely tied were the lives of mining community women across the Pacific. We began this project thinking that we would find many similarities in gender relations and practices, given the two communities' similar development histories, and even similar cultural practices, such as an obsession for domestic cleanliness and a strong group orientation. But our research suggests that Finnish immigrant women in Red Lodge used community-building opportunities to open up public spaces for creative, political, and spiritual as well as domestic roles. Yubari women, whether supporting families through working in underground mines, where they might obtain pride in working as men's equal, or in their domestic work, could not break out of the expected role as a good wife and good mother. Japanese paternalism and corporate and national hierarchies officially gave women little power, confined in their role as *ryosai kenbo*, but women nonetheless increased family economic sufficiency and developed social networks. Finnish women strode toward realizing their own *oma tupa, oma lupa* ideal in their adopted land in America by asserting greater autonomy through traditional ethnic associations.

NOTES

The authors would like to thank Debra Aoki, PhD, Professor, Hokusei Gakuen University Junior College, for her extensive advice and comments on the content of the paper. We also thank Robert Gettings and Marjorie Smith for their advice on earlier drafts.

1. Recent works in English regarding Japan's coal industry development and decline in Hokkaido clearly delineate the effects of mine closures on the community, but do not specifically detail the lives of women within the community. For example, see Suzanne Culter, *Managing Decline: Japan's Coal Industry; Restructuring and Community Response* (Honolulu:University of Hawaii Press, 1999).Works in Japanese regarding women's labor in the Hokkaido mining communities include Junko Yamamoto, *Labor Practices of Women Working in the Mines* (Sapporo: Hokkaido Labor Institute, 1961); Hokkaido Miners' Wives Association, *The Mines Know Everything* (Sapporo: Japan Miners' Wives Association Hokkaido Chapter, 1973); Sapporo Women's History Study Group, *History of Women in the North* (Sapporo: Hokkaido Shimbun Press, 1986).

2. Patriarchal power was clearly expressed in the Meiji Civil Code of 1898, which legally required that a wife must have her husband's consent before signing a legal contract. Additionally, in case of divorce the husband automatically took custody of the children, and the permission of the household head was necessary before women under twenty-five could legally marry.

3. Leona Lampi, *At the Foot of the Beartooth Mountains: A History of the Finnish Community of Red Lodge, Montana* (Coeur d'Alene, Idaho: Bookage Press, 1998), 52–53.

4. Great Britain first established legal restrictions on women's underground work with the Mines and Collieries Act of 1842. The first piece of protective legislation for women in Germany, which along with Japan was considered as a latecomer in joining the industrialized nations, was enacted in 1878, which prohibited women from working underground in mines. See Ulla Wickander, Allice-Kessler Harris, and Jane Lewis, eds., *Labor Legislation in Europe, the United States, and Australia, 1880–1920* (Urbana and Chicago: University of Illinois Press, 1995), 91–149.

5. Reiko Miyauchi, "Women Workers in Mines of Hokkaido," *Sapporo International University Journal* 31 (2000): 122.

6. Yubari Municipal History Editorial Committee, *Yubari Municipal History Vol. 2* (Yubari: City of Yubari, 1943), 513.

7. By the late 1980s, most of the women miners in Yubari, the coal kingdom of Hokkaido, were deceased. Reiko Miyauchi, then a journalist with a regional newspaper, interviewed the few surviving women miners and recreated their lives in the mines and in the mining community in a series of twenty articles called *Women in Yubari* (Sapporo: Hokkai Times, 1987). The information and excerpts for this essay come from that work.

8. Miyauchi, "Women Workers in Mines of Hokkaido," 123.

9. The Government of Japan enacted legislation, which prohibited women's underground work in the mines in 1928 (Ministry of International Affairs Law No. 30). However, it took another five years before all mines in Japan officially excluded female workers. Miyauchi, "Women Workers in Mines of Hokkaido," 122.

10. Masato Kuwahara, Makio Yano, Teruichi Tanji, *Modern Japan Seen from the Coal Development* (Tokyo: Societe, 1978), 160–185.

11. Ibid.

12. In 1946, Hokutan Sorachi Miners' Wives Organization was formed in Sorachi region where the Yubari mines were located as the first such organization in Hokkaido. Demanding "Immediate Distribution of Hidden Goods," "40 per cent Increase in Food Ration," "50 per cent Wage Increase," and "Wage Payment while on Strike," women fought together with the union workers in collective bargaining and demonstrations and supported the union activities by providing food for the workers. See Reiko Miyauchi, "Life in the Coal Mining Town" (unpublished working paper, 2000), 17.

13. As for the census figures quoted here, see Erika A. Kuhlman, "From Farmland to Coalvillage: Red Lodge's Finnish Immigrants 1890–1922" (MA Thesis University of Montana, 1987), 21–23.

14. The authors thank the four Finnish American women for their forbearance in allowing us to interview them in Red Lodge and Coeur d'Alene during the summer of 2000. Their willingness to share their life experiences in Finn Town and information they offered were most appreciated. We are indebted to Leona Lampi, in particular, for her support and the resource materials she provided.

15. As early as 1893, only a few years after the Red Lodge coal mine opened, the Finns were building a meeting hall. The first Temperance Society, incorporated by the Red Lodge Finns in 1895, organized on a strict religious basis and used this hall for various activities. The society also extended assistance to its members in the event of an illness or an accident and continued to provide the insurance even after unions finally won some benefits for the miners. See Leona Lampi, *At the Foot*, 13–20.

16. Ibid., 38–39.

17. The Workers' Building Association of Red Lodge built the Finnish Workers Hall in 1912 to replace the Temperance Hall (the Opera House) as the center for cultural activities for Red Lodge Finns. According to John Lampi, director of dramatics at the hall, by 1915 the hall was controlled by the IWW. See Leona Lampi, *At the Foot*, 20–36.

18. Interview with Lillian Lampi by Laurie Mercier, 1982, Montana Historical Society, Tape 1, 2; interview with Lillian Lampi by William Copeland, Red Lodge, Montana, July 12, 1976. Translated by Leona Lampi Hassen, December 1991.

19. Kuhlman, "From Farmland," 15–16.

20. One of the early activist women's groups was the Ladies of Kaleva (*Mielikin Tupa #1*), a woman's section of a lodge called the Knights of Kaleva. It was first founded in Red Lodge in 1904. A *maja* (local chapter) was to raise the status and goals of the immigrant women with education in Finnish culture. *Mialikin Tupa #1* remained active in the temperance movement in the early years and in the founding of the county's chapter of the American Red Cross in the 1910s. Lampi, *At the Foot*, 45–47, 89–90.

CHAPTER 8

Coal Mining Women Speak Out: Economic Change and Women Miners of Chikuho, Japan

Sachiko Sone

INTRODUCTION

History has not often been kind to the coal miners of Japan. They have as a group at times been characterized in economic labor histories as "illiterate peasant workers" or as "premodern laborers." Female coal miners have not only been described in extreme terms as shameless and lacking in feminine dignity, but they have also been celebrated as "super women," and as fulfilling the Meiji[1] ideal of "Good Wife, Wise Mother."[2] This essay looks beyond these stereotypical images into the reality of the lives of ordinary coal mining women, as seen through the eyes of two second-generation coal miners whose lives, with those of their families, span the final thirty years of the Japanese coal mining industry and encompass experience of its preindustrial and modern phases. The essay argues that categorization of the women miners under labels has overlooked their resilience and their capacity to adapt to their circumstances, and to exercise a degree of control over their lives.

My interest in the coal mining women was initially aroused in the early 1980s when I was conducting research into the Karayuki-san, Japanese women who were sold by their parents to work as prostitutes, mainly in western colonies. In the course of my fieldwork in 1988 I visited Kyushu, the area from which many women were smuggled by traffickers between the 1880s and 1920. They were commonly concealed in the holds of ships carrying coal, Japan's third largest export commodity at that time. In researching these women I discovered there was another group of whom I had no previous knowledge, the coal-mining women. I resolved to learn more about them.

Returning to Kyushu in 1996, I lived for three months in Fukuoka City, familiarizing myself with the local culture, dialect, and history. I researched all relevant sources in the Centre for Source Material on Coal Mining at Kyushu University, including government records, company records, and local history books. A chance encounter with a rare book of ex-coalminer Yamamoto Sakubê's drawings[3]—showing the miners, men and women, not only hewing and hauling by hand, but also using modern mining machinery—caused me to question the image of the miners as "premodern laborers." The research showed that regional history, especially where conventional research sources are complemented with oral and other alternative source material, presents a picture of the coal mining woman that is very different from that depicted in national histories. It revealed that in the Chikuho coalfield before the 1920s' mechanization of mining, women made up to nearly one-third of the mining workforce, with two-thirds of them working underground along-side men. This was true not only in small mines but also in large mines from the earliest days of coal mining in Japan, where the coexistence of large mines owned by the *Zaibatsu* (the giant financial corporate bodies), simultaneously with medium- and small-scale mines owned by local entrepreneurs and oper-ators, was the industry's most distinctive feature.[4]

Since existing national histories reveal little about regional and local circumstances, I determined to undertake research at the grassroots level in Chikuho,[5] the scene of some of the most profound economic and social changes in modern Japan. To gain the confidence of the local people, I lived for six weeks in 1998 with farmers in a former Naya (company housing) dwelling in Kawasaki machi, where there was formerly a concentration of small mines, and where I could record the stories of surviving coal mining women. In all, I interviewed ten former women miners, two of whose accounts I have selected for this paper because of their completeness, the power of the memories they evoked, and the extent to which their life expe-riences are typical of what we know of the lives of their contemporaries on the coalfield.[6] It was meeting surviving coal mining women such as these, and being impressed with their strength, intelligence, and dignity, that caused me to question, and perhaps help to correct, their portrayal in history.

COAL MINING WOMEN IN HISTORY

Despite the crucial importance of the coal mining industry for the creation of modern industrial Japan,[7] it wasn't until the 1960s that the Japanese popula-tion at large began to have any knowledge of the way of life of the men, women, and children on which the industry had historically depended.[8] Disturbances such as the massive strike in 1960 at the Miike Mine, in Kyushu, the nation's largest coal mine, coinciding as they did with a time of growing interest throughout Japan in local cultural history, began to excite interest in the lives and working conditions of Japanese coal miners. Chikuho, in Kyushu, as Japan's largest coal mining district,[9] attracted the attention of historians, journalists, and social activists who undertook field-work and published their findings in a series of books, articles, and papers.[10]

What surprised most investigators was the economic-political activism of the coal miners as, until that time, a negative image of coal miners had predominated in Japanese historiography and perceptions by the wider society.

The stereotypical image of prewar miners created by economic and labor historians had been that of "illiterate peasant workers." In the view of these researchers, the miners failed to meet two important conditions of "modern laborers": being free to sell their labor and services; and being free to migrate to secure reasonable employment.[11] Miners were also regarded as "premodern laborers" as they failed to form trade unions or to organize themselves to change their material conditions before World War II.[12]

Women, who constituted nearly one-third of the coal miners in the Chikuho region, the largest coalfield in Japan at the beginning of the twentieth century, received even less attention than their male counterparts, probably because they were mainly the wives and daughters of miners and were "family labor" in continuity with the peasant origins of many of the early mineworkers of Chikuho. Mathias encapsulates this view when she concludes:

> On the whole, female labor in the coal-mines has to be regarded as a remnant of the pre-industrial era. Therefore, in contrast to the "modern type" of female workers in textile industries, female colliers represent a more traditional type of working women. This traditional kind of female labor was—to some degree—successfully integrated into the early stages of industrial production in the coal-mines. It did not, however, fit smoothly into the modernized production process of the 1920s and 1930s. It was only then that, supported by public debate on protective labor legislation, the use of female labor in the coal-mines was questioned on the grounds of health and morals.[13]

The women were thus not regarded as independent laborers. By contrast, single women and girls in the textile industry, who had succeeded in developing unions and organizing strikes, were written about and discussed at great length. This imbalance in recognition was reflected in high school textbooks of Japanese history, where a 1985 text made no reference to coal mining women, and a 1991 edition featured only one small picture of coal mining women working underground but devoted two full pages to the factory women.[14]

From the 1960s to the 1980s the number of females in the workforce increased substantially in Japan.[15] As a consequence, in 1981 the Research Institute of Asian Economy, under the auspices of the International Federation of Universities, undertook a major new research project.[16] Three types of female labor were examined: textile factory labor between the 1870s and the 1900s; coal mining labor between the 1900s and the 1930s; and labor of the substratum in the large industrial cities from the 1870s to the 1920s. Thus coal mining women for the first time received significant attention in the labor and economic history of Japan. In the project's proceedings, leading Marxist economic historian Nishinarita Yutaka presented a historical overview of the female miners based on governmental data and statistics and contemporary research papers by notable economic and labor historians.[17]

He compared the characteristics of female coal mining laborers in the 1920s with those of female textile factory workers, using age structure, marital status, length of employment, educational background, place of origin, and wages and household expenses. He concluded that certain social characteristics, as well as a weak educational background, situated coal mining women in the lower strata of society. Thus even this innovative approach to labor history in the 1980s failed to reassess fully the image of coal mining women, framed as it was by the image of coal miners created by mainstream labor historians during the prewar period.[18]

From the 1960s to the 1980s, Japanese provincial historians portrayed a contrasting image of female miners.. They celebrated the female miner as an idealized "super woman" who selflessly fulfilled the role of "Good Wife, Wise Mother" while working harmoniously side-by-side underground with a male worker who was not necessarily her husband, as a codependent hewer-haulier pair, or even taking on the dominant role of hewer.

However, a starkly different image emerges from the account of Katô Shizue, wife of an engineer at the Miike mine and one of the leading Japanese feminists of the early twentieth century, who was able to observe the coal mining women daily between 1915 and 1917.

> Women who worked in the darkness had a pale complexion like the skin of a silkworm. They spoke and acted shamelessly, with the last sign of feminine dignity sloughing off. Often pregnant women, working until the last moment, gave birth to their children in the dark pit. It would be hard to tell the difference between the life of pigs and the life of these miners. Certainly the human beings were living like animals in barns.[19]

Stereotypical images usually have some basis in fact. So it is true that women labored in inhumane conditions, and that, particularly in small mines, the workers did not establish militant organizations. But, as the following accounts reveal, they did not lose their basic human dignity, and they took steps to improve their working conditions.

THE LIVES OF ÔNISHI MASAKO AND ISHIZAKI SHIZUKA

Ônishi Masako and Ishizaki Shizuka were second-generation coal miners whose mining experience was principally in small mines.[20] As was the case with many Chikuho miners, their families had migrated into the region, though in the case of Masako and Shizuka for very different reasons. Masako's account reveals the typical life pattern of a female miner in small-scale mines in the Chikuho region. By contrast, Shizuka's mining experience was much harsher than that of women miners in general as she belonged to a despised minority, the *Buraku*.[21] What is outstanding about Shizuka's story is that she became a radical activist for miners' rights and the rights of Koreans in Japan, environmentalism (especially relating to the Minamata mercury poisoning disaster), and other social issues. In addition, only she wrote a biography,[22] although it is not widely known outside Chikuho. Nonetheless, there are striking similarities in the experiences of the two women, and together their stories provide a collective portrait of the life and working circumstances of migrant female miners on the Chikuho coalfield.

Migrant Origins

Ônishi Masako was born in Nôgata City in December 1929. Her father owned a shop which made and sold wooden clogs in Niji-machi, a pleasure quarter in the city area. He migrated to Nôgata, the center of the Chikuho region in Fukuoka prefecture, from Kurume, a large town in the northern part of Fukuoka, to start his business. His shop was popular among *Geishas* and waitresses. Her mother, born in Nôgata, married her father when she was seventeen years old through an arrangement with a matchmaker. In 1936, her father died leaving his thirty-one-years-old wife with four children: sons of twelve, nine, and three years, and a seven-year-old daughter, Masako. Her mother and her eldest brother started working for a store that recycled old garments and household wares. Her brother therefore did not complete his secondary education. A year later, her mother heard from a neighbor that there was better paid work in a local coalmine, so both Masako's mother and her brother went to that mine to seek work. At first the mother was employed at coal sorting, but she soon went underground as the wages were better. In 1940, Masako's widowed mother married her work partner, a hewer, who used to be a peasant in Kagoshima prefecture, in southern Kyushu. Her eldest brother soon left home to work for a mine in Fukui prefecture in the eastern part of Japan's mainland, Honshu. The family then moved for the first time to a small mine in a town in another part of Nôgata City. They stayed only for a year as the mine was closed at short notice in 1941.

Most small mines were either shallow diggings or employed the strip-mining method, and once the surface mining became too difficult for manual labor or too much water entered from underground, the owners simply closed the mines. In the small mine to which Masako's family had moved, there were about one hundred employees, mostly husbands and wives who worked together and lived in the company houses. These miners had a good communication network for getting local and regional information by word of mouth, hence after the closure of the mine in 1941, Masako's family had no trouble finding new work and moved to another small mine in a nearby town. Within a year, however, the family had already returned to Nôgata City and then within a relatively short span of time moved from one mine to another in three districts: Kurate-gun, Munakata-gun, and Onga-gun, traversing an area of about 25 km by 15 km, traveling mostly by horse-drawn cart. Masako's recollection of these moves was as pleasant adventures, as if going on a picnic, as indeed they would have seemed for a small child about to be plunged into the daily grind of working life.

Miners often talked about other mines and were eager to look for better-paid work. One man would say that a mine in such and such place offered a better daily wage. Then somebody would go there to check. And next day the story would spread everywhere. Miners shared information and dreamt of a better life. Noone monopolized good fortune, at least that seemed to be the case. There was no means of transportation in the mountains at that time and so we had to rely on foot and cart horses. All we had were a little dining table, a small cupboard, a pan, an iron pot in which to boil rice, a woven trunk, and two futons and blankets. So, when we moved from Katsuki-machi with two other families, we hired two cart horses, which were enough to carry all the possessions of three families. It was just like a picnic, walking in the valleys and hills. When the children got tired the parents sat them on the household goods in the cart.[23]

The family finally settled down at the Ueki Yon-Kô (Ueki No. 4 mine), where the working conditions were better than in most of the small mines.

Whereas Ônishi Masako's family was forced by the death of her shop-keeper father to work in the mines in order to survive, the family of Ishizaki Shizuka had followed the path of many impoverished rural workers seeking to improve their lives. Shizuka was born in February 1930, in a village called Narimitsu-mura (village), Tagawa-gun (district), Fukuoka-ken (prefecture). She was the fourth daughter of miner parents. She did not know either when or where her father was born, but early in the twentieth century he came to Narimitsu-mura where his sister was working as a tenant farmer, tilling a small piece of land. Shizuka's father was an itinerant laborer and soon started working as a subcontracted miner for the Furukawa Mineji mine, a medium-scale operation in the region. Her mother was the daughter of a fisherman in a small village in Miyazaki prefecture, southern Kyushu. When she was eighteen years old she was seduced and lured away by Shizuka's father, who was working as a coolie along the coast of Hyûga Sea in Miyazaki prefecture at the time. She was a naive village girl and believed the promises of this drifter. Once she tried to kill herself and her newborn baby Shizuka, but her love for the first child prevented her from doing so. She was then only nineteen years old. Shizuka's mother soon started working as a hewer for a small mine in the village of Narimitsu-mura where the family was living.

Early Lives

From the age of eleven, Masako had assumed all domestic responsibility at home, including looking after her new younger sister. Masako explained to me how her day went more than fifty years ago:

I would get up at five o'clock in the morning and burn coal to cook rice. While my mother was feeding her baby, I quickly had my breakfast of cooked rice and Miso soup. Then my mother would strap the baby on my back and the real work began. I tidied up the table and washed bowls and chopsticks. I cleaned the room with a wet cloth. Then I walked to a river quite far away to wash nappies. After that, I returned to the well to wash other clothes belonging to family members. The river water was icy cold in wintertime. I used to get chilblains on my hands. When I was commuting to the school, the daily routine was not so bad. I had a break, a playtime between three and five o'clock with my brother and my classmates. We would play in the mountains and hills and enjoy the harvest of the wild fruit trees in autumn. Sometimes we did home-work together at a friend's house. After five o'clock I would dash to our hut to burn coal.

My important work as a full-time Komori, a nursemaid, was to take my youngest sister to the entrance of the mine before noon. My mother came up to feed the baby. She was so exhausted with work underground that she spoke not a single word.

At around half-past-five my mother would return home and go out to do shopping for dinner. As she was paid daily she had to take a bowl to buy rice each night. She therefore never took a day off except for a few weeks when she gave birth to her child. There was a fishmonger, a butcher, and a vegetable shop in Monzen-machi near Niji-machi where I was born. The meal was always sim-ple. A typical dinner would be grilled sardines and cooked vegetables with gristly pork meat. Mother cooked the food while I cooked rice. I cleaned the table and washed dishes. After dinner we walked to a public bath in the town, which took us 15 minutes. We had to walk fast in wintertime as it snowed often.[24]

Because of the need to support her family, Masako was able to complete only five years of her primary education, but whenever she found a little time she recounted how she read novels in the rental bookshop. She also taught herself cooking and sewing, including refurbishing futon mattresses and padded kimonos for winter by observing her mother's handiwork. Special skills for domestic work were also transferred from mother to daughter.

In 1943, at the age of fourteen, as the war came closer to Japan, she started working underground in the Ueki mine. It was the time when the state was desperately demanding that miners increase the supply of coal, the only local fuel the country could rely upon for the war effort, and women were called to work underground in both large and small mines in 1939. The war years were difficult for Masako as she had to finish all the domestic chores while her parents were working the first shift, and then she had to go under-ground for the second shift. She stated to me that she never questioned the basis of her way of life and never thought about the possibility of an alterna-tive lifestyle. This was because all the girls and young women around her were also working in the mines and at home in the very same manner, for family and country. Masako admitted that people like herself in the small mines were among the poorest families in the Chikuho region.

In 1947, however, women were again compelled to leave underground work by the authorities, so Masako's family moved to a smaller mine, the Yasutake mine in Onga district, further north from Nôgata, where she and her mother could continue to work discreetly below ground. Masako was then sixteen years old, and continued to work underground with her parents for another four years at that mine, where she first met her future husband.

Ishazaki Shizuka's early years had much in common with those of Masako. She started helping her mother when she was only five years old, by caring for her younger brothers. She recalled how her mother fed her newborn brother:

> I had to take my youngest brother to the entrance of the pit around lunchtime. It was the time of the day for my mother to feed him. The mine was so small that I was able to see my mother coming up the shaft. She was walking slowly while spitting on her nipples to clean them. Not only her breasts but her whole body was covered in pitch black coal dust. Her two arms just grabbed the baby. She never said "thanks" to me. She was so exhausted that she didn't have energy to even open her mouth.[25]

By the age of six Shizuka was already managing domestic household work such as washing and cleaning. She also looked after her two younger brothers while attending primary school. On the way home she usually remembered to pick up droppings of horse manure to sell to the farmers. Shizuka recalled the life of a daughter in the poorest miners' households:

> Every morning, we children carefully watched the iron pot in which the food was cooked. It was a mixture of 80 per cent wheat and 20 per cent rice. When it was cooked, rice subsided to the bottom of the pot, then my mother helped herself and came with a rice scoop and filled her lunch box with it, saying "Don't look at me like that. My work is so hard that I need some rice." My mother needed food in order to work and feed the babies. I was so small that I had no idea how painful it was for my mother to have to say this every morning.[26]

Shizuka attended primary school for five years. She was clearly a bright child, but her very intelligence unfortunately led to two incidents that gave her harsh lessons in authoritarianism and discrimination. The first one took place in 1939, when she was a third-year primary school student.

> It was the time of commemoration day, and the teacher asked each one of us about what sort of clocks we had at home. When it was my turn, I proudly answered saying that the clock in our house never broke down and never required winding. The teacher looked puzzled. So I explained that it was not a clock to tell time in the house but the sound of trains running behind our place. The sound varied depending on whether wagons carried coal[27] or the wagons transported army troops. These wagons passed by exactly at the same time every day. Surprisingly, my mother and I were soon called by the police in Soeda-machi to the station and were imprisoned for three days. I was accused of being a potential spy, for being able to predict the productivity of coal and military transport movement. I didn't know that my behavior would result in interference with the Military Secret Acts. What is worse, my mother was also detained leaving five children at home with their wayward father. The police had no concern for our household. Without my mother's daily wage we weren't able to buy rice. We were indeed the poorest and most hungry family. My brothers and sisters had nothing to eat for three days. My mother had no choice but to apologize to the police for my stubbornness. Nevertheless, I was

so disappointed with my mother because she didn't even try to understand the justification for my stance. My rebellious spirit began to grow from that incident at the age of nine.[28]

The second incident occurred a year later, and led to her decision to leave her home village.

My composition won the first prize in the grand contest for primary school children in Western Japan. But, on the day of ceremony for receiving the prize, my composition was read not by me, but by the class president in front of all the students, teachers, and the superintendent of the board of education. My name was not mentioned. After the ceremony I asked my teachers why such a mishap had occurred. Then the teacher told me that she was reproached by the headmaster for having been so imprudent as to select me. She said, "It can't be helped. You are from Narimitsu mura."[29] I was deeply hurt. When I returned home, my mother asked me how I went with reading my composition. So I explained what had happened. My mother said, "Don't bother with such a thing. Don't do anything that won't fill your stomach." I lost interest in school and began to look for work outside of the village.[30]

In fact, Shizuka wanted to get away from home as her father had already sold her two sisters. Her eldest sister was sold to a restaurant in Kita-Kyushu City, Fukuoka prefecture, where the Yawata Ironworks was established in 1901 as the first government iron foundry. Her second elder sister was sold to a brothel in Gifu prefecture. By then, Shizuka had three sisters and two brothers. Her father died of cancer in 1940, leaving nothing but debt for the family to pay, while his employer, the Furukawa mining company, gave her family no compensation as his death had not been caused by an industrial accident. Shizuka soon found a job that was advertised on the notice board of the local village office, in a silk reeling mill. She was not able to read every word but saw the figures: the wage for a male factory worker was eighty yen per annum, for a female factory worker fifty yen, and a girl could be purchased for three hundred yen. Shizuka did not hesitate to leave home straight away. She was then only eleven years old. As she did not have money to buy a train ticket she walked all the way to the mill in Ôishi-mura, Ukiha-gun, Fukuoka prefecture, which took her two-and-a-half days. Shizuka ruefully recollected that she must have looked an awful sight as her hair was dirty and untidy, her clothes ragged and her straw sandals worn out when she finally arrived at the mill.

The Ôishi Silk Mill was the largest mill in Kyushu, with extensive facilities, including a huge dining room, a big bathhouse, and a modern dormitory. More than 300 girls were working there, of whom about 100, like Shizuka, came of their own volition, while over 150 other girls were serving apprenticeships. All girls were under fifteen years of age and worked twelve hours a day. Shizuka noted that she had the happiest time of her life at the mill. She was better fed than ever before and she could spend most of her spare time in the library where an inspector tutored her and encouraged her reading and writing. However, all this came to an end too soon. As the war situation deteriorated the girls had very little food to eat. What is worse, the Japanese Imperial Army took over the mill and the officers forced girls to work fifteen hours a day. This forced labor ended when the Occupation Forces advanced into Fukuoka in 1945. Shizuka was repatriated against her will by the allied troops to her home village in Tagawa-gun when she was only fifteen years old. The local coal mining industry soon started to ride the crest of a boom under the new national energy policy to assert Japan's postwar rehabilitation. Shizuka started to work for the large-scale Mitsui-Tagawa mine as a *Hieki* (a day laborer), doing miscellaneous work aboveground. She recognized that Burakumin were only given certain kinds of work aboveground such as being a Hieki with low wages. There she met her future husband, Tomiji.

LATER LIVES

In 1949, when she was nineteen years old, Masako married a twenty-one-year-old miner who was also a member of a second-generation coal mining family. Harutoshi was born in 1927 as the second son of a farmer in Asakura-gun in the Chikuho region. He started working underground with his father when he was seven years old. He had moved around in Nôgata until he came to the Yasutake mine in Onga-gun. Masako fell in love with him because he was such a skillful and handsome miner. During the early months of their marriage they used to go to the theater in Nôgata City to see dramatic plays performed by local actors. However, Masako soon became pregnant, ending the initial phase of their married life. Between 1950 and 1954, Masako and her husband followed work to three mines, including the Akaji mine in Nôgata, where they stayed only half a year, as the mine was suddenly closed. Then they moved to Nôgata mine in Nôgata, and from there to Nichiman mine in a town in Kurate-gun where they stayed for three years. Between 1954 and 1961 they were also employed at the Kazamatsu mine in a nearby town in the same district.

Masako continued to work underground until 1954, the final year that women were allowed to work underground in small-scale mines. She soon found a new job with the Mitsubishi chemical and synthetic industrial company through the local unemployment office, and worked as a heavy construction laborer for six years. In 1961, they moved to the Buzen mine in Tagawa-gun, further south from Nôgata. Shortly afterward Masako's husband had a serious industrial accident when the mine roof collapsed, badly injuring his leg. He received official compensation for only a year, then was forced to relinquish the company house as he was no longer fit to work as a miner. They moved to a rented house nearby, and Masako now became the sole breadwinner of the family. She continued to work as a builder's laborer for the next nine years, during which period she raised her three children: the eldest daughter was born in 1949, the first son two years later, and the second daughter in 1954.

Masako was largely self-educated. Having not been able to complete her own primary schooling, she made a special effort to send her three children to high school. Her two daughters found jobs in the same company in Tokyo soon after they graduated and have lived there ever since. At the time of our interview Masako was living with her son and her husband in Chikuho where, at seventy-one years of age, she still worked, as an administrator at the public hall.

Shizuka also married a coalminer, Tomiji. Tomiji was the sixth of thirteen children in a poor Yokohama family, Kanagawa prefecture, around the mid-1920s. His parents were running a small dry-cleaning shop. After the end of the war in 1945, he returned to Yokohama from Palau in the Manua islands and soon found that his wife and children were dead and his parents, brothers, and sisters had disappeared without trace. While staying at a demobilization camp he saw a notice advertising for coal miners to work in the Mitsui Tagawa colliery in Chikuho. He was attracted by the working conditions whereby all miners received six *gô* (1 liter) of rice per day. It was just after the defeat and there was little food available for the nation to share. As soon as he arrived there he found that the advertisement was untrue. However, he had nowhere to go and ended up staying at the colliery for about five years. Unexpectedly, he received a letter from the Yokohama City Office telling him that his parents were alive and his name needed to be entered in the family register in Yokohama.

Miners like him were ordered by the government to return to their home-towns at the expense of the collieries, to reenroll on the family registers. He returned to Yokohama, taking Shizuka as his twenty-year-old fiancée. His father, however, did not approve of their being married. Shizuka did not tell me the reason why she was rejected by Tomiji's father. It was undoubtedly related to her social background and work in the mines. She returned to her village with a broken heart and started working as a daily worker above-ground in a small mine. By the 1950s, men with strong bodies had come from all over the country to work as coal miners in Chikuho. Some even lied about their academic background to gain employment, including some with a university education. Miners received special allotments of rice from the government as a reward for being industrial warriors. This special rice was called "lunch box rice" by miners.

Ironically, Shizuka's future husband, Tomiji, was recalled to work by the Mitsubishi-Tagawa colliery soon after she left Yokohama. He too returned to Chikuho, but left the mine shortly afterward and started moving from one small mine to another. Small mines were actively cooperating with the large mines at that time, and because of the existing pay system in the small-scale industry he was able to receive better wages than in the larger mines. Though the hazards were greater, the wages were higher. When he came to the Hôshû mine in Kawasaki-machi, he again found Shizuka. They at last got married and led a reasonable life for a while. He worked underground as a timberman, a specialist carpenter, and Shizuka worked aboveground as a coal-sorting woman. Her decent life, on this occasion too, did not last very long.

On September 20, 1960, the Hôshû mine experienced an environmental disaster when the bed of the Chûganji River collapsed into one of the old mining shafts, drowning sixty-seven miners. The rampaging water quickly ran into all the tunnels. The maelstrom took the lives of many miners who were believed to be of Buraku background, working in this most dangerous pit.[31] After the horrendous accident the mine was closed and Shizuka and her husband lost their jobs. They fell on further misfortune the following year. Her husband had contracted tuberculosis earlier and became so ill in 1961 that he was sent to a hospital. Shizuka was then around thirty-one years old. She had no money to pay for the hospital bills and medicine, so she started *Tanuki-Bori* (literally "raccoon mining") by herself, a shallow mining technique just like a raccoon digging holes into a hill. For a year or more she mined coal in this way at Daigahara hill in Kawasaki-machi. People in Chikuho called *Tanuki-Bori* "thief mining." She did this work out of desperation. She tried every possible way to earn money to save Tomiji, including working as a cleaner at the hospital where he was confined, but with little success in the end. There was no compensation for Tomiji's death as his illness was not seen as mining-related.

After Tomiji's death, Shizuka gradually established herself as a writer and a political activist in the 1970s and 1980s, although she continued to work for a living as a day laborer and in such employment as a building cleaner. Her strident criticism of the emperor system, which had created "racism" in Japan, often caused heated discussions among the audience at her public seminars, which were sometimes disrupted by ultra-conservative protesters. She appeared everywhere, from Minamata in Kyushu to a coalmine in Hokkaido, to be at the forefront of protests with people who were strongly questioning the way the country was being industrialized and modernized.[32]

Shizuka had piles of books on her desk, one of a few pieces of furniture in her small government subsidized house. On the occasion of the author's first visit she said that there is no end to education, as the more you study the more you learn how little you know. She was also a member of a local study group, *Yama no Kai* [The Association of Mountains], which has been working on the revision of the history of the coal mining industry in Chikuho since the 1980s. This involved interviewing former Korean forced laborers and Buraku people, many of whom, like Shizuka, had worked in the mines.[33] Her early-life autobiography stands silently on the corner of a bookshelf in the library of the association, waiting to be discovered by the world beyond Chikuho.

SOME CONCLUSIONS

The women's lives visited here illustrate the complex and dynamic nature of gender relations among the coal miners. As producers of many children, Masako was a "good wife." Rejection of this aspect of the Meiji ideal by the childless Shizuka would have been consistent with her attitudes toward convention, though she is not on record as making any such claim. Both women had little formal education in their early lives, but they valued education highly for themselves and for their own children in later life.

Shizuka and Masako demonstrated gender-role flexibility by their capacity to assume the role of independent breadwinner on the death or incapacity of their husbands. Both had been conditioned by early-life experiences to take control of their lives: Shizuka by the injustice she suffered as a child; Masako by the example of her widowed mother, and her childhood experience of constant movement in search of better working conditions.

The lives of these women cast doubt on the view that their kind were, in contrast to the textile workers, not "modern." Large numbers of women living and working together in textile factories had considerable advantages over the family mining teams in finding common cause and organizing themselves to act. Though the mining women may not have engaged in political or union activism, they by no means passively watched their lives unfold.[34] According to Marxist labor historians, the notion of resistance indicates opposition by an organized legitimate modern labor movement. This may be an interpretation of resistance discourse, but theorists of agency argue that individual acts of agency are a significant sign of political action.[35] The coalminers' responses to challenges in their lives are manifestation of this notion of agency.

The journeys of Masako's family were not about running away from the reality of the harsh economic circumstances of the depression; they were, rather, the act of a family seeking a better life, and could be considered pragmatic, economically rational, and "modern." Shizuka, admittedly an exceptional woman by any standard, journeyed far from home as a child to find work in a silk reeling mill before settling down in a conventional marriage, eventually providing sole support for her ailing husband, going back to the earliest type of preindustrial mining in order to do so. The life journeys of both women were in fact characterized by positive responses to the challenges that faced them, challenges that might see their role change from time to time or in different places: underground the leading worker, above ground the conventional mother.[36] And they survived to take their place in, and to launch the next generation into, Japan's modern era.

NOTES

1. Periods in Japanese history are named after the emperors who reigned in those spans of time: Meiji, 1868–1912; Taishô, 1912–1926; Shôwa, 1926–1988, Heisei, 1989–.

2. The concept, promoted by bureaucrats of the new Meiji government, defined womanhood at least partly in terms of motherhood. A "wise mother" would be one educated to better perform her home and child rearing duties. (Gail Lee Bernstein, ed., *Recreating Japanese Women, 1600–1945* [University of California Press, Berkeley, 1991], 7).

3. Yamamoto Sakubê was born in Kaho district, Fukuoka prefecture in 1892. He worked as a miner/hauler or blacksmith until 1955. During 1955 and 1963 he created his unique document—a detailed illustration of works underground and the miners' way of life aboveground, to pass on to his grandchildren. He received the 1977 "Western Japan Culture Prize" for the artistic merit and historical quality of his illustrations. His publications include: *Meiji Taisho Tankô Emaki* [The Picture Scroll of Coalmines in Meiji and Taisho Period] (Fukuoka: Private publication, 1963); *Chikuho Tankô Emaki* [The Picture Scroll of Coalmines in Chikuho] (Fukuoka: Ashi Shobô, 1973); *ôkoku to Yami* [The Kingdom and Darkness] (Fukuoka: Ashi Shobô, 1981).

4. **Table 8.1** Employment structure (male, female, child) of the large mines on the Chikuho coalfield between 1906 and 1930

Year (mines)		Hewer and haulier	Tim-berer	Misc.	Total underground	Total aboveground	Total & % female/male & child/male	Average labor per mine
1906	m	17,570	2,418	5,074	24,062	6,498	30,560	1,222
(25)	f	8,316	293	578	9,187	2,724	11,911 (39%)	586
	c	115		3	118	86	204 (0.7%)	8
1913	m	23,356	3,872	13,602	40,830	11,343	52,173	1,304
(40)	f	15,424	326	1,589	17,339	6,083	23,422 (45%)	476
	c	80		14	94	179	273 (0.5%)	7
1917	m	34,810	5,694	9,923	50,427	13,887	64,314	1,531
(42)	f	20,257	1,087	1,389	22,733	7,036	29,769 (46%)	709
	c	61		7	68	32	160 (0.2%)	4
1925	m	36,083	6,698	14,075	56,856	17,778	74.634	1.622
(46)	f	22,566	247	2,333	25,146	9,340	34,486 (46%)	750
	c	406		127	533	469	1,002 (1.3%)	22
1930	m	21,284	9,456	8,337	39,077	9,464	48,541	837
(58)	f	3,752	722	165	4,639	4,249	8,888 (18.3%)	153
	c	N/A	N/A	N/A	N/A	N/A	N/A	N/A

Sources: 1906 figures from *Kôfu Taigû Jire* 1913, 1917 & 1925 from *Hompô Jûyô Kôzan Yôran*. 1930 figures from Ogino Yoshihiro, *Chikuho Tankô Rôshi Kankei Shi*, p. 273 (originally cited in *Chikuho Sekitan Kôgyô Kumiai Shozoku Tankô Genkyô Chôsa Hyô*, December 1930).

5. The Chikuho coalfield occupies the northwest part of Fukuoka prefecture in Kyushu, the southern island of Japan. The field is 48 km in length and 12 to 28 km in width, covering an area of 816 sq. km. It is set in a low basin surrounded by mountain lands 300 to 600 m high on the south and northwestern sides, with a number of smaller parallel ranges within the basin. The population began to increase in the late 1880s when the central capitalists advanced into the Chikuho region. With the industry boom, population in Chikuho doubled from 260,000 to 520,000 between 1897 and 1915. It is claimed that two-thirds of employed miners had their families with them.

6. Evidence of the lives of the coal mining women of Chikuho is based almost entirely on oral accounts, of which more than one hundred have been recorded, mostly in the 1960s. Coal mining women of the generation of my two subjects were almost invariably born into coal mining families that had taken up the occupation out of economic necessity. Typically, the women's earliest recollections were of their domestic labors, and after little or no education they entered the mines as early teenagers or younger, usually working with a relative. They may have worked in as many as ten different small mines in their lifetime. See Morisaki Kazue *Makkura* [Pitch Dark] (Tokyo: Rironsha, 1961). Tanaka Hôichi, "Onna Kôfu no Kiroku." [Record of Mining Women] *Enerugî Shi Kenkyû Nôte*, no. 5 (June 1975): 86–96; Shindô Toyoo, *Chikuho no Onna Kôfutachi* [Mining women in Chikuho] (Kyoto: Buraku Mondai Kenkyûjo, 1978); Idegawa Yasuko, *Hi o Unda Onnatachi* [Women who gave birth to fire] (Fukuoka: Ashi Shobô, 1984); Hayashi Eidai, *Yami o Horu Onnatachi* [Women who dig the darkness] (Tokyo: Akashi Shoten, 1990); Tajima Masami, *Tankô Bijin* [Beautiful Coal mining Women] (Tokyo: Tsukiji Shoten, 2000).

7. Coal was the major source of fuel, though not a major employer. As a percentage of all manufacturing, employment in coal mining nationally peaked at 8.6% in 1914. Data from Tadashi Fukutake, *The Japanese Social Structure: Its*

Evolution in the Modern Century (Tokyo: University of Tokyo Press, 1989, 2nd edition), 18; and Shiozawa Kimio, ed., *Nihon Shihon Shugi Saiseisan Kozô Tôkei* [Statistics on the Structure of Reproduction in Capitalism in Japan], (Tokyo: Iwanami, 1973), 157, 159; and Kawahigashi Eiko, "Nihon Shihon Shugi to Joshi Rôdô" [Japanese Capitalism and Female Labor], in *Shin Joshi Rôdô*, ed., Takenaka Emiko (Tokyo: Yûhikaku, 1994), 55–56.

8. **Table 8.2**   The development of the Japanese coalmining industry

Stage	Period	Major Events
The preindustrial era	1600s–1800s	Wooden memorial dated 1723 marks site of a mining accident in which four male and two female miners perished. Fukuoka domain sets up official monopoly to control the production and distribution of coal.
The rise of the Zaibatsu and the coalmining industry	1880s–1900s	Sino-Japanese war, 1884–1885; Russo-Japanese war, 1904–1905
WWI boom	1916–1919	Dislocation in the West creates industrial opportunities
Recession	Early 1920s	International depression. Sekitan Kôgyô Rengôkai (Coal Owners Association) founded 1921. Nationalization of coal commenced. Restriction of coal production.
Rationalization	Mid-1920s, mid-1930s	ILO treaty, 1919; female labour prohibition underground, 1928–1933. Showa Sekitan Kabushiki Gaisha (pricing cartel) set up 1932. Increasing use of Korean labour.
State control	1938–1945	World War II Nihon Sekitan Sangyo Bunseki (sales cartel) set up, 1940.
Post WWII boom	1946–1950s	Reconstruction and rapid economic and industrial growth. Korean War, 1950–1953.
Demise of the industry	1960s–1970s	National energy policy change to oil and gas. Development of nuclear power industry. Free trade of oil began, 1960. "Scrap and build policy"—progressive dismantling of coal industry, 1962–2001 End of industry in Chikuho, mid-1970s.

9. See Smith in this volume for particulars of the Chikuho coalfield.
10. For example, Nakamura Masanori, *Rôdôsha to Nômin* [Laborers and Peasants] (Tokyo: Shôgakukan, 1976). Ueno Hidenobu, a leading activist in Chikuho, worked as a miner between 1946 and 1952. Soon after his earliest and moving book *Owareyuku Kôfutachi* [Miners being Forced out] (Tokyo: Iwanami Shoten, 1960) was published, a concerned group was established to help miners and their families employed in small- and medium-scale mines. At the time, among the most important female writers and members of the group working on labor issues and people's history, was Morisaki Kazue.
11. Nagaoka Shinkichi and Ishizaka Akio, *Ippan Keizai Shi* [A General Economic History] (Tokyo, Mineruva, 1988), 71.
12. See Smith in this volume on the role of women in industrial disputes.

13. Regine Mathias, "Female Labor in the Japanese Coalmining Industry," in *Japanese Women Working*, ed., Janet Hunter (London: Routlege, 1996), 119.
14. *Nihon Shi* [The Japanese History] (Tokyo: Tokyoshoseki, 1985). *Atarashii Shakai Rekishi* [The New Social History], (Tokyo: Tokyoshoseki, 1991).
15. There are a number of research papers and books about female labor published in the 1950s and 1960s, most of which take a Marxist viewpoint. See Ôkôchi Kazuo and Isoda Susumu, eds., *Fujin Rôdô* [Female Labor] (Tokyo: Kôbundo,1956), and Shakai Seisaku Gakkai, eds., *Fujin Rôdô*, (Tokyo: Yôhikaku, 1961). Female labor in the textile industry in relation to trade union activities has been the central concern among Marxist labor and economic historians since the 1950s. There are also a few studies of other female workers such as *Kangofu* (nurses), *Jimushokuin* (clerical workers), and *Tenin* (shop assistants). The main research in this period was undertaken on labor regulations as well as the wage system. See, Takenaka Emiko and Nishiguchi Toshiko, *Onna no Shigoto-Onna no Shokub* [Women's Jobs and Women's Work places] (Tokyo: Sanichi Shobô, 1962). As for the primary source, see the series of statistics published annually by Rôdô Shô Fujin Shônen Kyoku [the Office for Women and Minors in the Ministry of Labor].
16. Nakamura Masanori, (ed.), *Gijutsu Kakushin to Joshi Rôdô* [Technological Innovation and Female Labor] (Tokyo: Tokyo University Press, 1985).
17. Nishinarita Yutaka, "Sekitan Kôgyô no Gigyutsu Kakushin to Joshi Rôdô" [Technological Innovation in the Coal mining Industry and Female Labor], in *Gijutsu Kakushin to Joshi Rôdô*, ed., Nakamura Masanori, 71–105.
18. In a 1994 historical review of Japanese female labor, Kawahigashi Eiko, an expert in the field, devoted only one line to the role of coal mining women in Japanese industrialization between 1880 and 1900, while devoting six pages to factory women in the textile industry, detailing their wages, working conditions, and dormitory life. See Kawahigashi Eiko, "Nihon Shihon Shugi Kakuritsu Ki no Joshi Rôdô" [Female labor in the period of Establishment of Japanese Capitalism], in *Shin Joshi Rôdô Ron* [New Essays of Female Labor], ed., Takenaka Emiko (Tokyo: Yûhikaku, 1994) 37.
19. Katô Shizue, *Facing Two Ways* (London: Cassel, 1935), 167.
20. Both Masako and Shizuka were born after 1928 when the revised Mining Workers' Regulation, which prohibited underground work by women and young persons with a grace period of five years, was promulgated. The regulations resulted in a dramatic decrease in the number of female miners. This was especially the case for women miners in the larger mines where mechanization of mining had been underway. As table 8.1 shows, the number of women working underground in the larger mines in Chikuho shrunk from 25,156 in 1925 to 4,639 in 1930. Some were transferred to jobs on the surface, but many were dismissed. Some of them were driven into smaller mines.
21. The most recent work on women's history in Japan included the topic of Buraku women for the first time in a Japanese women's history work and it relied solely on secondary sources. Thus the interview material given here is very rare. See Yasukawa Junosuke, "Hisabetsu Buraku to Josei" [Segregated people and Women], in *Nihon Josei Shi* (Tokyo: Tokyo University Press, 1990), 185–222.
22. This covers only the first fifteen years of her life.
23. Author's interview with Ônishi Masako at her house in Kawasaki-machi in Chikuho in April 1998.

24. Ibid.
25. Author's interview with Ishizaki Shizuka at her house in Kawsaki-machi in Chikuho in March 1998.
26. Ibid.
27. This, incidentally, tallies with other evidence of the involvement of Buraku in the coal mining industry in the Chikuho region. Many mines opened before the turn of the twentieth century were located in areas of Buraku concentration, as these sites possessed abundant coal of high quality and were also situated close to the bank of the Onga river, which was especially convenient for transporting the coal from the mouth of the mines to the ports. Then, in the 1900s, some railroad lines were built right through the heart of the Buraku mining communities as it was the shortest way to transport coal from the mines to the central stations. See Nagasue Toshio, "Chikuho ni okeru Buraku no Keisei" [The Formation of Buraku in Chikuho], in *Kindai Buraku Mondai* (Osaka: Kaihô Shuppansha, 1986), 96–97; and *Buraku no Bunka Sôzô to Saisei* [For the Cultural Creation and Regeneration of Buraku], Fukuokaken Dôwa Kyôiku Kenkyû Kyôgikai (ed.), 1984, Vol. 2.
28. Author's interview with Ishizaki Shizuka at her house in Kawsaki-machi in Chikuho in March 1998.
29. It was known that only Burakumin lived in that particular village. Open acceptance in Japan that discrimination on social or ethnic grounds is part of the nation's history is relatively recent. The literature on the subject is mainly published in Japanese.
30. Ibid.
31. The monument in their memory with the names of the deceased stands silently near the Chûganji river in Kawasaki-machi. One of the former female miners I interviewed in Kawasaki-machi in April 1996 told me with tears streaming down her face that 200 miners were working underground on the day, and as usual, Burakumin were sent to the most dangerous coalface, only twenty or thirty meters below the river. On September 26, at ten minutes past twelve in the morning, she painfully recalled that the riverbed collapsed and killed sixty-seven miners, including her husband.
32. A measure of the esteem in which Shizuka was held is the tribute to her published in 1999, with contributions from forty-two environmental, social, and other activists throughout Japan: *Ishizaki Shizuka Tsuitô Ikôshû* [Ishizaki Shizuka Testimonial Anthology], privately published (in Japanese) by the contributors, Fukuoka, 1999.
33. The promoter of the group, Shiba Takeo, is a retired junior high school teacher who devoted half his life to the children whose parents were struggling with a declining industry in the 1960s and 1970s. He has published three books: *Hakugai no naka no Rentai* [Solidarity in Oppression], (Tokyo: Taimatsusha, 1977); *Chiisana Mune wa Moeteiru* [The Little Hearts are Burning], (Tokyo: Bunri Shoin, 1966); and *Tankô to Kyôsei Ronkôj* [The Coal Mines and Importation by Force], (Fukuoka: Chikuho Juku, 2000). Another local high school teacher, Yokogawa Teruo, also shares the same research interest and historical work. Their activities were still being pursued even in the 1990s. They were also extremely helpful to me during my fieldwork in Chikuho.
34. I agree with Molony (Barbara Molony, "Women in the Cotton Textile Industry," in Gail Lee Bernstein, *Recreating Japanese women*, 218) that the definition of what constitutes activism should include the opposite of passivity.

35. James C. Scott, *Weapons of the Weak: Everyday forms of Peasant Resistance,* (New Haven: Yale University Press, 1985).

36. My subjects were from the Chikuho coalfield on the southern island of Kyushu, but recent research on the women miners of Hokkaido in the far north of Japan (K. Yoshida and R. Myauchi, "Invisible Labor: Comparative Oral History of Women in Coal Mining Communities of Hokkaido, Japan, and Montana, USA, 1890–1940." Proceedings of the International Mining History Conference, Hokkaido, Japan, 2003, 159–164) reveal an identical duality in the lives of women miners of Hokkaido in the far north of Japan, where women who were good miners were called "goddesses of the pit," and where the women organized a support system for women in need well in advance of the introduction of union-based mutual aid systems in 1945.

PART III

Gender, Mining Communities, and Labor Protests, 1900–1960

As mining became more concentrated in the hands of corporations or the state, families drew on protest strategies that had been widely practiced for centuries in efforts to improve their individual situations. In the twentieth century, spurred by an international workers' movement, mining women and men increasingly relied on collective action to challenge corporate or state control of mining workplaces and communities. Labor solidarity was born, too, out of common suffering that all families experienced. This shared struggle and the particular challenges of the mining industry bound families and community together as they weathered mine closures, accidents, and hard times and envisioned more just futures.

The gendered division of labor, and the few economic alternatives, led women and children to see their interests closely tied to husbands and fathers. Women often initiated or threw themselves behind union efforts to demand the right to organize, reject wage cuts, or improve mine safety. Labor movements preserved the ideals of female domesticity and the male worker as head of household, but women creatively exploited these delegated roles to pursue their own interests and their own forms of protests. In Chile's El Teniente, for example, women used the "family wage" ideal to claim their rights to husbands' wages and benefits as well as work with men to extract economic and social concessions from Kennecott Corporation.[1] Abundant examples from the world's mining communities reveal how women exaggerated gender claims to secure solidarity for what they viewed as family and community, not just union, efforts. During the 1906 Windber, Pennsylvania strike, women hid their husbands' lunch buckets to insure that they stayed away from the mines. They also shamed strikebreakers by presenting them with pennies and breadcrumbs, challenging their indifference to family breadwinners.[2] In Chuquicamata, Chile, when the company tried to crush a strike, groups of women seized the scabs, dressed them in women's clothing, and marched them through the town to ridicule their lack of manhood in failing to support the strike.[3]

In their often dangerous confrontations with militia, police, or military regimes, mining women often relied on the presumed cultural protections that their gendered domestic roles allowed to protest more boldly than men. In late 1921 in Kansas, thousands of miners' wives marched, blocked mine entrances, and threw pepper in strikebreakers' eyes in efforts to support a four-month-old miners' walkout.[4] In the Witwatersrand, South Africa miner's strike and revolt in 1922, women confronted authorities and protected men from violence; wives of labor leaders in the Siglo XX mine village in Bolivia engaged in a hunger strike in 1962 to prevent a government massacre.[5]

Although their gender often protected them from brutalities that might be more openly directed at men, it did not always immunize women from violence or arrest. For example, during the 1891 strike in the coal community of Nanaimo on Vancouver Island, eighteen women led a "March for Female Suffrage" on the road where many had protested the company's evictions and militia outrages. The women criticized scabs' "unmanly" behavior in failing to join union miners; but one strikebreaker violently struck a woman leader, suggesting that he saw her behavior as "unwomanly."[6] Opponents of this militancy frequently labeled women as "men," "Amazons," and "disorderly," condemning their abandonment of appropriate feminine behavior and justifying rough treatment.

But in the process of supporting men's labor rights, women often came to contest the gendered rules for protest and question their own roles in unions, families, and communities. These miners' wives and daughters were motivated by their domestic roles to preserve family economies, and as such, they were "naturally" driven to the public streets and mine shafts to protest. Yet their public activism challenged the social order. Whereas the male mining workforce has been recognized worldwide for its militancy, the combative actions of miners' wives and daughters have not largely been credited for that reputation. This section features four examples from North America that illuminate how gender conventions structured labor protests, how men (husbands, managers, unions, and the state) reacted to women's militancy, and how gender often provided the nexus through which issues of class, race, ethnicity, and national politics were defined. But first, before turning to these case studies, we need to understand the global context for women and mining protests.

TRADITIONS OF PROTEST IN EUROPE, AFRICA, AND ASIA

Even before the outbreak of World War I signaled the dénouement of the old European empires, the influence of socialism and the rise of an international workers movement was being felt around the globe. In part, the international character of this movement may be attributed to the mass migrations that occurred in the last decades of the nineteenth century. As population growth outstripped the available land for farming and even the ability of industry to absorb new workers, nearly 26 million European migrants made their way to the "new world," principally Canada, the United States, South America,

Australia, and New Zealand. Although the immigrant populations sought new opportunities, they also brought with them the traditions of labor from their home countries, traditions that often led to even more radical responses to the exploitation they encountered in their adoptive or temporary homelands.

In Europe prior to World War I, socialist politics and labor organizations had been gaining strength. As the so-called aristocracy of labor, miners and their families were generally in the vanguard of these developments and provided examples of miltancy and organization that were legendary. In France, for example, conditions in the mining industry at least above ground were better for most miners than for other workers; nevertheless the first major miners' strike erupted there in 1884 under the leadership of Emile Basly, whose story became the basis for Emile Zola's *Germinal*.

In Germany, most trade unions under the Social Democratic banner tended to work for improved living conditions rather than the dismantling of the monarchy or capitalism; but the free trade unions tended to embrace the idea of class conflict as their model and to consider strikes a necessary weapon for achieving their goals. Polish migrants to the Ruhr Valley mining communities were so frustrated by the situation with respect to German unions that they formed their own "Zjednoczenie Zawodowe Polskie," which by 1912 had more than 50,000 members.[7] In both Germany and France, miners' wives supported their husbands' demands for a living family wage.

Perhaps ironically, Britain, despite the tradition of moderate socialism, developed the most radical and disciplined miners' union. In Wales and elsewhere major miners' strikes took place before World War I over hours and wages. Miners' wives and daughters followed the rural traditions of "white-shirting" scab laborers, challenging their manhood with embarrassing catcalls, and sometimes even going so far as pulling the trousers off the men enroute to work.[8] The coal owners began to bring in migrant workers, mostly from Spain, around the beginning of the century in an attempt to break the hold of the Miners' Federation of Great Britain (MFGB). But their plans were thwarted when it emerged that many of the Spanish miners were as committed to socialism as their fellow British miners. In the mining community of Abercrave, Welsh and Spanish miners learned each other's languages, and the MFGB promoted the use of "Esperanto" in the mines as the international language of communication.[9]

In the wake of World War I, new and cheaper sources of coal had been found outside of Britain and Europe in general. But labor expected a reward for the sacrifices made during the war. In 1926 the MFGB called a strike over wages and hours that lasted for a year. Financial support poured in from the USSR and other miners' unions from around the world. The miners called on the Trade Union Congress for support and for nearly a week a general strike was held that paralyzed the country. Despite the gesture of support from the major unions, the MFGB failed to win the day, and the miners returned to worse conditions of employment than before the strike. In 1927, British miners' wives organized the first Union of Miners' Wives in the Durham area, holding mass rallies for fund-raising.[10] British miners' wives fought for pit head baths and for better compensation for the widows of miners, and as always, for the principle of a livable family wage.

By 1929, when the Great Depression hit, conditions in British mining areas were desperate. In Maerdy (referred to as "little Moscow") in the Rhondda Valley of Wales, some miners' wives became active members of the Communist Party, while others without political affiliation, threw bricks at police during the violent strikes of the era. Even those with young children were sent to prison and some were even forced to relinquish custodial rights. It has been estimated that by the mid-1930s more than 100,000 people left the mining areas of Wales in search of employment opportunities elsewhere.

But the hard times had unified the British miners and in some areas a remarkable internationalism was forged. In the 1930s, unemployed Welsh miners were volunteering to fight against fascism in Spain, and miners' wives rallied to assist Basque refugee children that arrived in Britain. As the shadow of World War II hung over Britain, miners had the option of remaining in the mines as a vital war industry, and their wives and daughters took up work in the munitions factories, many of which were located around the more remote mining regions of the country. The virtual control of the industry by the government during the war led to nationalization of the mines in 1947 and the creation of the National Union of Mine Workers (NUM). For many miners and their wives this had been the ultimate goal of the union, and it was believed that nationalization was a guarantee of secure jobs and a decent wage. But their elation was short-lived as the government slowly began the task of closing unprofitable mines in the 1950s and 1960s.[11]

It should come as no surprise that with the legacy of British imperialism behind them, the MFGB and later the NUM, forged a vast network of international contacts with miners' unions elsewhere. In Australia, miners' wives followed in the tradition of their British counterparts, forming auxiliaries to the Australian miners' union as early as 1934 in the area of New South Wales. By the 1960s many of these miners' wives considered themselves socialists and through their organization protested everything from the racist implications of the "Gollywog" symbol on jars of imported British jam, to the war in Vietnam.[12] The story of their organization will be taken up in the epilogue of this book.

Elsewhere in India and Africa the legacy of European and British imperialism gave few reasons for optimism among the indigenous mining peoples. In South Africa racial tensions erupted in the early part of the twentieth century as the British, and later the Boer government, imposed policies of segregation against all "colored workers," indigenous black Africans and immigrants from India. In the gold mines of South Africa the black workers were introduced to trade unionism by white workers who began to form unions in the 1880s. The Chamber of Mines, a body of men who owned the gold mines, had set a low-wage policy to maximize their profits. From the very beginning of the trade union movement, bitter strikes emerged and white workers who had struggled for a better standard of living accepted an industrial color bar that allowed them to earn twelve times as much as black miners.[13]

The plight of black miners was magnified by the fact that their wives and children were forced to live, sometimes hundreds of miles away, on reserves. The government argued that black miners' wages were only intended to supplement their families' earnings from the land, but the reality was that the reserve land was unsuitable for farming and miners' families were literally being starved to death. In 1941 the African Mine Workers' Union was formed. The government's refusal to acknowledge the union and the right of black workers to negotiate for higher wages led to the African Miners Strike of 1946.

During the week-long strike hundreds of workers were arrested, tried, and imprisoned. An assembly of women workers who marched to a meeting to show support for the miners was attacked by police and one pregnant woman bayoneted. Despite its failure in terms of practical gains for the miners, the strike transformed the consciousness of a generation of black workers and the world overnight. When the leadership of the African National Congress and the South African Indian National Congress met with UN leaders in 1946 they appraised the member states of the strike and the ongoing struggle for equality in South Africa.[14]

Unlike the situation in South Africa, which forced the separation of black mining families, in the Zambian copperbelt the colonial governments and copper mining companies facilitated female migration by encouraging skilled miners to bring their families to the mines. But the migration of women to the towns created an independence that neither African chiefs nor colonial authorities found acceptable. As women moved in ever greater numbers to the towns, many came to favor casual alliances to formal marriages that might lead to divorce and a loss of both status and income. Despite attempts to restrict the sexual and financial independence of women through tribal laws and government regulations, the women of the mining community retained a certain level of autonomy. As Jane Parpart argues in her work, it was only during times of strikes that the men and women of the copperbelt were likely to join forces for a common goal.[15]

In India, the position of women in mining communities could generally be characterized as one of powerlessnes for the better part of the last two hundred years. During the years of colonial rule, both men and women were exploited as workers in the mines, but the men gradually organized trade unions to challenge conditions in the mines. Women miners were lower-caste Indian women who were generally excluded from the discourses of the labor movement, and eventually, in 1935 they were formally excluded from actual work in the mines, relegated to surface work during day time hours only. Before the 1935 Act outlawing women's work in the mines, the all-male trade union movement worked to insure that at least a widow would get the job of her deceased husband in the mine in order to support her family after his death. Since the nationalization of the mines in India in the 1970s, women's organizations have emerged, which question the displacement of indigenous people by the mining industry and the loss of traditional ways of life that have allowed women to sustain themselves and their communities.[16]

THE NORTH AMERICAN CONTEXT

Through their exploitation of mines in North and South America, by the early-twentieth-century North American corporations led the world in minerals production. The United States replaced Great Britain as the world's greatest coal producer by 1900. The Anaconda copper complex in Montana rivaled Rio Tinto in Spain and the Chilean mines, and the Phelps Dodge development in Arizona made the American West the world leader in copper.[17] Transcontinental railroads linked the mineral wealth of western Canada and the United States to markets in the East. The trust and cartel movement of the early twentieth century, which consolidated and vertically integrated technological and capital-intensive smelting and refining works, linked the largest corporations "that sat astride mineral activity throughout the world" and established the pattern of global mining.[18]

This North American expansion and dominance lured workers from around the world to its mines and smelters, merging many labor perspectives. Yet interethnic divisions at times hindered labor solidarity. Irish, English, and native-born American workers often rebelled against the hiring of southern and eastern European and Mexican workers, even when not employed as strikebreakers. But the Western Federation of Miners (WFM) and United Mine Workers of America (UMWA), the two unions that came to represent North American coal and hard rock miners, hired multilingual organizers in their bid to organize all workers. The multiethnic character of strikes in the early twentieth century reveals the success of this strategy. Despite employer efforts to foster ethnic divisions, a white ethnic class-consciousness developed in metal and coal mining communities through the early decades of the twentieth century, assisting the revitalization of the union movement in the 1930s. But racial exclusions and a dual system of labor remained entrenched in many American mining communities until the late twentieth century. Chinese on the Pacific coast, through exclusion legislation and intimidation, virtually disappeared from mining. Mexican Americans in the Southwest, and African Americans in the East were restricted to "unskilled" mining jobs or paid less than their white counterparts.[19]

Increased corporate power in the early twentieth century was met by fabled organizing efforts by miners and their families to gain a greater share of the wealth they produced. The place names of Ludlow, Matewan, and Butte symbolize the fierce and violent struggles that characterized the American mining industry. The frequency of miners' strikes reveals the importance of women for these actions, since the support of the entire community was necessary. A strong commitment to unions enabled women to hold together families despite the privations wrought by strikes and evictions. As Priscilla Long noted, the "concept of ideal womanhood—militancy combined with motherhood—ran wide and deep" in mining communities.[20]

If women and communities were central to the success of labor protests, mine owners stubbornly resisted union organization and employed sophisticated blacklists, police systems, state governments, and militias to assist them. Employers also created the ubiquitous company towns that controlled housing, stores, and credit, designed to effectively bind the miner and his family to the job. Despite these tactics, the UMWA successfully gained a toehold in the bituminous fields in 1898, and the WFM organized hard rock miners in western Canada and the United States in the early 1900s.[21]

In 1900 and 1902, John Mitchell and the UMWA launched a showdown with the nation's most powerful industry, leading 150,000 anthracite miners on strike. Mary Harris "Mother" Jones, already a particularly effective organizer of women, came to Pennsylvania to rally supporters of the union. Women led demonstrations and parades, and inserted themselves between National Guard soldiers and strikers to avert bloodshed. As Bonnie Stepenoff demonstrates in chapter 9, the organizing styles of Mitchell and Jones celebrated and reinforced traditional gender roles in efforts to win union goals. But despite the heroic stature and popularity of both figures, Jones remained outside the halls of power. The simultaneous celebration and marginalization of Mother Jones reveals how women were central to these protests, but male miners resisted any alterations of prescribed work, family, and union roles.

A decade later, Jones was in Trinidad, Colorado, to support thousands of East European and Mexican American strikers, where the Colorado National Guard promptly jailed her. Five hundred strikers' wives and daughters protested her treatment, and the militia attacked, justifying violence because of the protesters' "unwomanly" behavior. In chapter 10, Anthony DeStefanis links the Guard's brutal treatment of strikers and their families to the earlier conquest of Plains Indians, and explores how Guard beliefs in racial, masculine, and class superiority strengthened their vision of dominance over women and "others," in particular southern European immigrant workers. The Colorado Fuel and Iron strike of 1913–1914 was one of the nation's longest and most bitter industrial conflicts, becoming more violent when the National Guard attacked the Ludlow Tent Colony, killing eleven children and two women.

Five years later, the uprising of over ten thousand West Virginia coal miners, the largest armed insurrection since the Civil War, also ended after much violence and the sending of federal troops. Women played a critical role in this struggle, too, scrounging for food and shelter for families, attacking strikebreakers, ripping up railroad tracks, shooting in gun battles, and wearing the UMW insignia on their nurse's caps as they tended to the wounded. Their shared hatred of the company and desire for improved conditions such as running water led them to "'fight side by side with men'" and impressed observers with their courage.[22]

The militancy of male miners is understood in popular imagery, lore, and history, but many have assumed it was the transient, unattached male worker that characterized the workforce and a propensity for collective labor actions. Recent research has revealed that the presence of families must be integrated into an understanding of the early strength of mining unions and the willingness of them to strike. Miners with families could not protest with their feet and move on, but rather had a vested interest in improving wages and conditions. Ironically, company efforts to stabilize a workforce by providing housing and privileging married workers not only helped to unionize workers but also through women and children created a support system and more passionate defenders of the union cause.[23] As part of their "reproductive" roles, women instilled in a new generation the importance of militant solidarity.

Collective bargaining legislation in the United States in 1934 and in Canada in the mid-1940s enabled the UMWA and International Union of Mine, Mill and Smelter Workers (successor to the WFM after 1916) to unionize some of the most resistant company towns. Despite these gains, many union leaders and rank-and-file workers continued to believe that the association of masculinity with militancy aided their cause. Union iconography and rhetorical traditions championed masculine workers in contrast to weak and feminized bosses. Mining unions often acted autonomously of the rest of the labor movement in Canada and the United States, reflecting the fierce independence of the mining workforce. Even during World War II, company and union officials sought to preserve men's claims to traditional mining occupations, when much of Canada and the United States opened their industrial jobs to women. In the postwar period Mine Mill survived anticommunist hysteria partly through its embrace of a masculine regional identity to resist red-baiting by the United Steelworkers of America (USWA), Canadian and U.S. labor federations, governments, corporations, and the media. USWA organizers, in fact, contended that the nature of the mining industry and a masculine, militant heritage had made western locals more independent and less susceptible to red-baiting.[24]

Mine Mill's dependence on women's support but resistance to women's full involvement in union activities is the focus of the final two essays in this section. The 1951 Empire Zinc strike in New Mexico pushed masculine assumptions aside as a court injunction prevented male strikers from picketing, and Mine Mill wives took over in physically holding back deputies and scabs. As Ellen Baker documents in chapter 11, the reactions to the women's picket revealed the tensions inherent in the two models of unionism that had coexisted in this, and in many other, mining communities: one model based on a brotherhood of men as breadwinners, and the other model based on a larger union family that "helped consolidate the union's power beyond the workplace." As the strike continued and family responsibilities were questioned, women came to rebel not only against the company but also against their husbands.

In 1958 in Sudbury, Ontario, gender tensions within Mine Mill turned a strike against Inco into a contest over family values and the cold war. Mercedes Steedman illustrates in chapter 12 how red-scare propaganda convinced a significant number of union wives to lead a back-to-work movement, and because Mine Mill had failed to allow a more inclusive political role for women auxiliary supporters, it ultimately jeopardized the future of democratic unionism. In pursuit of their "manhood" in initiating the strike, union leaders to consider women's interests and found many women in the community pulled instead to an anticommunist faction that had framed the strike as an assault on the family. After a weak strike settlement, Mine Mill succumbed to these assaults and finally merged with the USWA in the mid-1960s.

The essays in this section demonstrate how labor actions can unsettle traditional gender arrangements and relations, and in the process affect union, mining, and family history. As women take to the picket line or streets, renegotiating who takes on household duties and the use of public spaces, the traditional social boundaries between unionized miners and their families collapse. Although most labor protests, informal and formal, involved men and women seeking improved wages for men as heads of households, as women recognized their collective power, they often asserted different needs and goals than men. Yet gender roles and identities have been remarkably persistent, not only in North America but in the rest of the world. The post-strike period often involved men reasserting their authority and control over public and private gender relations. Labor struggles, then, often evolved into private contestation over family roles and collective challenges, sometimes for specific material goals and sometimes for ideas about equality.

Notes

1. Klubock, *Contested Communities*, 221.
2. Mildred Beik, *The Miners of Windber: The Struggles of New Immigrants for Unionization, 1890s–1930s* (University Park, PA: The Pennsylvania State University Press, 1996), 209, 286.
3. Finn, *Tracing the Veins*, 145.
4. Ann Schofield, " 'An Army of Amazons': The Language of Protest in a Kansas Mining Community, 1921–22," *American Quarterly* 37, no. 5 (Winter 1985): 686–701.
5. Jeremy Krikler, "Women, Violence and the Rand Revolt of 1922," *Journal of Southern African Studies* [Great Britain] 22, no. 3 (1996): 349–372; Nash, *We Eat the Mines*, 114.
6. Allen Seager and Adele Perry, "Mining the Connections: Class, Ethnicity, and Gender in Nanaimo, British Columbia, 1891," *Histoire Sociale/Social History* 30, no. 59 (1997), 58–60. For many additional examples of women's activism during coal and hard rock mining strikes, see the lively discussions on H-Labor@H-Net.Msu.Edu, March 25–30, 2000.
7. V.R. Berghahn, *Imperial Germany, 1871–1914: Economy, Society, Culture, and Politics* (Rhode Island: Berghahn Books, 1994), 225.
8. Angela V. John, "A Miner Struggle? Women's Protests in Welsh Mining History." *Llafur 4.1* (1984), 72–75.
9. *The Miner,* November 12, 1927, 11.
10. *The Miner,* March 6, 1927, 3.
11. Raphael Samuel, Barbara Bloomfield, and Guy Boanas, *The Enemy Within: Pit Villages and the Miners' Strike, 1984–1985* (London: Routledge, Kegan and Paul 1986), 1–9.

12. Winifred Mitchell, "Women in Mining Communities," in *Women, Class, and History: Feminist Perspectives in Australia*, ed., E. Windshuttle (Melbourne: Dominion Press, 1980).

13. Alex Hepple, *South Africa, A Political and Economic History* (London: Pall Mall Press, 1966). See also John Temple, *Mining: An International History* (New York: Praeger Publishers, 1972), 111–115.

14. Gwendolyn Carter and Thomas Karis, *From Protest to Challenge*, vol. 2 (Stanford: Hoover Institute Press, 1973), 257–258.

15. Jane L. Parpart and Sharon B. Stichter, eds., *Patriarchy and Class: African Women in the Home and the Workforce* (Boulder: Westview Press, 1988), 115–116.

16. Kuntala Lahiri-Dutt, "Kamins Building the Empire: Class, Caste, and Gender Interface in Indian Collieries," in this volume chapter 4, p. 71.

17. Lynch, *Mining in World History*, 173.

18. Ibid., 189, 274, 280.

19. On the racialized and gendered notions of mining work and protests, see, e.g., Katherine Benton-Cohen, "Docile Children and Dangerous Revolutionaries: The Racial Hierarchy of Manliness and the Bisbee Deportation of 1917." *Frontiers: A Journal of Women Studies* 24, nos. 2 & 3 (2003), 30–50; Andrea Yvette Huginnie, " 'Strikitos': Race, Class, and Work in the Arizona Copper Industry, 1870–1920" (PhD diss., Yale University, 1991); Horace Huntley, "Iron Ore Miners and the Mine Mill in Alabama: 1933–1952" (PhD diss., University of Pittsburgh, 1977).

20. Long, *Where the Sun Never Shines*, 156.

21. Barbara Freese, *Coal: A Human History* (New York: Penguin, 2003), 137–138.

22. Robert Shogan, *The Battle of Blair Mountain: The Story of America's Largest Labor Uprising* (Boulder: Westview Press, 2004), 194; David Alan Corbin, *Life, Work, and Rebellion, in the Coal Fields: The Southern West Virginia Miners 1880–1922* (Urbana: University of Illinois Press, 1981), 92–93.

23. See, e.g., Belshaw, *Colonization and Community*, 73–74; Jameson, *All That Glitters*, Corbin, *Life, Work, and Rebellion*, 65–66.

24. For a discussion of Mine Mill's gendered heritage, see Laurie Mercier, *Anaconda: Labor, Culture, and Community in Montana's Smelter City* (Urbana: University of Illinois Press, 2001).

CHAPTER 9

"I'm a Johnny Mitchell Man": Gender and Labor Protest in the Pennsylvania Hard Coal Uprising, 1900–1902

Bonnie Stepenoff

> Right here I tell you
> I'm not a scabby fellow,
> I'm a good union citizen,
> I'm a Johnny Mitchell man.
>
> Lyric by Con Carbon, 1902[1]

In the first years of the twentieth century, Mary Harris "Mother" Jones stood out as the only woman attending national conventions of the United Mine Workers of America (UMWA). During strikes in 1900 and 1902, UMWA president John Mitchell asked her to come to northeastern Pennsylvania to help keep anthracite (hard coal) miners in the union. Mitchell and Jones had dramatically different public images, rooted in gender roles as much as in their individual personalities. Whereas Mitchell maintained a fatherly dignity, Jones nagged and scolded in a grandmotherly way. In these two charismatic figures, miners saw reflections of men and women they recognized and trusted. Their gendered organizing styles buoyed Pennsylvania hard coal miners through two militant seasons, but ultimately compromised worker solidarity by reinforcing stereotypes and linking males to a patriarchal power structure.

Under Mitchell's brilliant leadership, men in Pennsylvania's mountainous anthracite region overcame ethnic divisions and joined a mass movement to fight for better wages and working conditions in the mines. Mitchell became a national organizer in 1897 and union president in 1898. Previous attempts to organize the anthracite miners had ended in disillusionment, but by the end of 1899, local union halls in the valleys of the Susquehanna, Schuylkill, and Lehigh rivers were crowded with mine workers.[2] Mitchell appeared at district meetings, impressing delegates as "a man possessed of those sterling qualities which are so essential to a man in his position."[3]

Both Mitchell and Jones addressed a convention of miners in Hazleton on August 17, 1900, and stressed the importance of family. After the meeting adjourned, streetcars transported all the participants to the town of Lattimer, where police killed nineteen immigrant miners during a labor protest in 1897. Several speakers, including Mitchell and Jones, reminded the audience of the deaths of those men and the grief of their loved ones. One speaker later wrote in the *United Mine Workers Journal* that the memory of the "wails of the widows and orphans should stir the men to action, to be true members of their craft organization, helping to inculcate the spirit of true manhood into the hearts of others."[4] Implicitly, that spirit of true manhood had as its core the protection of women and children.

One month later, hard coal miners went on strike, with the blessing of their wives. In mid-September, Mitchell announced that the number of strikers topped 100,000, a figure exceeding "that of any other industrial context in the history of our country."[5] To keep the men on the picket lines, Mother Jones went to the local communities, calling the women into action. When striking miners came to a meeting in the town of McAdoo, she told them to go home and get their wives. The women's applause signaled their support for the men's militancy.[6]

Organized parades and mass meetings dramatized the numbers and solidarity of the striking miners. On October 2, 1900, fifteen thousand men and boys marched through the streets of Wilkes-Barre to the thumping rhythms of forty brass bands and drum corps. Marching four, five, and six abreast, the miners carried signs, saying, "We want our dinner pails filled with substantial food, not coal barons' taffy," "Our union must be recognized," and "We will no longer be slaves." Young boys who worked in the aboveground breakers, picking slate out of the coal, held banners reading, "We need schooling but must work," and "Down with oppression; we will stand by Mitchell."[7] A group of men from Pittston brought a float with four men representing "Coal Barons," drinking champagne. Following this was a float with miners consuming bread and water, and behind this paraders carried a stretcher containing a dummy representing a dead miner.

Labor parades reinforced gender stereotypes. After the massive parade on October 2, The *New York Times* reported that, "The great bulk of the parade was made up of stalwart men. As a rule they were well dressed, and some of them from their appearance might be taken for well-to-do farmers."[8] This allusion was revealing in that "well-to-do farmers" were the heads of traditional, patriarchal households.

Mother Jones was present at numerous demonstrations during the 1900 strike, capitalizing on her gender to draw the attention of the press. When she arrived in Wilkes-Barre on October 2, 1900, a huge crowd met her at the depot and paraded through the town. Four days later, more than a thousand striking miners, a fife and drum corps, fifty women in wagons, including

Mother Jones, and reporters, traveled from Hazleton to Lattimer, where they raided the two collieries of Calvin Pardee and Co.[9]

Furious women showed just how militant they could be during the activities at Lattimer. Early on the morning of October 5, twenty-five women attacked eight Italians working the night shift at the Calvin and Pardee colliery.[10] Two days later, with Mother Jones participating, a contingent of miners, musicians, and women entered the town at six o'clock in the morning and marched up and down the public road, preventing non-striking miners from going to work when the whistle blew. A short while later, another group of demonstrators entered the town; the two groups combined forces, organizing a spontaneous parade, with the women and girls heading the columns. For two hours, they marched in files, preventing any traffic from moving through the town, and frightening the occupants of the company houses, effectively shutting down the mine.[11]

Women played a peacekeeping role in subsequent demonstrations. In mid-October 1900, trainloads of company police and a regiment of the Pennsylvania National Guard converged on the Panther Creek Valley to stop 3,000 union marchers, who were trying to close down mines. With bayonets drawn, the militia forced the demonstrators away from the valley. A cordon of women, singing songs and jeering at the soldiers, formed between the troops and the strikers, averting bloodshed.[12] By the end of October, the miners accepted a 10 percent pay increase, and Mitchell became a regional hero, lionized by adult male workers and loved by the breaker boys. At a celebration in Wilkes-Barre, on October 29, 1900, young Benjamin Phillips presented Mitchell with a gold medal and said, "I represent the breaker boys of the anthracite region and have been selected by them to present to President Mitchell of the United Mine Workers of America a token of our respect and love for him. We respect him because we believe he is as good and just as any other president, either of states or railroads. We love him because he first loved us, because he is like Abraham Lincoln was, and cannot look down upon suffering and slavery without pitying and reaching out his hand to save."[13]

During a larger and much longer strike, which began in May 1902, Con Carbon's lyric, "I'm a Johnny Mitchell Man" gave voice to the miners' feelings for their Irish American leader. Realizing that ethnic divisions made solidarity impossible, Mitchell insisted that Slavic miners join the union fold, participating equally with their English-speaking brothers.[14] When eastern European immigrants sang Carbon's words, they expressed a complex set of ideas, asserting their courage, patriotism, and equality with their "American" union brothers. Rendered, as it often was, in Slavic-American dialect, the title became "Me Johnny Mitchell Man."

In the song's first lines, a miner named John sang, "Oh, you know Joe Silovatsky/Dat man is my brudder. . . ." As the narrative progressed, Joe came to John's "shanty," announced that there was going to be a strike, and urged him not to be "scabby." This was significant, in that Slavic workers had been seen as unreliable, easily intimidated, and willing to accept low pay, undercutting the wages of other miners. Because they remained outside the union, employers could use them as scabs. In response to his friend's call to join the strike, John replied, "Vell, I'm dunt fraid fer nottink/ Dat's me nevair shcare. . . ." Declaring his determination to stand up for the union, he said, "Me not scabby fella/ . . . I'm Johnny Mitchell man."[15]

"Scabby fellows," who reported to work during the strike, incurred the wrath and sometimes the violence of unionists. In September 1902, the conservative *New York Times* commented that "Like a plague the word 'scab' carries terror into every workingman's home. . . ."[16] Wandering bands of unemployed men and desperate women used threats, curses, stones, clubs, and sometimes guns, to intimidate miners on their way to the collieries. On September 26, 1902, the *Times* reported that a gang of Hungarian strikers attacked and clubbed James Winston on his way to work at Grassy Island Colliery near Olyphant. As Winston lay dying of blows to his head, a crowd of shouting men and women continued to beat him.[17] These incidents continued to happen, despite Mitchell's strong condemnation of violence.[18]

Strikers also had reason to be afraid. The Lattimer massacre remained a vivid memory.[19] Police and militia forces were a threatening presence at meetings, parades, and demonstrations. Immigrant miners regarded law enforcement officials with deep suspicion, and many miners carried weapons. In late July 1902 "tens of thousands of idle men and boys in this vicinity who had been gathering in large numbers and marching from place to place"[20] converged on the town of Shenandoah. Police and demonstrators fought a gun battle on the night of July 30. Four policemen and several strikers suffered bullet wounds. One man was clubbed to death, and at least twenty others were injured. On the following night, 1,200 state militiamen camped on a hill overlooking the town, attracting crowds of onlookers.[21] Recognizing the potential for disaster, in the summer and fall of 1902, union leaders, concerned citizens, and clergymen prevailed upon strikers and law enforcement officials to preserve the peace.

In addition to the constant threat of violence, idle miners faced hunger and homelessness. Without money to pay the rent, they had to depend on the charity of landlords, who often worked for the coal companies. By September of 1902, mine operators predicted that lack of food would force the miners back to work. Mitchell insisted they could hold out until Christmas. Labor organizations and other donors provided relief for destitute families. Every two weeks, mining families could draw $2.50 for a man and wife and 35 cents for each child. This was enough to buy a sack of flour, some beans, a bushel of potatoes, some salt pork, and small amounts of rice, coffee, tea, and sugar, with nothing left over for rent, fuel, and clothing.[22]

When conditions became intolerable, many anthracite miners left the region, or even the country, in search of employment in bituminous (soft coal) mines. Others roamed the countryside or jumped freight trains, riding from town to town. These rides became known as "Johnny Mitchell excursions." During the 1902 strike, miners sang these lines in a folk song:

The strike is nearly o'er
And with joy I'm near insane.

Here's health unto the union,
Which is very strong they say,
Likewise to the conductor
On Johnny Mitchell's Train.[23]

Clearly, there was an undertone of bitterness in this song, as idleness and suffering tested workers' loyalty.

Miners who stayed in the region depended upon support from their families. Almost all married women remained in the home, cooking, cleaning, and making limited resources stretch as far as possible. Clothes had to last an extra season, and children wore hand-me-downs. As winter approached, miners' wives salvaged fuel from the culm piles near every colliery, although some mine owners posted "No Trespassing" signs and even demanded police protection for their property.[24]

Unmarried daughters and sons brought wages home to help support their parents. Many girls and young single women found employment in the silk and lace mills that sprang up in the late nineteenth century in virtually every anthracite mining city, town, and hamlet.[25] During the strike, the *New York Times* noted, children's income became crucial for family survival.[26]

Miners and their families kept up their spirits by recognizing and celebrating, not only Mitchell, but also other leaders, including Mother Jones. The words of an anthracite folk song named a pantheon of worker heroes. Mitchell came first, and the songwriter invested him with many virtues, including honesty, fairness, selflessness, and most importantly, loyalty to the union cause. After Mitchell, the writer continued, "There's three more I'll mention; their names are well known,/John Fahy, John Siney and our beloved Mother Jones. . . ."[27] All these leaders were Irish American. John Siney organized the Workingmen's Benevolent Association (WBA) in the 1860s and the Miners' National Association in the 1870s. John Fahy led anthracite miners in the 1890s, although he did not welcome southern and eastern Europeans to the coalfields.[28] Mother Jones was new to the anthracite region in the early 1900s, but she quickly won people's affection.

Despite gender differences, Mitchell and Jones shared certain qualities that appealed to the miners' hearts. Both had lived very hard lives. Like many of the rank-and-file members of his union, Mitchell was the son of immigrants. Born in 1870 and orphaned at an early age, he became an apprentice to his stepfather in the bituminous mines of Braidwood, Illinois. As a boy of twelve, he descended into damp, noxious tunnels, where rats coveted his dinner pail. Notwithstanding his own lonely childhood, he constantly praised the warmth and endurance of working-class families. Having attended school irregularly for only five years, he regretted his lack of formal education and became an impassioned opponent of child labor and a champion of education for miners' children.[29]

Mitchell's union activities began in the late 1880s in Spring Valley, Illinois. After its inception in 1890, the UMWA sent organizers to this town, where operators and miners were at loggerheads. Mitchell was an influential citizen, president of a coal miners' athletic club, and supporter of the public schools. One of his most important friends was a Catholic priest with a pro-union viewpoint. When Mitchell's union affiliation cost him his job in 1894, he accepted a post as a UMWA organizer. Overcoming racial and ethnic hostilities, he successfully organized miners in Illinois and then played an important role in the momentous strike of 1897. By 1898, the union was looking for a new leader, who would bring an end to years of internal strife and external confrontation. With a mandate to defuse class warfare and develop peaceful contractual relations, Mitchell became president of the union.[30]

Although he was still a young man, the miners of northeastern Pennsylvania treated him reverently as a father figure. He dressed in dark suits and a soft black felt cap. Although he was a Protestant, he acquired an aura of sanctity by wearing priest-like clothing and by closely associating with prominent Catholic clergymen.[31] At a mass meeting in Scranton on August 1, 1902, he addressed a crowd of 7,000 miners. His district leaders appeared first, some speaking Polish and some Italian. The crowd cheered them all, but went wild over Mitchell. As the *New York Times* described the scene, as follows: "When he was introduced to speak some one shouted 'Hats off!' and although the sun's rays beamed down so intensely that many were carried from the crowd exhausted every man in the vast assemblage bared his head and remained uncovered until Mr. Mitchell's speech was concluded."[32]

Mother Jones was a former schoolteacher, more than twice Mitchell's age.[33] Educated in Toronto, Ontario, she taught in Canadian public schools, a convent school in Monroe, Michigan, and schools in Memphis, Tennessee.[34] In 1861, she met and married George Jones, an iron molder, devoted to his union. Six years later, her husband, son, and three daughters died in a yellow fever epidemic that devastated Memphis's Irish American section. A middle-aged widow, she moved to Chicago and worked as a dressmaker, until the great fire destroyed her home and shop. Recovering from this blow, she devoted her energies to the Knights of Labor, which held nightly meetings in Chicago and picnics on Sundays.[35]

When she joined the UMWA, she proved to be a gifted organizer. Although this was a strange occupation for a woman, she fit comfortably into the role because of her forthright speech and homespun wisdom. She could drink, cuss, and hurl venomous epithets, but so could many women who coped with the hard life of the mining community. Her early experiences in the classroom had taught her to boss unruly children, and she sometimes treated wavering strikers as errant boys in need of a good tongue-lashing. As a former teacher, and as a bereaved mother, she stood with Mitchell against child labor and in favor of education for miners' sons and daughters.

Her careworn face and tragic past gave her authority to speak, as a mother, to the hard-pressed women of the region. Many had lost husbands and sons to illness or injury in the mines. Some had to make their own living as seamstresses or laundry women, because male breadwinners were dead, laid off, or disabled. Many were forced to send sons and daughters out to work, because miners' wages could not support the family. These women knew the source of their troubles: the owners of the mines. Mother Jones voiced their rage by railing against fat capitalists, who dressed in silk spun by miners' children and feasted on the profits of the men's killing toil.

By 1902, she was a well-known figure in the region and the nation. In January of that year she made an unannounced appearance as the only female delegate at the annual UMWA convention in Indianapolis. According to the miners' journal, her arrival "was the signal for much rejoicing."[36] The reporter for the journal went on to comment that her "name [was] familiar to every member of the United Mine Workers" and that she "probably [had] a larger personal acquaintance among them than President Mitchell or any other official of the big organization."[37] Considering that this was the high water mark of Mitchell's career, this was high praise. The reporter was saying not only that Jones was well known, but also that people knew her, or felt they did, in a personal way.

Using her fame and star quality, she went on to rally miners' wives during the 1902 hard coal strike. At McAdoo near Hazleton in September 1902, Jones persuaded women wielding mops and brooms and banging on tin pans to follow male strikers on a fifteen-mile march through the Pennsylvania mountains.[38] The press may have accused her of arousing passions in women, but these passions were already close to the surface, as these lyrics from a local folk song, recalled by a Pottsville woman, attest:

> May God above,
> Send down a dove
> With wings as sharp as razors;
> To cut the throats,
> Of those old bloats,
> Who cut the poor man's wages.[39]

Marches and demonstrations provided outlets for miners' frustrations and spectacles for local citizens and members of the press. Organized parades featured drum and bugle corps, floats, and phalanxes of miners in sober black suits. Many of the spectators were women and children, also dressed in their Sunday best. A sentimental poem in the *United Mine Workers Journal* October 30, 1902, described a little girl watching a parade in celebration of the strike's end. The poet created a portrait of a storybook child with wavy golden hair and pouty lips. She responded to the music and the spectacle, as she waited anxiously for her father to appear. In the poet's words, "Her little feet were tapping as the band went booming by;/ The ever-flowing tide of men she watched with eager eye."[40]

The little girl's father conformed to the stereotype of the virile miner, tall and strong with muscles "like steel." But the sight of his little girl touched his heart, "A smile was on his bearded lips; a tear shone in his eye;/ He gently waved his massive hand as he went marching by."[41] Transparently, the poet meant to convey the image of the sturdy male provider and protector of the fragile female child, although many female children in the hard coal region reported to the mills every day to support their fathers.

Children growing up in the anthracite fields witnessed these spectacles and tried to emulate their militant parents. Writing for *McClure's* in 1903, Francis Nichols noted that every child of school age in the region had lived through two great strikes. Young boys, already employed in the breakers, formed junior locals of the miners' union. Nichols described their secret nighttime meetings, with elected officers, fiery speeches, and attentive members, all between the ages of ten and sixteen, in soft black caps and overalls, ready to "assert their manhood."[42] Factory girls also joined unions and held regular meetings, but they dressed as they would for church. Nichols, the middle-class reformer, expressed shock at the idea that "Pale-faced little girls 'assert their manhood' quite as often and as vigorously as do stalwart coal-begrimed miners."[43]

Nichols made a strong plea against child labor, arguing that these "Children of the Coal Shadow" were learning radical politics instead of reading, writing, arithmetic, and middle-class values. Meetings of the junior locals often took place in the schoolhouses, from which breaker boys and factory girls were notably absent during the day. When breaker boys did attend school, Nichols contended, their passion for unionism sometimes caused fights with the children of bosses or non-union men.[44] Deprived of their childhood and their education, these young boys and girls would grow up to be American citizens, but they would live forever under the "coal shadow" in a world far from the mainstream of American life.

Jones, Mitchell, and the UMWA shared Nichols's abhorrence for child labor. Like Nichols, Jones wanted to protect children from the influences of the breaker and the mill, but she believed the union had to take up their cause. Speaking in Indianapolis, Indiana, on January 25, 1901, she said, "When I look into the faces of the little toiling children and see their appealing eyes, it touches the chord of a mother's heart. Think of these helpless little things with no one to fight their battles but labor's hosts."[45] In fall 1902, the *United Mine Workers Journal* noted that the ongoing strike had prompted many of the former breaker boys to attend classes again, editorializing that, "President Mitchell is much pleased over the success of the schools. It has always been his ambition to get the boys out of the mines and into the schools."[46] (figure 9.1)

When young silk mill workers in Carbondale and Scranton emulated their fathers and spontaneously walked off the job in late 1900 and early 1901, they wrote to Mother Jones, asking her to help them form a local union.[47] At the time of the silk strike, Mother Jones plainly expressed her outrage at capitalist entrepreneurs who employed young girls in textile mills. Speaking to the UMWA in January 1901, she lamented the fact that fathers could no longer protect their daughters from capitalist exploitation. Pennsylvania hard coal miners had long been accustomed to sending young sons to work in the coal breakers. "But my friends," she announced, "the capitalistic class has met you face to face today to take the girls as well as the boys out of the cradle."[48]

As more and more girls and young single women walked out of the mills, male unionists tried to get control of the situation. In December 1900 and

WOMEN TAKING HOME COAL PICKED FROM CULM BANK

Figure 9.1 Miners' wives and children gathering fuel from the culm piles during the 1902 Pennsylvania strike. Courtesy of the Hagley Museum and Library, Wilmington, Delaware.

January 1901, various locals of the UMWA held meetings and offered their support. Committees of mine workers visited the fathers of silk hands and urged them to let their children join the strike.[49] Strikers and their supporters held mass meetings in Scranton. Male organizers urged weavers to form a branch of the Silk Weavers of America and all other workers to join a local of the Textile Workers. However, the Scranton daily paper commented: "To organize the silk workers is a difficult task, as the bulk are girls from 12 to 16 years of age and are very enthusiastic."[50]

With nearly three thousand silk workers on strike in mid-February, Mother Jones arrived in Scranton and organized several parades and demonstrations. A local headline noted that "She Roused Them Up" with mass meetings and fiery speeches. She said the girls were living under a system of robbery and demoralization of body and soul. She knew how they suffered and they would continue to suffer until they joined unions and remained firm. On wages, she understood that some of them were paid but $2 per week, which was "not enough to feed one of the dogs of the robbers."[51]

She characterized the silk insurgency as a children's strike and used it as an occasion to speak out against child labor. In one speech, quoted in the local newspaper, she castigated parents for bringing children to the Pennsylvania mills. In a speech in Scranton she said, "It is astonishing to find so many girls of exactly 13 years of age at work in the mills here, and we are going to look into it. The parents are really at fault. They make oath their children are 13 years old, when in many instances we can prove by the record of births that they are under 10."⁵² The conservative Scranton paper echoed Jones's sentiments, berating parents who filed false affidavits in order to place their children in the mills.⁵³

When the strike ended in April with modest gains for the silk workers, Jones continued to fight against the exploitation of children. During and after the strike, she organized parades and demonstrations that put the labor force on display. The youngest strikers headed a parade on March 8, prompting the *Scranton Republican* to comment that there were "nearly 500 of an age not beyond wearing short dresses."⁵⁴ Mother Jones led a group of older girls in the procession, which reportedly included nearly three thousand marchers. After strikers accepted the settlement, Mother Jones arranged another protest against child labor by staging a "victory" parade of little girls, accompanied by boys who belonged to the newsboys' and bootblacks' unions.⁵⁵

For Jones, Mitchell, and the UMWA, arguments against child labor rested upon a belief in the traditional family headed by a male breadwinner. Parades of factory girls, bootblacks, and breaker boys served to dramatize the evils of a system that exploited children while depriving adult males of a fair wage. The argument was simple: if miners earned enough to support their families, then young boys and girls would not have to work. Processions of stalwart miners, wearing dark suits, giving them the appearance of "well-to-do farmers," presented an image of patriarchal providers. In the words of the poet, labor parades, despite all the bombast and noise, had a sentimental meaning that, "more than banners, mottoes, bands, [spoke] Labor's love of home."⁵⁶

This traditional view of family and gender relations relegated mining women, including Mother Jones, to a secondary role. Women were not breadwinners or, except in dire circumstances, heads of households, and Jones was not a policy maker in the union. Miners' wives might be strong, courageous, outspoken, even physically violent in defense of family and home, but they were subordinate to their husbands. Jones, despite her flamboyance, remained, in the words of a biographer, a "supernumerary,"⁵⁷ outside the inner circles of power.

During the hard coal strikes of 1900 and 1902, Mitchell increasingly identified with a group of powerful and wealthy men. In December 1900, he addressed a conference on industrial conciliation, sponsored by a new organization called the National Civic Federation (NCF), which included representatives of capital and labor.⁵⁸ As time went on, he became more deeply committed to the federation's goal of replacing confrontation with negotiation, and he also became increasingly friendly with mine operators and railroad presidents in the organization.⁵⁹ Old friends noticed a change in his demeanor. He dressed differently and, when he attended the NCF conference in December 1902, he donned a derby hat.⁶⁰

In October 1902, President Theodore Roosevelt, the most powerful man in the United States, invited Mitchell and representatives of the anthracite mine owners to confer with him at the White House.[61] This conference resulted in no agreement on how to settle the strike. Within ten days, however, the president had appointed a panel of commissioners, all male, to consider both sides of the issue in a series of hearings at the courthouse in Scranton. With this promise of arbitration, the miners returned to work by the end of the month. Most of the miners were jubilant, but Mother Jones complained that Mitchell accepted a weak settlement because he had succumbed to the flattery of great men.[62]

Less than a year after the strike ended, Jones tried and failed to gain an audience with Roosevelt on the issue of child labor in Pennsylvania mills. During a Philadelphia textile strike in the summer of 1903, Jones organized a march of adult and child workers to the president's vacation home at Sagamore Hill at Oyster Bay, Long Island. After three weeks of marching in the heat and rain, with stops at various cities along the way and many desertions, a bedraggled group of workers arrived at the president's headquarters. Jones and three of the factory boys presented themselves at the executive offices, requesting a meeting with Roosevelt. He turned them down, and bitterly disappointed, they walked the hundred miles or so back to Philadelphia.[63]

Mitchell remained an icon in the anthracite region, even as he became more conservative and less sympathetic to the demands of his union's rank and file. By 1905, he faced strong criticism from socialists in the UMWA, as a consensus grew to censure him for his participation in the NCF. He retained his presidency until 1908, but his national power base rapidly vanished.[64] Miners in Pennsylvania's hard coal region remained loyal to him much longer than their brothers elsewhere. For a quarter of a century, until the 1930s, anthracite communities celebrated John Mitchell Day every October 29, the date the 1900 strike ended, with parades, demonstrations, and banners.[65]

Jones, who never gave up the fight for social justice, became a female icon, but never challenged traditional gender roles. She took no part in the women's rights movement. In fact, she vociferously opposed women's suffrage.[66] When she supported female strikers who walked out of the silk mills in 1900–1901, she turned from the issues of wages and hours to the issue of child labor, insisting that young single females did not belong in the factories.[67] Adult women, she believed, should be wives and mothers, whose proper place was either in the home or on the picket lines, standing behind their union men.[68]

During the Pennsylvania hard coal uprising of 1900–1902, John Mitchell and Mother Jones led a movement that demanded higher wages for male breadwinners, while reaffirming traditional gender roles. Mitchell brought thousands of men into the UMWA by insisting that ethnic divisions weakened the union and reaching out to recent immigrants. Miners from eastern and southern Europe declared their loyalty to the UMWA by singing, "I'm a Johnny Mitchell Man." Mother Jones used her charismatic personality to keep faltering strikers out of the collieries and, just as importantly, to rally wives and daughters for the cause. Mitchell personified manly pride and courage with his calm demeanor and dignified eloquence, while Jones railed at greedy mine owners, providing a conduit for female rage. Both these leaders spoke passionately of the importance of home and family and the need to protect miners' children.

The resolution of the 1902 strike reinforced the existing gendered hierarchy. Mother Jones remained with the union as a supernumerary—rallying, haranguing, and leading demonstrations—whereas Mitchell became increasingly involved in negotiations with powerful men in business and government. When Mitchell's power in the national union evaporated, many anthracite miners continued to regard him as a local labor hero—a hero whose actions and demeanor entangled him inextricably with the traditional male power structure.

NOTES

1. Con Carbon, "Me Johnny Mitchell Man," *Songs and Ballads of the Anthracite Miners* (Library of Congress Archive of Folk Culture, originally released as Recording Laboratory, Library of Congress, AFS L16, 1947), jacket notes, 12.
2. *United Mine Workers Journal*, January 4, 1900.
3. Ibid., April 19, 1900.
4. Ibid., August 23, 1900.
5. Ibid., September 20, 1900.
6. Ibid., September 27, 1900.
7. *New York Times*, October 3, 1900.
8. Ibid.
9. Ibid., October 7, 1900.
10. Ibid., October 6, 1900.
11. Ibid., October 7, 1900.
12. *United Mine Workers Journal*, October18, 1900.
13. Ibid., November 1, 1900.
14. See Victor Greene, *The Slavic Community on Strike: Immigrant Labor in Pennsylvania Anthracite* (Notre Dame, IN: University of Notre Dame Press, 1968).
15. Carbon, "Me Johnny Mitchell Man," *Songs and Ballads*, 12.
16. *New York Times*, July 27, 1902.
17. Ibid., September 26, 1902.
18. Craig Phelan, *Divided Loyalties: The Public and Private Life of Labor Leader John Mitchell* (Albany: State University of New York Press, 1994), 178–179.
19. Perry K. Blatz, *Democratic Miners: Work and Labor Relations in the Anthracite Coal Industry* (Albany: State University of New York Press, 1994), 55.
20. *New York Times*, August 1, 1902.
21. Ibid.
22. *New York Times*, September 5, 1902.
23. "On Johnny Mitchell's Train," in Carbon, *Songs and Ballads*, 14.
24. *United Mine Workers Journal*, October 2, 1902.
25. See Bonnie Stepenoff, *Their Fathers' Daughters: Silk Mill Workers in Northeastern Pennsylvania, 1880–1960* (Selinsgrove, PA: Susquehanna University Press, 1999).

26. *New York Times*, September 5, 1902.
27. George Korson, *Minstrels of the Mine Patch: Songs and Stories of the Anthracite Industry* (Philadelphia: University of Pennsylvania Press, 1938), 228–229.
28. Blatz, *Democratic Miners*, 46–54.
29. Phelan, *Divided Loyalties*, 1–5.
30. Ibid., 1–5, 41.
31 Robert H. Wiebe, "The Anthracite Strike of 1902: A Record of Confusion." *Missouri Valley Historical Review* 48 (September 1961): 235–236.
32. *New York Times*, August 2, 1902.
33. Mother Jones's birth date is often given as 1830, although records in County Cork, Ireland, indicate that she was born in 1837. See Elliott J. Gorn, *Mother Jones: The Most Dangerous Woman in America* (New York: Hill and Wang, 2001), 9.
34. Dale Fetherling, *Mother Jones, The Miners' Angel* (Carbondale: Southern Illinois University Press, 1974), 3.
35. Ibid., 2–6.
36. *United Mine Workers Journal*, January 23, 1902.
37. Ibid.
38. Fetherling, *Mother Jones*, 41.
39. Korson, *Minstrels of the Mine Patch*, 287.
40. *United Mine Workers Journal*, October 30, 1902.
41. Ibid.
42. Francis H. Nichols, "Children of the Coal Shadow," *McClure's Magazine* 20 (February, 1903): 441–442.
43. Ibid., 442.
44. Ibid., 442–444.
45. Mother Jones, *The Speeches and Writings of Mother Jones*, ed. Edward M. Steel (Pittsburgh, PA: University of Pittsburgh Press, 1988), 5.
46. *United Mine Workers Journal*, October 2, 1902.
47. *Scranton Republican*, December 8, 1900.
48. Mother Jones, *Speeches and Writings*, 4.
49. *Scranton Republican*, December 19, 1900.
50. Ibid., February 2, 1901.
51. Ibid., February 19, 1901.
52. Ibid., February 25, 1901.
53. Ibid., February 6, 1901.
54. Ibid., March 8, 1901.
55. Ibid., April 30, 1901.
56. *United Mine Workers Journal*, October 30, 1902.
57. Fetherling, *Mother Jones*, vii.
58. Phelan, *Divided Loyalties*, 124.
59. Ibid., 126–127.
60. Ibid., 200.
61. Ibid., 184.
62. Ibid., 187.
63. C.K. McFarland, "Crusade for Child Laborers: Mother Jones and the March of the Mill Children," *Pennsylvania History* 38 (1971): 283–296.
64. Phelan, *Divided Loyalties*, 212.
65. William J. Walsh, *The United Mine Workers of America as an Economic and Social Force in the Anthracite Territory* (Washington, DC: Catholic University of America, 1931), 105.

66. Priscilla Long, *Mother Jones, Woman Organizer, and Her Relations with Miners' Wives, Working Women, and the Suffrage Movement* (Boston: South End Press, 1976), 33; Gorn, *Mother Jones*, 232.

67. See Bonnie Stepenoff, "Keeping It in the Family: Mother Jones and the Pennsylvania Silk Strike of 1900–1901," *Labor History* 38 (Fall 1997): 432–449.

68. Long, *Mother Jones*, 27.

CHAPTER 10

Violence and the Colorado National Guard: Masculinity, Race, Class, and Identity in the 1913–1914 Southern Colorado Coal Strike

Anthony DeStefanis

On January 22, 1914, Trinidad, Colorado witnessed a protest that the *Pueblo Chieftain* called "the most remarkable demonstration of the kind ever witnessed in Colorado." "Lead [sic] by women, arranged by women, carried out by women," this protest demanded the release from prison of Mary "Mother" Jones, who was the United Mine Workers of America's most visible organizer at the turn of the twentieth century.[1] Jones was in Trinidad to lend her support to the more than 9,000 mostly southern and eastern European and Mexican immigrant and Mexican–American miners who had gone on strike in September 1913. As was so often the case in Colorado in the decades around 1900, the state's governor called out the National Guard, who, in turn, arrested and jailed Jones at the San Raphael Hospital on Trinidad's outskirts because, in the words of National Guard Adjutant General John Chase, she was an "eccentric and peculiar figure" who nonetheless was adept at "inciting the more ignorant and criminally disposed to deeds of violence and crime."[2]

Incarcerating Jones at the hospital was apparently an attempt to avoid making the Trinidad jailhouse a protest site and to steer clear of criticism for holding the seventy-six-year-old woman in a cold and damp jail cell. The protests came anyway. The 1,000 wives, daughters, sisters, and friends of the striking miners who turned out in Trinidad objected strongly to Chase's characterization of Jones and to the brutal treatment that the Colorado National Guard meted out while on strike duty. Most of all, they wanted the Guard to release Jones from custody. The protest began peacefully, but a line of soldiers confronted the marchers when they reached downtown Trinidad and turned out of town toward the hospital where Jones was held. A melee ensued between the Guardsmen and the women, and Chase later contended that only the cool and professional behavior of his National Guardsmen prevented the women's march from turning into a full-fledged riot.[3] In defense of his troops, Chase stated that they "disregarded the blows received, and bore themselves well and manfully, intent alone upon clearing the streets and dispersing the mob."[4]

Other accounts challenged Chase's view of the Guard's behavior. *The Rocky Mountain News* reported that saber-wielding soldiers slashed four women, one man, and one ten-year old boy, and used a rifle butt to smash the instep of a young girl. Protest organizer Mary Thomas claimed that a Guardsman grabbed her by the collar, pushed her down a set of stairs, and punched her, "as if he was a pugilist." When Thomas tried to resist, the soldier hit her several more times and then arrested her.[5] Sixteen-year old Sarah Slator testified that General Chase was himself involved in brutalizing the women protestors. She stated that Chase rushed up on his horse, told her to get back, and kicked her in the breast.[6] For his part, Chase pointed out that young Sarah was "playing truant from school" on the day of the protest.[7]

In an era where rigid assumptions about male and female gender identity made the image of a uniformed man on horseback kicking a young girl particularly troublesome, Chase had to explain this widely publicized behavior to a dubious audience. Chase and his charges, however, clearly believed that there was no reason to modify the violent tactics they regularly used against male workers when dealing with adversaries who wore dresses rather than trousers. They rationalized this behavior by denying that the women they faced in Trinidad were, in fact, women. Chase asserted, for instance, that Mary Thomas was a "belligerent and abusive leader of the mob" who "forcibly resisted orders to move on, responded only with highly abusive and, to say the least, unwomanly language. She attacked the troops with fists, feet, and umbrella . . . [and] made much of the awfulness of treating a riotous woman in the same way as a riotous man."[8] In Chase's telling, Thomas and the other protestors acted like the working-class men who were on strike— fighting, swearing, challenging authority, and taking over public space. If, as Chase believed, the strikers promoted the women's protest as an effort to "[hide] behind their women's skirts, believing it would be more embarrassing for the military to deal with women than with men," the Guard turned the tables by refusing to modify their brutal tactics.[9] A Guardsman's response to a woman protestor's question well encapsulated the soldiers' strategy. The protestor asked a soldier: "what right [did] they [the National Guard] have to chase women away like cattle?" to which the soldier replied: "When women sink beneath our respect, they need to be treated like cattle."[10] By questioning their honor and de-feminizing these working-class women, the Guard could more easily subvert gender conventions by attacking these women—and defuse the challenge to their own masculinity in the process.

The Mother Jones protest occurred during a strike that lasted more than a year and was one of the most brutal labor conflicts in American history. More than fifty people were killed during the 1913–1914 southern Colorado coal strike, and it resulted in the Ludlow Massacre in which two women, twelve children ranging in age from three months to eleven years, six miners and union officials, and one National Guardsman were killed in a day-long battle between the Colorado National Guard and residents of a tent colony near Ludlow, the Colorado railroad station.[11] Ludlow was the largest of seven tent colonies that the United Mine Workers set up to house families who were thrown out of company housing when the miners went on strike.[12] The massacre set off a ten-day-long war between National Guardsmen and incensed miners who became intent on exacting revenge for the Ludlow killings. Dozens more on both sides died during those ten days, before President Woodrow Wilson sent the United States Army to Colorado to restore order.[13]

Clearly, the Guard's behavior on Trinidad's streets was no accident. Guardsmen regularly perpetrated violence against both men and women, which was crucial to defeating the strike. Moreover, Chase's tactical and ideological approach to the Mother Jones protestors foreshadowed how the National Guard would explain the Ludlow Massacre. This essay examines the Colorado National Guard's deployment of ideas about gender, race, ethnicity, and class to describe and defend its actions at Ludlow. Just as General Chase sought to transform Trinidad's women protestors into riotous and dangerous men, other Guard officers insisted that the southern and eastern European immigrant miners who struck in southern Colorado were a much larger threat than they at first appeared. In the Guard's estimation, these miners were similar to the racially inferior but still formidable Plains Indians whom the Guard had helped defeat during the late nineteenth century. This understanding of the striking miners as "savages" was also evident in the Guard's depiction of the Ludlow tent colony's Greek residents as both menacing militaristic marauders and deviant cowards who had no understanding of manly duty. This portrayal of the striking miners resonated strongly because it conjured the Old West by portraying Guardsmen as defenders of white "civilization" while it also reflected the nativist thinking about the racial inferiority of southern and eastern European immigrants that had become so prevalent by the 1910s.

In a National Guard whose officer class was made up almost entirely of native-born, middle- and upper-class white men, the Guard's efforts to explain their adversaries' and their own actions reveal the intricate web of ideas about race, ethnicity, gender, and class that underlay the Colorado National Guard's understanding of their strike duty opponents.[14] A strong belief in their own racial, masculine, and class superiority helped Guardsmen create a vision of dominance that gave them a starring role in defending the "civilization" that white settlers had established in the American West. The Guard zealously protected this role with violence exercised against anyone who threatened the social, political, and economic order that they and their predecessors in the Guard had helped establish in Colorado.

*   *   *

Southern Colorado had long been caught up in the struggle for control of North America. Mexico gained control of the region when that country won independence from Spain in 1821, only to lose it to the United States twenty-seven years later in the Mexican–American War. Thousands of American Indians also lived on this land. Utes had lived in the mountains of southern Colorado for centuries before the 1913–1914 coal strike, only to be pushed aside by the Cheyenne and Arapaho tribes who came to the area in the late eighteenth century. The militias that the Colorado Territory originally raised to defend the Union in the Civil War found themselves fighting against these Indians in the battles that blazed on the western plains from the early 1860s through the 1880s.[15] These battles began the Colorado National Guard's education in comprehending strike duty.

As the Civil War drew to a close, John Evans, governor of the Colorado Territory, wanted to eliminate Indian claims to southeastern Colorado. Because Congress had just given the go-ahead for Colorado to apply for statehood, Evans thought that taking aggressive action against the Indians who lived in this part of Colorado would increase his popularity, and therefore, his chances of gaining election to the United States Senate once Colorado became a state. Evans found a willing partner in Colonel John M. Chivington, a former Methodist minister and Colorado militia officer who was positioning himself for a seat in the House of Representatives.[16]

Chivington and Evans, however, found that southeastern Colorado's Indian tribes were reluctant to fight. Chivington overcame this obstacle by gunning down Cheyenne Chief Lean Bear in May 1864 as he approached on horseback showing a letter from President Abraham Lincoln that he had received on a trip to Washington, D.C. The letter described the chief's friendly disposition. Chivington's men then opened fire on Lean Bear's people with artillery. Despite these atrocities, the Cheyenne remained reluctant to play the role Evans and Chivington had assigned them. After rejecting the efforts of several Cheyenne and Arapaho chiefs to make peace, Chivington attacked a Cheyenne and Arapaho camp at Sand Creek in late November. According to one of Chivington's soldiers, Chief Black Kettle ordered the Indians in his camp to stand around an American flag he had raised while others raised white flags. The troops ignored this gesture and in the massacre that followed, Chivington's third regiment killed 133 people, mostly women and children. The soldiers scalped many corpses and otherwise mutilated their victims' bodies. Many of these scalps were soon on display at a Denver theater during intermission.[17]

One of the most infamous Indian "battles" in American history, the Sand Creek Massacre established Colorado's military organizations' proclivity for indiscriminate violence.[18] After Sand Creek, the territory's military outfits fought Indians for another decade, and after Colorado achieved statehood in 1876, all these militia units were officially organized into the Colorado National Guard. In a fit of overzealousness, the Coloradan legislature authorized a 118-company Guard consisting of approximately 12,000 men. The legislature soon realized that a new state could not sustain financially such a large force and reduced the Guard's size to around 1,200 troops.[19]

This new National Guard saw less and less service against the Plains Indians as their capacity to resist conquest diminished in the decades following the Sand Creek Massacre. But while it was true that Colorado's militia and National Guard units often defeated the Cheyenne and Arapaho with ease, the Plains Indians staved off final conquest for almost thirty years after the Civil War. As the massacre of General George Custer and his troops at Little Big Horn, Montana in 1876 demonstrated, the Plains Indians were significant in number and capable of fighting—and beating—the United States military. Hence, the Plains Indians presented a formidable threat while they also lived in a world culturally at odds with the one white settlers occupied. These characteristics helped white Americans justify western conquest; they would also help Colorado National Guardsmen explain their actions when faced with "alien," immigrant working-class miners who seemed to threaten the American "civilization" that conquest had brought to the West.

The legacy of western conquest was most evident in the Colorado National Guard's official report on the Ludlow Massacre. In the immediate aftermath of the massacre, Colorado Governor Elias Ammons authorized a three-person board of National Guard officers to investigate. Adjutant General John Chase placed three lawyers, Major Edward J. Boughton, Captain William Danks, and Captain Philip Van Cise on this board, but Boughton, perhaps with some assistance from Danks, was most responsible for the Guard's findings. The final report these two officers produced depicted strike duty as a contest that would prove Guardsmen both racially superior to and manlier than their working-class adversaries.[20]

In their report, Boughton and Danks focused as much on the character of the people who resided in the Ludlow tent colony as on what happened there on April 20, 1914. Their judgments were not kind. They observed that the southern and eastern European immigrant families at Ludlow had "little in common . . . with the few Americans residents among them. The percentage of American citizens, even naturalized citizens, was small," and "it will readily be seen that these people did not possess much means of interchanging information or social ideas."[21]

Later in the report, Boughton and Danks described how Albert Martin, a private in the National Guard, died during the battle at Ludlow. Martin's body was found with his arms broken, and "he had been shot through the mouth, powder stains evidencing that a gun had been held to his lips. His head had been caved in, and his brains exuded on the ground." This act, the officers wrote, revealed "the savage blood lust of this southern European peasantry. In this connection we find also that without exception where dying or wounded adversaries, whether soldiers or civilians, had fallen into the hands of these barbarians, they were tortured or mutilated." In their conclusion, these officers laid some blame for Ludlow on the coal mine owners, but only for establishing a large "class of ignorant, lawless, and savage Southern European peasants" in an industrial community.[22]

Such sentiment was common among Colorado National Guardsmen. Adjutant General John Chase, for example, thought the striking miners possessed a "quiet, savage hatred."[23] As we have seen, however, the white American experience with "savage" and "barbaric" peoples did not originate with the immigration from southern and eastern Europe that began during the 1880s. Beginning with the fifteenth-century European invasion of the western hemisphere, Europeans justified expansion by casting the native inhabitants they encountered as racially inferior "others." By the late nineteenth century, when the Colorado National Guard helped complete the conquest of the American West, the idea that American Indians were savage and barbaric had become firmly entrenched in the country's consciousness. These ideas about the immutability of race and ethnicity, as much as the battle between capital and labor, influenced the Guard's account of the Ludlow Massacre.[24]

Although the medical examiner's statement and the Guard's report on Ludlow differ in their descriptions of Private Martin's corpse, it is probably true that the striking miners mutilated Martin's body.[25] It is also true, however, that this killing happened only after months of violent confrontations between private mine guards and National Guardsmen on one side and striking miners and their families on the other. These battles, which the miners and their families often lost, were topped off by the Ludlow tent colony's fiery destruction and the loss of life that accompanied it. Union leaders tried to keep their members from engaging in violent resistance once on strike, but they did not always succeed. The class resentment that these miners expressed through violence before, during, and after the Ludlow Massacre also helps explain why they came out on strike. Indeed, that class resentment was a deeply engrained part of who they were.

These violent deaths along with the many preventable deaths in mine accidents that preceded the strike—Colorado coal miners died at a rate that was three-and-a-half times the national average between 1909 and 1913—were the likely, if not justifiable, cause of the miners' own violence. The Colorado National Guard officers who sought to explain striker violence, however, obscured class anger in favor of a racialized understanding of their adversaries. Describing the killing of Private Martin as "savage" certainly recalled the sensationalism that often characterized reports of Indian atrocities during the Plains Indians Wars. Updating the language of western conquest for the world of industrial capitalism in this way forged a powerful tool because it allowed the Guard to portray strikers as savage threats to white "civilization"— a kind of threat that white native-born residents of Colorado understood very well. In this formulation, the miners' actions were not attributable to class resentment growing out of the horrific conditions in which miners and their families worked and lived, but were instead explained by the "fact" that immigrant, working-class miners were, like the Plains Indians, racially inferior savages.

By no means were Colorado National Guardsmen the first Americans to insist that immigrant workers were a threat to civilization similar to that posed by the "savage" Indian tribes of the western plains. In 1869, for instance, *Scientific American* welcomed the "ruder" laborers coming to the United States, but warned: "If some of these are likely to prove hard to assimilate into an homogeneous whole, the result will be a quiet but sure extermination. They will share the fate of the native Indian, who, unwilling to accept civilization, has been gradually driven away by its advance."[26] This warning in 1869 was aimed primarily at Irish Catholic and Chinese immigrants, for the "new" immigration for southern and eastern Europe had not yet started in earnest. Immigrant workers, moreover, were not alone in facing charges of savagery. As Richard Slotkin has shown, some popular press outlets described all the workers involved in the 1877 nationwide railroad strike as savage and barbaric.[27] In a strike that coincided with the Nez Perce Indian War in the Northwest, workers, like the Nez Perce, became the state's enemy. Other publications, however, insisted that the 1877 strike was evidence of a foreign proletariat promoting class war in the United States. *The Nation*, for example, argued that "Vast additions have been made to our population . . . to whom American political and social ideals appeal but faintly, if at all, and who carry in their very blood traditions which give universal suffrage an air of menace to many of the things which civilized men hold dear."[28] In this analysis, the strike and the violence that came with it could not be fully understood without acknowledging that immigrant participants had, like the Nez Perce, blood flowing through their veins that would forever prevent them from becoming worthy American citizens.

Observers of the many labor conflicts that followed the 1877 railroad strike continued to compare striking immigrant workers to Indians.[29] This focus on immigrants as the worst agitators in labor conflicts reflected the increasing concern that many nativist intellectuals, physicians, and journalists voiced about the threat that southern and eastern European immigrants posed to American "civilization." For example, John R. Commons, who spent his academic career as an economist at the University of Wisconsin championing labor's cause in the United States, supported the American Federation of Labor's position that Congress should restrict immigration from southern and eastern Europe. In *Races and Immigrants in America*, which he published in 1907 after President Theodore Roosevelt appointed him to the U.S. Immigration Commission, Commons argued that "the peasant of Europe, especially of Southern and Eastern Europe, have been reduced to the qualities similar to those of an inferior race that favor despotism and oligarchy rather than democracy."[30]

Commons's fears about southern and eastern European immigrants who had lived in "savagery" for centuries, and, therefore, also lacked the tools necessary for self-government, and were the cause of increasing labor unrest in the United States, were certainly widespread.[31] This is not to say that there was broad consensus on the question of immigrant racial inferiority. Immigrants, whether Irish, Slavic, Italian, or Greek, certainly did not believe that they were hopelessly backward "savages" unable to function in a democratic society, but it is clear that during the four decades before the 1907 publication of *Races and Immigrants in America*, the idea that southern and eastern European immigrants were less evolved, primitive, and "backward," and that savagery was rampant among these immigrants had became commonplace among the nation's many nativists and proponents of immigration restriction.

Social Darwinism and ideas culled from eugenics science, both of which enjoyed wide popularity at the turn of the twentieth century, led nativists to argue that these immigrants were racially inferior. The form of their inferiority, however, resembled something Americans had seen before. By engaging in labor strikes that produced violence, these immigrants—who often spoke little or no English, looked strange, dressed oddly, and, to some noses, even smelled funny—resembled the best example of a racially inferior, but formidable enemy capable of violent action and resistance that the country had ever known: the American Indian.

Still, comparing workers to Indians and describing them as savages was not strictly a means of indicating racial inferiority. Antonio Gramsci has pointed out that "for a social elite the features of subordinate groups always display something barbaric or pathological."[32] Gramsci's observation is certainly helpful in thinking about why images of warlike Indians violently resisting white conquest leapt into the minds of native-born Americans when they described workers who challenged the established social and economic order and, in the process, violated middle-class norms of decorum and civility by marching, picketing, and demonstrating in the streets.

Major Boughton and Captain Danks continued to combine class with race and added gender, as well, as they further described what was "barbaric and pathological" about the striking miners. The intersection of class, race, and gender was most apparent in Boughton and Danks's description of the Greek miners who lived at Ludlow. Guardsmen identified these Greek residents as troublemakers from early on in the 1913–1914 strike. In their report on Ludlow, Boughton and Danks characterized the Greeks as "aggressive fighting men" who "imposed their desire on the rest" and "were vociferous and insistent upon giving battle to the soldiers at once if they should appear."[33]

The Guard's uneasiness with the Greek miners reflected the significant role these miners played during the strike. Louis Tikas, a Greek immigrant who was murdered at Ludlow, was instrumental in maintaining the tent colony there and was popular among its residents.[34] In Boughton and Danks's report, the officers referred to Louis Tikas as the "master of the tented city" and asserted: "the Greeks were regarded as heroes, for many of them, we are told, had seen service in the Balkan wars."[35] Greece fought the First and Second Balkan Wars against the Ottoman Turks and then against Bulgaria in 1912 and 1913. That many veterans of these conflicts had made their way to the Ludlow tent colony by the fall of 1913 is not very likely, but some of Ludlow's Greek residents probably had served in the Greek military. As Gunther Peck has shown, furthermore, male Greek sojourners in the West built their community around a fraternal culture that rested on fictive kinship. New World friends became a New World family that these men depended on at work and in the often makeshift houses they occupied together.

Gun ownership was also common among Greek immigrants. The prevalence of guns in the turn-of-the-twentieth-century West reinforced an appreciation of guns as powerful symbols of masculine authority that was common among working-class men in Greece and other southern and eastern European countries. Young, working-class immigrant men also carried guns for more practical reasons. Guns were protection against the nativist attacks they occasionally encountered in the streets and saloons. Still, the most serious episodes of gun violence were the results of labor conflicts that occurred frequently in the West.[36] During the1913–1914 coal strike, the United Mine Workers spent $7,500 bringing more weapons to Colorado when it became clear that the Colorado National Guard and the mine operators—the CF&I alone spent between $25,000 and $30,000 on guns and ammunition during the strike—were bent on using violence to break the strike.[37]

The tight bonds between the single Greek men living in the Ludlow tent colony were evident to anyone who spent time there. This fraternalism, along with the fact that these men were armed, probably explains the Guard's concerns about the Ludlow tent colony's Greek contingent. Transforming these circumstances into a claim that Ludlow's Greeks residents had fought in the Balkan Wars allowed Boughton and Danks to deflect attention away from the women and children killed at Ludlow, while highlighting the presence of a formidable, male enemy who, like themselves, had military experience. Lieutenant Karl Linderfelt, another Guard officer, followed a similar logic when he asserted that "an Apache Indian belonging to the WCTU [Women's Christian Temperance Union]" could not match what "the Greeks and the Bulgarians had done to each other in the Balkans."[38] By exaggerating the Greeks' previous military experience, and by highlighting the Greek military's behavior in the Balkans, Boughton, Danks, and Linderfelt attempted to evade responsibility for killing women and children, an act they certainly considered unmanly, by casting the tent colony's Greek residents as a fierce, savage, masculine foreign army that had "invaded" southern Colorado.

Contending that many Balkan Wars veterans who lived at Ludlow helped bolster this position, Boughton, Danks, and Linderfelt were not the only ones who found this story compelling. Mine owners and local newspapers also highlighted the supposed presence of these "fierce" Greek "warriors" in the Ludlow tent colony. *The Rocky Mountain News*, for instance, had published letters from Greek soldiers to their families describing atrocities they committed in the Balkan Wars just a few weeks before the 1913–1914 coal strike began. These letters, which allegedly fell into the hands of the Bulgarian army during battle, described the murders of children and various torture methods Greek soldiers employed before killing prisoners. One letter from a corporal writing to his brother said: "Not even a cat has escaped where we have gone. We have burned every Bulgarian village through which we have passed. This is all I can tell you."[39]

While it is not clear if these letters were authentic or merely a propaganda tool manufactured by the Bulgarian government, *The Rocky Mountain News* told Denver's residents that Greek soldiers were guilty of conducting "savage" warfare. Given warfare's inherent barbarism, it would not be surprising if the letters published in the *News* were real. Whether or not they were, such accounts clearly influenced the Guard. When the National Guard was called out on strike duty in late October 1913 several weeks after the *News* story appeared, Captain Philip Van Cise told his troops on the train ride to southern Colorado: "You are on serious business. There are 1,000 Greeks, veterans of the Balkan war, in the strike district. They are trained soldiers and they are heavily armed, armed to the teeth. If you have to shoot, shoot to kill."[40] *The Trinidad Chronicle-News* bolstered Van Cise's claim when it reported early in the strike that Louis Tikas was "shrewd and fearless—a veteran of the Balkan war, and he controls the Greeks at the tent colony with a spoken word, a lift of the eyebrows or a gesture of his hand."[41] In fact, Tikas had come to the United States half-a-dozen years before the Balkan Wars began and became a U.S. citizen just after the southern Colorado coal strike began in September 1913.[42] Nevertheless, this myth about the savagery of the Ludlow miners continued to spread. Jesse Welborn, president of the Colorado Fuel and Iron Company—the largest coal mining company in southern Colorado—wrote in his company's 1914 annual report that the Ludlow tent colony's population was "largely veterans of the Balkan Wars of various nationalities."[43]

Residents of the tent colony, on the other hand, remembered no more than a few Balkan Wars veterans among them, but it is perhaps more important that contemporary observers did not realize that Greek sojourners in the American West were ambivalent about both their country's involvement in the Balkan Wars and about military service in general.[44] In fact, many young men left Greece for the United States seeking to avoid military service.[45] Many of the Greek men who had so recently come to the United States certainly looked proudly on the success that their native land had enjoyed in the Balkan Wars, but that pride certainly did not make these men experienced combat soldiers.[46] Publicizing the "presence" of Balkan War veterans at Ludlow was aimed more at creating an enemy that the Guardsmen and the mine owners who wished to defend them could use to justify the Guard's actions at Ludlow.

Even as Boughton and Danks sought to portray the Greek miners as a formidable, masculine, yet "savage" adversary, they also questioned the Greeks' manliness and raised questions about their racial identity. "The strange thing, and one that we found important," Boughton and Danks wrote, "is that there were no Greek women or children in the colony."[47] They were correct about the absence of Greek women in the Ludlow tent colony. The 300 to 350 Greeks (not the 1,000 that Captain Van Cise claimed) working in southern Colorado's coal mines were predominantly young, without family in Colorado, and therefore, fairly mobile.[48] That mobility influenced how native-born Americans defined the Greeks' racial identity. The racial status of "new" immigrants to the United States at the turn of the twentieth century varied widely, but native-born, white Americans often saw transience as evidence of racial inferiority and an inability to assimilate.[49] Writing in 1914 about Italian immigrants, another group widely represented among the miners who struck in southern Colorado, the sociologist Edward Ross asserted that "not being transients, the north Italians do not resist Americanizing influences," but "the South Italians remain nearly as aloof as did the Cantonese who built the Central Pacific Railway. Navvies who leave for Naples when the ground freezes and return in April, who huddle in a 'camp' or a box-car, or herd on some 'Dago Flat' are not really *in* America."[50] To Ross, the sedentary north Italians were "more intelligent, reliable, and progressive than the south Italian" and well on their way to becoming Americans.[51] The transient southern Italians, on the other hand, whom Ross categorized as a "race" separate from and inferior to northern Italians, had more in common with the Chinese, a group that many turn-of-the-twentieth-century Americans saw as clear racial inferiors with no chance of ever successfully assimilating themselves into American society, and who had been excluded from legally emigrating to the United States since 1882.[52]

The transience that made working-class immigrants racially suspect also called their manliness into question. Their lack of wives and children in the New World, and therefore, of domestic attachments and responsibilities that defined middle-class, native-born manhood in the United States, made them seem unmanly and uncivilized.[53] Many single, Greek working-class men, however, came to the American West to earn dowries for their sisters and ensure the economic security of their families. These were duties that many native-born, middle-class American men certainly would have seen as "manly." Only in a literal sense, therefore, was it true that Greek immigrants did not have their families with them.[54]

The Guard's account of the Ludlow Massacre, therefore, demonstrates their ignorance about Greek immigrants' lives in southern Colorado. The report also reveals an overwhelming desire to escape blame for Ludlow. Boughton and Danks blamed not only the Greeks, but also all the striking miners for leaving their women and children behind in the utter chaos that reigned in the tent colony once fighting began.[55] For these officers, this was a cowardly act that allowed them to praise other National Guardsmen because they risked their lives rescuing, as they put it, "these deluded people," as the battle raged around them. Boughton and Danks sought to show that their fellow Guardsmen were more masculine than their adversaries in the tent colony. They wrote: "We find that the work of rescuing these women and children . . . was under the circumstances, truly heroic and must stand out boldly in contradistinction to the abandonment of the helpless women and children by their own people." The officers, finally, lamented their comrades' inability to find the two women and eleven children who died before fire consumed their tent.[56]

Colorado Fuel and Iron Company president Jesse Welborn took a similar position when he sought to explain the events at Ludlow. He wrote that the women and children who "lost their lives in this affray were smothered in a covered cave through the foolish, if not criminal, act of their own men who put them here and sealed the cover with dirt."[57] That the Guard fired their machine guns into the Ludlow tent colony and eventually burned it to the ground had nothing to do with the deaths, according to Welborn and the two officers who wrote the Guard's official report on the event.

* * *

By 1913, violence had become a way of life for the Colorado National Guard. Over a fifty-year odyssey that began at Sand Creek and wound through more than a half-dozen labor disputes before the 1913–1914 coal strike, Colorado National Guardsmen had violently defended the civilization that their organization had helped create. Violence undoubtedly helped defeat the 1913–1914 strike, but Guardsmen had to constantly justify their brutality. As we have seen, those justifications consistently used the Guard's shifting understanding of masculinity, race, and class to transform their adversaries into deviant, "savage," and unmanly enemies of civilization.

The attributes of the enemies Guardsmen created in their public comments on the strike were not complete fabrications. The women who stomped their feet and hollered in Trinidad's streets certainly broke Victorian gender conventions by acting assertively in a public space, and therefore, appeared masculine to many onlookers. It was also likely that the striking miners mutilated Private Martin's body on the day the Guard destroyed Ludlow, and they certainly did kill other Guardsmen in the ten-day war that followed the Ludlow Massacre. A few Greek Balkan War veterans were present in the Ludlow tent colony, and they, along with the other immigrant men who lived at Ludlow, did leave without their women during the battle at Ludlow.

The Colorado National Guard used these facts to attack all of these groups with words and with weapons because they all, in different ways, challenged the Guard's sense of masculine, racial, and class dominance. The immigrant, working-class Trinidad women tested the Guard's position both as an enforcer of the state's will and as men who enjoyed an unquestioned ability to control women. The striking miners at Ludlow—Greek and otherwise—presented a different problem. They challenged Guardsmen's manhood by going on strike and taking up arms against a National Guard commanded by Colorado's middle and upper class. Seen in this light, the Greek men at Ludlow did not appear dangerous solely because Guardsmen believed that they were Balkan War veterans. They appeared dangerous because they were strangers in Colorado who dared to challenge their "betters," and because they were men who lacked the civilizing presence of women. They built tents, collected weapons, and refused to end their strike no matter how brutally the Guard treated them. They also appeared dangerous because they were desperate, and their desperation only became more apparent as they toughed out a Colorado winter living in tents. It is no coincidence that the Ludlow Massacre happened in late April 1914, after the relationship between the Guard and the striking miners had become increasingly poisoned over the course of a long, cold winter.

How the Guardsmen understood both the challenge that immigrant, working-class men and women made to their authority and the desperation that challenge created tells us much about the Colorado National Guard and its role in breaking strikes. On one level, it is useful to think of the Guard as a modern institution, as a product of the modern state and modern industrial capitalism. In 1913, National Guards were relatively new institutions, created by many states after the nationwide 1877 railroad strike to counter what many observers saw as the inevitable labor unrest that would accompany the second industrial revolution.[58] The Colorado National Guard, however, did not talk and write entirely in the new terms of class and class conflict that shaped the battle between labor and capital during the Gilded Age and Progressive Era. The Guard often obscured class in favor of gender and race, and thus invoked not the modern industrial world, but the West's romantic past when they sought to describe their adversaries in the 1913–1914 coal strike. When Adjutant General Chase accused Trinidad's vocal and assertive women of being "unwomanly," he looked back longingly to the nineteenth century, when, for him and his fellow Guardsmen, white manly men, unfettered and unquestioned by women, wrested control of the West from its "inferior" and "savage" Indian inhabitants. Continually asserting the white man's masculine superiority over Ludlow's Greek residents while equating the striking, immigrant miners with the "savage" Plains Indians also allowed the Guard to cast strike breaking as a continuation of their frontier-era efforts to defend the "civilization" that white settlers had brought to the West, rather than as the brutal use of state power against working people at capital's urging that it actually was.

Reading these same descriptions, however, as a reflection of the eugenics-influenced scientific racism that enjoyed widespread popularity by the 1910s shows that Guard officers were capable of using the new tools that the modern world offered. Whether the Guard invoked the past or placed itself squarely in the debates about modernity that divided the nation at the turn of the twentieth century, likening labor conflicts to Indian battles and asserting that striking immigrant workers were unmanly and racially inferior did not guarantee the Guard's victory over southern Colorado's coal miners in the 1913–1914 strike. Still, such comparisons were powerful rhetorical strategies in the hands of Guardsmen who sought to garner public support while maintaining the new order that industrial capitalism had established. The constant presence of this rhetoric in strikes that occurred throughout the late nineteenth and early twentieth centuries, furthermore, reveals how those who defended capital used race and gender, as well as class, to fight their battles. More importantly, it shows how they viewed their working-class adversaries. Indeed, their conviction that labor unrest threatened white native-born supremacy over the North American continent also suggests why late nineteenth- and early twentieth-century labor conflicts were so intense. Though economic concerns certainly drove the actions of employers and state actors in these strikes, it is also clear that the challenge workers made to the established economic, political, and social order convinced many that nothing less than American civilization was at stake.

NOTES

The author would like to thank Tim Barnard, Wendy Gonaver, Kelly Gray, Cindy Hahamovitch, Jennifer Luff, Mark Long, Leisa Meyer, Emily Mieras, Scott Nelson, and James Spady for their comments, suggestions, and support.

1. *Pueblo Chieftain*, January 23, 1914; George S. McGovern and Leonard F. Guttridge, *The Great Coal Field War* (Boston: Houghton Mifflin Company, 1972), 173; On Mother Jones, see Mary Harris Jones, *Autobiography of Mother Jones* (New York: Arno Press, 1969); Philip Foner, ed., *Mother Jones Speaks: Collected Writings and Speeches* (New York: Monad Press, 1983); Elliot J. Gorn, *Mother Jones: The Most Dangerous Woman in America* (New York: Hill and Wang, 2001).

2. McGovern and Guttridge, *The Great Coal Field War*, 172; *The Military Occupation of the Coal Strike Zone by the Colorado National Guard, 1913–1914, Report of the Commanding General to the Governor for the Use of the Congressional Committee, Exhibiting an Account of the Military Occupation to the Time of the First Withdrawal of Troops in April, 1914* (Denver, CO: The Smith-Brooks Printing Company, 1914), 46. Hereafter cited as *The Military Occupation of the Coal Strike Zone*.

3. Several Colorado newspapers made the same argument in their coverage of the protest. See, e.g., *The Pueblo Chieftain*, January 23, 1914, and *The Trinidad Chronicle-News*, January 23, 1914.

4. *The Military Occupation of the Coal Strike Zone*, 29.

5. *The Rocky Mountain News*, January 23, 1914; See the testimony of Minnie Hoghart and Mary Thomas in House Committee on Mines and Mining, *Conditions in the Coal Mines of Colorado*, 63d Cong., 2d sess., 1914, H. Res. 387, part 6, 794–802; McGovern and Guttridge, *The Great Coalfield War*, 174.

6. The testimony of Sarah Slator in House Committee on Mines and Mining, *Conditions in the Coal Mines of Colorado*, part 6, 988.

7. *The Military Occupation of the Coal Strike Zone*, 59.

8. Ibid., 58.

9. Ibid., 28.

10. Priscilla Long, *Where the Sun Never Shines: A History of America's Bloody Coal Industry* (New York: Paragon House, 1989), 284–285.

11. "Those Killed in the Colorado Strike," The Papers of Edward Doyle, box 2, envelope 18, Western History Collection, Denver Public Library, Denver, Colorado.

12. McGovern and Guttridge, *The Great Coal Field War*, 103.

13. The literature on the southern Colorado coal strike of 1913–1914 begins with George S. McGovern, "The Colorado Coal Strike, 1913–1914" (PhD diss., Northwestern University, 1953). He published this study with Leonard F. Guttridge as *The Great Coal Field War*. Also see Barron B. Beshoar, *Out of the Depths: The Story of John R. Lawson, A Labor Leader* (Denver, CO: Golden Bell Press, 1958); Zeese Papanikolas, *Buried Unsung: Louis Tikas and the Ludlow Massacre* (Salt Lake City, UT: University of Utah Press, 1982); Manfred F. Boemke, "The Wilson Administration, Organized Labor, and the Colorado Coal Strike, 1913–1914" (PhD diss., Princeton University, 1983); Priscilla Long, "The Women of the Colorado Fuel and Iron Strike, 1913–1914, in *Women, Work, and Protest: A Century of U.S. Women's Labor History*, ed., Ruth Milkman (Boston: Routledge & Kegan Paul, 1985) and Long, *Where the Sun Never Shines*, chapters 12–14.

14. "Minutes of the Court of Inquiry Established by an Executive Order of his Excellency, George A. Carlson, Governor of the State of Colorado, August 28, 1915" in the Papers of Hildreth Frost, Colorado Historical Society, Denver, Colorado, contains over 1000 pages of testimony from National Guardsmen and provides much information about the previous military service and socioeconomic background of many National Guard officers. Also see "Official List and Directory: The National Guard of Colorado, October 6, 1912, Office of the Adjutant General," the Papers of Hildreth Frost, Western History Collection, box 1, envelope 2, Denver Public Library, and "The Rosters of the Colorado National Guard, 1912–1915," Colorado State Department of Military Affairs, Colorado State Archives, Denver, Colorado. These sources show that almost all the Guard's commissioned officers were business owners, professionals—attorney, physician, and engineer were common occupations among the Guard's officers—or white-collar workers who held jobs as clerks, bookkeepers, accountants, civil servants, or managers.

15. Richard White, *"It's Your Own Misfortune and None of My Own": A New History of the American West* (Norman, OK: University of Oklahoma Press, 1991), 77–83; Long, *Where the Sun Never Shines*, 172–174.

16. Robert M. Utley, *The Indian Frontier of the American West, 1846–1890* (Albuquerque, New Mexico: University of New Mexico Press, 1984), 87–88; White, *"It's Your Own Misfortune,"* 95–96.

17. John H. Nankivell, *History of the Military Organizations of the State of Colorado, 1860–1935* (Denver, CO: W.H. Kistler Stationary Company, 1935), 28–34; Richard Maxwell Brown, ed., *American Violence* (Englewood Cliffs, NJ: Prentice-Hall, 1970), 67–68; Utley, *The Indian Frontier in the American West*, 88–93; White, *"It's Your Own Misfortune,"* 96.

18. Governor Evans lost his job as territorial governor in the fallout that followed the Sand Creek Massacre and never succeeded in becoming a U.S. senator. See the Colorado State Archives biography of Evans at http://www.colorado.gov/dpa/doit/archives/govs/evans.html.

19. Jerry M. Cooper, *The Rise of the National Guard: The Evolution of the American Militia, 1865–1920* (Lincoln, NE: University of Nebraska Press, 1997), 31.

20. The testimony of Lieutenant Colonel Edward J. Boughton in the U.S. Senate Commission on Industrial Relations, *The Colorado Coal Miners' Strike*, 64th Cong., 1st sess., 1916, S. Doc. 415, vol. 7, 6840–6841.

21. Major Edward J. Boughton, Captain W.C. Danks, and Captain Philip Van Cise (of the Colorado National Guard), *Ludlow: Being the Report of the Special Board of Officers Appointed by the Governor of Colorado to Investigate and Determine the Facts with Reference to the Armed Conflict Between the Colorado National Guard and Certain Persons Engaged in the Coal Mining Strike at Ludlow, Colorado, April 20, 1914* (Denver, CO: Williamson-Haffner Company, 1914), 6–7. Hereafter cited as *Ludlow: Being the Report of the Special Board of Officers*.

22. Ibid., 16–17, 24.

23. Adjutant General John Chase to The Commission on the Church and Social Service of the Federal Council of the Churches of Christ in America," October 9, 1914, "Business Interests," Papers of the Colorado Fuel and Iron Company, RG 2, folder 186, box 20, Rockefeller Foundation Archives, Rockefeller Archive Center, Sleepy Hollow, New York.

24. See Robert F. Berkhofer, Jr., *The White Man's Indian: Images of the American Indian from Columbus to the Present* (New York: Alfred A. Knopf, 1978); Richard Drinnon, *Facing West: The Metaphysics of Indian-Hating and Empire-Building* (Minneapolis: University of Minnesota Press, 1980); Reginald Horsman, *Race and Manifest Destiny: The Origins of American Racial Anglo-Saxonism* (Cambridge, MA: Harvard University Press, 1981), esp. 189–207. Richard Slotkin's trilogy, *Regeneration through Violence: The Mythology of the American Frontier, 1600–1860* (Middletown, CT: Wesleyan University Press, 1973); *The Fatal Environment: The Myth of the Frontier in the Age of Industrialization, 1800–1890* (New York: Atheneum Books, 1985); *Gunfighter Nation: The Myth of the Frontier in Twentieth-Century America* (New York: Atheneum Books, 1992) is also excellent in demonstrating how western conquest has shaped the American consciousness.

25. McGovern and Guttridge, *The Great Coalfield War*, 222.

26. Quoted in Herbert Gutman, *Work, Culture, and Society in Industrializing America: Essays in American Working-Class and Social History* (New York: Alfred A. Knopf, 1976), 71–72.

27. Slotkin, *The Fatal Environment*, 477–498. The 1877 strike was a massive nationwide walkout that began on the railroads and quickly spread to other industries. Several states called out their militias, but they were mostly ineffective in putting down the strike. After the United States Army succeeded in defeating the strike, many states began reorganizing their militias and forming National Guards for the purpose of having a strikebreaking force on hand. See Philip S. Foner, *The Great Labor Uprising of 1877* (New York: Pathfinder Press, 1977) and David O. Stowell, *Streets, Railroads, and the Great Strike of 1877* (Chicago: University of Chicago Press, 1999).

28. Quoted in Slotkin, *The Fatal Environment*, 495.

29. For example, see Paul Krause, *The Battle for Homestead: Politics, Culture, and Steel* (Pittsburgh: University of Pittsburgh Press, 1992), 188, 247 for a comparison of immigrants from all over Europe to Indians during an 1882 strike in Homestead, Pennsylvania. Also see Carl Smith, *Urban Disorder and the Shape of Belief: The Great Chicago Fire, the Haymarket Bomb, and the Model Town of Pullman* (Chicago: The University of Chicago Press, 1995), 121, 150–151 for his account of how the German anarchists accused of the 1886 Haymarket Square bombing in Chicago were portrayed as "wild" Indians, and see Frederic Remington, "Chicago Under the Mob," *Harper's Weekly*, July 21, 1894, 681, and "Chicago Under the Law," *Harper's Weekly*, July 28, 1894, 703, for Remington's equation of immigrant strikers with Indians during the 1894 Pullman strike. On Remington and Pullman, also see Richard Slotkin, *Gunfighter Nation*, 95.

30. John R. Commons, *Races and Immigrants in America* (New York: The Macmillan Company, reprinted edition, 1911), 11. In 1911, after several years of research, the U.S. Immigration Commission, or the Dillingham Commission, published a forty-one-volume argument for restricting immigration from eastern and southern Europe. See U.S. Senate, Immigration Commission (Dillingham Commission), *Reports of the Immigration Commission*, 61st Cong., 2d and 3d sess., 1911.

31. In *Whiteness of A Different Color: European Immigrants and the Alchemy of Race* (Cambridge, MA: Harvard University Press, 1998), 88, Matthew Frye Jacobson observes that men and women across the turn-of-the-twentieth-century

American political and intellectual spectrum expressed ideas that comfortably complemented the arguments Commons made in *Races and Immigrants in America*. Also see James Barrett and David Roediger, "In between Peoples: Race, Nationality and the 'New Immigrant' Working Class," *Journal of American Ethnic History* 16 (Spring 1997), 3–44; Desmond King, *Making Americans: Immigration, Race, and the Origins of the Diverse Democracy* (Cambridge, MA: Harvard University Press, 2000); Gary Gerstle, *American Crucible: Race and Nation in the Twentieth Century* (Princeton, NJ: Princeton University Press, 2001); Gwendolyn Mink, *Old Labor and New Immigrants in American Political Development: Union, Party, and State, 1875–1920* (Ithaca, NY: Cornell University Press, 1986).

32. Gramsci quoted in Charles Tilly, "Collective Violence in European Perspective," in, *Violence in America: Historical & Comparative Perspectives*, ed., Hugh Davis Graham and Ted Robert Gurr (London: Sage Publications, 1979), 89.

33. *Ludlow: Being the Report of the Special Board of Officers*, 7, 13.

34. On Tikas, see Papanikolas, *Buried Unsung: Louis Tikas*.

35. *Ludlow: Being the Report of the Special Board of Officers*, 7.

36. Gunther Peck, *Reinventing Free Labor: Padrones and Immigrant Workers in the North American West, 1880–1930* (Cambridge: Cambridge University Press, 2000), 135–143.

37. *The Military Occupation of the Coal Strike Zone*, 12–14; Long, *Where the Sun Never Shines*, 278.

38. Office of the Adjutant General, Records, 1887–1914, "Record of the General Court Martial, Military District of Colorado, in the Matter of Karl E. Linderfelt," vol. 20, 280, Western History Collection, Denver Public Library. Native Americans' susceptibility to alcohol abuse was well known by 1914. Many Anglos, furthermore, believed that the Apaches were one of the fiercer tribes in the American West. Lieutenant Linderfelt's reference seems to be to what he thought a sober, and therefore, particularly "savage" Apache could accomplish on the battlefield, and how he thought Greeks and Bulgarians were capable of equaling such "savagery."

39. *The Rocky Mountain News*, September 4, 1913.

40. *The Denver Post*, October 28, 1913.

41. *The Trinidad Chronicle-News*, November 13, 1913.

42. Papanikolas, *Buried Unsung*, 9, 88, 90.

43. *Twenty-Second Annual Report of the Colorado Fuel and Iron Company*, "Business Interests," RG 2, box 25, Rockefeller Archive Center.

44. In *Buried Unsung*, Zeese Papanikolas interviewed Greek miner Michael Lingos who remembered three Balkan veterans in the Ludlow tent colony on the day of the massacre. See pgs. 119 and 297, endnote 119.

45. Peck, *Reinventing Free Labor*, 171–172.

46. Papanikolas, *Buried Unsung*, 119.

47. *Ludlow: Being the Report of the Special Board of Officers*, 7. In the "Findings of the Board" section of this report, Boughton and Danks repeated this observation when they wrote: "The Greeks, always warlike and obstreperous, had no women or children in the colony." See p. 25.

48. Louis Tikas estimated that between 300 and 350 Greeks were working southern Colorado's coal mines just before the 1913–1914 strike began. See

Papanikolas, *Buried Unsung*, 72. This figure is in line with number of Greeks (589) the United Mine Workers estimated worked in all the state's coal mines. See "Nationalities Employed in Mines of Colorado During the Year 1912" in The Papers of E.L. Doyle, box 2, envelope 18; also see Peck, *Reinventing Free Labor*, 158–173.

49. Peck, *Reinventing Free Labor*, 166–173.
50. Edward Alsworth Ross, *The Old World in the New: The Significance of Past and Present Immigration to the American People* (New York: The Century Company, 1914), 111. "Navvies" or "navvy" is a British term for unskilled laborers. The term was most commonly applied to men working on road or railroad construction.
51. Ibid., 101.
52. Peck, *Reinventing Free Labor*, 166–173.
53. For a general discussion of definitions of middle-class manliness at the turn of the twentieth century, see E. Anthony Rotundo, *American Manhood* (New York: Basic Books, 1993), 222–246; Gail Bederman, *Manliness and Civilization: A Cultural History of Race and Gender in the United States, 1880–1917* (Chicago: The University of Chicago Press, 1994).
54. Married men had different motivations for emigrating. In Greece, brides commonly moved into their father-in-laws' houses after marriage. Some husbands came to the United States to earn extra money for their fathers' newly expanded household. Both duties paid off for men who carried them out successfully. For single men, earning dowry money meant accomplishing a task that was expected of them. Married men, on the other hand, received the benefits of marriage and helped maintain their fathers' estate, which they hoped to inherit in the future. See Peck, *Reinventing Free Labor*, 127–129.
55. One resident of the Ludlow tent colony testified later that Charlie Costa, a striking miner who was killed at Ludlow, led his fellow miners out of the tent colony when the fighting began in an effort to draw the National Guard's fire away from the women and children in the tent colony. It is not clear if Major Boughton and Captain Danks were aware of this testimony when they wrote their report on Ludlow. See the Affidavit of Margaret Dominiske in Commission on Industrial Relations, *The Colorado Coal Miners' Strike*, vol. 8, 7380.
56. *Ludlow: Being the Report of the Special Board of Officers*, 19–20.
57. *Twenty-Second Annual Report of the Colorado Fuel and Iron Company*, "Business Interests," RG 2, box 25, Rockefeller Archive Center.
58. See William H. Riker, *Soldiers of the State: The Role of the National Guard in American Democracy* (Washington, DC: Public Affairs Press, 1957); John K. Mahon, *History of the Militia and the National Guard* (New York: Macmillan Publishing Company, 1983); Cooper, *The Rise of the National Guard*; Jerry M. Cooper, *The Army and Civil Disorder: Federal Military Intervention in Labor Disputes, 1877–1900* (Westport, CT: Greenwood Press, 1980).

CHAPTER 11

"I Hate to Be Calling Her a Wife Now": Women and Men in the *Salt of the Earth* Strike, 1950–1952

Ellen Baker

A Crisis in the Union

Word spread fast. On the afternoon of June 12, 1951, sheriff's deputies came to the union hall with an injunction issued by New Mexico's Sixth District Court: officers, agents, and members of Mine-Mill Local 890 had to stop picketing the Empire Zinc Company or face immediate arrest.[1] This court order, coming just a day after a fight between striking miners and sheriff's deputies at Empire Zinc, electrified the mining district in this southwestern corner of New Mexico. Phones rang, cars threaded their way to the picket, and women hurried to tell their neighbors. Men starting their shift in other mines told workers who were just leaving. That night, crowding into the biggest dance hall that could be found, hundreds of union members and supporters confronted their dilemma: if the union obeyed the injunction, replacement workers could enter the mine and the ten-month-long strike would be lost; if it disobeyed, all of the picketers could be arrested—and the strike would be lost.

Everyone agreed that the stakes were very high. The late 1940s and early 1950s were a period of fierce class conflict in the United States, and companies used anticommunism as a battering ram against left-wing unions like Mine-Mill.[2] Elsewhere, and in other industries, companies had succeeded; in Grant County they had failed. Confronted in 1948 by companies willing to negotiate new contracts only with "good Americans," Mine-Mill Local 890 successfully used walkouts, sit-downs, and strikes to force companies to the bargaining table.[3] Local 890 challenged the "dual-wage" system that kept Mexican Americans in "Mexican" jobs, and it pressed a similar agenda beyond the workplace by entering local politics. Mine-Mill members and leaders understood that Empire Zinc Company was only one of the six or so important mine operators in Grant County, but they believed that the other companies were colluding with Empire Zinc to destroy the militant, left-wing union.[4] The Empire Zinc strike of 1950–1952 was a showdown. From October 1950 to March 1951, the company tried to outlast the strikers, but even the shrinking strike funds did not drive strikers back to work. Then it launched a back-to-work movement, which failed to lure strikers back to work. The court injunction was the company's next step: using the power of the state to force the strikers back to work.

At the union meeting on June 12, men first wanted to stay on the pickets and hold their ground against the sheriff. But then they heard an unexpected alternative from three women. Aurora Chávez, Virginia Chacón, and Virginia Jencks had met ahead of time and arrived at the meeting ready to advance an unusual strategy.[5] They pointed out that the injunction referred only to union officers, agents, and members. Perhaps women, then, could picket with impunity. Surely no judge would think women belonged to the union? Surely no union man could object to a way to obey the injunction and simultaneously circumvent it?

But union men did object. "What are you gonna do with the children?" they asked. "I'm sure not gonna take care of them!"[6] Some men were afraid their wives would be injured on the line, and others thought that "shenanigans" would take place on the line—that their wives would run off with other men.[7] But most of the women were soon fired up by the chance to take over the picket, eager to help defend the union.[8] The "stronger" women, in Anita Tórrez's words, were not stymied by the problem of childcare. They would "do [their] own problem-solving [if] the men didn't want to share in solving the problem."[9] Braulia Velásquez commented later that "we had a hard job convincing the men but we finally did it by a vote."[10] Around 2:30 the next morning, with women voting alongside men—a provision granted to them by the International union—Local 890 decided that women would take over the pickets.[11] The women started planning their shifts.

Early in the morning on June 13, scores of women arrived at the Empire Zinc picket lines in the small town of Hanover. Sheriff Leslie Goforth may have been among those county officials who "opined that the women were not technically union members and therefore would not be affected by [Judge A.W.] Marshall's order."[12] In any case, Goforth chose to watch carefully rather than act hastily. His twenty deputies harassed the women, but scabs could not pierce the women's barrier and enter the mine.[13] Women were thrilled by their victory and swept into the next union meeting eager to tell stories of the pickets. It was hard "catching the sneaking scabs crawling through the pine trees," Braulia Velásquez reported. But "no scabs were crossing our lines," declared Aurora Chávez. "We don't need men."[14] More women were needed on "our line," and Elvira Molano and Daría Chávez exhorted them to come to the pickets the next morning.[15]

The hundreds of women who answered the call came from all over Grant County. Dolores Jiménez, for example, carpooled with neighbors for the twelve-mile drive north from Hurley. Her husband Frank worked at

Kennecott's smelter, not at Empire Zinc, but she had heard about this strike and had been encouraged to join by her friend, Clorinda Alderette.[16] Elvira Molano, married to an Empire Zinc striker, was several years older and fearless in the face of the deputies. Before the women's picket, in fact, she had walked the men's picket and been arrested in the fight that prompted Empire Zinc to seek the court injunction.[17] All the women found the pickets an exciting place to be. On the line they sang, they danced (with their husbands playing guitars on the hillside), they laughed, and they crocheted. And they often wanted to stay beyond their shift.[18] Away from the line, women staffed all the strike committees except the negotiating committee; they wrote publicity materials, spoke on the union's weekly radio show, persuaded local newspaper editors to publish union letters, and divvied up the strike relief funds. They tightened their own organization, meeting regularly on their own and electing picket captains and other leaders.[19] "The way people are moving now," Evelina Vigil predicted, "shows that we will win this strike. I'm ready to be there any time."[20]

But perhaps Vigil should have said, "the way *women* are moving now," for the men were not always moving alongside them. Physically, perhaps, they were, for men stayed near the pickets; but many were stalled in their moral support for the women's action, uneasy over their wives' willingness "to be there any time." While both women and men believed that the union needed to be defended, their differing reactions to the women's picket came out of gendered understandings of the union that needed this defense and of the families who could provide it.

Two models of unionism had coexisted until the injunction crisis forced their differences into the open on June 12. One model was based on a brotherhood of men—and exclusively men—who protected one another against the dangers of mining and exploitation by management. This was a brotherhood of equals, whose equality rested on their shared status as breadwinners in their individual families.[21] By interrupting the normal workings of the family, the women's picket appeared to threaten male authority and power, which in turn cast doubt on the breadwinner system that defined men's purpose in the workplace and cemented union solidarity. The other union model was based on a larger union family, whose members endured sacrifices during strikes for long-term economic security, and who helped consolidate the union's power beyond the workplace, partly through the activities of the ladies' auxiliary.[22] Taking over the picket followed logically from women's recent auxiliary work and, most importantly, promised to defend the union against the latest company assault. Those who thought in terms of the union family saw the threat to normal family life as merely temporary and saw men's resistance as divisive precisely when unity was most needed.

The vote on June 12 was a victory of the union family over the union brotherhood, and this decision set the parameters for the events to follow. But the vote did not wipe out the underlying differences that had generated the two visions. On the contrary, it simply set those differences in sharper relief once the implications for families became clear: women would let their household duties take second place to their picket duties, and men would not willingly take on women's work. Out of that juxtaposition came a new situation that demanded attention to gender relations. Individual homes and the union hall became the spaces in which new arrangements between men and women were hammered out; the picket lines and courthouse became the places where women developed a new political consciousness and solidarity that they brought to these household negotiations.

Women did not begin their picket with gender relations on their mind; they only aimed to defend the union community. But their husbands' resistance looked childish given the stakes of this union battle, and the story of the women's picket thus became a story of women's rebellion, not just against the Empire Zinc Company, but also against their own husbands. What grants this story even greater significance is that it became the theme of a remarkable movie made in 1953—*Salt of the Earth*—starring these same union men and women; indeed, making *Salt of the Earth* reveals their effort to make sense of what had happened to them.

THE UNION AS A MILITANT BROTHERHOOD

Men resented the women's picket because they sensed its threat to the "natural" order: their wives expected them to move to the sidelines of their own strike and even to take on women's work, both of which publicly eroded men's status. But there was more to union men's resistance than a defense of male authority for its own sake. This authority was also a dimension of the masculinity that shaped Mine-Mill Local 890's structure and infused its battle for workplace power. As miners built their union in the 1940s, they used, deliberately or not, models of the family to shape their relationships with one another. Already familiar with the horizontal and vertical relationships inherent in families, union men drew upon three sets of relationships—those of brothers, husbands, and fathers—in structuring the union. The union became a brotherhood made up of equals bound to one another by mutual needs and reinforced by the exclusion of women; the workplace danger that required mutual help also required individual courage, and women's absence from mines and mills ensured that this courage would be associated with men.

Union men's fraternal equality (the *kind* of brotherhood they felt) was itself partly based on another set of family relationships: these men were equals not only because they had the same experiences at work, but also because they each headed their own household, or aspired to do so. Male breadwinners exercised their authority over the women and children in their private families, away from this fictive family in the union hall; yet men achieved the status of breadwinner, from which their authority at home derived, in the workplace. The democratic structure of the union was rooted in this brand of social equality. Yet another dimension of their fraternity was its grounding in shared ethnicity and, at the same time, its capacity to transcend ethnic barriers, to attract Anglo workers to a brotherhood that affirmed the social equality of Mexicans and Anglos.

The miners' union was much more than a fraternal club, of course. Its central purpose was to deal collectively with a powerful adversary. Here, too, family relations and masculinity came into play, but with a twist. Management insisted that a family relationship structured the workplace. As Kennecott labor relations expert James K. Richardson instructed the New Mexico Miners and Prospectors Association, "[l]abor negotiations should be, in my opinion, family affairs."[23] As in any industry, it was common for managers to speak of the company as one big family, working together, headed by a father; this corresponded to a notion that any differences between labor and management were "merely a misunderstanding by each party of the aims of the other. Each has a basic willingness to promote a free enterprise system."[24] In exerting paternalist control, management assured workers that it knew best what workers' interests were (because they were the same as the company's) and how best to protect them. Managers were parents and workers were children.

In the Southwest, paternalism took on another dimension: Anglos were parents and Mexicans were children. Companies had long characterized Mexican workers as docile, prone to laziness, and indifferent to work conditions that "American" workers would not tolerate; lazy workers needed the firm, fatherly governance that a mining company provided. Thus when miners joined Mine-Mill, demanded better wages, and pursued grievances, they challenged both the cultural definition of Mexicans as ethnically inferior and the paternalistic labor relations in local mines and mills. Their combative, militant stance vindicated both their manhood and their Mexican ethnicity.

THE UNION AS A LARGER FAMILY

Women drew on a competing vision of the union, one that also came out of the "militant" tradition but existed in some tension with it. In the late 1940s, Local 890 began to campaign against segregation in local schools, businesses, and housing. The impetus to expand the union's activism beyond the workplace came from Mine-Mill organizers Clinton and Virginia Jencks, who moved to New Mexico from Denver in 1947. Having studied the history of mining struggles, the Jenckses believed that without women, the union was acting with one hand tied behind its back.[25] Moreover, the Jenckses belonged to a left-wing tradition that, in the 1940s, criticized male chauvinism and theorized the political significance of housework.[26]

Inspired by views like this and with experiences from years of political organizing, Virginia Jencks pushed hard for the union to hold regular family meetings. She walked from house to house and struck up conversations with miners' wives, encouraging them to come to union meetings where families would eat and then play games, watch a movie, or talk about political issues. Virginia Chacón, who soon joined Jencks, found that "some women were interested, but it sounded like they were scared" of their husbands.[27] Indeed, it took some doing to get men to invite their wives to union meetings, but Mine-Mill's structure and political orientation made these invitations a bit easier to extend. The Mine-Mill International allowed women to vote, which very few male-dominated unions did and which probably came in tandem with the union's move toward the Left in the 1930s.[28] Miners' wives further developed the union family model when they formed a ladies' auxiliary in the summer of 1948. Like other union auxiliaries, Auxiliary 209 was based on the principle that anything affecting a male breadwinner necessarily affected his family. With a wife in the union, a union man like Juan Chacón could come home and say, "this and this is happening, we're gonna do this, you gotta help." The auxiliary would be the backbone of the union, just "like a wife [was] the backbone of [her] husband."[29]

Gender functioned, albeit differently, in the two models of unionism, serving to unify the "brothers" and marking out appropriate realms of action for union "family" members. The auxiliary was the realm in which women joined the union effort. Many women's historians have interpreted auxiliary activities along axes that stretch from the "domestic" to the "social" and then to the "political," or from the "traditional" to the "non-traditional." Traditional activities projected women's domesticity onto the union community; they included organizing socials and dances, cooking, offering medical care to wounded strikers, and buying only union-made products and services. They were often associated with domestic life and, importantly, with countering the "nagging wife syndrome"—the hostility of wives toward their husbands' union, and especially toward strikes.[30] Non-traditional, political activities, by contrast, could broaden women's perspective and turn women into staunch unionists; these activities included demonstrating, speaking in public, picketing, and joining political campaigns.[31] Auxiliary 209 can be understood this way, for it took up the typical tasks of a union auxiliary; through raffles and enchilada suppers, women aimed to nourish the union family. And auxiliary members became more politically active over time, in registering voters and boycotting discriminatory businesses, as well as during each strike that Local 890 conducted.

But another way to consider gender in the union is to look at the issues the union considered within its purview. That is, apart from the gendered composition of the union and women's own activities, we can see gender in the sorts of issues that became union business. From this perspective, it is clear that before the Empire Zinc strike, the auxiliary was precisely that: an auxiliary, always ancillary and subordinate to union men. Women believed, in fact, that it was this union family that they were defending when they stepped onto the Empire Zinc picket line. But by inverting family responsibilities, the women's picket forced union members to confront the thorny question of male dominance in families. No longer did gender function only as an organizing principle for the union's composition and activities. Now gender relations themselves became a union issue.

HOUSEHOLD CONFLICT

The union had to deal with those power relations because couples immediately began to argue about the picket. Aurora Chávez, for instance, had a big fight with her husband, even though (or perhaps because) she had been one of the women to propose the picket. He "didn't like it at all," she recalled. "He knew how it was gonna be and he didn't like it." Aurora was pregnant, and Agustín feared the violence that his wife would face.[32] As a husband and father, he took his responsibility to protect his wife and children seriously. A married, pregnant woman facing down a leering, armed deputy could mean only that her husband had failed: either he would not or could not protect them, and either way he looked bad. Agustín Chávez also feared—correctly— that he would have to take care of their three children, all under the age of ten.[33] The women's picket meant, then, not only that he would be failing to meet one of his responsibilities, but also that *she* would fail to meet hers.

Fighting over the performance of duties, Aurora and Agustín Chávez nonetheless agreed on how a family should be run. Every family is, in some respects, a unit with clear objectives, bringing together cash and noncash resources to feed, house, clothe, educate, and discipline its members. In the breadwinner model—widely accepted by working-class families at that time and especially powerful in mining districts, which were built around an industry whose workforce was male—husbands provided wages and security while wives cared for children and kept house.[34] These responsibilities complemented one another and corresponded to realms of authority, particularly over children.[35]

But necessity often demanded flexibility in the breadwinner model. Every miner's wife faced the possibility of her husband's absence, whether by injury, death, or desertion. Approximately 17 percent of Hanover's households in 1930, for example, were headed by women, three-quarters of whom were widows and most of whom were in their forties with children.[36] In these instances women had to find ways to support their families, usually by taking in laundry or boarders; women with sons old enough to work in the mines could rely on that income. As historian Laurel Thatcher Ulrich has shown of colonial New England women, under extraordinary circumstances a wife could become a "deputy husband" who performed men's work and exercised a husband's power.[37] Local 890 women saw their picket in a similar light: if men were incapacitated by the injunction, it fell to women to sustain the union effort.

Yet while the Empire Zinc strike circumstances were extraordinary, there was one key difference: these husbands were alive, they were present, and they were not interested in assuming the role of a "deputy wife." There was, in fact, no deputy wife that mirrored a deputy husband. This discrepancy results from the critical asymmetry of family power relations; while husbands' and wives' duties complemented one another, they were not commensurate, nor interchangeable. A household may share goals, agree on the way to reach them, and allocate power to do so, but it nonetheless comprises distinct people with distinct interests exercising different kinds of power, and the apparent unity of the family results from struggles of power. In systems of male dominance, male authority can override female authority at critical moments, by virtue of cultural prerogative or physical force, although women are not without resources of their own.[38] In the Chávez home, Aurora prevailed over her husband, but not because Agustín took on childcare: her father sent her teenage sister Rachel to help out while Aurora walked on the line.[39] Neither husband nor wife had to give in because their extended family was on hand to make up the difference.

Not all families resolved this conflict the way the Chávezes did. Chana Montoya, for example, appealed to a different kind of authority: the union community. Just two days after women began their picket, she insisted upon "more help from men on the jobs off the line. We need more help on the job, we cannot do at home while we are doing this job."[40] Montoya spoke with some authority. She was married to Local 890 President Cipriano Montoya, so her words probably carried weight in a union meeting. But her comments stand out even more when we learn that she regularly suffered abuse at her husband's hands. Many people knew this; no one discussed it. She was probably speaking from her own experience at home, and for her even to hint at domestic conflict is astonishing. Perhaps her call was made easier by Cipriano's absence from that particular meeting.[41]

Cipriano Montoya presided over another important union meeting, though, and hinted at his idea of women's duties. In October 1951, Local 890 celebrated the first anniversary of the Empire Zinc strike. While strike committee chairman Ernesto Velásquez praised the women as "veterans," a term fully laden with masculine honor, Cipriano Montoya first congratulated the entire membership and then commended the women for "knowing that they have . . . work to do at home."[42] At this meeting, meant to reflect upon the difficulties they had faced and the victories they had won, Montoya chose to remind women of their household duties. His praise extended only so far as they met those obligations. Chana Montoya did not speak at this meeting.

SOLIDARITY ON THE PICKET LINE

When women and men confronted one another at home, men brought the force of their customary authority. Women brought the strength of the solidarity they generated on the picket lines and the new light it shed on their husbands' behavior. Their recent history of auxiliary organization and the tremendous energy unleashed by the unusual strike conditions together forged the solidarity that enabled women picketers to respond to threats, the most important of which were direct violence and unfair treatment at the hands of local law enforcers. Successfully meeting those threats changed their understanding of local political economy and of their husbands' claims to authority.

More than anything else, women created solidarity by resisting law enforcers. Sheriff Goforth was ordered to break up the roadblocks on June 16, and he found himself in an ordeal that strengthened the women while it left him helpless. When a deputy pushed Virginia Chacón aside to let strikebreaker Francisco Franco through, a crowd of women pushed Franco's car right back down the road.[43] Other women threw rocks. The scabs were angry, Chacón reported, and "began calling us names, and were just dirty to us."[44] Into this tense scene one of the deputies lobbed a tear-gas grenade, which "skewered and rolled among the pickets, spewing the white gas and dispersing the screaming women."[45] But the wind favored the women, who soon reorganized their line, cursing the sheriff and jeering at his deputies. Deputies arrested dozens of picketers and sent three carloads to the county jail in nearby Silver City. The arrests did not destroy the picket line, though, for three hundred women remained on the line in Hanover. "We can keep arresting them," Undersheriff Lewis Brown commented, "but they keep moving in."[46]

In all, fifty-three women were arrested that afternoon, many taken to jail with their children in tow. Few had seen the inside of a jail before, and all were nervous until the sheriff made a critical mistake. He promised to release them if they agreed not to return to the picket. Instantly, they announced that they would not "go home, [they would] go back to the picket lines," and after that the women "had a very good time" playing cards, singing, and making "all kinds of noise."[47] Only the filth, and a miserable lunch of cold beans, dampened their excitement. The women made such a racket in the county jail—"the worst mess" that jailer Jim Hiler had ever seen—that Goforth released them that night. "It looks like an endless job," he admitted. And indeed it was, for the women returned to the picket that night, building a "picket tent" that housed food, a stove, and cots.[48] High spirits continued during the arraignment of forty-five women on June 18. Over a hundred women filled the corridors of the county courthouse. "It's like a picnic," one woman declared. "We're having fun—and we're going to stay on the picket line, too."[49] Goforth's effort to intimidate the women only succeeded in uniting them.

Throughout the summer of 1951, violence continued between the picketers on the one hand and the sheriff, his deputies, and strikebreakers on the other. On July 11, deputy Robert Capshaw tried to arrest Antonia Rivera and immediately found himself the target of rocks and red pepper. "The whole bunch ganged up on about seven deputies," Sheriff Goforth reported. "The battle wound up as a standoff."[50] The next day, deputy Marvin Mosely tried to drive his car through the picket line. He hit fourteen-year-old Rachel Juárez, crushing her foot and sending her to the hospital.[51] Juárez "deliberately threw herself on the left fender of my car," Mosely explained. "I stopped to get her off and she cussed me."[52] And an even more serious conflict flared on August 23, when five cars of strikebreakers approached the line of forty women and children. Everyone waited, tense and uncertain. Then the cars began to move slowly, "bumper to bumper," into the line.[53] Bone and muscle strained against steel and engine as the picketers tried to hold the cars back, but one car and a pickup truck made it through and injured two women.[54] A call to the Kennecott company hospital at Santa Rita, which the public had often used for emergencies, met with stony refusal to send an ambulance. "If this call is for the picket[er]s," the hospital operator allegedly declared, "we have no ambulance. The picket[er]s will have to take care of themselves."[55] And for the first time the deputies' guns were used for more than brandishing. Denzel Hartless "jumped out of a car" and "shot about five shots, apparently wildly, during the peak of the fracas."[56] He wounded Agustín Martínez, a young veteran discharged from the army just nine days earlier.[57]

The cumulative effect of this violence was not to inure picketers to it, to make them dismiss it as the normal course of events, but rather to discredit the police; encounters with the local judiciary furthered this process. One June afternoon, for instance, strikebreaker Jesús Avalos discharged his rifle near the pickets. Lola Martínez confronted him at once and was told that he was only out "shooting rabbits," an account that Assistant District Attorney Vincent Vesely credited when he declined to prosecute Avalos. Martínez angrily declared that "justice was not for the working people" in Grant County.[58] Elvira Molano was also radicalized by her experience with law enforcement. She was repeatedly injured by deputies—shocking enough for a law-abiding woman, but compounded by being charged with crimes while her attackers went free. "I had never in my life been involved in courts or the law until the Empire Zinc strike," she declared after deputy Marvin Mosely was acquitted of assault charges. "I thought the law of Grant County was to protect us, not throw us in jail like animals and beat us with blackjacks."[59] Some deputies keeping "order" on the picket line even did double-duty as strikebreakers. Daría Chávez was outraged to see Mosely and Robert Capshaw sneaking to work at Empire Zinc on the morning of August 10. "It certainly seems funny to us women on the line," she said, "to see these so-called peace officers, who are supposed to be neutral, now working as scabs. And these are the men the court told us we should respect. They have gone from one dirty job to another. What could be lower than a scab?"[60]

Experiences on the line gave women a taste of power. Not only did they resist physical assault, but they usually did so without any help from men. And they were exhilarated by it. Moreover, acting in two settings—the picket lines and their own houses—and crossing from one to the other placed both sets of actions in relief. This perspective enabled women to question why issues of justice and equality were limited to relations between the union and the company. In short, throughout the summer and fall of 1951 women undertook two kinds of defensive actions. The first was to defend their community against the company and its allies; the second to defend their actions against the resentment and active opposition of their husbands, who believed that domestic relations and gender roles should stay constant lest the community be fractured. Convinced that their motives and actions were just, women bristled at their husbands' antipathy and insisted that the real threat to unity lay in men's "backward" ideas.

UNEASY CHANGE

Over time, and through the struggle, men accepted being sidelined on the picket lines. Local 890 officials Bob Hollowwa, Clinton Jencks, and Cipriano

Montoya explained the union's involvement in this process to the Mine-Mill's International Executive Board in August:

> In the past few weeks considerable improvement has been made in organizational problems which have come up from time to time. Some problems such as the participation of strikers in helping the women with work in and around the picket line—such as hauling water, chopping wood, furnishing transportation to women pickets, carrying out the numerous odd jobs required at the picket line. Solving these problems have [sic] been accomplished by and thru "frank" discussion of all the people involved.[61]

Some men went even further, accepting changes in their own households as well as at the picket lines, but they did so equivocally. Ernesto Velásquez provides a good example of the complexities bound up in men's experiences of the women's picket. An employee of Empire Zinc since 1948, he quickly assumed leadership within the Empire Zinc unit of Local 890 and chaired the strike negotiating committee. In this capacity he addressed the September 1951 convention of the International Union of Mine, Mill and Smelter Workers. Joking about the role reversals effected by the women's picket, Velásquez revealed some of his discomfort and, perhaps, his way of easing it.

> We will see what my wife says—and I hate to be calling her a wife now—she's the boss of the family. It so happened the 13th of June she took over the household. We have a little baby and she said you go home and wash the dishes and change the diapers. That puts me in an embarrassing situation. I have washed the dishes and I have swept the house, but one thing I cannot get myself to do and that is change a diaper. Let's see what Sister Velásquez has to say.[62]

Sister Velásquez had nothing to say about "taking over the household"; instead, she described the picket and her time in jail. There are any number of reasons for her to have remained silent on the topic that her husband had so clearly and so publicly raised. Perhaps she believed that nothing of substance had changed, or that the changes were too touchy to be aired in this public setting. Perhaps she felt that Ernesto had used humor to trivialize the extent and meaning of changes in gender relations and had thereby won over the largely male audience to his own perspective. For what could be more ridiculous than a female "boss of the family"? And how could a man boss the family if he had to change diapers? What, indeed, could changing diapers represent, if not the debasement that necessarily accompanies wifehood?

Still, Ernesto Velásquez proved one of the women's most consistent supporters. Unlike Cipriano Montoya, who generally referred to the strikers as "brothers," Velásquez acknowledged women as full-fledged union members. He frequently and publicly encouraged women to participate, and his own wife's steady participation speaks of his sincerity. On the strike's anniversary, he described how he felt "as a newborn, . . . good as to how solid everything has been over the past year. . . . The women . . . knew nothing about strikes but [now] they are veterans. The women were tear-gassed, jailed, these women have suffered."[63] In stressing women's suffering, Velásquez did not dwell on men's failure to protect their wives. Instead he cast it as women's strength in the face of company assaults; such a picture drew on an unassailable cultural value, that of women's patient strength, and imbued it with the masculine honor accorded to veterans. His comments are quite remarkable for their imagery, too. He felt "as a newborn"—interesting, given that he and his wife Braulia had a newborn at home; perhaps he was imagining his own child's future in a more equitable society.

Prodded by comrades like Ernesto Velásquez and, most importantly, forced by their wives, men ultimately stood behind the women's picket even if they remained ambivalent. This unsteady commitment proved enough impetus for the strike to succeed. In January 1952, the Empire Zinc Company finally returned to the negotiating table and agreed to a contract that granted many of the union's demands. Some weeks later, the company quietly agreed to add indoor plumbing to all of its company houses—a demand raised as early as 1949, but one which the male negotiating committee had quickly abandoned when challenged.

CARRYING THE STRUGGLE TO A NEW LEVEL

It was the dramatic conflict between wives and husbands, in the course of a heroic fight of workers against management and against racism, that attracted blacklisted filmmakers to southwestern New Mexico in the summer of 1951. Recently expelled from Hollywood studios for refusing to disavow a Communist past, they wanted to project "real stories of real working people" onto the silver screen. The strike going on at that very moment in New Mexico provided appropriate material. *Salt of the Earth* (1953) resulted from an unusual worker-artist collaboration in which screenwriter Michael Wilson consulted the families and changed the script in response to their reactions. The film was shot in Grant County, where a committee consisting of six representatives each from the film company, Local 890, and Auxiliary 209 managed the daily production work. The cast featured seven union members in leading roles and hundreds more in group scenes.[64]

Mining families' contributions to the movie took place at a moment when they had space to reflect on the strike; working on the film allowed them to work out what the women's rebellion meant and to resolve, through an artistic medium, the contradictions and conflicts that still faced them. This process took place on an organizational level, too: in choosing two sets of representatives (from Local 890 and Auxiliary 209), union families recognized that no single perspective could claim to represent the whole community.

Salt of the Earth tells the story of a fictional married couple, Ramón and Esperanza Quintero, who are driven apart when Esperanza joins the women's picket. Ramón does not care to see women on the picket line. Not only does he disdain "hiding behind women's skirts," but he cannot bear having his authority eroded as Esperanza transforms herself from a meek housewife into a vibrant union activist. In the movie's climax, Ramón confronts Esperanza after she returns from jail. They cannot "go on in this way," he insists. Esperanza agrees, but concludes something quite different.

> The Anglo bosses look down on you, and you hate them for it. "Stay in your place, you dirty Mexican"—that's what they tell you. But why must you say to me, "Stay in *your* place"? Do you feel better having someone lower than you? . . . Whose neck shall I stand on, to make me feel superior? And what will I get out of it? I don't want anything lower than I am. I'm low enough already. I want to rise. And push everything up with me as I go.[65]

Ramón is furious and raises his hand to hit her. But Esperanza stands defiant, and he lowers his hand. "That would be the old way," she tells him icily. "Never try it on me again—never."[66]

Salt of the Earth carried a powerful feminist message and prescient analysis of what later feminist theorists would call the intersections of race, class, and gender. It owes much to the men and women of Independent Productions Corporation, especially screenwriter Michael Wilson, who marveled at the "battles for equality taking place there on so many levels [that he could] hardly unskein them" himself.[67] The movie's opening scenes, for example, visually established the equal dignity and worth of women's housework and men's wage work, a perspective that probably came out of Wilson's own discussions with fellow Communists about "the Woman Question."[68] But the strong feminist message owes even more to the mining families' own understandings of the changes they had undergone, and gender was the lens through which they wanted viewers to see them. If Wilson had Esperanza bravely confront her husband, it was because the women in Grant County told him to do so. His script reflected their recent history and the leverage they had gained in representing their strike. Performing the story of the strike—reenacting more than acting, in Clinton Jencks's words—allowed a cathartic and triumphant conclusion that settled the power relations between men and women, regardless of how such changes played out in real life.

For the nature of the union community was not, in fact, a settled issue. Some women sensed a genuine and a permanent change; others found the changes between themselves and their husbands only temporary.[69] Ladies' Auxiliary president Mariana Ramírez noted "a certain respect for the ladies" after the strike.[70] Dolores Jimenez continued to suffer abuse from her husband, yet she felt that the strike had made her "ten feet tall." She stayed in her marriage for the sake of her children, and she always appreciated that her husband Frank was a good provider, even as he was having an affair with another woman. When Frank left her after the boys were grown up, she went to beauty school and opened her own shop.[71]

The story of Chana and Cipriano Montoya shows some of the heartbreaking complexities of these changes. In 1954, Chana Montoya divorced her abusive husband, although they continued to live together off and on for several years. She finally broke off from him by moving to Los Angeles with their children, and soon she landed a job in a hospital. Cipriano was unhappy to see her go, and he followed her to Los Angeles. She did not want to return to New Mexico with him, and she quickly got a restraining order against him.[72] Then the story took a tragic turn. He waited for her at a bus stop one morning in July 1961, and he shot her dead when she approached. She was thirty-three years old. His defense: that his wife was a Communist, and he wanted to save his seven children from such an upbringing. He accused her of joining the Communist Party in 1948 and leading him into it as well. And from that moment, he said, "we had a very sorrowful marriage." He resented her joining the Empire Zinc picket, attributing her participation entirely to a supposed Communist Party order. It made him angry, for "it was no job for a woman."[73] Moreover, he claimed that authorities at a party school had charged him in the mid-1950s with "exercising undue 'masculine control' over his wife." Montoya was convicted and imprisoned. Upon release he told Virginia and Juan Chacón that he had been forced to testify in that manner. He ended up committing suicide.

CONCLUSION

The Empire Zinc strike and *Salt of the Earth* together show how gender mattered in the power structures that operated both across class lines and within the working class, and in the union whose mission was to transform those structures of power. Gender served as an organizing principle for the union's activities until an unusual situation, the injunction, propelled women to the center of the strike. Mining wives' awareness of the interdependent nature of the family, and their appreciation of the contributions they made through the work that defined each day of their lives, proved essential to their ability to imagine, contemplate, and eventually insist upon playing an active and ultimately transformative role in the Empire Zinc strike. Men's sense that their family authority was linked to the union's power made it hard for them to picture even a temporary inversion of family responsibilities as anything other than an irreversible diminution of men's authority; men's reaction ensured that this inversion brought gender relations into focus for union men and women. It was this story that strikers wanted to share with an audience, and making *Salt of the Earth* was an unusual opportunity to reflect on changes that had taken place and to imagine a "new way" in which men and women could regard each other as equals.

NOTES

1. *Silver City Daily Press* (hereafter cited as *SCDP*), June 13, 1951.
2. In 1947 Congress passed, over President Truman's veto, the Labor-Management Relations Act, better known as the Taft-Hartley Act. Taft-Hartley affirmed workers' right to not join a union, made it easier to get a court injunction against strikers—a return to the years before the 1932 Norris-LaGuardia Act, which had limited such injunctions—and specified unfair labor practices thenceforth forbidden to unions. It required all union officials to sign affidavits

stating that they did not belong to the Communist Party. The unions that did not file noncommunist affidavits lost access to the National Labor Relations Board (NLRB). Congress of Industrial Organizations (CIO) leaders refused to sign these affidavits for over a year; Mine-Mill and other left-wing unions held out even longer. Anticommunism was more than a weapon of the companies; political battles over communism and anticommunism tore many unions apart during this period. For this process in Mine-Mill, see Vernon H. Jensen, *Nonferrous Metals Industry Unionism, 1932–1954: A Story of Leadership Controversy*, Cornell Studies in Industrial and Labor Relations, vol. 5 (Ithaca, NY: Cornell University Press, 1954).

3. Mining companies operating in Grant County refused to negotiate with Mine-Mill and fostered "independent" union organizing, hinting that its workers should be "good Americans." (The term *good Americans*, of course, referred both to noncommunists and aliens.) Letter from Clinton Jencks to Maurice Travis, June 26, 1948, Western Federation of Miners/International Union of Mine, Mill and Smelter Workers Collection, box 868, folder 9, Archives, University of Colorado at Boulder Libraries, Boulder (hereafter cited as Mine-Mill Papers), box 867, folder 1; *SCDP*, June 24, June 30, and August 20, 1948; Arthur Flores, B.G. Provencio, José T. Morales, and Clinton Jencks to W.H. Goodrich, July 10, 1948, in Mine-Mill Papers, box 870, folder 7.

4. Clinton Jencks, telephone interview by author, May 10, 1997; Lorenzo Tórrez, interview by author, tape recording, October 4, 1995, Tucson. Grant County's biggest operation was Kennecott's open-pit copper mine in Santa Rita, accompanied by its smelter in Hurley. American Smelting and Refining Company (ASARCO), Peru Mining Company, U.S. Smelting, Refining, and Mining Company, and Empire Zinc all ran lead-zinc mines in the towns of Hanover, Vanadium, and Bayard.

5. Braulia Velásquez, quoted in *Proceedings of the 48th Convention of the Mine, Mill and Smelter Workers in Nogales, Arizona, September 10–15, 1951* (Denver: International Union of Mine, Mill and Smelter Workers), 64; Aurora Chávez, telephone interview by author, May 9, 1997. Chávez was married to Empire Zinc striker Agustín Chávez; Chacón to Hurley worker Juan Chacón, and Jencks to union organizer Clinton Jencks.

6. Anita Tórrez, interview by author, tape recording, Tucson, Arizona, October 4, 1995.

7. Aurora Chávez interview; Virginia Chacón, interview by author, tape recording, Faywood, New Mexico, September 30, 1995.

8. Historian Jack Cargill reports that the discussion split along gender lines, with International representatives Bob Hollowwa and Clinton Jencks joining the women. Jack Cargill, "Empire and Opposition: The 'Salt of the Earth' Strike," in *Labor in New Mexico: Unions, Strikes, and Social History since 1881*, ed., Robert Kern (Albuquerque: University of New Mexico Press, 1983), 203.

9. Anita Tórrez interview.

10. Braulia Velásquez, quoted in *1951 Mine-Mill Convention Proceedings*, 64.

11. Ernesto Velásquez, quoted in *1951 Mine-Mill Convention Proceedings*, 64. A few women and children had already begun picketing casually with men even before the injunction, but women's picketing on a large scale presented quite a different picture to men's (and women's) imaginations.

12. *SCDP*, June 13, 1951.

13. Cargill, "Empire and Opposition," 204.
14. Minutes of Local 890, International Union of Mine, Mill and Smelter Workers, June 14, 1951, Mine-Mill Papers, box 868, book 9.
15. Ibid.
16. Dolores Jiménez, interview by author and Sam Sills, March 2, 2003, Santa Fe, N.M.
17. *SCDP*, June 11, 1951.
18. Anita Tórrez and Lorenzo Tórrez interview; Elena Tafoya and Daría Chávez, interview by author, tape recording, Hanover, New Mexico, March 14, 1996.
19. Local 890 minutes, June 14 and 28, 1951; and Local 890 press and radio release, July 24, 1951, Mine-Mill Papers, box 873, envelope 1.
20. Local 890 minutes, June 28, 1951.
21. Recent work on masculinity in the mining and railroad industries has shaped my understanding of Local 890's gender politics. Thomas Miller Klubock enhances Gramsci's concept of hegemony with an incisive gender analysis to explain miners' acceptance of and resistance to corporate power in *Contested Communities: Class, Gender, and Politics in Chile's El Teniente Copper Mine, 1904–1951* (Durham, NC: Duke University Press, 1998). Michael Yarrow has marked out two different kinds of masculine identities corresponding to different periods of workers' mobilization. Unionized coal miners of the 1930s defined true manhood as a worker's vigorous challenge to management prerogative (and to management's paternalism), but in a period of union retrenchment, these miners articulated and acted upon a different definition of manhood, one marked by hard work and the breadwinner ethic. Michael Yarrow, "The Gender-Specific Consciousness of Appalachian Coal Miners: Structure and Change," in *Bringing Class Back In: Contemporary and Historical Perspectives*, ed., Scott G. McNall, Rhonda Levine, and Rick Fantasia (Boulder, CO: Westview Press, 1991), 285–310. See also Steven Penfield, " 'Have You No Manhood in You?' Gender and Class in the Cape Breton Coal Towns, 1920–1926," in *Gender and History in Canada*, ed., Joy Parr and Mark Rosenfeld (Toronto: Copp Clark, Ltd., 1996), 270–293; Mark Rosenfeld, " 'It Was a Hard Life': Class and Gender in the Work and Family Rhythms of a Railway Town, 1920–1950," *Historical Papers/ Communications Historiques* (Windsor, Ont., 1988), 237–279; Paul Michel Taillon, " 'What We Want is Good, Sober Men': Masculinity, Respectability, and Temperance in the Railroad Brotherhoods, c. 1870–1910," *Journal of Social History* 36, 2 (2002), 319–338.
22. Women's historians from the 1970s onward have recast American labor history to account for community-based unionism, not just the workplace unionism that had long dominated institutional labor histories. See Elizabeth Jameson, *All That Glitters: Class, Conflict, and Community in Cripple Creek* (Urbana and Chicago: University of Illinois Press, 1998); Elizabeth Faue, *Community of Suffering and Struggle: Women, Men, and the Labor Movement in Minneapolis, 1915–1945* (Chapel Hill: University of North Carolina Press, 1991); Ardis Cameron, *Radicals of the Worst Sort: Laboring Women of Lawrence, Massachusetts, 1860–1912* (Urbana and Chicago: University of Illinois Press, 1990); Laurie Mercier, *Anaconda: Labor, Community, and Culture in Montana's Smelter City* (Urbana and Chicago: University of Illinois Press, 2001).
23. James K. Richardson, Address to 1946 Meeting of New Mexico Miners and Prospectors Association, reprinted in *New Mexico Miner and Prospector*

(June 1946), 4. Richardson was a labor relations specialist at Kennecott's Utah operations, and in the early 1950s he was transferred to New Mexico.

24. Ibid.

25. Clinton Jencks interview.

26. In general, the Communist Party held that women's oppression would evaporate under the enlightened conditions of socialism; "feminism" meant one thing—the bourgeois feminism that masked real class relations and sacrificed working-class women for their bourgeois "sisters." See Van Gosse, " 'To Organize in Every Neighborhood': The Gender Politics of American Communists between the Wars," *Radical History Review* 50 (Spring 1991): 109–141; Rosalyn Baxandall, "The Question Seldom Asked: Women and the CPUSA," in *New Studies in the Politics and Culture of American Communism*, ed. Michael E. Brown et al. (New York: Monthly Review Press, 1993), 141–161; and Robert Schaffer, "Women and the Communist Party, USA, 1930–1940, *Socialist Review* 45 (May–June 1979): 73–118. In the 1940s, some women challenged this simplistic view, and groups like the Congress of American Women pushed a leftist agenda without trivializing women's issues. See Amy Swerdlow, "The Congress of American Women: Left-Feminist Peace Politics in the Cold War," in *U.S. History as Women's History*, ed. Linda Kerber et al. (Chapel Hill and London: University of North Carolina Press, 1995), 296–312; Kate Weigand, *Red Feminism: American Communism and the Making of Women's Liberation* (Baltimore: Johns Hopkins University Press, 2001); Linn Shapiro, "Red Feminism: American Communism and the Women's Rights Tradition, 1919–1956" (PhD diss., American University, 1996); Harriet Hyman Alonso, "Mayhem and Moderation: Women Peace Activists during the McCarthy Era," in *Not June Cleaver: Women and Gender in Postwar America, 1945–1960*, ed., Joanne Meyerowitz (Philadelphia: Temple University Press, 1994), 128–150.

27. Virginia Chacón interview.

28. Mine-Mill Auxiliary women from the United States and Canada reported that women in other auxiliaries were astonished by, and jealous of, women's voting rights in Mine-Mill. See *Mine-Mill Convention Proceedings*, 1942 and 1944. Mine-Mill auxiliary members probably exercised this right only in circumstances that already favored it and on issues already deemed to concern them; that is, it was a formal right that only occasionally, and imperfectly, became a substantive right.

29. Virginia Chacón interview.

30. Patricia Yeghissian, "Emergence of the Red Berets," *Michigan Occasional Papers in Women's Studies* 10 (Winter 1980), 1–2.

31. For other examples of the movement from domestic to political, see Neala Schleuning, *Women, Community, and the Hormel Strike of 1985–1986* (Westport, CT and London: Greenwood Press, 1994); Lynda Ann Ewen, *Which Side Are You On? The Brookside Mine Strike in Harlan County, Kentucky, 1973–1974* (Chicago: Vanguard Books, 1979); and Judy Aulette and Trudy Mills, "Something Old, Something New: Auxiliary Work in the 1983–1986 Copper Strike," *Feminist Studies* 14 (Summer 1988): 251–268. While Schleuning and Yeghissian posit a sharp division between "public" and "private," other historians have acknowledged the permeable boundaries between the two and have expanded the scope of the "domestic" to include neighborhoods. See Ann Schofield, "An 'Army of Amazons': The Language

of Protest in a Kansas Mining Community, 1921–1922," *American Quarterly* 37 (Winter 1985), 686–701; Temma Kaplan, "Female Consciousness and Collective Action: The Case of Barcelona, 1910–1918," *Signs* 7 (Spring 1982), 545–566; Sylvie Murray, "A la jonction du mouvement ouvrier et du mouvement des femmes: La ligue auxiliaire de l'Association Internationale des Machinistes, Canada, 1903–1980" (MA thesis, University of Québec at Montréal, 1988); and Ardis Cameron, *Radicals of the Worst Sort: Laboring Women in Lawrence, Massachusetts, 1860–1912* (Urbana and Chicago: University of Illinois Press, 1990).

32. Aurora Chávez interview.

33. Ibid.

34. Louise A. Tilly and Joan W. Scott developed the concept of the family wage economy in their influential *Women, Work, and Family* (New York: Holt, Rineholt and Winston, 1978; reprint, New York: Routledge, 1989). Analyzing reactions to married women's employment during the Great Depression, Alice Kessler-Harris has shown that women as well as men strenuously upheld the breadwinner model, in which men earned a "family wage" and could thereby provide for their families. Alice Kessler-Harris, *A Woman's Wage: Historical Meanings and Social Consequences* (Lexington: University Press of Kentucky, 1990). Miners' wives daily felt the power of companies, which often controlled housing, utilities, and social institutions like schools. Every aspect of their own household work bore the marks of class and ethnic injustice. Only the "Anglo" houses in Kennecott's two company towns, Santa Rita and Hurley, had running water; Mexican American tenants had to haul water from wells. Hanover, the site of the Empire Zinc strike, was similarly segregated. As Anita Tórrez complained, "Empire thinks us second class citizens—no plumbing as in Anglo houses." Anita Tórrez, letter to editor, *Silver City Daily Press*, April 5, 1951.

35. Children did whatever chores they could handle; teenagers went either to school or to work depending on their family's situation and their parents' decisions.

36. Manuscript Census, Precincts 11 and 16, Grant County, N.M., Fifteenth Census of the United States, 1930, in National Archives Microfilm Collection T-626-1395. 1930 is the most recent date for which the manuscript census is available, and the statistical abstracts for 1940 and 1950 do not indicate the sex of heads of household for Grant County or its subdivisions.

37. Laurel Thatcher Ulrich, *Good Wives: Image and Reality in the Lives of Women in Northern New England, 1650–1750* (New York: Knopf, 1982).

38. Linda Gordon, *Heroes of Their Own Lives: The Politics and History of Family Violence* (New York: Penguin, 1988), v–vi.

39. Aurora Chávez interview.

40. Local 890 minutes, June 14, 1951.

41. Domestic abuse was rarely on the public radar screen, but it set the terms for many families' power relations. Dolores Jiménez, for example, dealt with Frank's violence by running out of the house. She did not want to leave him permanently, even though she knew he was also unfaithful to her, because he was a good provider.

42. Local 890 minutes, October 17, 1951.

43. *El Paso Herald-Post*, June 16, 1951; Virginia Chacón, quoted in 1951 *Mine-Mill Convention Proceedings*, 63.

44. Virginia Chacón, quoted in 1951 Mine–Mill Convention Proceedings, 63.

45. *SCDP*, June 16, 1951.

46. *New York Times*, June 17, 1951, 26; *SCDP*, June 16, 1951.

47. *New York Times*, June 17, 1951, 26; Virginia Chacón, 1951 *Mine-Mill Convention Proceedings*, 63.

48. *New York Times*, June 18, 1951.

49. *SCDP*, June 18, 1951. All forty-five women pleaded not guilty to the charge of unlawful assembly and were released pending trial. Children under the age of sixteen were not charged. One girl complained: "But I fought the sheriffs. I fought 'em good. I hit one real hard and I spit in another's eye."

50. *SCDP*, July 12 and 13, 1951.

51. Juárez was none other than Aurora Chávez's sister, who had been sent to Hanover by their father to help Aurora with the children.

52. *SCDP*, July 13, 1951.

53. *SCDP*, August 23, 1951.

54. Ibid.

55. Local 890 press and radio release, August 23, 1951, Mine-Mill Papers, box 873, envelope 1.

56. Ibid., and *SCDP*, August 23, 1951.

57. Local 890 press and radio releases, August 23 and 25, 1951; *SCDP*, August 23, 1951.

58. Local 890 minutes, June 28, 1951.

59. Local 890 press and radio release, July 27, 1951.

60. Local 890 press and radio release, August 10, 1951.

61. Bob Hollowwa, Clinton Jencks, and Cipriano Montoya to Maurice Travis et al. re: Empire Zinc strike, etc., August 19, 1951, Mine-Mill Papers, box 294, folder 11.

62. Ernesto Velásquez, quoted in 1951 *Mine-Mill Convention Proceedings*, 64.

63. Local 890 minutes, October 17, 1951.

64. Juan Chacón, Henrietta Williams, Angie Sánchez, Joe T. Morales, Clorinda Alderette, and Charles Coleman played seven of the eight leading roles. Rosaura Revueltas, an award-winning Mexican actress, played the lead female role, Esperanza.

65. Michael Wilson and Deborah Rosenfelt, *Salt of the Earth* (New York: The Feminist Press at the City University of New York, 1978), 81–82.

66. Ibid., 82.

67. Herbert Biberman, *Salt of the Earth* (Boston: Beacon Press, 1965), 39. Biberman directed the movie, which was in many ways a family affair: his sister-in-law, Sonja Dahl Biberman, served on the production committee; producer Paul Jarrico was Wilson's brother-in-law, and his wife Sylvia worked on the film production as well. The Jarricos had first discovered the Empire Zinc strike in the summer of 1951, when they met the Jenckses at a ranch in northern New Mexico.

68. *The Woman Question* was Wilson's first title for the screenplay, and hardly anyone besides Communists continued to use this nineteenth-century term. Based on her interviews with several of the people involved with *Salt*, Deborah Rosenfelt suggests that the Hollywood Communist Party clubs were more likely to discuss women's issues, including housework, than CP clubs elsewhere. Wilson and Rosenfelt, *Salt of the Earth*, 102.

69. See Deborah Rosenfelt's interviews with women picketers in *Salt of the Earth*, 142–143.

70. Mariana Ramírez, quoted in Deborah Rosenfelt, *Salt of the Earth*, 142.
71. Frank's reputation among men was damaged—not by his infidelity, or even his leaving a wife, but for taking the furniture and cutting her out of his insurance; the breadwinner ethic had hardly disappeared, but it took on new aspects. Dolores Jiménez interview.
72. *SCDP*, July 26, 1961.
73. *Los Angeles Times*, July 28, 1961; *SCDP*, August 25, 1961.

Godless Communists and Faithful Wives, Gender Relations and the Cold War: Mine Mill and the 1958 Strike against the International Nickel Company

Mercedes Steedman

We need a new recipe for Christmas cake, for the one the union baked. We can't eat it, we can't digest it. We need a union of fair-minded men ready to fight for the working men, we don't want a union that starves and degrades our men.

Dorothy Dolman, striker's wife[1]

Soon after a strike at the huge Sudbury mining operations of the International Nickel Company—also known as Inco—had begun on September 24, 1958, a wave of anticommunist hysteria swept the northern Ontario mining town of Sudbury. The press depicted miners' families held ransom by union bullies and the events as a battle between Godless communists and faithful Catholics: "Two thousand Inco miners' wives urge men to return to work"; "Inco wives defy goons, yell 'Go back to Russia' "; "Inco wives form anti-Red faction."[2] Reports by "faithful" workers' wives challenging the members of the union and their "Ladies' Auxiliary" dominated the media. They claimed that the union's "communist leaders" were being unreasonable in their unwillingness to accept the nickel giant's offer. "It's time we heard the truth from the union," declared Mrs. Regina Talbot. "We want our men to go back to work, and they should have some say in the matter." Ethel Lasalles, acting secretary for the Back to Work movement, a wives' oppositional group, told the local radio station: "We women have taken the initiative and we feel that it is up to the men to follow through on our resolutions. How much longer are you going to permit yourselves to be hidden behind the Red Curtain?"[3] The International Union of Mine, Mill and Smelter Workers (Mine Mill), led by left-wing unionists, was under siege in both the United States and Canada. The strike challenged capitalist control of an essential sector of the economy; and gender tensions within the union provided an opportunity for its opponents to reinvent the "traditional family" as a means of fighting subversive influences. The company, local civil and church leaders, the press, and the cold war transformed an all-male strike of nickel miners into a contest over family values.

If the "enemy within" was to be fought with all the vigor and moral right-eousness the community could muster, then who was better placed to carry on the fight than the wives and mothers of the community?[4] The dominant view of postwar working-class women portrayed them as politically conserva-tive, living in a narrow world of patriarchal and church control, unable to understand the political world of trade unionism that their husbands, broth-ers, and fathers inhabited. But recent scholarship has challenged this con-struction. Working-class women, especially ethnic working-class women, had long traditions of active participation in community and labor struggles.[5] They understood their domestic roles in larger terms and considered their normal responsibilities to engage in direct political action and support the union activities of their men. The 1958 labor crisis in Sudbury thus offers an opportunity for a close examination of working-class gender relations in a mining community—as well as of how the cold war political discourse shaped gender, union, and community politics.

THE ROOTS OF THE BATTLE

Soon after the discovery of mineral deposits in the Sudbury Basin in 1883, the Canadian Copper Company of Cleveland, Ohio, was formed to mine and smelt nickel ore; in 1902 it became part of International Nickel, a company controlled by J.P. Morgan of New Jersey. In 1928 the British-controlled Mond Nickel Company, which processed metals for the British market from its smelter in Coniston, merged with International Nickel. Two years later another producer, Falconbridge Nickel, started operations in the region. Although the industry experienced a decline in the 1920s and 1930s, by the 1940s the Sudbury basin ore deposits accounted for close to 90 percent of all nickel production in the noncommunist world, and production expanded during the cold war.[6] U.S. capital dominated production in the Sudbury basin, and the United States was the major market for the metals produced.

In 1910, Finnish and Ukrainian immigrant workers organized the first Western Federation of Miners (WFM) local, but for the next 40 years the mining companies kept unions out of the region by blacklisting, intimidat-ing, and firing those with union sympathies. In 1936, when the CIO began an organizing drive in many industrial sites, Mine Mill (successor to the WFM) moved in to northern Ontario. Led by a small group of communists and left-wing activists, the union again tried to unionize Inco and Falconbridge miners. These efforts met with limited success. In 1942, Mine Mill used its support in Sudbury's ethnic communities to launch a secret sign-up campaign. Taking advantage of new wartime federal government labor regulations, Local 598 certified at Inco in 1944, to become one of the largest locals in the international union.[7]

In 1947 the Taft-Hartley Act became law in the United States, requiring anticommunist pledges from unions, but the Canadian government relied on the Canadian Congress of Labour (CCL) to eliminate communists from the labor movement.[8] Still, the U.S. requirement and the refusal of Mine Mill to identify communists in its midst—instead the union went on to fight the act for many years—had sharp repercussions in Canadian mining communities. In 1948 a strong business lobby orchestrated by mine owners and joined by the Chamber of Commerce and the Catholic Church demanded that suspected Communist trade unionists from the United States be kept out of Canada and that any Communist organizers were to be removed from office.[9] In 1949 the social-democratic, reformist, CCL responded to intense anticommunism among its member trade unions and expelled Mine Mill, thus opening the door to raiding by the rival United Steelworkers of America (USWA).[10] In the strike situation of 1958, the combination of forces that rallied against Mine Mill would make it difficult for the union to get its message out to its own workers, their families, and the general public.

The anticommunist hysteria that swept the community during those few months in 1958 offered an opportunity for conservatives, both in the labor movement and in the community at large, to defeat the left-wing leadership of the local.[11] Within months of the culmination of the strike, activists from the CCL had their first real success. The local union executive went down in defeat and the USWA raids began in earnest.[12]

LIVING AND WORKING IN A COMPANY TOWN

Sudbury in the 1950s was a typical company town. Some 160,000 people spread out through the basin, clustered in communities around the ten or so mining heads of the region's two main employers, Inco and Falconbridge. Mining companies employed almost half of Sudbury's 80,000 people. Company housing marked the contours of each regional center. The company supervisors' homes offered workers a visual reminder of the relations between labor and capital and their distinct places in the community hierarchy.

Sudbury's dependence on nickel mining made it a place where the traditional male breadwinner predominated. With few jobs available for them, women found it difficult to support themselves and their children outside the confines of traditional marriage. In 1958 few women in the community had paid employment. Less than 22 percent of the labor force was female, and most of that employment was in sales, clerical, or domestic work. Although women were unlikely to be wage earners after marriage, their unpaid work in the family and in the larger community was essential to working-class family well-being.[13]

Immigrants, recruited to work in the mines and smelters, created a multi-ethnic working-class society.[14] In 1951, French Canadians made up 39 percent of the population, and Italian, Ukrainian, German, and other European immigrants comprised another 17 percent. The large numbers of newly arrived immigrants brought with them new political ideas of both the left and the right. The local Anglo-Celtic elite still dominated local politics, and while mining companies continued to assert their influence, the prewar hierarchical community relations that placed the Catholic Church and company officials at the center of social life were waning.

Traditionally the Francophone population worked on farms surrounding the mines, but as the pollution from the mines destroyed their farms, they sought alternative employment. Albert Ouellet, a Francophone miner, recounted his experience of finding work at Inco in 1936: "Like hundreds of other young French Canadians here in the valley, I got into Inco with a letter from my priest. I could never have had a job without it." According to Ouellet, "That was the beginning of the terrible alliance between the French priests and Inco . . . the priests got together and made a deal with Inco. They decided to sacrifice the farming communities in the valley for jobs in the mines. They sold us like sheep!"[15] By the 1950s, Mine Mill had put a stop to such practices. Former Mine Mill president Jim Tester described the effect of collective agreements in the mining sector: "Fear and favouritism were largely wiped out, overnight. Employees were no longer subject to the whim and caprice of supervision."[16]

Although cold war anticommunism was already providing a vehicle for the Anglo-Celtic business class to undermine the popularity of the town's most powerful union, Mine Mill's expansion of cultural and social activities offered working-class Sudbury its first union-centered community infrastructure. Beginning in March 1952, under union cultural director Weir Reid, the Sudbury Mine Mill local carried trade unionism beyond the close confines of the bargaining process.[17] Its members built union halls that served as community centers for dances, drama, and various other cultural events, which brought together people from various social, economic, and ethnic backgrounds. The union sponsored Labor Day picnics, films, and radical folk singers, such as The Travellers and Pete Seeger. It developed a summer camp on union-owned lakefront property, offering workers a chance to take their families out to swim and picnic on the shores of a local lake.[18] Ruth Reid, Women's Auxiliary activist and long-time volunteer at the Mine Mill summer camp, described the centrality of the union to Sudbury: "This was a Mine Mill town in the 1950s. All the community activities were run by Mine Mill. Everyone from the Mayor and his family to the local doctors' wives and children were at the Mine Mill hall for some activity or another."[19] In a company town where the Catholic Church and company worked closely together to ensure a stable community respectful of corporate power and family values, Mine Mill offered an alternative vision of family and community. The union's presence in the town challenged Inco's right to define the community in the company's terms.

Although Mine Mill gained community support, municipal politics and the media remained firmly in the hands of local business. In 1952, for instance, when Mine Mill ran a weekly radio program and criticized the local newspaper and the Chamber of Commerce for their role in local politics, the owner of the radio station banned the program, claiming it was "communist propaganda." The union then signed a contract with another station, but after one show that station dropped it, stating that the program was "too hot an issue."[20] The union's ability to express its point of view within the community was thus restricted. In response to this curtailing of freedom of speech, Mine Mill president Mike Solski declared, "The powers that be, who have now seized control of our community, have no intention of permitting any effective criticism." These same forces would line up again during the strike of 1958.

Despite the significant bargaining achievements of Mine Mill, which had by the 1950s transformed hard rock mining from one of the most exploited into one of the best paid blue collar occupations in the region, the cold war anticommunist campaign threatened its success in Sudbury as in the rest of North America. Successful purges of leftists in labor unions, media, and government offices in the United States reverberated through the Canadian political scene.[21]

Mining communities received incessant anticommunist propaganda. Press coverage of Mine Mill's 11th annual national convention in Sudbury in 1956 included red-baiting headlines such as "Breath of Communism cools city welcome," and "Delegates have left, Red stigma remains." When a small group from the Canadian League for Liberation of the Ukraine picketed the union meetings, the *Sudbury Star* made it front-page news. The newspaper's photo of picketers focused on a graphic of a hammer and sickle on their sign, which read, "welcome to Mine Mill convention comrades!"[22]

BUILDING THE WOMEN'S AUXILIARY

Women who wanted to support the union in some active way outside the home faced both red-baiting and male resistance. As Lukin Robinson pointed out, "Few women in Sudbury had heard of feminism, you could cut male chauvinism with a knife. The union men never thought they might need organizational help from the women and were indifferent, at best, to the Ladies Auxiliary."[23]

Many of the women who persisted in building a women's auxiliary recognized the importance of unions and had been involved in the early organizing of the Mine Mill local. Millie McQuaid of Creighton came from a strong union family and joined the Auxiliary to support her husband: "I knew why my husband was there at the union hall. If you don't understand what your husband was doing, why he's doing it (he went all out once he started learning about it) then you wouldn't support him. He didn't have a clue about unions when he married me. I did, because I grew up with it. I cut my teeth on a union button."[24] Another active Auxiliary member, Val Billoki, recalled how wives joined husbands in the late 1930s and early 1940s to help organize members into the local:

> We used to go out at ten or eleven o'clock at night and put the leaflets in the
> mail boxes. We couldn't do that in the daytime. One time Alice and Larry
> Bennett were picked up by the police and brought down to the police station
> and their pamphlets and everything were taken away from them and they were
> warned, but they found us and got more pamphlets and we just continued
> the rounds. We put them in everybody's house, we just went all up and down
> the streets and put the leaflets in the mail boxes.[25]

The base for the Mine Mill Women's Auxiliary, established in the organizing drives of the 1930s, relied on sympathetic and trusted members of
left-wing ethnic organizations and the Women's Labor League of the
Communist Party of Canada. Many women, like Ann Macks and Patrica
Chytuk, came from the Finnish Organization of Canada (FOC) and the
Ukrainian Labor Farmer Association (ULFTA). Ukrainian and Finnish
Auxiliary members, especially those from nearby Coniston and Copper Cliff,
where the Ukrainian and Finnish societies had active memberships, canvassed
homes and encouraged wives to support the union and join the Auxiliary.[26]

This group of women was persistent in part because of their long experience of red-baiting. Women who became active in the Auxiliary were aware of
the tensions in the union over its suspected communist domination; and they
were wary of red-baiting as a defensive tactic used by the union's enemies to
weaken and divide the union. Still, as Millie McQuaid suggested, the Auxiliary
members faced ostracism because of their ties to the red-tainted union and
this hurt their organizing efforts:

> I mean, when I was working with the church auxiliary you admitted that very
> freely, but you didn't as far as being in the union auxiliary. Because . . . society
> didn't accept it to the extent that probably would now. . . . I think the ones of
> us who were really prominent, if you want to use that word, were people who
> had a base in union activity, that knew something about it. Because it really was-
> n't a popular thing.[27]

By the late 1940s, the Canadian leadership of the auxiliaries under Kay
Carlin, the Mine Mill auxiliaries' first women's organizer in northeastern
Ontario, saw how red-baiting had decimated their American counterparts.
The investigation and eventual banning of international Auxiliary president
Mary Orlich of Butte for red-baiting in 1947 left a permanent mark on
women's organizing in the union. In the shadow of this earlier red-baiting,
the U.S. auxiliaries moved cautiously, at the same time as the Canadian aux-
iliaries pushed for a stronger position within the union.[28]

In 1953, Canadian auxiliaries began to challenge Mine Mill for greater
participation in the union at its 49th Convention. Dorothy McDonald,
a Timmins, Ontario, housewife, then chair of the international Mine Mill
auxiliaries, proposed that union papers introduce women's columns "written
by and for women, explaining to them the current issues of special interest to
union men's wives and informing them of the activities of the Auxiliaries."

She also urged that the men "continue to give cooperation and financial assistance to the Ladies Auxiliaries and more attention to the problems of organizing and leading this body of union women."[29] The "Women's Plank" demanded social space and legitimacy within Mine Mill. In 1956, when Mine Mill established autonomy for its Canadian section, its first annual convention offered Auxiliary women the opportunity to mobilize for greater representation and amended the constitutional bylaws to reflect this.

The Mine Mill constitution outlined the main purpose of the Ladies' Auxiliaries as "the education and training of women in the labor movement and to assist their Local Unions in time of need and labor disputes, to support the union in its legislative efforts and to provide educational and cultural activities for our members and their children."[30] Although the auxiliaries construed their role as supporting the union's members, Mine Mill's commitment to social unionism ensured that women's activities, although separate from those of the male union members, were regarded as legitimate (at least by the leadership). Yet the space the women were able to claim within the Canadian Mine Mill still reaffirmed the male breadwinner's role and limited women's activism to the cultural prescriptions of domesticity. Mine Mill women walked a fine line between unfeminine behavior and supportive militancy with their men, leaving them in a restrictive social position. Their public activities were rarely accepted as legitimate, respectable womanly activities in the broader community, and the men did not accept their attempt to extend their political franchise within the larger Mine Mill movement.

Still, Mine Mill's form of social unionism did provide women with a distinctive social space in the trade union movement, and it gave credence and legitimacy to women's forms of organizing and participation in the development of a working-class culture in the Sudbury basin. But the masculinist assumptions that underpinned union culture remained evident. Many Mine Mill men only paid lip service to the leadership's attempt to draw women into the union. Millie McQuaid, president of the Local 117 Women's Auxiliary, recalled its role, on the whole, as being very limited: "We had no vote in the 598 meetings, or anything like that. But we could speak in the part of the meeting dealing with welfare. But I don't think it meant a heck of a lot. They listen but they don't hear. They don't hear what they don't want to hear."[31]

THE 1958 INCO STRIKE

In 1958 some 14,500 members of Mine Mill Local 598 engaged in one of the largest industrial disputes of the decade.[32] Prior to that point, union relations with Inco had been relatively harmonious. When Mine Mill Local 598 (along with Port Colborne Local 637 in Southern Ontario) prepared to negotiate a new contract, the nonferrous metals market had slumped (with nickel stockpiled as a result); and the federal Progressive Conservative government led by Prime Minister John Diefenbaker had announced a "hold-the-line" policy for labor that translated into a wage freeze.[33] Furthermore, the introduction of a new tariff policy in the United States—a tariff favorable to U.S. labor but not Canadian—had driven a wedge between Mine Mill leaders in the two countries.[34] Also, after years of major strike actions, legal battles and USWA raids, the international leadership of Mine Mill was not in a financial position to adequately support a large and lengthy strike.[35]

Soon after the certification of Mine Mill, a small faction in the Sudbury union had begun to push for merger with the USWA. The opposition's strong run against the leadership during the 1952 local election clearly threatened Mine Mill partisans.[36] Throughout the 1950s the dissidents continued to work to undermine the local. Coupled with this internal battle, many of the rank and file felt loyal to Inco and were reluctant to demand higher wages.[37] "It was a terrible situation," Mine Mill activist Tom Taylor maintained. "The union itself was divided at a convention in Winnipeg [over whether the local should strike]. The '58 strike was a strange phenomenon—anybody who was party to what was going on will tell you that." Only 13 years old, the union had just won over many members.

All of these factors—internal conflicts, a defensive union movement crippled by anticommunism, lengthy legal battles, raids by USWA, and an uncertain economic climate—challenged strike supporters. With markets depressed and nickel stockpiled, a strike was more in the interests of the company than the workers.[38] When contract negotiations got underway in March 1958, Inco announced production cutbacks and laid off 1,000 employees in Sudbury. In April the company announced decreased profits for the first quarter of the year and made further layoffs.[39] On September 19th, one of the last days of bargaining, several wildcat strikes, led by pro-USWA workers, broke out at the mines in nearby Garson and Levack. Solski went on the radio saying, "There are deliberate attempts to cause dissension among our members and some men have taken action on their own." He appealed to these men to go back to work, but Inco wasn't going to budge from its position of no wage increases.[40] In a last-ditch effort, the union leadership persuaded the provincial Premier Leslie Frost to arrange a meeting with the company on September 23, but the meeting was of no use; the company was ready to strike.

Workers were ready to strike, too, if only to prove their manhood to company and community. Lukin Robinson, research director for the national Mine Mill office, recalled the situation:

> The guys wanted to take on the company. The company had been having things easy, and they were beginning to ride the men individually. So we wanted to take them on. It was sort of a way of proving our manhood, to show the militancy of the union. . . . But we weren't aware of the change in Inco's strategy . . . and the impact this recession might have on their bargaining strategy.[41]

Robinson's invocation of labor militancy as an expression of manliness drew on the long-standing assumptions that have defined unions as male terrain and diminished women's participation in labor struggles. The male-dominated labor force in Sudbury utilized this depiction of militancy, but the equation of union strength with manhood also denied the importance of women's support for the strike or the family dynamics that, as a number of community studies have demonstrated, are so often crucial in determining who wins a strike.[42]

Family economics were crucial factors in determining who could and would support the strike. In the company towns, opportunities for alternative employment were scarce, and because the company experienced a post-war labor shortage, there had been a recent influx of immigrant men into Inco operations. There were multiple factors that weighed heavily against the strike's success. Tom Taylor noted,

> It was the wrongest year in the world to take a strike because the steel plants were on strike, the railroads were on strike, the forest workers were on strike. . . . I think we were something like 15,000 to 16,000 workers and that is a terrible amount of guys to throw out onto the workforce of an area that has no work. No one could go out and get a job to support their families, they were completely reliant on the money the local gave them for strike support.
>
> Stressing the importance of families in enduring a strike, Taylor added, "A whole bunch of people had no families to fall back on, because to a lesser degree our people were imported from Newfoundland and Nova Scotia. So they had no immediate family unless they went home to it, but they didn't have the money to buy the train fare."[43]

Financing a strike of nearly 16,000 workers was a gargantuan task. The Mine Mill international provided $100,000 and the Canadian union provided $44,256.38 as the basic strike pay, but the strike cost the union $1,038,189.00.[44] Wives' support for the strike depended, in part, on their ability to manage the family economy on the limited strike pay provided by the union. It was just this issue, strike pay, which caused the greatest dissension among the strikers.[45] The union's decision to withhold strike pay until four weeks into the strike and the procedures it established requiring workers, rather than wives and family members, to register in the union hall, generated widespread complaints.

Letters from disgruntled union members and their wives started to appear soon after the strike started. One woman wrote, "This is a hell of a spot you have got us into. No money coming in till 28 days after the strike started. They are going to shut off our electricity and the oil company will not give us credit. What are we going to do?"[46] By focusing on the men, the union appeared to give short shrift to the needs of families and risked losing the support of the strikers' wives, who managed the family economy. The union set up over 13 subcommittees to deal with the hardships caused by the strike, but with limited funds and no experience dministering to the needs of such a large number of miners and their families, resentments continued to grow among the rank and file.[47]

THE WOMEN'S ROLE IN THE STRIKE

The local's Women's Auxiliary 117 was unable to address this growing resentment. While it had been actively recruiting members since the late

Figure 12.1 Mine Mill Auxiliary Women singing labor songs during the strike of 1958. Courtesy of Sudbury Public Library, Mike Solski Collection, Sudbury, Ontario.

1930s, by 1958, the auxiliary only had a few hundred members in sub-branches in Sudbury and in the nearby towns of Coniston, Levack, Chelmsford and Creighton-Lively, compared to some 15,000 to 16,000 unionized men (figure 12.1).[48]

During the early days of the strike, the Auxiliary provided sandwiches and coffee for the picket lines and helped families in need (figure 12.2). Auxiliary members interacted widely with the community of strikers' wives, and they were successful in generating practical forms of community support. They visited 636 homes, distributed 514 boxes of groceries, drove to rural homes using donated gasoline, and provided nutritional and household management advice.[49] The Auxiliary took a leading role in organizing outside aid for striking workers and their families by sending strikers' wives to solicit cash, food, and clothing donations at meetings of local union auxiliaries throughout Ontario. At the national level Mine Mill auxiliaries appealed to the cross-country network of union wives who they had supported during previous strikes, who, in turn, organized local women's committees in aid of the Local 598 women.[50] Millie McQuaid recalled:

> We knew that if we were going to go on strike, we were going to have to ask for outside help from other locals. And with the different truckloads of things coming into the union we had to have committees to handle it to get it ready. We had to make lists of the people who really needed help and find ways for them

Figure 12.2 Women in Local 117, Mine Mill Auxiliary, Sudbury, serving food.
Courtesy of Sudbury Public Library, Mike Solski Collection, Sudbury, Ontario.

to either come and get it or take it to them. All of this. I am not an organizer,
I was just doing it. That's the things we had to do. Of course all the Mine Mill
people were really concerned and all of the other unions, the Autoworkers, the
Electrical workers, all of them, they really helped. They had to, I guess.[51]

While women worked on community support, the male union leadership
concentrated on pushing Inco back to the negotiating table. When talks
broke down, the leaders appealed to the provincial government for media-
tion. Then, in November, they organized a car cavalcade to Toronto provincial offices to protest the further breakdown of the talks with the Department
of Labor and Inco. Focused on these efforts, the union did little to mobilize
the community and the rank and file.

By December 1958 the strikers and their families were beginning to experience the material hardships imposed by the strike. On December 2, after
talks had again broken down, Inco went directly to the membership with its
"final offer": a three-year contract that would increase the wage scale by
1 percent as of August 15, 1959, and by an additional 1.5 percent on August 15,
1960. The union's negotiating committee refused to accept this offer.[52] With
strike funds now very low, an early and severe winter, the beginning of the
Christmas season, and the Inco letter expressing firm resolve, the public relations aspect of the strike, always important in a company town such as
Sudbury, became more important to both the company and the union.[53]

Both sides tried to gain the support of the community through the
press. The company placed full-page advertisements in the Toronto, Port
Colborne, and Sudbury papers.[54] The union, by contrast, had only issued
weekly bulletins to the picket lines and paid for local radio and television spots

out of union reserve funds. The local and national press reaffirmed the cold war political discourse that in effect cut off Mine Mill's ability to engage in dialogue with the community and fueled anticommunist sentiments. The *Sudbury Star* ran anticommunist editorials and blamed irresponsible union leaders for the strike, who, it claimed, were willing to sacrifice the well-being of families in their battle with the company.[55] Newspaper stories of hardship, particularly about women and children, pointed an accusing finger at the union. The medical director of the Sudbury District Health Unit said that there would be dire cases of need if the strike continued.[56] Father J.J. Delaney, who operated Sudbury's Catholic Charities, stated, "This has become a knock down drag-out battle and the average man with his despairing wife and his hungry children is the ammunition."[57] On December 6, 1958, the *Globe and Mail*, in an article entitled "The Prisoners of Sudbury," declared: "The Inco strikers, in short, are prisoners of their own leadership. This is nothing new in Ontario, but has been developing since the war, with the closed shop, the union shop, the compulsory check-off and all the rest contributing to it. So now we find union members appealing for liberation—from whom? From their own officials."[58]

The political authority invested in the forces opposed to Mine Mill extended well beyond the media. The Canadian Congress of Labor refused direct aid to the union.[59] The Catholic Charities, established by Algoma Diocese Bishop Alexander Carter, openly opposed Mine Mill.[60] Prior to the strike in 1958, CCL president Claude Jodoin and the Steelworkers had met with local clergy selected by Bishop Carter to plan the Steelworker raids on Local 598.[61]

The Catholic Church regularly ran anticommunist articles in its publications attacking Mine Mill, and local priests frequently warned parishioners of the dangers of communism in the mining union. In this community where about 60 percent of the inhabitants were Catholic, local priests held study groups specifically directed at miners and their wives.[62] During the strike, Catholic anticommunist forces mobilized lay women through the Catholic Women's League (CWL), which played a leading role in the Back to Work movement. Their motto included the phrase "For God and Canada and its members who should be in one fold, due to all the communism that is in the world today." Since early December, the CWL had vigorously opposed the strike and extended the organization's charitable mandate to include the fight against communists. At the end of the strike, CWL minutes congratulated their members for their leadership in the Back to Work movement.[63] The women in the movement were largely representative of French, English, and Irish Catholic Inco families who were part of the prewar class hierarchy that was uneasy with the new influx of European immigrant workers and their families.

The Back to Work women fastened on the apparent inflexibility of the Mine Mill leadership and claimed that the Auxiliary women were placing their families in jeopardy by continuing to support the union.[64] While they wanted to get their men back to work, the Back to Work women also had another agenda—to purge the union "communist" leadership. While their initial efforts—a letter campaign among the miners and local reeves—failed, the wives of some of the miners opposed to Solski's leadership and the local's handling of the strike persevered in their campaign.[65] It was indeed the reach of cold war anticommunism that allowed this small group of women, who had never previously participated in union affairs, to become effective. Influenced by the Catholic Church through weekly sermons, social study clubs, and labor schools run by local priests, female parishioners mounted a campaign to ensure that all good Catholics were aware of the threat that communism posed within the community and nation.[66]

The Back to Work movement highlighted the union's failure to adequately address the direct interests of a crucial part of their union membership—the wives and families—by privileging men's concerns over wages at the bargaining table. On December 7 and 8, a top-level conference of all Mine Mill leaders met in Toronto and discussed the wives' opposition movement, which had received media coverage.[67] On December 8, the union issued a strike bulletin denouncing the Back to Work movement and passed a resolution to "strenuously" oppose it. They announced plans to organize a women's parade and generally get women involved in, and backing, the strike.[68]

For the women of the Local 117 Mine Mill Auxiliary, standing by their men carried the contamination of communism. The gendering of cold war politics in the highly charged atmosphere of the Inco strike immediately marginalized the Mine Mill women, who were perceived as dupes of a communist-led union.[69] Men and women in Mine Mill were targets of community rumors and hearsay, which had a damaging effect on all of the strike participants. "The strike of 1958 was a bitter battle," explained Pearl Moir, an Auxiliary member in Levack. "It separated us from some of our friends. They didn't want to have anything to do with us because we were all Communists, that was all there was to it, you know."[70]

Women's loyalty to the union made them direct targets for anticommunist accusations and threats of violence, recalled one Auxiliary activist: "I was sick all the time. I didn't get any sleep, crackpots phoning into the night, they were threatening us. It was awful. . . . Everything was taken away from you, your security, what you felt, you know, you just didn't know if someone was going to hurt you or your children, what was going to happen to you. It was very bad."[71] Although tensions continued to rise and further involvement posed risks, Mine Mill women felt they had to act.

STRIKE SUPPORTERS VERSUS THE BACK-TO-WORK MOVEMENT

In the weeks before Christmas, the struggle between the company and the union men shifted from the bargaining table to the community, where the Auxiliary women tussled with the Back to Work movement women. On December 10, the Auxiliary called a meeting of strikers' wives. Some 900 women listened as Millie McQuaid proposed that a mass delegation of as many as 2,000 wives would march on City Hall on Friday, December 12, "to demand full support for efforts of the union to bring about a speedy settlement of the strike." A second resolution ordered the women's strike committee to address a letter to the Inco president asking for new bargaining with the union.[72] The majority of women supported the motion, but about twelve left the meeting in protest. It was this small group that received the attention of the media. The *Sudbury Star* quickly capitalized on the discord:

> There were sure signs of dissension among the strikers' wives last night as the women endorsed the action of a small group of women who had met Tuesday night (December 9) by secret invitation. Mrs. Leon Breen, wife of a striker who works underground at Frood Mine, told the Star "the meeting tonight was called solely for the purpose of backing the union executive's decision not to accept the Company's November 26 offer. We understand from the Company's letter that this is a fair offer. The officers at this meeting were hand-picked by the union leaders. We know that, we also know that this meeting was rigged."[73]

With the dissent growing daily, the Women's Auxiliary's planned march to City Hall became more problematic. The women had turned opposition to the strike over to anticommunist Mayor Joe Fabbro's hands. When the Mine Mill bargaining team in Toronto heard what the Auxiliary had done, they were furious, believing the decision to meet the mayor was ill advised. As Local president Solski recalled, "Mine Mill staff representative, Ray Stevenson, had organized a group of women at the Mine Mill Hall. That was fine, but they got the bright idea that they were going to march on City Hall. When we found out, we were ready to hang him from the first damn tree. You never place yourself in a position where you let a guy like Fabbro turn the table on you!"[74] Mine Mill's outrage at the women's efforts to support the union reflected men's ambivalence at women's involvement and a belief that women had to be directed in appropriate union tactics.

Mayor Fabbro recognized an opportunity to challenge the Mine Mill leadership and arranged for the use of the community arena for the meeting with the women. "The women [and their children] will not then be forced to stand in sub-zero weather," he declared, "and they will be in a position so all can hear." Mine Mill local officers Solski and McQuaid went on radio to try to cancel the event. "We appreciate the support by our women in Sudbury," they said, but the event would be "improper at this time."[75] Leola Breen and her faction were able to use the union strike committee's attempts to stop the wives' march as further evidence of the undemocratic nature of Mine Mill. Breen went on radio to appeal to women: "Is this a scare movement or something? After all, the meeting was called for strikers' wives and I think the strikers' wives should still be there." Rita Baker added, "Does the phone call from one man change all of our minds? We are still free thinkers. Come on women, you are still strikers' wives."[76] The Back to Work women portrayed the Mine Mill women as being blinded by the dogma of the union men, rendered incapable of carrying out their family responsibilities.

At two o'clock on December 13, some 2,000 women and children gathered in the community arena to hear Breen and her supporters. The mayor and local district reeves were on the platform to greet them. Under the mayor's direction, Breen and Baker passed four motions supporting a return to work with no raise in the first contract year. The Back to Work women's motion affirmed their domestic situation: "As wives and mothers we are shocked by the way [the strike] is destroying our homes. But most of all we are upset by the fact that our children are suffering and many are in need of food and clothing."[77] Claims to defend the family supported their efforts to discredit the union—by blaming Mine Mill, not the company, for the hardship. Not surprisingly, then, the majority of women at the arena supported the motions. But the manner of voting was also controversial. All women in agreement with the motions were asked to remain in their seats, while those dissenting had to stand and make their way to the floor of the arena, so that they were thus visually placed outside of the dominant political framework of the meeting. Any woman wanting to voice her opinion had to identify herself by her name, address and her husband's position at Inco. When the 100 Auxiliary members attending the meeting tried to voice their opposition the mayor announced that the meeting was over.[78] Millie McQuaid recalled the impossibility of changing the situation:

> We knew [Breen and the Back to Work Movement women] were going to be there. There was no sense in us fighting, you know you don't fight them, you fight the company. Everybody other than our own people seemed to be saying, "Well, the company's right, accept what the company's offering." . . . We felt we were right because we wanted our men to have decent wages, we wanted them to have the security they needed, the safety, especially the safety. Because when you are underground, good God, I don't think men were made to be ground hogs, really.[79]

Every step of the opposition now played to a national audience as the press descended on the community. The next day a *Toronto Telegram* headline screamed out "Black Day for Red-led Union as Wives in an Uproar."[80] The *Globe and Mail* capitalized on the alleged threat of violence from Mine Mill supporters, suggesting, "If violence does not flare up in Sudbury it will be because rank and file opposition has been crushed by threats against miners' wives."[81] Leola Breen's husband claimed he feared for his life and the safety of his family. "We have had 25 to 30 threatening phone calls, but they don't worry me. I don't need any [police protection], I have a gun."[82]

After the arena meeting, the union and the auxiliary tried to revive support by holding strike rallies at the local union halls.[83] But the control of public discourse, now more visibly out of the hands of the union, muffled these efforts. The strike was settled on December 19, 1958, with the union accepting what was generally considered to be a weak offer.[84]

CONCLUSION

The pervasive power of cold war anticommunist discourse and the union men's inability to see their wives as legitimate participants in the strike became decisive factors that defeated the strike. While Mine Mill tried to build a workers' culture that extended the franchise of trade unionism, including women and pensioners in its constitution and extending union activities beyond the bargaining table, it did not sustain that broad inclusion of women and the rank and file during the strike crisis. A political and social climate that condoned the place of women as primarily in the home and saw family life as peripheral to the labor movement weakened union efforts. While Mine Mill proclaimed "a union without the women is only half organized," in reality its acceptance of the traditional position of working-class wives worked to undermine the effectiveness of the union defense against cold war oppositional forces. Despite the larger vision of community, union men still privileged hierarchical and patriarchal political structures of the union. The Back to Work movement legitimized its members' political power through their appeal as the moral protectors of the family. This political authority awarded women's domesticity, while the fears of the potential destructive forces of communism undermined Mine Mill. The Auxiliary employed the same traditional familial rhetoric, but in cold war Sudbury, the Back to Work movement could draw support from the press, the CCL and the Catholic Church and claim that the Auxiliary members were nothing more than mouthpieces for the union leadership, which did not represent most of the strikers' wives.[85] As Lukin Robinson remarked, the strike was "a struggle for the uncommitted middle."[86] In cold war Canada, it was not by any means a fair fight.

After the strike, the USWA, with the assistance of conservative politicians and the Catholic Church, began raiding Mine Mill in earnest and pushed aside the Back to Work wives. Ruth Reid recalled the rapid demise of the union: "The community of Sudbury was almost destroyed. Mrs. Breen's women were no longer needed. The anticommunist crusaders in the Catholic Church moved directly into the center of the dispute immediately after the strike." Professor Boudreau, of the Jesuit-run University of Sudbury, mobilized a group of workers to lead the anti-Solski slate for local elections in 1959.[87] The role of women in the 1958 strike proved critical in setting the stage for the next seven-year period of resistance to and championing of the anticommunist USWA. By 1965 the forces pitted against Mine Mill's left-wing leadership had won. The workers at Inco in Port Colborne joined USWA, and eventually the 1,500 members of Local 598, the last remaining local of the once strong union, merged with the Canadian Auto Workers Union, ending a turbulent period of Canadian labor history.

NOTES

1. *Sudbury Star*, December 13, 1958.
2. *Globe and Mail* (Toronto), December 13, 1958; *The Telegram* (Toronto), December 13, 1958; *Hamilton Spectator*, December 13, 1958.

3. CKSO Radio, "News Broadcast," December 12, 1958, David Lehto Collection, National Archives of Canada, Ottawa.

4. Elaine Tyler May, *Homeward Bound: American Families in the Cold War Era* (New York: Basic Books, 1988), 16; Franca Iacovetta, "Making New Canadians, Social Workers, Women and the Reshaping of Immigrant Families," in *Gender Conflicts: New Essays in Women's History*, ed., Franca Iacovetta and M. Valverde (Toronto: University of Toronto Press, 1992), 261–303; Veronica Strong-Boag, "Their Side of the Story, Women's Voices in Ontario Suburbs, 1945–1960," in *A Diversity of Women, Ontario, 1945–1980*, ed., Joy Parr (Toronto: University of Toronto Press, 1995), 46–74.

5. See, e.g., Ruth Frager, *Sweatshop Strife* (Toronto: University of Toronto Press, 1992); F. Iacovetta, *Such Hardworking People: Italian Immigrants in Postwar Toronto* (Kingston: McGill University Press, 1992); Carmel Patrias, "Relief Strike: Immigrant Workers and the Great Depression, in Crowland, Ontario, 1930–1935," in *A Nation of Immigrants: Women, Workers, and Communities in Canadian History*, ed., Franca Iacovetta, Paula Draper and Robert Ventresca (Toronto: University of Toronto Press, 1998), 322–358; Varpu Lindstrom, *Defiant Sisters: A Social History of Finnish Immigrant Women in Canada* (Toronto: Multicultural Historical Society, 1992); Frances Swyripa, "The Ideas of Ukrainian Women's Organization of Canada, 1930–1945," in *Beyond the Vote: Canadian Women in Politics*, ed., Linda Kealey and Joan Sangster (Toronto: University of Toronto Press, 1989), 239–257.

6. John Deverell and the Latin American Working Group, *Falconbridge: Portrait of a Canadian Mining Multinational* (Toronto: James Lorimer Press, 1975), 14. See also Wallace Clement, *Hardrock Mining: Industrial Relations and Technological Changes at Inco* (Toronto: McClelland and Stewart, 1981).

7. Local 598 was certified as the bargaining agent at Inco on February 4, 1944 and at Falconbridge on March 7, 1944. Jim Tester, "The Shaping of Sudbury, A Labour View," paper, Sudbury Historical Society, April 18, 1979. Canadian autonomy for Mine Mill was established in 1955. Clement, *Hardrock Mining*, 103.

8. For an extensive discussion of the impact of cold war activities in Canada, see Reg Whitaker and Gary Marcuse, *Cold War Canada: The Making of a National Insecurity State, 1945–1957* (Toronto: University of Toronto Press, 1994).

9. Whitaker and Marcuse, *Cold War Canada*, 193, 277 (Toronto: University of Toronto Press, 1994).

10. Mercedes Steedman, Peter Suschnigg and Dieter Buse, eds., *Hard Lessons: The Mine Mill Union in the Canadian Labour Movement* (Toronto: Dundurn Press, 1995), 6–9. See also John Lang, "A Lion in a Den of Daniels: A History of the International Union of Mine, Mill, and Smelter Workers in Sudbury, Ontario, 1942–1962" (MA thesis, University of Guelph, 1970); Mike Solski and John Smaller, *Mine Mill: The History of the International Union of Mine, Mill and Smelter Workers in Canada since 1895* (Ottawa: Steelrail Publishing, 1984); Al King, *Red Bait! Struggles of a Mine Mill Local* (Vancouver: Kingbird Publishing, 1998). The American CIO expelled Mine Mill in 1950.

11. For a discussion of the impact of the cold war on Canadian labor, see Irving M. Abella, *Nationalism, Communism, and Canadian Labour: The CIO, the Communist Party and the Canadian Congress of Labour* (Toronto: University of Toronto Press, 1973), chapter 6; Franca Iacovetta, "Making Model Citizens:

Gender, Corrupted Democracy, and Immigrant and Refugee Reception Work in Cold War Canada," Julie Guard, "Women Worth Watching, Radical Housewives in Cold War Canada," and Mercedes Steedman, "The Red Petticoat Brigade, Mine Mill Women's Auxiliaries and the Threat from within, 1940s–1970s," all in *Whose National Security? Canadian State Surveillance and the Creation of Enemies*, ed., Gary Kinsman, Dieter Buse, and Mercedes Steedman (Toronto: Between the Lines, 2000), 55–90.

12. For a discussion of attacks on Mine Mill in the United States, see Vernon Jensen, *Nonferrous Metals Industrial Unionism, 1932–1954* (Ithaca, NY: Cornell University Press, 1954); and Laurie Mercier, "Instead of Fighting the Common Enemy: Mine Mill versus the Steelworkers in Montana, 1950–1967," *Labor History*, 40, no. 4 (1999): 459–480.

13. J.R. Winter, *The Sudbury Area: An Economic Survey* (Sudbury: Sudbury and District Industrial Commission and University of Sudbury, 1967).

14. Oiva Saarinen, "Sudbury: A Historical Case Study of Multiple Urban Economic Transformation," *Ontario History* (March 1990): 59.

15. As quoted in Sheila McLeod Arnopoulos, *Voices from French Ontario* (Montreal: McGill-Queen's University Press, 1982), 108–109.

16. Jim Tester, "The Shaping of Sudbury: A Labour View," paper, Sudbury and District Historical Society, April 18, 1979, 28.

17. For example, the union tried to recognize the Sudbury Basin's large Francophone population by publishing the union newspaper and information leaflets in both French and English and holding union meetings in predominately French communities, such as Chelmsford, in French. These efforts paid off, for during the Steelworker raids in the late 1950s and early 1960s, Francophone workers remained loyal to Mine Mill. See Arnopoulos, *Voices from French Ontario*, 108–109. Mike Solski, President, Mine Mill, Local 598, interview with Mick Lowe, December 1995.

18. Deiter Buse, "Weir Reid and Mine Mill: An Alternative Union's Cultural Endeavours," in Steedman, Suschnigg, and Buse, *Hard Lessons*, 285.

19. Interview with Ruth Reid, President, Mine Mill Women's Auxiliary, May 1993 (all interviews conducted by author unless otherwise noted).

20. Lang, "Lion in a Den of Daniels," 160–162.

21. Solski and Smaller, *Mine Mill*, 125–132; Frank Southern, *The Sudbury Incident* (Toronto: York Publishing Co., 1978). See also M.J. Heale, *American Communism: Combating the Enemy Within, 1830–1970* (Baltimore: Johns Hopkins University Press, 1990); and, Paula Maurutto, "Private Policing and the Surveillance of Catholics: Anti-Communism in the Roman Catholic Archdiocese of Toronto, 1920–60," in Kinsman, Buse, and Steedman, *Whose National Security?* 37–54.

22. *Sudbury Star*, February 27, 1956, March 3, 1956.

23. Interview with Lukin Robinson, Research Director, Mine Mill and Smelter Workers Union, Toronto, 1993.

24. Interview with Millie McQuaid, President, Mine Mill Women's Auxiliary, March, 1992.

25. Interview with Val Biloki, member, Mine Mill Women's Auxiliary, December 6, 1992.

26. Denise Thibeault, " 'A Union without Women is Only Half Organized': A History of the Sudbury Mine, Mill and Smelter Workers' Union, Local

598 Ladies Auxiliary," unpublished paper, York University, Toronto, April 1987, 64.

27. McQuaid interview.

28. For a discussion of anticommunism in the U.S. women's auxiliaries, see Mercier, "Instead of Fighting the Common Enemy," 460; Colleen O'Neil, "Womenfolk and Union Men: The Gendering of Class in IUMMSW, 1947–1957." Paper presented at Berkshire Women's History Conference, 1993.

29. 49th Convention of the International Mine Mill and Smelter Workers Union, 1952.

30. Bylaws of the Ladies Auxiliaries of the International Union of Mine Mill and Smelter Workers in Canada, adopted February 27, 1956; radio talk by Agnes Gauthier, Mine Mill Ladies Auxiliary, April 23, 1950.

31. McQuaid interview.

32. Stuart Jamieson, *Task Force on Labor Relations, Study no. 2* (Ottawa: Queens Printers, 1968), 372.

33. In March 1958 the company reported that unsold stocks would reach one-third of the company's annual productive capacity. See Paul Comtois, Natural Resources Minister-Canada from Marc Boyer, Deputy Minister, April 1, 1958, National Archives of Canada, RG27, vol. 3473, file 1-101-1-4. Lang, "Lion in a Den of Daniels, 199–202; Solski and Smaller, *Mine Mill*, 132–134.

34. Ibid., 199–202.

35. Clements, *Hardrock Mining*, 306–310; Lang, "Lion in a Den of Daniels," 199–202; Solski and Smaller, *Mine Mill*, 132–134; interviews with Lukin Robinson, Ray Stevenson, May 1993 suggest this.

36. Lang, "Lion in a Den of Daniels," 155.

37. "Crank letters," 1958 strike file, MU8247, Box 7, series 2, file 8, Ontario Archives, Toronto.

38. See Clement, *Hardrock Mining*, 305–307; Lang, "Lion in a Den of Daniels," 201.

39. *The Gazette* (Montreal), March 17,1958. See also Lang, "Lion in a Den of Daniels," 203–208; Solski and Smaller, *Mine Mill*, 133; *Sudbury Star*, 1958.

40. CHNO radio report, September 19, 1958, David Lehto Collection, Laurentian University Archives, Sudbury, Ont. See also Solski and Smaller, *Mine Mill*, 133.

41. Robinson interview.

42. Elizabeth Jameson, *All That Glitters: Class, Conflict and Community in Cripple Creek* (Urbana: University of Illinois Press, 1998), 139; see also Mary Murphy, *Mining Cultures, Men, Women and Leisure in Butte, 1914–1941* (Urbana: University of Illinois Press, 1997); Laurie Mercier, *Anaconda: Labor, Community and Culture in Montana's Smelter City* (Urbana: University of Illinois Press, 2001), 160–172.

43. Interview with Tom Taylor, Mine Mill member, May 14, 1993, Mine Mill centenary collection, Laurentian University Archives.

44. Official Report on Financial Contributions made to members of Local 598 and Local 637 of the Mine, Mill and Smelter Workers during the Inco Strike (September 24, to December 19, 1959), Ann Morrison Papers, Laurentian University Archives, Sudbury.

45. Local 598 President Mike Solski claimed that the union membership was made aware that there wasn't enough money to pay everyone strike pay before

the strike vote was even taken. Mike Solski, interview with Mick Lowe, December 1995.

46. "Crank Letters, 1958 strike," M. Solski Collection, MU8247, Box 7, Series II, file 8, Ontario Archives.

47. CKSO radio, "News report," March 10, 1959, David Lehto Collection, National Archives Canada and Laurentian University Archives.

48. IUMMSW Papers, UBC Box 3, 1957; Dorothy McDonald, Report of Coordinator to the Eleventh Canadian Convention of the IUMMSW, Mike Solski Papers, Series 18, Box 74, file 7, 1959, Ontario Archives.

49. Reid interview; Dorothy McDonald, "Report to the Eleventh Canadian Convention of the IUMMSW," 6.

50. Interviews with local 598 Women's Auxiliary members, November 1986, in Thibeau, "Union without Women," 98.

51. McQuaid interview.

52. "To our employees in the bargaining units, Sudbury and district and Port Colborne," *Sudbury Star*, December 5, 1958.

53. *Globe and Mail*, December 16, 17, 22, 1958; *Sudbury Star*, December 11, 1958.

54. Canada, National Archives, press clippings, RG 27, vol. 3473, file 1-101-1-1.

55. *Sudbury Star*, December 2, 1958.

56. *Sudbury Star*, December 11, 1958.

57. *Sudbury Star*, December 8, 1958. See Brian F. Hogan, "Hard Rock and Hard Decisions: Catholics, Communists and the IUMMSW—Sudbury Confrontations," paper presented to the Canadian Historical Association meetings, Montreal, May 30, 1985, 9–10.

58. *Globe and Mail*, December 9, 1958.

59. *Sudbury Star*, December 15, 1958.

60. Thibeault, "A Union without Women," 95.

61. Hogan, "Hard Rock and Hard Decisions." See also James Kidd Papers, Laurentian University; "Course outline for Northern Workers Adult Education Programme," Jimmy Kuehl Papers, Laurentian University Archives.

62. Hogan, "Hard Rock and Hard Decisions," 8–12.

63. The Catholic Women's League dates back to 1932, when the first church women's organizations were formed in the Algoma Diocese. Minutes of the Annual Meetings, Catholic Women's League, May 1932; minutes of the Creighton Mine Catholic Women's League, St. Michael's Parish, May 1960, Archives of the Diocese of Algoma, North Bay, Ontario.

64. This echoes similar behavior in the 1960 Mine Mill strike in Kellogg, Idaho. K. Aiken, "When I realized how close Communism was to Kellogg, I was willing to devote day and night: Anti-communism, Women, Community Values, and the Bunker Hill Strike of 1960," *Labor History* 36, no. 2 (1995), 182.

65. "Back to Work Movement Fizzles, Strikers Visit District MPPs," *Sudbury Star*, December 9, 1958.

66. The role of the Catholic Church is well documented by Paula Maurutto, "Private Policing and Surveillance of Catholics: Anti-communism in the Roman Catholic Archdiocese of Toronto, 1020–1960," *Labor/Le Travail* 40 (Fall 1997), 113–136.

67. Lang, "Lion in a Den of Daniels," 214; *Sudbury Star*, December 6, 1958.

68. Joint meeting of Executives of National, International, Locals 598 and 637, December 7, 1958, Mike Solski Papers, MS ll, Series 3, Box 9, MU 8251. See also Lang, "Lion in a Den of Daniels," 214; Mine Mill 598 Strike Bulletin,

December 8, 1958, M. Solski papers, Mu 8247, Series 2, Box 7, file 9, Ontario Archives.

69. The Royal Canadian Mounted Police (RCMP) had long targeted Mine Mill and sent regular surveillance reports on the local union and Auxiliary activities to Ottawa. See Steedman, "Red petticoat brigade," 65.

70. Interview with Pearl Moir, May 1993.

71. Interview with Mine Mill Women's Auxiliary member, name withheld, March 1992.

72. *Sudbury Star*, December 11, 1958, 1.

73. Ibid.

74. Mike Solski interview with Mick Lowe, December 1995.

75. Lang, "Lion in a Den of Daniels," 216.

76. CHNO "News report," December 12, 1958, David Lehto Collection.

77. *Sudbury Star*, December 12, 1958, 1.

78. Thibeault, "A Union without Women," 92.

79. McQuaid interview.

80. *Toronto Telegram*, December 13, 1958.

81. *Globe and Mail*, December 15, 1958; *Sudbury Star*, December 15, 1958.

82. *Toronto Telegram*, December 12, 1958. The threats added to the sensationalism, but according to Solski and Smaller, *Mine Mill*, the allegations were ridiculous.

83. *Toronto Star*, December 15, 1958, as quoted in Thibeault, 93.

84. The strike settlement became known in the popular memory as the "three cent strike." See Clements, *Hardrock Mining*; Lang, "Lion in a Den of Daniels."

85. *Globe and Mail*, December 15, 1958.

86. Robinson interviews.

87. Reid interview.

PART IV

The Division of Mining Labor Revisited: Cultures of Solidarity, Deindustrialization, and the Globalized Economy, 1945–2005

The mining world has always been characterized by shifting investments and fortunes, creating boom and bust communities. This pattern continued in the post–World War II period, when despite unionization, "modernization," and national liberation movements that at times transformed the world's mining communities, multinational dominance of global markets more often left communities with strained labor relations, uncertain economic prospects, and environmental devastation. Women's fortunes varied, too, with the political and economic changes affecting the industry. In North America and Europe, new wage opportunities emerged for women at the same time that the mining industry mechanized or moved out, introducing new survival and gender role challenges to mining families. Elsewhere in the world, the gender division of labor was often maintained or even became more pronounced as mining capital forged or expanded new sites of production. In this section, the final three essays and epilogue of the book address the impacts of mining openings and closings for women in the industrial North, how women negotiated new work and family arrangements, and how men and women built on a labor internationalism that was embedded in the past.

By the late twentieth century the industrial powers of North America, Western Europe, and Japan increasingly looked to the southern hemisphere for new ore sources to fuel their enterprises. Yet other than steel, metals held declining importance in industrialized economies. With the growth of hydropower, nuclear, and oil and gas technologies, coal played even a less important role. Industries downsized and mechanized, closing older mines even when expanding giant open-pit mines. The numbers of workers and families supported by mining dropped dramatically. The oil crisis of 1973, when producing countries dramatically increased the price of oil, brought into sharp focus the world economy's dependence on this other resource.

Deindustrialization and mine closures disrupted families and gender relations. Miners' wives had always contributed to family survival through their productive and reproductive roles, but since mining was dominated by men, women had few wage-earning opportunities outside the home. In the industrialized North, postwar mine shutdowns often altered these work and domestic relations as women pursued new employment opportunities to help families survive, increasing tensions at home.[1] As Yong-Sook Jung reveals in chapter 13 about the Ruhr mining region of Germany, women had historically been excluded from the industrial workforce. But the decline of coal production in the late 1950s brought new industries to the area, expanding education and job opportunities for women. This new generation of miners' wives, born after World War II, Yong-Sook argues, embraced a modified version of the domestic ideology that suited the exigencies of a deindustrialized economy. The readjustment of gender roles to accommodate economic circumstances is typical of a marginalized female work force. Historian Gwyn Williams recorded similar developments in the Welsh mining valleys in the 1980s.[2] As the number of male miners declined and pits were closed, miners' wives and daughters could be found taking up jobs in the tertiary sector, usually low paid and nonunionized.

In the United States and Canada, women won the legal right to enter male mining workplaces just as the industry began to decline in the 1970s. Federal affirmative action mandates opened coal and hard-rock jobs to women, and for the first time since World War II, women entered production jobs in large numbers. For women in places like Arizona, Montana, Appalachia, and Ontario, despite male resistance and harassment, the good wages offered made competition stiff for the few mining jobs available. That competition called into question as to who was entitled to a breadwinning wage. In 1974, miners' wives in Logan, West Virginia, protested a local mine's hiring of women, and elsewhere in the state, male miners voiced greater support for affirmative action quotas than did their wives.[3] Despite initial opposition, female miners broke barriers in the UMW and created the Coal Employment Project to combat discrimination, work on health and safety issues, and form an international network of coalfield women.[4]

In chapter 14, Jennifer Keck and Mary Powell outline how a hundred pioneering women took jobs at Inco in Ontario in the 1970s. Motivated primarily by higher wages, the women Inco workers found that "men's" jobs offered a great deal of satisfaction as well as greater financial independence. They endured the physically hard work, sexual harassment, and difficulties finding child care to better support themselves and families. In adapting to masculine work culture, they had to prove they could "do the work of a man" in order to be treated the "same as a man." In the process, they could achieve "manhood" regardless of sex, breadwinner status based on family need, and respect for fighting back. During the strike of 1978–1979 women workers saw themselves as workers first and declined to join wives in making sandwiches, instead joining their brothers on the picket line and in negotiating committees. Yet these challenges to the gender division of labor became muted as the minerals industry downsized in the late twentieth century; women and minority workers with the least seniority were laid off first.[5]

The Arizona copper mining strike of 1983–1985, involving the large multinational Phelps Dodge and the USWA, represented a watershed moment in North American labor and mining history. Once again, women assumed a dominant role in maintaining the strike, loyally and passionately picketing for the same reasons they had in years past—to improve their families' living conditions, and to support striking men (and some women miners) who were legally enjoined from action.[6] The Miners Women's Auxiliary mobilized its members to protest evictions, organize food banks, and win wider national support. The strike ultimately failed and the company successfully decertified the union with its permanent replacement workers, ushering in a new non-union era in the American mining industry. Yet the thousand female strike supporters emerged with a moral victory and new consciousness that "cut the apron strings" to assert themselves both at home and in public.[7]

A similar watershed strike in Britain transformed labor and domestic relations and mining communities. The NUM. was at the pinnacle of its power in 1972 when the miners called a strike and shortages of coal led to blackouts across Britain. The war between the miners union and the National Coal Board had begun. More than a decade later, under Margaret Thatcher, the government and the union would face a rematch in the Great Miners' Strike of 1984–1985. The miners' wives would achieve near iconic status as the real heroines of the strike through the first nationwide mining women's organization, Women against Pit Closure (WAPC), the history of which is discussed in the Epilogue.

Despite what appeared to be inexorable forces pushing against the fortunes of mining women and men during the 1980s, the weight of traditions of sacrifice and community struggles helped mining families stick together to confront powerful corporations. In chapter 15, focusing on the tens of thousands of miners and supporters who maintained Camp Solidarity during the 1989–1990 Pittston coal strike, Camille Guerin-Gonzales explores how cultures of solidarity take root. She unravels the history of organizing and cross-ethnic, cross-regional, and transnational support for labor strikes in the coal fields of the eastern and western United States from the 1910s through the 1930s. Helped by memories, these alliances persisted and endured state-corporate collusion, company-hired armed mercenaries who inflicted violence and intimidation, red-baiting of union activists, and exploitation of racial divisions. Despite union masculinist rhetoric, women labored in the mines and at home, and were often at the forefront of sacrifice and struggle in these conflicts. Ultimately, Camp Solidarity supporters won a Pyrrhic victory; miners' benefits were saved, but ten years later, Pittston closed permanently many of its mines. But, as Guerin-Gonzales argues, these mining men and women contributed to a foundation of struggle that is poised to champion justice again.

Women's and men's actions mattered in their efforts to design their communities; but the depletion of ore reserves, increasing privatization, and the

Figure IV.1　Miner's wife and son during the 1984–1985 British Miners' Strike—poster behind her reads "Save the Pits."

rise of the importance of oil in multinational and global politics, hurt their hopes for solidarity and economic security in the twenty-first century. In the postcolonial world, mining men and women continue to play an important role in their regions' destiny, as witnessed by the militancy of copper miners

Figure IV.2   Three women from the South Wales Women's Support Group of the Swansea, Neath, and Dulais Valley's on the picket line with their husbands during the 1984–1985 Miners' strike. Original photographs taken by Abigail Porter.

that helped topple the Pinochet regime in Chile and successes of the National Union of Mineworkers in challenging apartheid and low wages in South Africa. Yet the mobility of capital and the quality and exhaustibility of ore continue to threaten the stability of mining communities. The World Bank and the International Monetary Fund have facilitated structural adjustment programs that have introduced or expanded large-scale mining operations in the third world through liberalized mining codes and privatization of state resources. Despite its attractive wages, mining continues to disrupt women's and indigenous people's agricultural practices, cultural traditions, and extended kin and community networks; mining displaces communities, introduces disease, and pollutes lands and water.

Women and men in mining communities across the globe continue to mount protests to challenge the ways in which multinational corporations extract resources. In the twenty-first century, environmental concerns have led to heightened awareness of the legacy of toxic groundwater, erosion, pollution of farmlands, and high disease rates. Once led to extract better wages and working conditions from mining companies, more recent protests often attempt to keep mining *out* of an area. Tibetan protests against Chinese mining, Australian protests of uranium production, and Honduran, Sri Lanka, and Indonesian protests of U.S. corporate mining reveal the growing "cultures of solidarity" between environmentalists, indigenous peoples, mining communities, and international human rights organizations.

Since the 1990s, several international conferences involving women in mining countries have met and an International Women and Mining Network has formed to protest the unsustainability of mining and its harm to women and communities. Others have called worldwide attention to the devastating impacts of cyanide leaching, mercury poisoning, open-pit mining, and corporate efforts to privatize state resources.[8] Where governments and mining companies once openly collaborated to grant mining operations exemptions from environmental laws, these global protests have complicated investment strategies. For example, Peru has become the world's third largest copper producer, but its recent militant protests against environmental degradation have lowered its investment attractiveness. Women continue to play an important role in these protests.[9] In the epilogue, Jaclyn J. Gier addresses how women's protests in mining communities have evolved since the 1980s. The final section of the book turns to these more recent struggles that confront changing gender roles and changing economic realities in the world's mining communities.

NOTES

1. See, e.g., Laurie Mercier, *Anaconda: Labor, Culture, and Community in Montana's Smelter City* (Urbana: University of Illinois Press, 2001), 184, 204. Thomas Dublin and Walter Licht show how women's entry into wage employment in the declining anthracite region of Pennsylvania increased household tensions over child care, control over family finances, and the need to leave the

area, in "Gender and Economic Decline: The Pennsylvania Anthracite Region, 1920–1970," *Oral History Review* 27, no. 1 (2000): 81–97. Margaret Williamson finds that in the ironstone mining district of East Cleveland in Britain, women who took jobs in the declining mining area used strategies to preserve the image of the male provider, in " 'I'm Going to Get a Job at the Factory': Attitudes to Women's Employment in a Mining Community, 1945–1965," *Women's History Review* [Great Britain] 12, no. 3 (2003): 407–420.

2. Gwyn Williams, "Mother Wales Get Off Me Back?," *Marxism Today*, (December 1981): 14–17. As Williams notes, a turn toward conservative politics followed in the wake of the break up of traditional unions and the onset of a working-class consumer culture—a similar pattern emerged among Ruhr Valley miners and their wives in Germany.

3. Marat Moore, *Women in the Mines: Stories of Life and Work* (New York: Twayne Publishers, 1996), xxxvii–xxxviii.

4. Ibid., xl–xlvi.

5. Dona G. Gearhart notes that some women were displaced because of revived gender discrimination and the attraction of other work alternatives, in "Coal Mining Women in the [American] West: The Realities of Difference in an Extreme Environment," *Journal of the West*, 37, no. 1 (1998), 60–68.

6. Barbara Kingsolver, *Holding the Line: Women in the Great Arizona Mine Strike of 1983* (Ithaca, NY: Cornell University Press, 1989 and 1996), 1st ed., xi, 5.

7. Ibid., 102.

8. "Halting the Rush Against Gold: Big Mining and Its Increasingly Radical Opponents," *Economist* (April 10, 2005). <http://www.economist.com/displaystory.cfm?story_id=3627092>.

9. In February 2005, as a result of a spate of fatal mining accidents in the Copperbelt of Zambia, 300 wives and widows of Mopani Copper Mines workers staged a protest where they blocked entrances to several plant areas and demanded that the government intervene and stop MCM from contracting firms with little or no mining background and enforce safety regulations. Claudia Nombuso and Kingsley Kaswende, "Mopani Miners' Wives Protest Over Working Conditions," *Zambezi Times Online* (April 11, 2005) <http://metals.zambezitimes.com/fulltxt.php?id_news=2605>.

CHAPTER 13

Just a Housewife? Miners' Wives between Household and Work in Postwar Germany

Yong-Sook Jung

Introduction—The Ruhr Area of Proletarian Housewives

"The Ruhr area is really a region of proletarian housewives," wrote Georg Schwarz at the beginning of the 1930s in his book on life and labor in the "Ruhr coal pit."[1] In his opinion, the wife of the coal miner was a slave in two senses: she was the "slave of her husband" on the one hand, with her "total dependence on the husband's wage because of the impossibility of self-sustenance by her own earning"; on the other hand, she was the "slave of the industrialist" due to her "blessing of fecundity, petit bourgeois livestock husbandry, and the hostility toward the husband's class consciousness and class struggle."[2] What interests me is not so much the way a social democrat viewed "petit bourgeois" proletarian women from a critical angle, as the overall image of working class housewives in the Ruhr area imprinted on the populace arising from historical reflections. His statement reveals what a Ruhr miner's wife was like at that time: underemployed, with high rates of fertility, and reliance on agricultural sub-economic activities at home.

Working outside the home was highly uncommon for a miner's wife, although additional earnings of the wife were much needed by working-class families at that time.[3] It was a matter of pride for the miner who stood at the top of the wage hierarchy that his wife did not go out to work: "As soon as we got married we had a household of our own. We didn't have to go out to work any more, even if we wanted to. Our husbands were against it. This was possible, only when worst came to the worst, in the true sense of the word, or when the work was compatible with housekeeping."[4] A miner's wife was expected to be subordinate to patriarchal rights, to fulfill her role as a mother to a number of children while at the same time contributing to the household's economy, by means of managing the household's expenses and the self-sufficient production of food and clothing. It fell to the wife's lot to take care of vegetable patches and raise livestock, which were indispensable to the matter of "making both ends meet" in the household.[5] Social historians define this way of life as the "heavy-industrial form of existence," which arises from the special demographic constellation and industrial structure in mining communities.[6]

In the period of industrialization during the late nineteenth and the early twentieth centuries, the population of the Ruhr mining cities was exploding because of a massive influx of immigrants. Catholic immigrants from northeast Prussia brought with them rural family cultures and a preindustrial way of life into the Ruhr area, by keeping in touch with their old homes in their choices of wives.[7] Most of all, the characteristic of the mining communities that featured only one single industry, was responsible for low female employment rates. In mines and smelters, which employed the bulk of the labor force in the Ruhr area, women's work was strictly forbidden for health and moral reasons.[8] Alternative industries virtually did not exist due to the administrative measure whereby the progress of installing other industries including the service sector was at an embryonic phase in the Ruhr area. The limited number of middle-class families living in working-class regions also provided few domestic jobs. Accordingly, young women moved to those cities in the lower Rhine province featuring the textile industry or to the farms in North Germany to seek employment.

The industrial structure has changed since the late 1950s, when the coal mining industry began to lose its dominant position in the regional economy. This study traces developments in the female employment situation in the postwar Ruhr area, thereby exploring the changes in the woman's roles in the miner's patriarchal family system. The study is made up of three sections. The first section explores the question: How did women fare in the deindustrializing process? The next section deals with the role of educational expansion in motivating women to wage work. The last section discusses the extent of the women's integration into the labor workforce and their opportunities and limitations in the job market. The changes in social attitudes toward paid employment of married women will also be addressed.

"Feminization" of the Male-Dominated Labor Market

The major factor that influences a married woman's decision to go out to work is opportunities, that is, suitable jobs within their reach.[9] These had been absolutely lacking in the structurally underdeveloped female labor market of the Ruhr area. A frequently quoted example of this is *Hamborn*, a mining and smelter city on the Rhine incorporated into *Duisburg* in 1929: a study by *Eckert-Fischer* on the socioeconomic situation of the women at the turn of the century, which surveyed 495 families, including 281 miners' families, shows that only one married woman found employment as a dressmaker.[10] Until World War II, taking in boarders or lodgers seemed to be the most ideal source of supplementary income for a miner's wife. Not only were there enough single young miners seeking room and board, but the practice was considered appropriate for a housewife in an extension of her domestic duties. In addition, the job was financially rewarding for families with young children. A representative study on the Ruhr miners' housing at the end of the nineteenth and beginning of the twentieth century shows that every other house took in lodgers in the company-owned housing quarters of *Essen*, and more than two thirds of the families who took in lodgers had young children.[11]

In the immediate years after World War II, the increase in the number of women in the workforce was becoming an emerging trend in West Germany. First, the war resulted in a lack of male workers especially in the most economically active generation: in 1946 in the Ruhr area, women aged 20 to 35 outnumbered the men of the same age group by 1.6 to 1.[12] The housing shortage in the industrial cities bombed out by the allied forces aggravated the existing shortage of workers. Finally, the extreme financial exigencies forced women to work. The women who had lost their male breadwinners or who simply had never had anyone to support them, had to earn a living on their own.[13] However, the "forced emancipation" was just a brief matter. As the living conditions slowly returned to normal after the war, women were expected to return home and assume their traditional gender role, with the result that the employment rate of West German women in 1950 was lower than during the Nazi regime.[14] The fifties saw the ideal of the modern nuclear family gaining ground across the social spectrum. The household structure based upon differentiated gender roles, with the husband as the breadwinner and the wife as the housekeeper (*Hausfrauenehe*), was accepted as the only norm of the day.[15] At the same time, the shortage of workers caused by rapid industrial reconstruction gave rise to new demands for the female workforce: over the period 1950–1959, the number of employed women in West Germany rose by 22 percent from 7.6 million to 9.3 million, whereas the number of the whole working population grew by 16 percent from 21.5 million to 25 million.[16]

In the Ruhr area, the coal crisis in 1956/57—a drastic slip both in the exploitation of coal and in the number of employees—was the first decisive moment in the gradual influx of female workers into the labor market. This change was driven by competition from North America and by the introduction of other alternative energy resources, mainly oil. This resulted in a radical drop in mining jobs: between the twenty years spanning 1950 and 1970, the number of Ruhr miners declined from approximately 415,000 to 225,000, in other words, from 55.2 percent to 24.7 percent of the whole working population within the area.[17] This regional employment crisis triggered monumental social and political discussions on how to reform the structure of industrial employment predominantly driven by a single sector, namely, coal mining. This included the introduction of alternative industries and, most of all, the creation of female jobs.

Among the examples of the settlement of alternative industries in favor of women is *Herne*, a typical mining town in the North Ruhr area. In 1950, nearly 80 percent of Herne's job openings belonged to the mining industry; ten years later, the number of employees in other industries exceeded those employed by the mining industry.[18] In the center of this development was the textile and clothing industry. Textiles represented the classical "women's industry," and the seamstress course topped the list of vocational training courses that the miners' daughters could take. Although the coal mining industry had frowned upon the introduction of other industries for fear of losing its workforce, the textile and clothing industries were tolerated because of their minimum wages: the average wage level in the new industries was no more than half as much as that of mining.[19] A couple of small and medium-size textile factories established in Herne in the immediate postwar years assisted widowed and single women left alone after the War.[20] With the opening of a nylon stocking factory in 1961, the textile and clothing industry became the biggest employer in Herne outside the mines.[21] The work in textile factories was considered appropriate for married women, whereby they could contribute to the household's budget with "a reasonable income."[22] During the sixties, however, the West German textile industry underwent a radical restructuring process in the face of strong competition from low wage countries. The restructuring process included the introduction of machinery and rationalization of work. For example, in 1962, the above mentioned stocking factory introduced newly invented machines from Italy, which turned out more than twice as many pairs of stockings as with the conventional technique.[23] Consequently, the textile industry of Herne lost half of its employees.[24]

Beginning in the late sixties, the electronics industry replaced the textile industry as the largest job provider for women. Unlike the textile and clothing industries, it was a sector that had high growth rates. It was also a typical "women's industry" with a high number of women in the workforce. The electrical assembling work was thought to be appropriate to women: expressions such as "skillful" and "tender woman's hands" frequently found their way into the local newspaper reports at that time.[25] The plentiful women's labor reserves in the Ruhr area was one of the most attractive incentives for big electronic companies, whose factories were destroyed by bombing during World War II, to build new ones here in the fifties.[26] As a result, the electrotechnical sector grew to be the fourth largest employer in the Ruhr area by 1971 with 6.2 percent of the employed workforce.[27] In Herne, between 1953 and 1970, the electronics industry created nearly two-thirds of all the newly emerging jobs outside the coal mining industry. *Blaupunkt*, a company affiliated with *Bosch*, is credited for this new development. It grew rapidly to become the second largest employer in Herne by 1970 after the coal mining industry, absorbing around two thirds of all employees in the electronic sector.[28] Women accounted for about 80 percent of the total workforce at *Blaupunkt*. These jobs were so immediately popular for area women that it resulted in a short-term shortage in the workforce making it necessary to recruit nearly half of their female employees from neighboring cities.[29]

Table 13.1 Employed women in Herne and (in all of) West Germany

	Herne		West Germany	
	1951	*1979*	*1950*	*1980*
Female employment rate (in %)	**19.6**	**32.3**	**31.1**	**37.6**
Distribution of total employed in the working sectors (in %)[a]				
Agriculture and Forestry	0.9	0.3	7.3	6.5
Producing industries[b]	**34.4**	31.6	**41.2**	27.4
Commerce and Traffic[c]	31.1	24.9	20.7	19.4
Other Services[c]	33.4	43.2	30.8	39.3
Percentage of women in each sector (in %)				
Agriculture and Forestry	27.2	29.9	33.9	49.1
Producing industries[b]	7.6	16.9	23.1	24.5
Producing industries without mining, iron and steel, and construction	29.5	29.4	–	28.7
Commerce and Traffic[c]	45.7	47.4	33.7	44.8
Other services[c]	67.9	54.8	51.0	42.2
Other services without domestic services	44.7	–	37.1	–

Notes: (a) Percentages do not always add up to 100% due to round up calculation.
(b) Producing industries include [the Federal Employment Institute] the coal mining industry, iron and steel industries, construction, and manufacturing industries.
(c) Banks, credit institutes, and insurance companies are included in the statistics for the commerce and traffic sector in 1950–1951, but in 1979–1980, they are listed as "other services."

Sources: Compiled and calculated (partially own) from *Statistisches Jahrbuch Nordrhein-Westfalen* (1950–1951), pp. 252f.; *Statistische Berichte. Versicherungspflichtig beschäftigte Arbeitnehmer in Nordrhein-Westfalen am 30. Juni 1979. Ergebnisse der Beschäftigten- und Entgeltstatistik nach Verwaltungsbezirken*, 58; *Statistisches Jahrbuch deutscher Gemeinden*, vol. 38 (1950), pp. 80ff; *Statistisches Jahrbuch BRD* (1981), 95.

The discussion of women's employment would not be complete without discussing the service sector. Like other industrialized Western countries, West Germany transitioned to the service-oriented economy in the last three decades of the twentieth century.[30] At the same time, as shown by table 13.1, the weight of the women's employment shifted from manufacturing industries toward the service sector: in 1950, producing industries which acted as a driving force of the economic reconstruction of postwar West Germany still absorbed 41.2 percent of the female workforce, in 1980 only a quarter; in contrast, the service sector increased its distribution of female workforce during the same time from 50 percent to 58.7 percent. The Ruhr area was no exception in this development, but its peculiarities must be pointed out. Although the service sector here also expanded so much that it employed more than half of the total employees by the beginning of the nineties, the development of the sector never did overtake the national level. During the seventies and the eighties, the Ruhr area lost more than a quarter of the jobs in manufacturing industries, compared with the gains in service jobs at no more than 27 percent, which was far below the national growth rate, an estimated 40 percent. The main reason was the high dependency of service business here on traditional heavy industries, such as the transportation and distribution of coal and steel products, which declined continuously.[31]

Although this barely influenced the number of jobs available to women, since commerce and traffic were actually male dominated in the Ruhr area, the female employment rate in the Ruhr area always remained far lower than the national average.[32]

However, it cannot be denied that the number of women in employment increased tremendously in the process of deindustrialization. In 1950–1951 only every fifth women in Herne was in the labor market, far below the national average of nearly a third; thirty years later, the gap narrowed considerably (refer to table 13.1) The service sector played a much more significant role in women's employment in Herne than throughout the rest of West Germany. In 1925, domestic services employed every third woman working in the Ruhr cities. In 1950, of the working women only less than one in every fifth working women was employed in this job, whereas commerce and modern service jobs absorbed 45 percent.[33] In the fifties and sixties, a great part of newly created service jobs here came from retail sales, as well as from cleaning and hygienic service businesses, all based on the escalation of consumption in the working class.[34] Women's wages increased family purchasing power of consumer products and services. In the seventies, the service sector expanded due to increasing job openings in educational and public administrative institutions.

EDUCATION AND PROFESSIONALIZATION OF WOMEN

In an empirical study of the German women who had vocational training during the immediate postwar years, Claudia Born concluded that the social appreciation of the job and the kind of vocational training is more influential on the woman personally rather than the number of children or the husband's income.[35] A report from the labor exchange office at Duisburg written in 1953 pointed out that the insufficient educational and vocational qualifications of women was the major reason for their failure to find employment: "We usually see lack of vocational qualifications among the jobless. Many of them lost their knowledge or, at least, whatever qualifications they have are not competitive enough to be employed."[36]

Data of 1997 points to a considerable gap in qualifications between gender: 34.8 percent of women but only 22.4 percent of men in the Ruhr area had not acquired vocational qualifications.[37] This is explained by the fact that many of those women surveyed belonged to the older generation, who had not benefited from higher education. The generation of the miners' wives who grew up in the forties had limited chances for schooling and vocational training, not only because of the traditional prejudices of parents against their daughters' education, but also due to a relatively large number of children, more than they could often manage, as well as the father's inability to get all the children through upper rungs in the school system.[38] This is illustrated in an example of a miner's daughter who was born in Essen in 1901: although she wanted to be a dressmaker or a nurse, she had to get a job as a housemaid when she left school at the age of 14, because her parents who had eight children to raise were not able to pay ten marks for the vocational school.[39] In case the family could support only one of the children, normally the son was the main beneficiary of the financial support: "My elder brother should necessarily have a better start in life than the others. Grandmother said, 'He should have it better,' counting the few pennies she has. He was allowed to go to middle school, and we had to cut down on the other household budget for his school fees. At that time nobody ever thought of going to middle school other than those kids of civil servants, businessmen or those from well-off families in the next community."[40]

Women were the main beneficiaries of the educational reform in the sixties and seventies in West Germany under the slogan of "equal opportunities."[41] Data on education shows that the schooling level of Germans was gradually rising in the fifties, but rose more rapidly from the sixties.[42] Most of all, the educational reform touched off an increase in the number of girls aiming for advanced secondary level, that is, in the intermediate school ("Realschule") and the grammar school ("Gymnasium"). While more than two thirds of the girls who entered school in 1962 left it before reaching the advanced secondary level, every second girl of the cohort of 1970 stayed.[43] The increase in the number of graduates from the grammar school ("Abiturient") also serves as a frequently quoted indicator in assessing the schooling level. In 1961, only 5.9 percent of the young people aged 18–21 in North Rhine-Westphalia left school with the "Abitur", that is, the secondary school prerequisite for an admission into university studies. But twenty years later, school graduates with the Abitur nearly quadrupled in their share of the age cohort. The proportion of women among them also increased from 38.7 to 47.9 percent, which nearly reached the integrated gender rate of 49 percent.[44] We can say that the gender differential between boys and girls at advanced secondary school had disappeared in the latter half of the seventies.

The educational reform in the Ruhr area resulted in the formation of universities in Bochum (1965), Dortmund (1968–1969), Duisburg and Essen (1972). In the Ruhr area, in spite of its high density of population, in the earlier days, there were very few higher educational institutions. This can be attributed to the historical result of a political consideration made under the German Empire.[45] The number of students in the Ruhr area increased from around 4,000 in the mid-sixties to more than 40,000 during the winter term of 1972–1973, and doubled up again in 1979–1980.[46] At the end of the seventies, a sociological study on the social background of the students at the Ruhr University Bochum showed that the women's share of the total students was 28.9 percent, definitively under the national average of 32.8 percent.[47] This can be attributed to two factors: one, the Ruhr University, in keeping with the industrial heritage of the region, offered more courses for science, technology, engineering, and economy, where the women's share remained traditionally low. On the other hand, only a minority of workers' daughters probably benefited from the third level education, since they had to overcome barriers such as lack of funds, parents' prejudices, and even commuting problems: "Her parents did not let her go to grammar school. Firstly, they thought they just couldn't afford it. Secondly, they believed that she would not make it through grammar school. In addition, girls had to go to grammar school or intermediate school by bus. At that time, there were no cheap monthly tickets available."[48]

Women have also played an increasingly prominent role in the so-called second educational track (*Zweiter Bildungsweg*). Evening classes provided courses for adults who wanted to complete secondary schooling or *Abitur* examination. In the Ruhr area and in the vicinity of Düsseldorf, the state capital of North Rhine-Westphalia, women took advantage of this, since most of the classes of these state institutions, that is, special preparation course for the *Abitur* ("Kolleg") and evening grammar school ("Abendgymnasium"), were located nearby.[49] During the later sixties and the seventies, the number of women in evening classes increased more radically than the number of men: in the school year 1979–1980, women represented 44.8 percent of the high school graduates attending evening classes in North Rhine-Westphalia.[50]

The secondary school qualification serves as the base for further qualified vocational education. In accordance with the rise in the schooling level of women, the imbalance of gender in vocational education was largely corrected. In 1970, 29.6 percent of 17 year-old girls in West Germany neither entered advanced secondary school nor finished vocational training; ten years later, the share of young women who found their jobs without completing vocational qualifications dropped to 14.4 percent.[51] In the seventies, the schooling level of female apprentices grew a lot more than before, and this development was more obvious compared to that of their male counterparts. According to data collected by the Social Research Institute in Dortmund, 60.9 percent of male and 51.2 percent of female graduates from the main school (*Hauptschule*) in North Rhine Westphalia in 1973–1974 preferred the dual system of apprenticeship training, where an apprentice works under a contract with an employer while attending vocational school part-time to study on a curriculum of general and work-related subjects. In 1981–1982, only 56.5 and 39.7 percent of men and women respectively took this course. On the contrary, the share of the main school graduates who wanted to enter the full-time vocational school, *Berufsschule* or *Fachschule*, in place of the dual system increased from 22.5 to 35.7 percent of women, but from 13.6 to a slim 16.3 percent of men during the same period.[52]

However, this trend must not be interpreted only as the result of educational expansion for women. Rather, it reflects the critical situation of the labor market for women, as a state government report pointed out.[53] Young men could easily enter an apprenticeship directly and therefore had to rely less frequently on full-time vocational courses. Moreover, the labor market in the seventies was not favorable for young women who benefited from the educational reform and swept across the labor market in a great mass. Due to the oil and steel crises, the economy of West Germany, especially in the Ruhr area, slipped into long-term stagnation. Under such circumstances, women needed a higher level of education or vocational qualifications to be able to enjoy equal opportunities with their male competitors.[54]

COMPROMISES: JOB, MARRIAGE, AND CHILDBIRTH

During World War II, the armament industry in the Ruhr area minimized the break up of families here, because a large part of its male workforce was exempted from conscription and therefore the traditional family norm was kept almost unchanged. This was also the case even after the tumultuous postwar years, which are thought to have been destabilizing for traditional family structure and values.[55] The economic growth in the postwar era had fortified the traditional sense of values, especially in the working class that was more prosperous than it had ever been.[56] At the same time, the steadily growing volume of the female workforce—among them a growing percentage of married women—pushed male workers—the central supporters of the familial conservative value—into a cultural dilemma by tarnishing their patriarchal pride as breadwinners. The solution for the conflict came from a new social consensus on women's paid work, by the demands of modern consumption, and part-time jobs.

The expansion of modern consumption was an important motive for married women to go out to work. The sixties were the period when modern "luxuries" were expanding into the working class: modern household appliances like the refrigerator and washing machines were introduced to the miners' households. In 1962–1963, among West German working class four-person households, 26.8 percent had a refrigerator and 42.3 percent a washing machine.[57] The popularity of car ownership, the privatization of mining companies' rental houses, children's education, and vacations provided prime motives for women to work.[58] Women did not work to make up for a loss of income, but to achieve a standard of living desired in a modern consumer society, which they otherwise could not afford. In a documentary novel written in 1963, a miner's statement demonstrates the relationship between consumption and women's work: "We want our own house, and who doesn't? . . . We want a TV set, and who doesn't? Finally, we want to watch soccer games and [we want] a washing machine, too. It's necessary that our wives work in order to buy those things that I just listed. Do they have to stand in line for a Laundromat on Saturday or on Sunday? Nobody wants this. . . . "[59] Husbands tolerated the new situation, in which their wives worked not because of economic pressure, but to satisfy a personal "need" or to achieve a "better life," even though there is no clear distinction between the two.

Part-time jobs were the result of the "economic miracle." Confronted with a constant labor shortage, employers and the government were forced to recruit the "silent reserves," that is, married women, for industry, while at the same time they tried to prevent them from doing so. Women were increasingly expected to alleviate the shortage, even though the improved standard of living for families made it unnecessary for the wife to work. Therefore, special institutions for them were introduced: childcare facilities in the workplace, a day-off per month for household duties (*Hausarbeitstag*), and part-time jobs (*Halbtagsarbeit*). Part-time jobs drastically increased the employment rate of married women: in 1950, 9.6 percent of married women

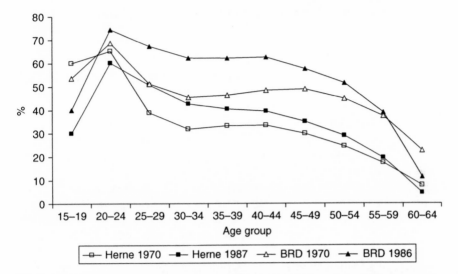

Figure 13.1 Women in employment in 1970–1986/87 by age in % of age group

Source: Compiled from Hans-Viktor von Hoff, *Die Entwicklung der Wirtschafts- und Bevölkerungsstruktur in der kreisfreien Stadt Herne von 1950 bis 1970*, 2 vols, vol. 2 (Frankfurt am Main: Peter Lang, 1974), 99; Stadt Herne (ed.), *Frauen in Herne. Bericht zur Situation der Frauen in Herne 1993* (Herne; Gleichstellungsstelle der Stadt Herne, 1993), 57; *Statistisches Jahrbuch NRW* (1988), 220; *Statistisches Jahrbuch BRD* (1988), 97.

were employed in West Germany, rising to 27.4 percent in 1970.[60] This was most influential upon the shift in social awareness of women going to work, since women's part-time work was no longer thought to be a destabilizing factor in the gender hierarchies, neither within the family nor in society.[61]

It is difficult to figure out the precise number of miners' wives who joined the labor workforce. There are no aggregate statistics. Neither the community statistics nor the documents from the mining companies and associations provide sufficient information. Even if statistics did exist, they failed to cover the whole scope. Since women were primarily engaged in casual work, which was usually grouped under the "grey zone" of an informal labor market, they were not included in employment statistics.

The general statistics of employment present the real influx of females into the labour market only to a limited extent, since the degree of the participation in the labor force varies from age group to age group. In 1970, the employment rate in the 15–19 year group was relatively high in Herne (figure 13.1). That means many teenage girls here left full-time education earlier than those in other districts and began to work. The high employment rate in this age group and the radical drop in the period following marriage reflect that women's paid work in Herne required neither high educational qualifications nor skills that necessitated lengthy training. In the seventies, the educational reform for equal opportunities reduced the qualification gap between the mining cities and the rest of the nation. This is confirmed by a dramatic decline in the employment of teenage girls from 60 to 30 percent in the age group less than twenty years: young women tended to remain longer in full-time education or training and entered the labor market later than in the past.

In 1970, the employment rate of Herne's women in their twenties was not only below the national average, but also dropped much more sharply. (refer to figure 13.1). This can be explained by the trend toward early marriage and the consequent distancing of married women from paid employment in the miner's family. Communal statistics in the fifties indicate a trend toward early marriage among miners as well. They married in large numbers between the ages of twenty and twenty-five, while white-collar workers and the self-employed preferred to marry in their late twenties. The typical age difference between miner couples was one to five years, but it was not unusual for wives to be more than five years younger than their husbands.[62] In 1987, both in Herne and throughout all of West Germany, employment of women in their early twenties decreased to a lesser extent than it had seventeen years earlier. This is traceable to a shift in the marriage age: between 1970 and 1987, the average age at which West German women first got married rose from 23.0 to 25.2 years.[63]

Employment patterns between Herne's and West German women, all in all, considerably differed especially in the family phase, that is, the 30- to 45-year-olds. In 1970, West German women largely followed a three-stage life pattern that set out the stages of employment before and after childcare. Employment rates tended to decrease until they reached their early thirties, and then increased again in their late thirties and forties, when they were, to some extent, freed from the burden of childcare. In 1987, with the exception of the youngest age cohort that remained in education, women became more active in the labor market than in the past, with an increase in those engaged in family care. In the Ruhr area however, women's employment proved to be transitory: more women tended to give up their jobs after marriage or child-birth and then did not or could not return to work after the intensive child-care stage. In 1970, employment of Herne's women tended to remain at about the same level as during the family phase. In the mid-eighties, it even fell continuously in the same age groups. A similar pattern also prevailed in other Ruhr cities, such as Duisburg, Gelsenkirchen, Dortmund, and Bochum.[64]

In the figure 13.1, the difference in the employment rates between Herne's and West German women's in general age groups 45+ reflects the traditionally passive attitudes of Herne women toward paid employment. They had been socialized in the conventional miner's milieu in the earlier twentieth century and influenced by the motherhood ideology of National Socialism. For them, it was natural for a wife to be responsible only for the household and to adjust her daily life to the shift-work schedule of the husband. Women, who had entered the labor market at the end of World War II, seldom had much success with it, even after their children had grown up. The struggle for existence at the end of the war and during the immediate post-war years offered them little chances for education: in some cases they could not even complete compulsory schooling. Places for apprenticeship were lacking as a result of massive unemployment immediately after the end of the war. In the figure, the gradual fall of employment in the same age groups shows a new trend that people retire at an earlier age than in the past.

Data on the average number of family members in a miner's health insurance plan indicates indirectly a reduction in family size during the seventies: in 1971, every insured active miner had 1.82 family members to support, until in 1987 it dropped continuously to 1.13.[65] This evidently reflects a trend toward dwindling instances of marriage of miners on the one hand, and the decline in the number of children per household on the other hand. Detailed statistics on the average number of children in miner families in this period are not available. A face-to-face interview points to the trend of having fewer children: younger women had only one or a maximum of two children; the older generation also tended to have fewer children than before.[66] Some women consciously tried to reduce the number of children, so that they could enjoy life: "We had wished we could relax a little more than our parents and that our children have it better than we used to! For this, you better not have so many kids."[67] Clearly, the introduction of contraceptive pills must have significantly facilitated this trend. Hence, a drop in the birthrate at the beginning of the seventies can be traced to it. Although many attempts were made to find them, there is no clear evidence proving relationships between fertility and female participation in the labor force.[68] Nevertheless, considering that childcare was the most important factor preventing married women from going out to work, the trend toward fewer children gave a new "freedom" to women, and opened the possibilities for them to work outside home.

The attitudes of miners' wives toward wage work outside the home substantially differed from generation to generation. The generation influenced by the "motherhood" ideology of National Socialism had an unambiguous sense of family orientation and a limited personal interest in the job. They considered it "normal" for women to earn money as early as possible before marriage, and then ultimately give up the job upon marriage. A husband's low income and low standard of living were crucial factors that allowed them to return to work. For the younger generation, women's work could be accepted, as long as someone else cared for the children and housekeeping was organized mostly to the satisfaction of their husbands, which was very uncommon for older generations. This was not unrelated to the increasing instability of their husbands' jobs due to a decline in the mining industry. The growing instability of their husbands' jobs in the declining mining industry encouraged many women to seek paid employment.[69] The social security benefits in the case of labor disability still remained unfavorable, placing the family's financial situation in jeopardy in case of an illness or accident of the breadwinner.

Even in the younger generations, the attitudes of women themselves toward wage work varied from person to person. Many of them looked at working women in the light of economic benefits. "I go to work not for pleasure, but because I earn money, which I can buy things with that were beyond my reach otherwise. If one says she goes to work because she doesn't want to stay at home, I would not consider this to be normal. I think it is normal that a woman works in order to earn money so that she can maintain a certain standard of living. If I had a fantastic job, for example in a public office or in an institution, and if I had only one child, I would give up such a job in any case. . . . It was not difficult for me to say: I'll stay at home. I would be willing to remain a housewife."[70]

Nevertheless, it is clear that the "domesticity," which had been regarded as a privilege as well as responsibility of wives in the earlier days, was no longer the dominating rule among them. A record of a miner's wife from a book about Recklinghausen-Hochlarmark, a small mining village in the north Ruhr area, records a typical life course of women who shuttled between household duties and the place of employment. She married when she was twenty years old, and then gave up her job as a salesperson to bring up her children. In the late sixties, when Blaupunkt in Herne introduced part-time jobs for women, she began to work again. As a part-timer, she could take turns in caring for her children with her husband. After the rationalization of employees in the factory in the early seventies, she stayed at home until she found a new job as a part-time assistant salesperson. Although her husband accepted her working at these jobs with some reluctance, they needed money to buy the rental house in the company's housing quarters where they were living. However, economic necessity was not the only reason why she wanted to go out to work: "When I got married, I thought: just a housewife? I could never imagine that I should remain one."[71]

CONCLUSION: INDIVIDUALIZATION OF LIFE CYCLE

In the postwar period, the process of a growing influx of women into the workforce seemed more dramatic in the Ruhr area, where the rate of female employment had been much lower than in the rest of the nation for structural as well as cultural reasons. Two overlapping developments are observed here. First, the diminishing dependence of the economy on the coal mining and smelting industry since the mid-fifties weakened the male dominance on the labor market in the Ruhr area. The need for multiple industries in order to compensate for the loss of workplaces by declining heavy industries facilitated the establishment and enlargement of alternative industries in favor of women. From the seventies, the service sector expanded steadily within the whole economic structure of the old mining communities which resulted in the increasing integration of women into the workforce, by providing them with more and better opportunities for work outside home than was previously available.

Second, this process was also supported by a growing interest in women themselves in finding employment. The revolutionary extension of education for women positively influenced them, too, motivating them toward paid employment. The generation of women born since the sixties could enjoy equal opportunities for education. Part-time jobs, which were introduced to alleviate the shortage of an appropriate labor force caused by the economic reconstruction, made women's work compatible with their duties in the household. Therefore the necessary flexibility served as a base for individual compromises between paid work by women and the conservative notion of family as well as women's role in postwar West Germany in general. The spread of modern consumption not only motivated women to go to work, but also made their employment acceptable both in the family and society, shifting the argument about women's work from making both ends meet to achieving a certain standard of living.

However, this change is not to be exaggerated, since it does not mean substantial changes in the differentiated gender roles in the family and society. First, the main reason women left their jobs for some time was still childbirth and childcare. Second, in the gender-segregated labor market, women's employment was limited exclusively to a few "women's sectors," where the wage level was lower than the male one and women had always outnumbered men. Finally, in order to be accepted, working women had to contribute to the maintenance of, or increase in, the standard of living, because it was the husband's job to support the family financially rather than the wife's.

In the postwar era, through the decline of the coal mining industry and increasing social mobility, the "traditional miner's milieu" that had been distinct in the Ruhr mining area since the nineteenth century has faded away. The size of the miner's family is now "normalized"; the patch garden has lost its economic indispensability in the household. The traditional definition of the woman's role in a miner's family as mother and housewife only was also modified. Women's paid work outside the home was hardly constrained by family reasons as before. The traditional attitude toward this employment has shifted and become individualized. Although the diversification of the life cycle of miners' wives cannot be interpreted as a direct result of deindustrialization in the mining area, it contributed at least to a shift away from the traditional role of women, by freeing them from the forced "domesticity."

NOTES

1. Quoted from Georg Schwarz, *Kohlenpott 1931. Reportage aus den 30er Jahren* (Essen; Klartext, 1986: the original version entitled: *Kohlenpott. Ein Buch von der Ruhr von Georg Schwarz* (Berlin 1931), 170.
2. Ibid., 171.
3. On the necessity and condition of employment for working class women see, Heidi Rosenbaum, *Proletarische Familien. Arbeiterfamilien und Arbeiterväter im frühen 20. Jahrhundert zwischen traditioneller, sozialdemokratischer und klein-bürgerlicher Orientierung* (Frankfurt am Main: Suhrkamp, 1992), 422.
4. Quoted from Jutta de Jong, ed., *Kinder, Küche, Kohle—und viel mehr! Bergarbeiterfrauen aus drei Generationen erinnern sich* (Essen: Klartext, 1991), 110.
5. Carl Jantke, *Bergmann und Zeche. Die sozialen Arbeitsverhältnisse einer Schachanlage des nördlichen Ruhrgebiets in der Sicht der Bergleute* (Tübingen: Mohr, 1953), 11.

6. For further details see Klaus Tenfelde, "Klasse und Geschlecht," *Geschichte und Gesellschaft* 18 (1992): 179–203 and Thomas Welskopp, "Leben im Rhythmus der Hütte," *Westfälische Forschung* 45 (1995), 205–241.

7. On the demographic development of the Ruhr area since industrialization, see Wolfgang Köllmann, Frank Hoffmann, and Andreas E. Maul, "Bevölkerungsgeschichte," in *Das Ruhrgebiet im Industriezeitalter: Geschichte und Entwicklung*, ed., W. Köllmann, 2 Vols, vol. 1 (Düsseldorf: Schwann, 1990), 111–197.

8. See Evelyn Kroker, *Frauen und Bergbau: Zeugnisse aus 5 Jahrhunderten. Ausstellung des Deutschen Bergbau-Museums Bochum vom 29. August bis 10. Dezember 1989* (Bochum: Deutsches Bergbau-Museum, 1989), 116.

9. Alva Myrdal and Viola Klein, *Women's Two Roles* (London: Routledge and Kegan Paul, 1956), 79.

10. Li Eckert-Fischer, *Die wirtschaftliche und soziale Lage der Frauen in dem modernen Industrieort Hamborn im Rheinland* (Hagen: Verlag von Carl Stracke, 1913), 77–95.

11. Franz J. Brüggemeier and Lutz Niethammer, "Schlafgänger, Schnapskinos und schwer-industrielle Kolonie. Aspekte der Arbeiterwohnungsfrage im Ruhrgebiet vor dem Ersten Weltkrieg," in *Fabrik, Familie, Feierabend. Beiträge zur Sozialgeschichte des Alltags im Industriezeitalter*, ed., J. Reulecke and W. Weber (Wuppertal: Peter Hammer Verlag, 1978), 135–175, at 152.

12. Own calculations from Statistisches Landesamt Nordrhein-Westfalen, ed., *Volks- und Berufszählung vom 29. Oktober 1946* (Düsseldorf, 1950), S. 15.

13. Almost every second woman born between 1913 and 1928 was single, widowed or divorced. Ingeborg Marx, *Frauenarbeit in der Zeitenwende* (Essen: Ludgerus, 1961), 54–55.

14. Walter Müller, "Frauenerwerbstätigkeit im Lebenslauf," in *Strukturwandel der Frauenarbeit 1880–1980*, ed., Walter Müller, Angelika Willms, and Johann Handl (Frankfurt/M. and New York: Campus, 1983), 55–106, at 63.

15. The Marriage Law in 1957 maintained patriarchal authority of the Civil Code in a revised form, by allowing a wife to work principally where her husband was "not solvent" and as long as the work was compatible with her duties in the household and family. See Gabriele Müller-List, *Gleichberechtigung als Verfassungsauftrag. Eine Dokumentation zur Entstehung des Gleichberechtigungsgesetzes vom 18. Juni 1957* (Düsseldorf: Droste, 1996), 78.

16. Klaus-Jörg Ruhl, *Verordnete Unterordnung. Beschäftigte Frauen zwischen Wirtschaftswachstum und konservativer Nachkriegszeit 1945–1963* (Munich: Oldenburg, 1994), 287.

17. "Der Strukturwandel in der Industrie des Ruhrgebiets," in *Statistische Rundschau für das Land Nordrhein-Westfalen*, 25 (1973): 155–159.

18. Hans-Viktor von Hoff, *Die Entwicklung der Wirtschafts- und Bevölkerungsstruktur in der kreisfreien Stadt Herne von 1950 bis 1970*, 2 vols, vol. 2 (Frankfurt am Main.: Peter Lang, 1974), 16, 19, 21.

19. Ibid., 97.

20. Leo Reiners, *Herne 1945–1950. Fünf Jahre Wiederaufbau* (Herne: Oberstadtdirektor, 1950), p. 280; Hoff, *Die Entwicklung der Wirtschafts,* p. 21.

21. "Es-De-Strumpffabrik baut schon die zweite Halle," in *Ruhr Nachrichten*, November 19, 1960.

22. Ibid.

23. "Italienische Wundermaschine ersetzt viele hundert Kräfte," in *Herner Rundschau*, March 29, 1962.
24. Hoff, *Die Entwicklung der Wirtschafts*, p. 20.
25. For example: "Zweigwerk Herne ist schon unentbehrlich," in *Westfälische Rundschau*, March 26, 1969.
26. Wilhelm Dege and Winfried Dege, *Das Ruhrgebiet*, 3rd edn. (Berlin and Stuttgart: Gebrüder Borntraeger, 1983), 109.
27. "Der Strukturwandel in der Industrie des Ruhrgebiets," in *Statistische Rundschau für das Land Nordrhein-Westfalen*, vol. 25 (1973): 157.
28. "Blaupunktwerk: Schon 1968 Arbeit für über 1000," in *Ruhr-Nachrichten*, November 10, 1967; "Produktionsausweitung erfordert mehr als 1000 neue Arbeitsplätze," in *Ruhr-Nachrichten*, June 12, 1970; "1000 Mitarbeiter bei Blaupunkt," in *Westfälische Rundschau*, February 12, 1968; "Stadtväter lockten Weltfirma an," in *Westfälische Rundschau*, November 10, 1967.
29. Hoff, *Die Entwicklung der Wirtschafts*, p. 21, 43, 58.
30. Hartmut Häußermann and Walter Siebel, Dienstleistungsgesellschaften (Frankfurt am Main; Suhrkamp, 1995).
31. On the development of the service sector in the postwar Ruhr area, see Dietmar Petzina, "Wirtschaft und Arbeit im Ruhrgebiet 1945 bis 1985," in *Das Ruhrgebiet im Industriezeitalter*, ed., Wolfgang Köllmann, vol. 2 (Düsseldorf: Schwann, 1990), 492–567.
32. Still at the beginning of the nineties, it was said that the Ruhr area was around twenty years behind the national average in women's employment. Heike Jacobsen, *Arbeitsmarktsituation von Frauen im Ruhrgebiet. Zum Stand der Frauenerwerbsarbeit in zehn Städten der Montanregion zu Beginn der neunziger Jahre* (Dortmund; Sozialforschungsstelle Dortmund Landesinstitut, 1993), 68.
33. Karin Hertewig, *Das unberechenbare Jahrzehnt. Bergarbeiter und ihre Familien im Ruhrgebiet 1914–1924* (München: Beck, 1993), 213f.; Reiners, Herne 1945–1950, 281.
34. On the expansion of consumption in the West German fifties and sixties, see Michael Wildt, *Am Beginn der "Konsumgesellschaft." Mangelerfahrung, Lebenshaltung, Wohlstandshoffnung in Westdeutschland in den fünfziger Jahren* (Hamburg: Ergebnisse, 1994).
35. Claudia Born, "Das Ei vor Kolumbus. Frauen und Beruf in der Bundesrepublik Deutschland," in *Frauen arbeiten*, ed., Gunilla-Friederike Budde (Göttingen: Vandenhoeck & Ruprecht, 1997), 46–61.
36. Quoted from Gertrud Braun, "Wege zur Bekämpfung der Frauenarbeitslosigkeit aus der Sicht eines Ruhr-Arbeitsamtes," in *Bundesarbeitsblatt* (1953), 342.
37. Ruth Kamphern, *Frauenatlas Ruhrgebiet. Analyse der Lebens- und Arbeitssituation von Frauen im Ruhrgebiet* (Essen: Kommunalverband Ruhrgebiet, 2000), 17.
38. Ursula Röhder-Zang and Susanne Zander, *"Gelernt hab' ich gar nicht groß." Arbeits- und Lebenserfahrungen von Sprockhöveler Bergarbeiterfrauen* (Wuppertal: Forschungsinstitut für Arbeiterbildung, 1994), 28.
39. Hartewig, *Das unberechenbare Jahrzehnt*, 190.
40. Hans Dieter Baroth, *Aber es waren schöne Zeiten* (Köln; Kiepenheuer & Witsch, 1978), 51.
41. On the educational reform, see Christoph Führ and Carl Ludwig Furck, eds., *Handbuch der deutschen Bildungsgeschichte, Vol. 6: 1945 bis zur Gegenwart,*

Erster Teilband: Bundesrepublik Deutschland (München; Beck, 1998); on women's education, see Eva Kolinsky, *Women in Contemporary Germany. Life, Work, and Politics* (Providence/Oxford: Berg, 1989), 100–150.

42. See detailed data, Strukturförderung im Bildungswesen des Landes Nordrhein-Westfalen, ed., *Statistik des Bildungswesens 1950–1985*, 3rd edn. (Köln; Greven & Bechtold, 1987).

43. *Statistische Rundschau NRW*, vol. 32 (1980), 852.

44. Ibid, vol. 24 (1972), 283; vol. 32 (1980), 854.

45. It is said that William II believed that the "arms manufacturer" of the Empire (the Ruhr area) needed no higher educational institution.

46. Kamphern, *Frauenatlas Ruhrgebiet*, 18.

47. Werner Voss, Rolf Meyer, and Immo Rausch, *Bericht zur sozialen Lage der Studenten an der Ruhr Universität Bochum*, 2 edn. (Bochum: Brockmeyer, 1978), 36.

48. Quoted from; Anne Schlüter, "Arbeitertochter des Ruhrgebiets im Studium. Naturwissenschafts- und Technikkompetenzen und sozialer Aufstieg—oder: 'Obwohl Papa Schlosser war, haben wir Kinder studiert!.' Eine Exploration," in *Arbeitertöchter und ihr sozialer Aufstieg. Zum Verhältnis von Klasse, Geschlecht und sozialer Mobilität*, ed. A. Schlüter (Weinheim; 1992), 82–123, at p. 101.

49. *Statistische Rundschau NRW*, vol. 25 (1973), 253–257.

50. Ibid., vol. 32 (1980), 854.

51. Jürgen Strauss, *Strukturen und Entwicklungen der Ausbildung und Beschäftigung junger Frauen in Nordrhein-Westfalen: Gutachten des Landesinstituts Sozialforschungsstelle Dortmund* (Düsseldorf; Minister für Arbeit, Gesundheit u. Soziales d. Landes Nordrhein-Westfalen, 1985), 29.

52. Ibid.,1, and 115.

53. Ibid,. 4.

54. See, Kolinsky, *Women in Contemporary Germany*.

55. On the theory of continuity in the Ruhr area through the war, see Lutz Niethammer, "Privat-Wirtschaft. Erinnerungsfragmente einer anderen Umerziehung," in *"Hinterher merkt man, dass es richtig war, dass es schiefgegangen ist." Nachkriegs-Erfahrungen im Ruhrgebiet*, ed., L. Niethammer (Berlin, Bonn: Dietz, 1983), 17–105, at 54.

56. Josef Mooser, "Arbeiter, Angestellte und Frauen in der nivellierten Mittelstandsgesellschaft' Thesen," in *Modernisierung im Wiederaufbau. Die westdeutsche Gesellschaft der 50er Jahre*, ed., A. Schildt and A. Sywottek (Bonn: Dietz, 1998), 362–376.

57. Wildt, *Am Beginn der Konsumgesellschaft*, 392.

58. Between 1958–1970, e.g., the number of cars jumped by 413% in the Ruhr cities, e.g. Bochum, Herne, Castrop-Rauxel, Recklinghausen, and Wanne-Eickel. "Kraftfahrzeugbestand 1958–1964–1968–1970 in Herne und seinen Nachbarstädten," *Herne in Zahlen* (1970): 52–53.

59. Quoted from Max von der Grün, *Irrlicht und Feuer*, 5th edn. (Hamburg: Rohwolt, 1967: first edition in 1963), 53.

60. The figure excludes women engaged in the family business. Müller, Willms and Handl, *Strukturwandel*, p. 35.

61. A recent study on the theme is Christine von Oertzen, *Teilzeitarbeit und die Lust zum Zuverdienen. Geschlechter-politik und gesellschaftlicher Wandel in Westdeutschland 1948–1969* (Göttingen: Vandenhoeck & Ruprecht, 1999).

62. See e.g., *Statistisches Jahrbuch der Stadt Bochum*, 1959–1970.
63. *Statistisches Jahrbuch für das vereinte Deutschland* (1991), 76.
64. Jacobsen, *Arbeitsmarktsituation*, 24.
65. These statistics are available from 1963. See, "Mitglieder und Familienangehörige/Familienkoeffizient je 100," Dezernat V.1.6–7211/7279, Bundesknappschaft.
66. Jong, *Kinder, Küche, Kohle* 88.
67. Ibid., 89.
68. See, for a case study in West Germany, Herman Schubnell, *Der Geburtenrückgang in der Bundesrepublik Deutschland. Die Entwicklung der Erwerbstätigkeit von Frauen und Müttern.* Schriftenreihe des Bundesministers für Jugend, Familie und Gesundheit, vol. 6 (Stuttgart Kohlhammer, 1973)
69. See, Jutta de Jong, "Zur Dialektik von männlicher Arbeitswelt und weiblicher Alltagskultur am Beispiel von Bergarbeiterfamilien," *Arbeit und Kultur*, vol. 7 (1988): 108–113; Jutta de Jong, "Sklavin' oder, Hausdrache'? Frauen in Bergarbeiterfamilien," in *Eine Partei in ihrer Region. Zur Geschichte der SPD in westlichen Westfalen*, ed., Bernd Faulenbach and Günther Högl (Essen: Klartext, 1988), 45–50.
70. Quoted from Jong, *Kinder, Küche, Kohle*, 116.
71. Quoted from Stadt Recklinghausen, ed., *Hochlarmarker Lesebuch, Kohle war nicht alles. 100 Jahre Ruhrgebietsgeschichte* (Oberhausen: Asso Verlag, 1981), 294.

CHAPTER 14

Women into Mining Jobs at Inco: Challenging the Gender Division of Labor

Jennifer Keck and Mary Powell

INTRODUCTION

In 1974 Sue Benoit was a single mother with a five-year-old daughter living in Levack, a small mining community outside Sudbury, Ontario. After leaving an abusive marriage she was living with her parents and working as a cashier at the local grocery store. She worked long hours for low pay: "That was rough because the total pay to take home was seventy dollars a week and I had to pay $25 for the babysitter and $25 for rent. You'd have to be there at eight and the store didn't close until six and then you'd usually have to balance the tills . . . by the time you got home it was seven o'clock. It was hard, really hard with a baby." When she heard that Inco was hiring women for the blue-collar jobs at the Levack mill for the first time since World War II, "it was just like heaven."

It was an historic occasion when Benoit and other women were hired as hourly workers at Inco in the 1970s because they were the first women to enter as full-time, permanent workers. But they did not set out to be pioneers; these women took newly opened jobs at Inco for ordinary reasons—better pay, benefits, and job security. Their experience became extraordinary because they entered a male-dominated workplace and, consciously or not, challenged the sex/gender division of labor. By hiring on at Inco, the women were confronting powerful ideologies of masculinity and femininity on the shop floor, at home, and in the community. This chapter focuses on the women's experiences during their first decade on the job: getting hired, adapting to male work culture, and being "men" at work and "women" at home.[1]

Blue Collar Jobs and Mining in Sudbury

Inco (formerly the International Nickel Company) is in many ways typical of companies that dominate the mining industry in Canada: it is old (its Sudbury works were established in 1902), with a largely unskilled, well-paid labor force. Historically, the combination of single industry dominance, high wages, and dangerous work contributed to Sudbury's image as a "man's town." For decades, Sudbury was also a "company town" with management living in the town of Copper Cliff (now a part of Sudbury) and the workforce living in Sudbury or in the cluster of villages (also company towns) on the edge of the Sudbury Basin.[2]

Inco's share of the market has diminished considerably in recent years, but it remains the world's second largest supplier of nickel, accounting for about 20 percent of the global supply. The mining, milling, smelting, and refining complex in Sudbury is the largest in Canada and one of the largest in the world; when women were hired in the mid-1970s, it was one of the largest industrial sites in the country, employing between 14,000 and 16,000 hourly rated workers. Falconbridge, the second largest employer in Sudbury, had a smaller mining workforce but with wages competitive with Inco's.

Male domination in the mining industry reflected social convention and the historical hiring practices of mining companies in Canada. What was conventional elsewhere was compulsory in Ontario: the first *Ontario Mining Act* in 1890 prohibited female employment in mining. Amendments to the legislation in 1912 and 1913 allowed companies to hire women in a "technical, clerical or domestic capacity"[3] but still barred them from any mining work. During the World War II labor shortage, a temporary order allowed women to work at surface jobs (in groups, each supervised by a matron), but the order was rescinded as soon as the war ended to ensure that the jobs were open for men returning from military service.

During the 1970s, however, Inco and the wider mining industry faced significant changes. Increased international competition, attractive overseas mining opportunities, and militancy among its unionized workers in Sudbury, led Inco to invest heavily in new technology.[4] With increased mechanization and automation in the workplace, fewer workers were needed, and physical strength and endurance were less critical for job performance. The company's workforce reached a peak of 18,966 workers in 1971, but at that point employment began a long-term decline.[5] By the end of 1972, the company had reduced its workforce by 3000, mainly through layoffs. The company began rehiring in late 1973 but announced major layoffs again in 1978 and 1982.[6] It was in this context—a temporary expansion in a period of employment decline—that the first women were hired in the postwar period.

A number of factors set the stage for Inco to begin hiring women in the 1970s, including the broad pattern of social change affecting the status of women, the postwar increase in women's labor force participation, changes in the structure of the family, and the emergence of a vigorous second wave women's movement with its demands for economic equality and employment equity. Public policy both reflected and influenced these changes as governments increasingly viewed women as full-time participants in the labor force.[7] In 1970 human rights legislation in Ontario included gender as grounds for discrimination for the first time. Also, that year the Sudbury Women's Business and Professional Association and other groups helped push the government to amend the *Ontario Mining Act* to allow mining companies to hire women for production jobs at surface operations. The amended act removed the prohibition against women working at surface jobs, but there was no immediate reaction to the legislative change.

DECISION MAKING BY PRESS CONFERENCE

Inco's decision to hire women for its hourly rated workforce in Sudbury can be traced to the early months of 1974. On January 23 the *Globe and Mail's* business section reported that several mining companies had begun to hire women as mill workers and truck drivers on surface to address a continuing shortage of male workers in the industry. But in Sudbury a spokesperson for Inco indicated the company planned to recruit 100 men "from district sources."[8] Two days later a local reporter asked Inco's public affairs director in Sudbury to clarify the company's policy on hiring women. In an article that received front-page coverage in the *Sudbury Star*, Don Hoskins announced that he was "all for women." The only reason that women had not been hired at Inco's operations in Sudbury was simple: "they just haven't applied."[9]

The response to the company's "willingness and definite intention" to hire women was described in *The Triangle*, the Inco's in-house publications, as "immediate" and "overwhelming."[10] Within days of the announcement, women began to flood the company with applications. The prospect of women being hired for a "man's job" in mining attracted widespread media coverage as outraged radio talk show hosts debated whether women could do the work and whether they should be allowed to take "men's jobs."

In its public statements the company stressed that it was "business as usual" at its recruitment office. Standard policies applied and female applicants would be "treated exactly as males." Women who were interested in a job would have to meet basic qualifications, pass a medical examination, and undergo established training. If hired they could expect to receive "equal opportunities, equal benefits and equal pay."[11]

"IT WAS GOOD MONEY AND I THOUGHT I COULD DO THE JOB"

Women heard about the jobs from family, friends and the media. While some women thought they would be the only ones interested in such work, they were surprised to find that hundreds of women applied, revealing how desirable these jobs were. In a company town like Sudbury, "getting on at Inco" was a ticket to a good paying job for as long as you could work, and a good pension at the end of it.

It was clear from the outset that women were not expected to apply for laborers' jobs at the employment office. One woman who applied during the first few days recounted that she had to insist on getting an application, when male office employees resisted women's inclusion into "men's" jobs:

> He reached under the counter and threw an application at me . . . I looked at it and it said it was for office work and I gave it back to him and I said no, I don't want to do office work; I want to be a laborer. So anyway, he thought that was a big joke and the whole place burst out laughing and I reminded him that he couldn't refuse me an application. So he reached under the counter and threw another one at me and I filled it out and was called a few weeks later for an interview.

Far from assuming the equality of women and men, the male interviewers at the Inco employment office had strong assumptions about women, their capabilities, and sensibilities. They asked women how they would adapt to conditions in the industry and the masculine work environment, warning "it's dirty work over there." One woman applicant referred to her previous job as a nurse's aide and replied, "Well you know if I can wash men that have poohed and peed themselves, and I can lift men by myself to their geriatric chair I'm pretty sure I can handle any thing you dish out over there. So I guess he was impressed with that because I was hired." Other women were asked how they would react to sexual advances: "One of them asked me what I would do if one of the men in the plant made a pass at me . . . that was such a big deal . . . every other woman that went after was asked that question too . . . I said I'd slug the guy . . . I ended up with the nickname 'slugger.' "

While the interviewers at the employment office were concerned with how the women would adapt to the new work culture, the women—like most of the men standing in line with them—were motivated first and foremost by the prospect of a "good job" at Inco and its promise of better pay, benefits, and job security. At the time, process laborers (the mandatory entry-level job) at Inco earned $3.99 an hour and miners $4.74, while secretaries were paid $2.50, sales clerks $2.39, and waitresses $2.25.[12]

All the women we interviewed stressed how important the pay was: "Like we all went there for the money. I mean nobody in their right mind would go and work in a dirty place like that for nothing. It was good." Many of the women considered this their only option for earning a good wage: "where else would I make this kind of money with a grade ten education?" The prospect of earning a "man's" wage was particularly important for women who were struggling to support themselves and children on women's wages. Of the 26 women we interviewed 18 had children or other dependants to support when they were hired. One recalled how concern for her children motivated her: "I had no idea what it looked like inside of the place. I just knew they paid really good. They paid good money and I had two kids to support and it had all these benefits if the kids get sick." Another woman noted her critical breadwinning role: "I had just asked my husband to leave. I had two sisters and my two kids to support. He was supposed to give me support but he didn't. I had to find a job, a good paying job."

For many of the women, financial security was associated with independence from male partners, creditors, and the state. Several women described how the job at Inco became their "ticket" out of an abusive relationship: "I was scared of him because I used to get beat up every other day . . . so I thought I wanted to get out of here . . . I waited and applied at Inco . . . when I found out I got the job friends helped me move me and the kids out." For others it meant being able to escape the rules and regulations of state assistance: "I was living in a low rental and on Mother's Allowance . . . I didn't want to raise my son there . . . my first check I moved out."

While financial security was the primary motivation, there were other reasons for seeking a blue-collar job at Inco. Some rose to the challenge of going after the best job in town; others thought the work itself might suit them. One woman explained, "I've always been working with Dad when he was working on a car . . . I could change a carburetor by the time I was 14 . . . I taught my husband how to change the brake shoes on our car . . . so I guess I'm mechanically inclined."

All the women hired were from the local area and many of them came from families with ties to Inco that extended back for generations. Often fathers, brothers, uncles and even mothers and grandmothers had worked for the company. Many parents were ambivalent about their daughter's decision to enter a man's job in mining. While some fathers were proud that their daughters were joining them at Inco, others wanted "better" for their children, both male and female: "I have two brothers, and when I was growing up [my father] had always encouraged them to get a university education because he didn't want them to wind up working at Inco, like he did . . . he was also concerned for my safety."

Sometimes, parental concern came from familiarity with the workplace and the response their daughters could anticipate on the shop floor: "My dad thought that this was not a world that I wanted to be in. I think my father knew that some men couldn't get over my being female and that would cause me problems. I don't think he had any doubt in his mind that I was capable of doing the work and that I probably would run into situations." Even mothers who had worked at Inco during World War II expressed their concerns. One woman who had worked at Inco during the war expressed her dismay at her daughter taking a job at Inco: "It was ok when we worked there during the war . . . there were no men for the jobs . . . but mining isn't a place for a woman."

MINING, MASCULINITY, AND WHY WOMEN "DON'T BELONG"

The belief that mining was not for women had several distinct components. Many doubted that women were capable of doing the very physically demanding work. With technological change, brute strength was no longer an essential job requirement, but there was no question that women would have to be strong and physically fit. Another concern was that the workplace itself was not only dirty but also dangerous, requiring constant awareness of and attention to one's physical environment. Without this skill from previous jobs, women were at greater risk. However, all new employees learned how to negotiate a dangerous worksite, and the women learned just as other workers had.

Third, and probably most important, allowing women into mining contravened a long-held belief that mining was men's work and represented an affront to its masculine work culture. As Cockburn, Willis and Luxton point out, the equation of work with masculinity is often an integral part of a large-scale industrial setting where the work involves manual labor and heavy machinery and where the work environment is noisy, dirty, and noxious.[13] The idea that the work is men's work reflects the view that men and women are inherently different and that difference is attributed to biology. The cultural assumption that men are more suited to performing heavy, physical work, and their status as primary wage earners means that they are regarded as having a greater right to high-paying jobs in the industry.[14]

This strong belief in gender difference and male breadwinner privilege, reinforced by the industry, union, and community, immediately confronted the new women recruits. One woman described a lunchroom encounter that revealed the widespread view that Inco jobs were men's by right: "One of the men found out that I took my husband back. He said you got hired on here because you were separated; now you're married. I said, no I did not get hired on here because I was separated. But he got all upset over that. He says, what are you doing in here, you've got a husband to support you." Single mothers were somewhat more acceptable because they were supporting children, but even they found themselves having to defend their breadwinner status: "You could feel the tension in the lunchroom especially . . . the women are taking our jobs away and they're taking food out of my kids' mouths . . . it didn't take very long before I'd say look, I'm a single parent, would you rather see me on mother's allowance and you're supporting me through your taxes or get me working."

Newly hired women found they had to defend their jobs in the community, even among other women who alleged that the women were stealing men's jobs and having sexual affairs with male workers. One woman described her reaction to a radio talk show:

> This guy had his own talk show; the women would call in and the names that we were called. We were going to sleep with their husbands. And I called in one day, and I was just so angry and upset, I had been on welfare, too, with four children and I told them a man can work anywhere in an office . . . and if he's going to run around, he's going to run around.

But as one woman worker observed, this opposition stemmed from a deeper cultural aversion to female heads of households:

> Down the street, believe it or not I've had women call me an Inco whore. And this really ticked me off because before I got hired on at Inco, about a month and a half before they hired me, I had asked for welfare assistance, and then I got called welfare bum. Then when I got on I got called Inco whore and I stopped a woman one time and I told her, you're never satisfied, people like you, you're got nothing better to do with your time than put us down, now I'm working and they thought we took showers with the men.

It is ironic that these latter objections—women are invading a masculine work culture, stealing men's jobs, and may initiate or welcome sexual advances—focus on women as women. Yet as we shall see, the essence of their work was to become like a man.

GETTING STARTED: "YOU GOT DIRTY AND TIRED BUT YOU SHOWERED . . . AND THE PAY WAS GOOD"

Like their male coworkers the women began as process laborers. The work involved shoveling, sweeping, hosing down dirty areas and in some cases painting and unloading supplies. The women responded to the first day with more than the usual apprehension: "You have no idea what to expect . . . when we first walked in we saw these flotation cells and they're all bubbling and it seems like it's really hot, it was very scary . . . walking over the grating and looking down three floors . . . I had never seen this kind of machinery in my life." Another woman described her adjustment to the heavy machinery and the noise, dirt, and smell of an industrial work environment: "In the mill it was really dirty; from the time you walked in you were dirty. Like I got dirty just looking at it. There was a smell of lime, varsol and sometimes when the gas was coming in you'd have to sit in the lunch room. Lots of noise." One woman defined a process laborer as "a technical term for seeing how dirty you could get by the end of the day!"

Despite their initial trepidation, most of the women discovered that their jobs were not difficult to learn. Process laborer was the entry-level classification for all blue-collar jobs and most of the training was on-the-job:

> I'm really pigheaded, I figured they wanted me to shovel, I'll shovel this damn stuff, and there's got to be a knack to everything . . . so one of the foremen came by and I'd ask what am I doing wrong? So he'd say well use your foot, cause if you just used your arms if you start at the top of the pile you just [move] two rocks . . . use your foot to push the shovel underneath.

While their first few weeks were difficult, the first pay check reminded the women why they had taken the job: "I remember my first pay check that I came home with . . . I was making double plus what I was making at my other job . . . I didn't want to cash it right away. I brought it home and showed it to my husband and his eyes went wide. He said 'Wow, we're in good times now, eh baby?' "

A Woman in a Man's Job: "This was Their Place"

The women soon discovered that being treated the same as men meant having to become more "like a man" and adapt to masculine work culture. From the outset the women were sensitive to the fact that this was an exclusionary workplace and many of them initially felt out of place: "Just like you are intruding. Like you are going someplace that where you are not supposed to be. Like wow what am I doing here and these guys how are they going to take it." The company warned the men to adjust their behavior when women joined their work crews, but the situation was tense at first: "It was bad because nobody else would talk, the men were too afraid to talk to the women and we of course were scared . . . we found out later the company had a long talk with the men before we came and warned them about pictures and whatever . . . to make sure they were dressed properly and that nothing was hanging out . . . to urinate in the proper place."

The reception the women received depended a great deal on the reaction of frontline supervisors and the culture of the particular work site. Many supervisors did not want the responsibility of supervising the women because they anticipated that there would be problems, and they had little training or preparation for dealing with the integration of the new workers.[15] One woman recalled one of these reluctant supervisors: "It was a thing that he didn't want. I mean nobody wanted to be in charge of the women, because they didn't want to be, you know, 'hey you're having a good time with those women.' " Others were blunt about their opposition. These were men's jobs; if women were going to take these jobs they would have to prove they could be "men": "He said he didn't want us new four girls; he didn't want women working there at all. He pulled us in the office and told us from this day on you're going to have to prove you're a man." (figure 14.1)

While some men were supportive and helped women adapt, many resented the fact that women were being hired in what was for them a "man's job." Opposition to the women took many forms. Most of the men challenged whether or not women would be able to do the work and there was a constant testing of their abilities. They complained that the women were getting "cushier jobs" and had better dry facilities (shower and change rooms). Other men tried to undermine the women by telling crude jokes, refusing to help train the women, and ostracizing them. There were also more hostile forms of harassment in the form of threats and physical assaults. The situation was particularly tense during layoffs or when their seniority allowed women to compete successfully against men for positions: "One guy with less seniority threatened us with a shovel . . . he was peeved off because we had a month

Figure 14.1 Inco Miners, 1979 (labeled "woman with buddies in mine"). Courtesy of Mercedes Steedman and Jennifer Keck.

more than him and we had the choice of the jobs before he did. And he was a big guy."

Men also used sexual harassment, another reminder that the women were "different," to maintain masculine dominance in the workplace. Harassment took many forms. One woman was assigned extra work shoveling asphalt after she refused the invitation to go to her foreman's summer cottage after work. Another woman described a more threatening situation that involved a shift supervisor and her own courage to resist his advances:

> He would say to me, okay come with me and he would take another guy and bring us to this god-forsaken place where no one's ever going to work there because it's full of dust and much and he'd say, oh, I forgot to get the tools and he'd send the guy down, then he's left alone with me and he'd try rubbing his private area against my knee and I told him, if he appreciates talking in a deep tone he wouldn't ever do it again. But then he tried calling me at home and asking me if I would meet him and I told him I'm not desperate for company and that I don't sleep with a pig.

Men used sexual language to describe working conditions, make jokes, and in the course of everyday conversation, often unconsciously or to provoke, shock, or insult women workers. One woman described frequent verbal assaults that made her feel "like your whole body was insulted . . . it was either your breasts, or like they knew you were separated . . . so it was you're not getting it. I wasn't used to that." Men also posted pornography and pin-ups to claim their male workplace:

> The first thing that went up in the lunch room when we were there were pic-tures of naked women. Well two of us were quite upset. We didn't think that it was appropriate but we were the minority, this was their lunchroom. But two other women came in the next morning with *Playgirl*. Well it didn't take long for the pictures to disappear because the men no more wanted to look at other naked men than we wanted to look.

Male workers delighted in harassing new, vulnerable women. One woman described her first experience in the lunchroom:

> Some guy yelled out, "Hey Shera," and I thought maybe it was one of the gen-tlemen that were teaching us so I turned around to look and this guy yells out, "Do you suck cock?" No one corrected him for it, nothing was said to him, but I didn't leave the lunchroom either. I stood my ground by sitting down and ignored it. But I thought I was going to die. I had tears in my eyes.

Most of the women we interviewed stressed that the more hostile behavior tended to come from individual men, rather than groups of workers, that it did not exist at every site, and that it depended on the reaction of supervisors, whether or not the women were the first at the work site, and the response of individual women to taunts.[16]

Shift Work and the Double Day: "Shift Work means Missing Your Family"

The struggle to be a woman in a man's job extended beyond the shop floor to the women's lives at home. Like other working women—and unlike most of their male coworkers—the women had to balance their paid work at Inco with unpaid labor at home. Many women found their double duty hard on them physically, especially in terms of lost sleep.

> No matter what shift I was on I wouldn't stay in bed all day just because I worked grave yard all night. I had to get up . . . do the laundry . . . make them supper. Then I would get a couple hours sleep before I go to work at night and they were in bed by the time I left. It was just a mad run. It was no easy chore . . . I had to do baking and cooking and cleaning and doing floors. I told the guys they were really lucky all they had to do is go home and eat. I even had to buy the groceries before I could cook.

Shift work presented major problems for women with family responsibili-ties. Continuous production in industrial workplaces is organized around the assumption that workers are male and that their incomes support women who perform unpaid domestic labor. None of the women had enough sen-iority to be eligible for steady day shifts, which meant that they had to work on rotating eight-hour shifts. It took some time to get used to the schedule and women found that it wreaked havoc on their bodies and caretaking responsibilities. One woman described the impact of shift work on family life:

> The 7–7–6 schedule where you work 7 days in a row . . . was a horrendous schedule, it was terrible for families. You never saw your children . . . you had no choice you just had to work, but I mean you saw your family on day shift but on graveyard you slept, or 4–12 was the worst for me, because when I left for work he'd be in school and when I got home he'd be sleeping of course. I'd get up in the morning and he would have gone back to school.

Many of the women felt that they missed out on important events: "You couldn't get them to an arena first thing Saturday morning [to play hockey] . . . and I had to book off sick to make it to my son's first communion."

Securing child care also proved to be an ongoing problem. There was no organized child care available for shift workers in the community. Most of the women relied on informal support from family members or sitters from the neighborhood, but arranging child care could be difficult, especially for single mothers. When there was a breakdown in these arrangements it was difficult to explain the problem at work: "You would be getting ready for work at 11:00 pm and your sitter would not show up. My daughter would be in bed and I would be desperately trying to find someone who could come and look after her. Your foreman would never believe that you didn't show up because you didn't have a sitter." For most of the women, the problem was not just the logistics of getting reliable care, but that they were missing parts of their children's lives. Yet, a job at Inco could provide for their children in a way no other job could.

GETTING ACTIVE IN THE UNION LOCAL

Like most of the men they worked with, the majority of the women were not radical. They were prepared to challenge conventional gender prescriptions to earn a man's wage but few of them considered themselves feminists or were interested in broader political struggles. Still, few women working in USWA Local 6500 were untouched by the militancy of mining work culture and the impact of the women's movement in the 1970s. It was not long before a small number of women emerged who were willing to hold the company—and union—to the original promise that they would be treated the same as men and receive equal treatment and opportunities.

Women became active with the union under much the same conditions as new male workers. They were recruited early, often after complaining about conditions on the shop floor, and put on health and safety committees at the various plants. The first two women union stewards took office in 1975; women were also elected as delegates to the Ontario Federation of Labour convention the following year. While the union gave early support for the women to become active, it assumed women would work on traditional union issues rather than challenge differential treatment based on gender.

A women's committee was formed in 1977 to address this problem. One of the organizers challenged the company and the union in an article that appeared in the union's newsletter, *The Searcher*: "Over the last three years women have had to prove themselves to the company and the union. As women workers we share and support the concerns and struggles of our brothers . . . now we want to be active so we can have a voice in our local . . . that is not our privilege, it is our right."[17]

The strategy of separate organizing based on gender met with mixed reviews from men active in the local. While the committee had the support of the local president and other key activists, many men wondered why women needed a special committee to represent their interests when the union represented the interest of all workers. Even some of the women disagreed with the need for a separate committee. One woman who was involved at the time remembered being accused of being a "women's libber." Activists with the committee remained convinced that there were problems "peculiar to women" that needed to be addressed including maternity rights, child care, job opportunities, company attitudes toward women and the aspects of health relating specifically to women.[18]

The committee tackled maternity leave as one of its first most pressing issues. The women were concerned that pregnant women workers did not receive the same treatment as workers who were injured on the job.[19] Under the collective agreement the company could ask a pregnant employee to go on an unpaid leave of absence at such time as she could not, in the opinion of the company, perform her normal duties. This meant that a woman could be without income for nine or ten months if she were asked to leave early in her pregnancy. This was in sharp contrast to provisions that obliged the company to find alternative employment for workers who were unable to perform their regular jobs owing to age, disease, or occupational injury. In the first few years, the fear of being laid off led a number of women who became pregnant not to tell managers that they were pregnant as long as they could manage to work. The women's committee proposed changing the policy to be more consistent with the policy for injured workers. While the management rejected this proposal during bargaining that year, it marked the first time the union had addressed issues specific to women in negotiations.

The prominence of the women increased dramatically during the 1978–1979 strike. In September 1978, the Steelworkers Local 6500 rejected Inco's latest contract offer, which for the first time demanded concessions from the union and began the longest strike in company history, lasting eight-and-a-half months. At first, the women in the local were assigned to work with the strikers' wives to turn out a daily quota of 800 to 1000 sandwiches in the kitchen at the Steelworkers hall. But many of the women rejected the assignment as traditional women's work and joined their brothers on the picket line. Women also played a prominent role on committees responsible for distributing vouchers, general information, and aid to striking workers and their families.

The strike became a politicizing and empowering experience for many of the activists. One of the women worked on the emergency drug and benefit committee and helped organize the workers in the kitchen. She remembers the first time she went on a speaking tour: "They wanted someone to speak to the University of British Columbia students and another group for International Women's Day . . . I told Harvey [Wyers] that I couldn't do it. I didn't know anyone there . . . here I was from a small town and I'd never done that kind of thing . . . I ended up going there for five weeks." Another activist remembered meeting the president of the local for the first time when she was walked into his office to complain about kitchen duty. He responded by putting her on the committee allocating aid to striking families. She later became the only member of Local 6500 to join the Wives Supporting the Strike Committee. Like many of the women who became active during the strike, she had never spoken in public before. She found her political voice before 500 people in Toronto where she spoke on a panel with some of the wives, about being a woman and a worker on strike at Inco. The strike ended with substantial gains for Local 6500; not only were the concessions dropped, but the union won a significant wage increase, improved cost-of-living benefits, and a stronger pension plan that for the first time included a 30-years-and-out provision.[20]

After a few years on the job, the women had enough experience that they began to challenge gender discrimination on the shop floor with the support of the union's grievance procedure and human rights legislation. Three cases received high profile attention in the media. The first case involved a struggle over washroom facilities. After bidding on a job as conveyor man at the Clarabelle Mill, Shirley Brown was told that she would not get the job despite her qualifications because there were no washroom and dry facilities for women at the mill. Brown had worked with the company since 1974 and had worked at an older mill in Copper Cliff. She wanted the job at Clarabelle because it offered the possibility of being assigned steady day shifts, a priority for Brown who was a single parent. With the support of a grievance officer from the union, Brown launched a complaint with the Ministry of Labour and in 1978 the Ministry ordered the company either to build a dry or to transport Brown, on company time, to the nearest facility with a washroom for women. Brown never did work at the Clarabelle Mill but the company was forced to build washroom facilities and a dry for the women at that plant.[21]

A second case involved two women who filed grievances after the strike in December 1979 because company officials blocked their attempts to transfer to the Cottrell area of the Copper Cliff smelter.[22] Marie Emery and Olive Richer bid on the trainee jobs and qualified on the basis of seniority. They were refused on the grounds that the company did not want men and women to work alone at a remote location. Under pressure from the union and the human rights commission the company reversed its position in January 1980. The smelter manager told the *Sudbury Star* that it had been "past practice not to allow a man and a woman working together without additional supervision . . . However contractually women are entitled to those jobs and we have an obligation."[23]

The third case set an important precedent in the area of reproductive hazards. Laurene Wiens launched a human rights case in 1984 over the company's refusal to let her work at the Nickel Carbonyl Plant in the nickel refinery. Wiens had the necessary seniority and qualifications to bid on a job as an operator at the Nickel Carbonyl Plant, but under a policy endorsed by the company and union, women of child-bearing potential were excluded from work in this section because occasional small leaks of toxic gases could damage the fetus of a woman who was unaware that she was pregnant; in other words, to be eligible any "female [had] to have reached menopause or to be sterile."[24] On the grounds that Wiens was of childbearing age, she was denied the job. In 1988 the Ontario Human Rights Commission ruled that, while Inco had acted in good faith in developing and applying the restrictive policy, the risk of exposure was small. It was up to women to decide whether or not they wanted to take it. The Commission also noted that some rules "protecting" women are "based on sex role stereotypes premising that since women can bear children they will bear children."[25]

CONCLUSION

In many respects the story of the move of women into blue-collar jobs at Inco is a very ordinary one. A new group of workers applied for and were successful in getting jobs that paid them more than they could earn at virtually any other job. With the income from these jobs they were able to support themselves, raise children, buy homes and pay for their children's education. What makes this story significant is that the workers were female and the jobs they applied for were historically male jobs in mining. In going to work at Inco, women like Sue Benoit left the minimum wage non-unionized jobs available to women and moved into the well-paid jobs that had in the past been available only to men.

While they were largely unaware of the struggle they were about to undertake, the women who were hired at Inco during the 1970s ended up confronting the gender division of labor and did so without a local campaign by the union or the women's movement. For them, there were few role models or support systems to help the women make the transition to a male dominated workplace.[26]

The experience of the Inco women underscores that it is the social construction of gender that has kept women out of these jobs. Male domination in mining reflects factors that are historic and structural. Women were excluded from the mining industry as a matter of law beginning in the nineteenth century, a prohibition that remained in place for surface jobs until 1970 and for underground jobs until 1978. Women were hired for the first time mid-decade, but many workers, men and women, lost their jobs during the period of restructuring and downsizing in the 1980s. Because women were among those with least seniority, they were among the first to go.

Finally, the example of the Inco women serves to remind us of the importance of vigilance in challenging the gender division of labor and the occupational segregation it supports. It also stands as a clear example that a masculine work culture will not easily accept women, but it is very much in women's interests to gain access to such jobs because of the pay, benefits, and pension they offer. This is particularly the case in the absence of any government commitment to supporting full employment and the current climate of official distaste for employment equity in Canada.

NOTES

The authors gratefully acknowledge financial support from INORD, USWA (Local 6500 and District 6) and HRDC. We also thank our research advisory committee, our research assistants, and in particular, the women of USWA Local 6500 who opened their homes and their stories to us.

1. This research is part of collaborative project with Women's Committee of USWA Local 6500 to commemorate the 25th anniversary of the women hired in 1974. The project has since expanded to include women in three periods: World War II, the 1970s and the 1990s. This essay is based on a series of in-depth interviews with 26 of the 100 women who were hired between 1974 and 1976, including 17 women who were still with the company in 1998. An earlier version of this paper was presented at *Genderations: Women's Worlds '99*, Tromso, Norway, June 21, 1999.
2. The Sudbury Basin is the geological formation that has pushed metals to the surface and has made mining a profitable industry. Mines (and towns associated with them) are dotted around the edge of the basin.
3. *Statutes of Ontario*, 1890, Chapter 10, S. 4.
4. Inco blue-collar workers have been unionized since 1944, first with the International Union of Mine Mill and Smelter Workers, and later after a bitter struggle between the two unions, with the United Steelworkers of America (USWA) in 1965.
5. In 2004, only 4560 people were employed by Inco in Sudbury. This figure includes management, technical and clerical staff, as well as hourly rated workers at the surface and underground.
6. Employment figures are based on the company's annual reports. See also Jennifer Keck and Mary Powell, "Working at Inco: Women in a Downsizing Male Industry," in *Changing Lives: Women in Northern Ontario*, ed., Marg Kechnie and Marge Reitsma-Street (Toronto: Dundurn Press, 1996), 147–161, and Dieter Buse, "The 1970s," in *Sudbury Rail Town to Regional Capital*, ed., Carl Wallace and Ashley Thompson (Toronto: Dundurn Press, 1993), 242–274.
7. Barbara Cameron, "From Equal Opportunity to Symbolic Equity: Three Decades of Federal Training Policy for Women," in *Rethinking Restructuring: Gender and Change in Canada*, ed., Isa Bakker, (Toronto: University of Toronto Press, 1996), 55–81.
8. Lawrence Welsh, "Mining Executives Claim Labor Shortage now at Critical Stage," "Mines Turning to Women for Work in Operations," *The Globe and Mail*, January 23, 1974, B1.
9. "May welcome women in area mines," *Sudbury Star*, January 25, 1974, A1.
10. "Ladies/First Ladies," *Inco Triangle*, August, 1974.
11. Ibid., "May Welcome Women in Area Mines," *Sudbury Star*, January 25, 1974.

12. Keck and Powell, "Working at Inco," 156.
13. Meg Luxton and June Corman, "Getting to Work: The Challenge of the Women Back into Stelco Campaign," *Labour/le Travail* 28 (Fall 1991): 149–185; Cynthia Cockburn, *Brothers: Male Dominance and Technological Change* (London: Pluto Press, 1983); Paul Willis, "Shop Floor Culture, Masculinity and Wage Form," in *Working Class Culture: Studies in History and Theory*, ed. J. Clarke et al. (London: Hutchison, 1979), 185–198.
14. See the special issue of the *Labour History Review* 69, no. 2 (August 2004), which explores "key features of working-class masculinities . . . in the twentieth century," 129. See also Marat Moore, *Women in the Mine: Stories of Life and Work* (New York: Prentice Hall, 1996).
15. Mick Lowe, "Hard Rock Women," *Financial Post Magazine*, January 1995, 24.
16. Meg Luxton and June Corman make similar observations in their study of workers at Stelco. See *Getting by in Hard Times: Gendered Labour at Home and on the Job* (Toronto: University of Toronto Press, 2001).
17. *The Searcher*, 1977.
18. Ibid.
19. While for some years women have struggled to ensure that pregnancy is not treated as a sickness or illness, in the mid-1970s the conceptual model for remuneration during health-related inability to perform regular work was the ill or injured worker.
20. The local went out on strike with the support of 58% of the membership. After 8 months on strike, the membership voted 65% to reject an offer with some improvements and no concessions. Two weeks later, the company agreed to a proposed settlement with significant improvements over the earlier offer.
21. "Jobs shut to women at Levack," *The Sudbury Star*, July 10, 1978.
22. The cottrells are huge vessels that accumulate dust and gases from the furnaces that lead to the superstack. The Cottrell jobs were "cleaner" and paid a higher rate than the women's regular jobs.
23. Tony Van Alphen, "Moms Work in Smelter following lengthy struggle," *The Sudbury Star*, January 25, 1980.
24. Lorne Slotnick, "Barring women from refinery illegal, Inco told," *The Globe and Mail*, March 7, 1988, A1.
25. Ibid., A2.
26. Educational programs promoting the move into nontraditional jobs did not emerge in Canadian cities until the late 1970s. See Luxton and Corman, "Getting to Work," 149–185.

CHAPTER 15

From Ludlow to Camp Solidarity: Women, Men, and Cultures of Solidarity in U.S. Coal Communities, 1912–1990

Camille Guerin-Gonzales

VISITING CAMP SOLIDARITY

Fifteen years ago, I joined a caravan of union supporters and students of labor who descended on a working-class community in Appalachia.[1] In 1989–1990, this community became a gathering place for thousands of coal miners and their supporters from around the world. Over 50,000 people visited Camp Solidarity during a year-long strike against the Pittston Coal Group. In a tent and trailer village established by striking miners and their allies in the Appalachian Mountains near Castlewood, Virginia, supporters gathered to give one another assistance, share information, and strategize. Some came to learn more about the strike and to see for themselves whether news reports concerning the struggle were accurate. Most came because they believed that the outcome of the strike against Pittston would determine the fate of labor unions—and laboring people—in the United States. Many union members and supporters, as well as labor commentators, were convinced that, should the coal miners fail, employers across the nation would use the Pittston Coal Group's actions before and during the strike as a model for transforming their own relations with workers—ultimately bringing about the end of organized labor in the United States.

When striking coal miners and their supporters christened their tent and trailer village Camp Solidarity, they exposed the glue that held this unlikely community together. The struggle with Pittston arose out of a culture of solidarity that stood like a stately tree, its wide branches reflecting its broad contemporary reach and its massive trunk indicating its deep historical roots. In this essay, I first examine the contours of the culture of solidarity during the Pittston strike, and then some of the early twentieth-century coalfield labor struggles that served as both precursors of and historical touchstones for Camp Solidarity.[2] I am especially interested in how women have negotiated and helped to create cultures of solidarity in mining communities, although this is not my exclusive focus. Indeed, in coal communities, gender has been so profoundly embedded in other economic and social relations that an exclusive emphasis either on women or on gender more broadly defined would preclude a full assessment of how coalfield cultures of solidarity developed in the twentieth century. Still, no assessment of such cultures would be complete without a consideration of women's participation, in particular, and gendered matters more generally. Camp Solidarity included both women and men, and it reflected a long history of gender relations in coal communities.

Working people from nearly every industry in the country passed through Camp Solidarity at one time or another. Steelworkers, flight attendants, auto workers, teamsters, garment workers, printers, railroad workers, and coal miners from all over the world converged at the site. They were joined by union supporters and activists, including students, teachers, and members of religious groups, as well as by reporters, photographers, and others interested in bearing witness to the conflict between Pittston and the United Mine Workers of America (UMWA). Many remained in the camp overnight and shared meals, conversation, and music with striking miners and their friends and families. Of these, a good number stayed on—for days, weeks, and even months—helping to build and maintain this new community of working people dedicated to defending both the striking miners and the hard-fought gains achieved by organized labor over the last hundred years.

At Camp Solidarity, worlds of difference came together as coal miners from Russia, Poland, Australia, the United Kingdom, Belgium, and South Africa joined miners from every coal-producing region in the United States. Women miners from the United States shared stories about working underground with miners from countries that prohibited women in the mines. Men, too, swapped tales about their lives as miners, finding some surprising differences in their experiences. Miners from the Soviet Bloc—Poland in particular—remarked at the abysmal working conditions they discovered in some Appalachian mines and compared them unfavorably with those in their own countries, though the men also noted that most Appalachian mines were far superior to those in eastern Europe.[3]

Although coal miners discovered much that was strange in one another's experiences, they met on what they saw as common ground at Camp Solidarity. Here was a place where workers could realize their utopian visions of working-class solidarity. Here too was a place where civil rights advocates could test their assumptions about social justice, where students of labor could witness firsthand a historic confrontation between capital and labor, and where journalists could see for themselves what life was like for coal miners in an increasingly postindustrial society. Women miners from around the world joined their sisters and brothers in Camp Solidarity not only to demonstrate their support for the strike but to become part of a community—to experience solidarity in a place created by and for working people.[4] Religious leaders came and stayed to offer solace as well as support and, in doing so, became members of the Camp Solidarity collectivity.

For all these participants, Camp Solidarity was a place where they could join together to celebrate commonalities. For some, however, the camp was a place of uneasy truce. For others it was a place where romantic notions of egalitarianism and democratic unity hid deep racial and gender tensions. Women miners and their male counterparts sat together at campfires to ward off the evening chill, ate together in the common dining hall, and stood side by side at rallies and protests. Their public unity belied women miners' ongoing struggle for acceptance and legitimacy in an industry long dominated by men. Men and women miners' public expressions of solidarity that ignored gender distinctions contrasted sharply with other public expressions that celebrated customary gender differences—and supported and perpetuated differences among women in coal mining communities. For example, the communal meals in Camp Solidarity's dining hall were served by male miners' wives, daughters, mothers, and sisters—women who did not work in the mines. The long serving counter behind which such women worked was as much a symbolic as a physical barrier between these women and those who worked underground with their husbands, sons, fathers, and brothers.

No such physical or symbolic barrier signaled racial divisions at Camp Solidarity, but divisions did exist. Although the small number of African American and Latina/o miners and supporters who visited Camp Solidarity ate alongside their brothers and sisters and joined them in fireside songfests and union rallies, such expressions of solidarity did not extend to the mining communities outside the camp. Only a few blacks worked in the Pittston mines, alongside an even smaller number of self-identified Latina/o miners. A UMWA film publicizing the strike played on racial fears and stereotypes by assigning tall, physically imposing African American actors to play the roles of state police supporting the Pittston Company. African Americans in Castlewood lived in a segregated neighborhood that white miners called "Nigger Town." Black people were present in white miners' neighborhoods as gardeners and domestic workers, but they were also symbolically present in the blackface lawn jockeys decorating some white miners' front yards and the "Aunt Jemima" cookie jars in many mining family kitchens. Latinos/as occupied a similar place in the Appalachian coal communities. Although Latinos and Latinas had migrated to the region decades before to work in the mines, most were sojourners, working and living in Appalachia for a period of months or years and either returning home—to northern New Mexico–southern Colorado or to Mexico—or moving on to other mining regions. But some remained. Most of them married into white Appalachian families and subordinated their ethnic and cultural identities to those of white Appalachia—if they were able to pass for white. Others employed the strategy of emphasizing their European ancestry, becoming "Spanish" in the hope of tempering racial discrimination against them. Some of these joined Spanish American communities that had been established by immigrant miners from Asturias, Spain, in the early years of the twentieth century.[5] Still others lived in segregated neighborhoods alongside African Americans.

Racial tensions complicated the public performance of unity and solidarity during the Pittston Strike, as did conflicts over gender. Behind the scenes of working-class harmony, on the stage that was Camp Solidarity, residents of long-standing coal communities engaged in contests over how community membership would be defined—over the definition and composition of coal communities. Ultimately the struggle was one over working-class identity, over citizenship in a working-class community, and over access to working-class places. For many, Camp Solidarity was less a common ground, upon which similarities overshadowed differences, than it was a middle ground—a place where common cause operated to mediate power differences between women and men and among different racial groups—a process that was always in flux and never completed.[6]

Uniting the disparate groups that came together at Camp Solidarity was a belief that the economic survival of working people and their right to live with dignity depended on forming alliances around shared class interests and playing down racial and gender differences. Pittston miners seemed genuinely puzzled when questioned about race-baiting in the UMWA publicity film and the residential segregation of blacks. Some state police were, in fact, black, they explained, and black residents lived in "Nigger Town" by choice. They pointed out that class, not race or gender, determined access to camp resources, inclusion in camp functions, and eligibility for respect from others in the camp. Those who had no claim to the working class but offered their support were welcome, too, but their presence was conditional on the goodwill of those who had legitimate working-class credentials. Coal miners shared an understanding of the working class that embraced those who earned wages for their labor, those whose income placed them among the lowest paid of employees, and those who had little or no direct, individual power over their working lives. Included in this definition were professionals, such as teachers and university professors, whose eroding social status and power over their work placed them in a class borderland of late capitalism, presenting them with the possibility of claiming legitimate alliance with other wage workers. Indeed, the mechanization of many aspects of coal mining and agreements entered into by unions and management in the industry had resulted in a highly-specialized, highly-paid workforce that was difficult to replace. As a consequence, the experiences of some professionals, whose social and economic position had deteriorated, and those of some coal miners, who enjoyed greater social and economic power than their predecessors, had become, by 1989, more similar. Rather than demonstrating a blurring of class lines, these similarities heralded a widening of boundaries between classes that created a borderland where class alliances and identities could be reconfigured to meet new relations of production and reproduction. The vision that united the inhabitants of Camp Solidarity was one that invited wage workers to come together in solidarity and that offered a conditional welcome to those who could further the cause of the striking miners and of the working class in general. In addition, as the presence of supporters from around the world indicates, both citizenship and ties to place were global in scope, rather than limited to an individual nation.[7] Thus, working people at the camp belonged to an international labor community, the borders of which were class-determined, utopian, and imaginary.[8]

CULTURES OF SOLIDARITY

The utopian impulse that inspired the formation of a working-class community at Camp Solidarity and sustained it during the strike drew on a long heritage of class struggle and a strong belief in the intransigence of class divisions. This was not a middle ground in the sense that those with opposing class interests negotiated how they were to live together. Coal operators and their allies were neither welcome nor tolerated at the camp. And it was not the common ground for which the Pittston Coal Group called in its appeal to the striking miners to turn away from class interests and toward a different kind of community based on a shared cultural heritage and on residential ties—an admonition to striking miners to privilege racial solidarity over class unity. Michael Odom, Pittston Coal Group Chief Executive Officer, sought to situate the miners' union outside the community—thereby challenging the legitimacy of Camp Solidarity—by appealing to a particular construction of place, Appalachia, rooted in ideas about who could or could not claim legitimate ties to the region. He wrote: "From their national perspective, the UMWA leaders must find a common ground with all of us because this region—and its communities—is our home. This is where we wish to work and to prosper in the years ahead."[9] From the title of its counterproposal to union demands—A Common Ground Pact—to the repeated invocation of the term in official correspondence, Pittston operators sought to claim both symbol and place by appropriating the term as a company slogan that represented an alternative collectivity based on regional and kinship ties. Odom wrote:

> Those of us who live here in the southern Appalachian coal fields must go to work to see that solutions are found, that a *common ground* is reached so that we can grasp firmly these opportunities for community growth, expanded employment, and economic health for our families. All of us must find the will and wisdom to work together because when all the shouting and arguing is finished, we shall still be here living and working together.[10]

At issue for operators and miners alike was how "we" would be defined and how a community that encompassed a whole way of life, a "structure of feeling," might be expanded.[11]

Camp Solidarity became a battleground for contests between coal miners and operators over definitions of citizenship and community, and ultimately over power and how it would be deployed to legitimize economic relations. Striking miners and their supporters worked to create a culture of solidarity founded on shared class interests that crossed boundaries of region, race, gender, ethnicity, and nation. Mine owners and operators, for their part, turned this strategy on its head in their efforts to create a community of supporters whose sense of place and identity rested on shared racial, ethnic, and national bonds. They viewed Camp Solidarity as a hotbed of radicalism and a haven for "outside agitators." Meanwhile, striking miners and their allies celebrated Camp Solidarity as a utopian village dedicated to social change that drew its strength from both the commonalities and the differences among working-class people from around the globe.

How was it that, at a time when deindustrialization had transformed the landscape of production and eroded the power of organized labor, striking Pittston miners and their supporters were able to tap into a reservoir of shared ideals and values about the meaning of work in an industrial capitalist society?[12] How was it that Camp Solidarity could become a symbol of possibility—a "dreaming and acting out of new kinds of social solidarity" that drew on older notions of oppositional class relations untroubled by boundaries of race, gender, and nation?[13] How was it that coal miners generated such an outpouring of support not only from workers in every major industry but also from those not customarily associated with the working class—students, professionals, and religious leaders? And how was it that a strike in this particular industry, coal mining, galvanized organized labor around the world and became the bellwether of the labor movement in the United States? An understanding of the material and cultural repertoire upon which the Pittston miners and their supporters drew can help answer these questions and, in the process, begin to untangle the complex social, cultural, and economic relations that give rise to new cultures of solidarity and shape their expressive forms.

MATERIAL BASES FOR SOLIDARITY

Coal miners in Appalachia tapped a long history of conflict in devising effective strategies with which to defend themselves. The greatest number of worker protests and the most violent strikes in the United States took place in coal mining communities during the early twentieth century. The reason for these protests lies in the nature of coal production and in the cultural relations that developed among miners and between miners and mine owners. For example, the quality, location, and geography of coal deposits, as well as the unpredictability of demand for coal given the vagaries of climate, limited the ability of mine owners to systematize and mechanize production. Similarly, the coal industry's tendency to expand production quickly in response to high consumer demand coupled with its resistance to reducing production during periods of low demand thwarted industry efforts to control production and contain competition. The relatively low capital required to begin mining operations meant that many new mines opened in response to increased consumer demand. When demand decreased, however, mine owners were loath to shut down mines or reduce production.[14] Instead, they lowered prices. Since their capital outlay for equipment and other material necessary for coal production remained fixed, they turned to their expenditures for labor to reduce costs and lowered miners' wages. One consequence of this peculiar character of coal production was that pressure on wages remained high during times of both high and low consumer demand. Competition among coal producers increased during periods of high consumer demand, resulting in pressure to reduce costs in order to remain competitive, and reducing miners' wages was the surest way to cut costs. Miners were caught between a rock and a hard place.

Coal mining requires a high skill level and a working knowledge of geology and engineering. It is dangerous labor. Both miners who worked for extended periods of time underground and residents of coal mining communities, even those who did not enter the mines, could expect to develop one or more respiratory diseases from breathing the coal dust that blanketed both the mines and nearby towns. In addition, miners were vulnerable to cave-ins, drowning, falling rock, malfunctioning equipment, lack of oxygen, exhaustion, and explosions—caused either by the build up of dangerous gasses emitted by minerals and decaying matter or by faulty blasting techniques or materials. One of the most effective strategies miners developed to protect themselves was to work in pairs. Survival often depended on the reliability and skill of one's partner. As a result, miners formed close bonds with one another, and often members of the same family teamed together to work in the mines. But miners learned quickly that their knowledge and expertise and the great risks they took would not guarantee them a living wage and protection from the dangers of mining. Not surprisingly in the face of the unrelenting pressure on wages, the dangerous nature of mining, and the strong bonds that miners developed with one another, coal miners came to form the most militant, tight-knit labor force of all industrial workers in the nineteenth and twentieth century.[15]

GENDER AND MINING LABOR

The self-image that coal miners came to adopt was one that reified male gender. It was also grounded in ideas about whiteness and blackness. Coal miners constructed their masculinity through a rhetoric that assigned dignity to hard work and dependability.[16] Theirs was a male world in the mines, where physical strength provided the last defense against injury and death. In the United States, the widely shared notion that it was bad luck for a woman to be in a coal mine was coupled with the belief that women's sexual purity had to be protected from contamination by unsupervised contact with men in the mines. Further, many believed that white women should not be allowed in mines where they would be dirtied by coal dust and where they would be transformed into "black" workers. White men, according to this argument, could be temporarily blackened because they had the physical strength to defend their racial honor. As long as white women remained above ground in their homes, men could protect their sexual and racial honor. Once women left their homes to work underground, however, they entered a public space where both their racial and sexual honor were at risk. Those opposed to women working in mines argued that women's sexual purity would be tainted if they spent long hours underground with men. Thus "blackness" takes on ironic and contradictory meanings in the context of coal mining communities, where racialized class identities were always at issue but also always in flux. The word "black" conjures up images of miners and their communities blanketed with coal dust, which turned everyone "black." It also refers to the relative purity of grades of coal. These multiple and conflicted meanings had particular resonance for women in coal towns, where racialized meanings of "black" and associations of "blackness" with filth came together to invoke the sexual purity of its opposite, "whiteness." In Europe, British legislation passed in 1842 had excluded women from underground mining for these same reasons. And in 1874 women were barred from working underground in French mines. Although similar legislation was never enacted in the United States, the idea that it was bad luck for a woman to be in a mine and the notion that women had to be protected not only from men in general but, in particular, from the supposed hypersexuality of black men who worked in the mines, resulted in women's de facto exclusion from mine work.

These ideas obscured the long history of women who had worked both openly and surreptitiously in mines. And they contributed to the mystification of mining as an inherently male enterprise. Women worked alongside men in coal mines during the industrial revolution in Great Britain, Japan, France, China, India, and the United States.[17] This is not to say that they held an equal position in the work force. Often these female miners, many of whom were young girls, worked with other family members under the direction of male heads of households. Images that circulated in popular culture reinforced gender relations that subordinated women. For example, in the nineteenth century, Emil Zola's widely read *Germinal* critiqued the social relations of capitalist industrial production by demonstrating that the exploitation of French women and children who were miners undermined the social fabric of a patriarchal society responsible for the well-being of its weakest members—women and children.[18] In Britain, photographs depicting Welsh "pit girls," women who worked above ground at mining pits after the passage of legislation banning them from underground work, became the rage among middle-class men who found such images erotic. "Pit girls," blackened by coal dust, dressed in "mannish" clothing, and engaged in work gendered male, transgressed both racial and gender norms. The seductive value of the photographs lay in their presentation of white women in blackface, wearing men's clothing, who made themselves sexually available by venturing into male spaces.[19] As these European representations suggest, the presence of women in and around coal mines provoked strong cultural reactions.

"YOU HAVE TO HAVE SPUNK TO WORK IN A MINE": U.S. MINING WOMEN

In the United States, women were absent from most representations of mining. Yet they played an important role in the development of the coal industry. They mined alongside men and they worked in their own mines. Audrey Smith Hawkins, for example, began working in a coal mine when she was nineteen, shortly after she married a miner. She and her husband first leased and later, in 1936, bought a mine in Badgersburg, Ohio. Hawkins found she needed to learn a wide range of skills, since the enterprise was relatively small: "I've cut coal, shot coal, load[ed] coal, run the loader, and delivered coal in a truck." Her work was both physically demanding and dangerous—as well as exciting. In 1982, she told an interviewer, "I should have been a boy. . . . It was interesting for me to go twelve or fourteen miles in there [to mine]." She and her husband used a cutting machine, which, if operated improperly, could cause serious injuries:

> First, you have to cut the coal, dig out and under, then you would have to draw a hole and tamp that with powder, let the shot and we'd go in another room. [After the explosion had loosened the coal,] then we'd shovel it and had a horse that pulled it out in a car. Back then they didn't have motors like they do today. Then we'd load the car. You'd have to push the cars out to where the pony was. . . . It was heavy, heavy work.

Hawkins left mining briefly in 1943, when she joined the military and worked in a motor pool as a mechanic. Mining prepared her for military life: "the motor pool girls were supposed to be rough and tough." She fit right in.[20]

Alice Crawford, who began working underground in Pennsylvania coal mines when she was thirteen years old, in 1936, was equally "rough and tough." Once, after she had worked in the mines for a few years, a supervisor "got a little funny" with her, and she "cracked him in the head with a paperweight [and] knocked him out." A cousin introduced her to mining. By her own assessment, she "was just so damn stubborn" that she "didn't care what it was like [in the mines]. I was never afraid." She dressed in men's clothing: "I took some of my cousin's clothes and wore them in," she told Marat Moore, a writer and editor for the *United Mine Workers Journal*, even though "they were a little big." From afar, she and her male partner looked like any other pair of men working together. The cousin who gave her his clothing to wear taught her the skills she would need to be productive and stay alive. Crawford was the only woman working in the mine at the time. The supervisor in charge when she first began mining respected and protected her:

> The boss always called me his daughter. I didn't know him before, just my cousin. But he'd say, "That's my daughter back there." Nobody never said nothing to me. When I first went up there, he said, "Hello, little girl. . . . What are you gonna do?" I said, "Gonna work in the mine." And he never said a word, just stood there and looked at me. And I went in every day my cousin went in.

She loved mining: "I just took a liking to it. You have to have spunk to work in a mine—nerves."

Crawford worked among neighbors and friends who watched out for her. Although only thirteen, she "made pit cuts and used the auger. You had to take and drill your holes back in the ground so far," she explained, "then put your powder in and your squibs, then when you light that fuse you'd have to run." "I'd outwork some of the men," she recalled. She earned the respect of supervisors and her fellow miners: "One of the bosses would say to one of the men, 'How come that woman's doin' more than you're doin'? Why don't you go over there and help her?' And the man would say, 'Why that's her job.'" After she married, she continued mining and assumed responsibility for the household, too:

> I'd get up early in the morning, about 4:30 or 5:00, and do my milkin'. Then I'd go to the mines and be down there at 8:00. Go in and work 'til 5:00. Go home and do my work: milkin' and feedin' [the family] and get a bite to eat. Then I'd go back and make my pit cut for the next morning. I'd get out of there about 11:30 or 12:00. I'd not get much sleep. I needed it but I didn't take it. I was always healthy.

Crawford continued mining into her fifties. She became a celebrity of sorts in her later years and expressed interest in participating in the coal heritage festivals that honored miners: "They tell me they want me to be in one of those parades . . . in the Coal Festival. If I had me an open truck, I'd have some coal on there, and my tools, and my light. Be sittin' on the load of coal."[21]

Many other young women became coal miners while in their early teens. Billy Hepler began mining in 1931 near Dawson, Pennsylvania, at the age of twelve or thirteen. She continued to attend high school, and worked after school and on Saturdays. "We'd get home from school, and I'd go in around four o'clock. I'd get my pick and shovel and go on over to the mine." She worked alongside her father. "There was nobody working the mine but me and Daddy. I was a tomboy. That's why I got the name Billy! My dad got me out of dishes."[22] Ethel Day Smith, too, began mining at a young age, in Harlan County, Kentucky. She was only fifteen in 1928 when she joined her father and brother in a mine, and she continued working with her father even after she married. She reported that her father had never treated her differently because she was a girl: "My dad never said anything special to me about being a girl. He'd just say, 'Let's go, children.'" Smith never questioned working in a mine or using dangerous materials like dynamite: "my dad had worked us children at so much, at so many hard things, that it just seemed like another job to me."[23]

These women gained expertise as coal miners during the Depression of the 1930s. By the end of the decade, when men began leaving the mines just as coal production increased dramatically to meet wartime demands, women constituted a skilled, experienced source of labor. Few mining companies, however, hired women openly. The UMWA fought hard against women joining the ranks of coal miners. Consequently, most women miners worked in the shadows of the industry, where their contributions went unnoted. They continued to work in small mines alongside family members, in their own mines, or in mines where supervisors turned a blind eye to their presence or where they were able to pass as men by wearing men's clothing. Yet there were exceptions to this rule. One was Ethel McCuiston, who started mining as a young wife in 1939. She began helping her husband, who worked for a large mining company in Benham, Kentucky, by preparing boxed lunches for miners and delivering them to the mines: "Whenever I'd come over there and find out no one wasn't helping my husband, I'd get me a lamp with a big ole battery on my hip. I'd climb the deck of the motor, and go hunt my husband up." Although she was afraid to go underground, she overcame her fears: "I thought well, fiddle, there's my husband in there making our living, working for me and the children. I'm not no better than him. I had him to check me in one day." The war buildup was draining the mining work force, and so the mine operator agreed to hire McCuiston, who continued mining for fourteen years.[24] She was not the only one among women who worked for extended periods in coal mines. But she was one of the few hired by large mining operations during World War II to meet the labor shortage.

In one instance, in 1942, the Algoma Coal and Coke Company in West Virginia experimented with a policy of hiring women to replace the young men who had joined the military. The plan originated with the president of the company, William Beury, Jr., who later told reporters that, although initially he had harbored doubts about whether women were capable of working in a coal mine, he was persuaded differently by "reports of our superintendent and tipple foreman [who] have dispelled any thought that they would not be able to do the work."[25] The company hired five women to work as "bone pickers." This task was among the most menial and least prestigious in coal mining. "None of us worked inside the mine," Alice Fulford, one of the miners, explained, and then went on to describe the work of the bone pickers:

> we were in the tipple on the outside, where they brought the coal through. In the mine they would shoot the coal down with dynamite and load it in cars and pull it out with an electric motor car. Then it would come down through the tipple, onto these shaker tables. The table would shake this-a-way, back and forth, and we would pick the bone out of the coal. The bone was the part that wasn't any good. Then the coal went down on through a chute and into the railroad cars at the bottom of the tipple.[26]

Despite the disdain most miners held for this task, men at Algoma Coal & Coke protested the presence of women in the workforce. A UMWA representative visited Alice Fulford and tried to persuade her to quit working for the company: "He said, if I would quit work, he would get my daughter into the movies. She was a real good-looking kid." Fulford declined the offer: "I . . . him I needed work to support my children." Finding that Fulford was more interested in the immediate needs of her family than embracing a fantasy of stardom for her daughter, the union official tried a different approach. He appealed to social norms that relegated women to household labor and defined paid labor outside the home in industries like mining as a male preserve, offering to arrange for her husband to be hired by the coal company—even though her husband had lost one of his legs. The choice for Fulford, given that her reason for working was to provide basic necessities for her family, was clear. She agreed to quit: "The union got my husband a job at the tipple. He wore that artificial leg to work. The union didn't make me quit. They asked me if I would quit if they got him a job, and I told them I would." Fulford could not draw on an organized movement that promoted working women's rights in making her decision. Nevertheless, her brief employment in a large mining company at the same wages paid to men helped pave the way for later generations of mining women.[27]

The experiment with women miners at Algoma Coal & Coke was short-lived. The UMWA threatened a strike if the five women working as bone pickers "were not dismissed and men given employment in their place." Since the women earned the same wages as men, the charge that women depressed wages, usually leveled against women hired in industries dominated by men, had no weight. Instead, the UMWA argued that "the employment of women violated the union agreement because the 'wage classification set out in the contract is for men and not women.'" Under threat of a shutdown of operations while the U.S. Labor Department investigated the allegations, the company acquiesced to UMWA demands. A local paper reported, "Out of work were Mrs. Viola Vickere, 44, mother of five (two of them in the armed forces); Mrs. Alice Fulford, 39, mother of three; Mrs. Minnie Sauders, 53, mother of five; Julia Power, 20, unmarried; and Mrs. Fannie Turner, mother of five."[28] Years later, Alice Fulford told Marat Moore, "After that I worked for the government in a sewing room, making quilts and overalls, and I took in ironing at fifty cents a bushel. I did a lot of housework. The job at the tipple was just another job to me, except that the pay was better."[29]

"No Business at the Tipple": Justifying the Exclusion of Women

The UMWA's actions were part of a well-established pattern of excluding women from coal mines. Audrey Hawkins knew that "people didn't . . . think it was a woman's place to go out and work like that. They would tell me that." Dominick Morelli, who worked at the Algoma mine in 1942, disapproved of the five women hired to sift impurities from coal, though he acknowledged their ability to do the work: "They just didn't have no business at the tipple, and the men started complaining, and they finally got rid of them. It wasn't the hard work. The women could do it."[30] Some women actively resisted such exclusionary attitudes. Alice Crawford described the response of another mining woman, a close friend, to efforts by inspectors to shut down her mine: "She took [the inspector] to court, saying she was going back into the mines, because housework was monkey's work for her. So she fought the case and got to go back in."[31] The exclusion of women from coal mining did not go uncontested.

The widely held belief that it was bad luck for a woman to enter a mine provided a foundation for exclusionary practices. Madge Kelly, who worked at a mine near Rock Springs, Wyoming, in 1945, lamented not being able to go underground: "They would never let us [women miners] go underground. . . . they said it was bad luck for women to go down in a coal mine. . . . they thought there would be an accident, so they never let us go down."[32] Similarly, Alice Crawford recalled, "I heard my brothers and different people say it was bad luck for a woman to be in the mines. I never minded it. I just went in."[33] As Kelly and Crawford's remarks suggest, mining women could both articulate and reject justifications for their exclusion.

Sexual fears and tensions also worked to keep women out of the mines. Some women who worked underground themselves expressed disapproval of women working alongside men in mines. Audrey Smith Hawkins told an interviewer, "I do not believe in a woman going into the mines and working with other men." It was one thing for a woman to work alongside family members and quite another for her to work with men to whom she was not directly related:

> I was with my husband. I wouldn't have thought for one minute about going in there and working with those other men, and him not there. . . . I'd be in the mine, but not in the same place with them. . . . There's plenty of jobs for women outside—secretary and restaurant and things like that. I don't think a woman should go in with other men that are married—now if they were all single, why maybe it would be different. But I don't think a woman should go in and work with other wives' husbands.[34]

Similarly, Dominick Morelli explained that pressure to fire women working at the Algoma mine tipple in 1942 came not only from men but from their wives: "During the war, men had to leave. [The mine owners] had to get anybody they could. . . . The wives were kicking."[35] And, although Ethel Day Smith worked for many years as an underground miner, she reacted strongly to women joining the mining work force in large numbers during the 1970s: "I couldn't believe when [women] started going into the mines. It made me feel funny. It made me feel that the end time is coming closer. The Bible is fulfilling itself every day. It seems like a lot of women are trying to take over." She worried that a woman working with men, unsupervised by a father or brother, posed a threat to a woman's sexual honor: "Now, children, I believe women has to help, and work, because times is hard. But I think you ought to be where a woman could work decent. I just don't believe in going in them big mines with them men."[36] Particularly when it came to issues of sexuality, some women themselves agreed that women were better off if they stayed out of the mines.

THE MULTIPLE BONDS OF MINING WOMANHOOD

For the most part, women in coal communities shared a set of ideas about proper gender behavior. They believed that women's primary responsibility was to provide for their families. They generally accepted the idea of separate spheres of work for men and women; some tasks were appropriate for men and others for women. But there were instances when gender lines could be blurred. Providing for their families took precedence over strict adherence to gender divisions of labor. These mining women led hard lives. They grew up working alongside their parents and were accustomed to taking on a variety of jobs in order to survive. In doing so, many gained a strong sense of their own worth and of their entitlement to a living wage. Many continued to do "men's" work because they could earn higher wages and win greater respect. In the process, these women learned the demands of coal mining. They experienced the hardships, the danger, the excitement, and the camaraderie of working with other highly skilled laborers.

Mining women forged complicated bonds with men and with other women, bonds that were sometimes strained by competing interests. When a woman worked with a man in the mines, each relied upon the other to stay alive and avoid injury. Women miners often earned the respect of male coworkers. But women also challenged the masculine rhetoric of coal communities, a rhetoric that gave meaning to the sacrifices men made to earn a living underground and offered them prestige for risking their lives and damaging their health. The shared experiences of men and women in the mines provided a common ground for alliances across gender lines. At the same time, mining women were part of a community of women, most of whom did not work in mines, but who had intimate knowledge of the demands and risks of mining. Most women in coal communities cooked, cleaned, and made it possible for miners to work. And they worried about the dangers miners faced every day. Most women miners were also responsible for household labor. They understood the conditions of work both in the mines and in mining households. Commonalities of experience nurtured bonds among all women, miners and non-miners alike. At times, these bonds were tested—by jealousy, envy, or competing interests. But they could also be remarkably strong. It was bonds such as these, among women and between women and men, that formed the tendons of cultures of solidarity in coal communities, cultures that found their expression in a series of twentieth-century struggles that culminated at Camp Solidarity in 1989–1990.

CULTURES OF SOLIDARITY IN SOUTHERN COLORADO, 1913–1914

These bonds often extended across regional boundaries, as miners traveled from one region to another in search of work, or as union organizers traveled to publicize the plight of miners and the benefits of union membership. The intertwined experiences of two women in southern Colorado in the 1910s illustrate the forging of such bonds. One of the women, Mary Harris "Mother" Jones, gained a national reputation for her work as a labor organizer, while the other, Helen Krmpotich, was an ordinary member of a coal community. But the actions of both helped to constitute a culture of solidarity in

Colorado. And it is telling that Krmpotich, a lifelong supporter of coal miners and the UMWA, continued to defend the cause of mining labor as late as the 1980s and 90s, when, as a resident of Rock Springs, Wyoming, she collected donations for miners striking against Pittston.

Krmpotich was one of the last survivors of the infamous 1914 Ludlow Massacre in southern Colorado's Huerfano County. Mother Jones visited Colorado in 1913 to help organize a strike of miners, many of them immigrants, against Colorado Fuel and Iron Company (CF&I), owned by John D. Rockefeller, Jr. The miners found in Mother Jones an indefatigable champion of their right to organize. Krmpotich, whose father was a CF&I miner, remembered Mother Jones's visit as a transformative moment:

> She come . . . and [made a] speech for our rights, [telling us] not to go and work for the company for nothing . . . you want your wages and a decent living. . . . We called her Grandma Jones. She was so sweet. . . . I loved her. She was a great work person . . . and she [worked] for people to have better lives. And that's what we worshipped.[37]

Krmpotich remembered Mother Jones visiting: "Grandma Jones used to come all the time . . . to give us clothes and everything." Mother Jones and other UMWA organizers collected clothing, provisions, and the promise of support from coal communities in Appalachia for the miners' struggle in Colorado. As a result, coal miners forged cross-regional bonds.

Conditions for Colorado miners were some of the worst in the nation. They risked dust explosions because of the dry climate and low-moisture content of the coal. Mine operators openly violated state safety laws. Between 1884 and 1912, 1,708 miners died in Colorado mines, most in explosions or as a result of falling rock. Colorado's death rate from 1887 to 1897 was nearly double that of the other coal producing states, and more than twice the national average.[38] In addition, miners earned low wages. When Lamont Montgomery Bowers took over as vice president of CF&I in 1907, he vowed to improve the company's record of low profits, which he suspected stemmed from miners' high wages. He found, however, that low earnings the year before had been caused not by high wages but by graft, waste, and inefficiency in company management. By 1909, he had cut operating expenses by 10 percent. He then set out to increase profits even more by cutting wages.[39] In 1909, he wrote to Rockefeller, "I always regret cutting wages of laborers who have families to support, but considering these foreigners who do not intend to make America their home, and who live like rats in order to save money, I do not feel that we ought to maintain high wages in order to increase their income and shorten their stay in this country."[40] The result was a bonanza for CF&I. Several years later, one of Bower's successors, J.F. Welborn, testified to a congressional commission that CF&I's annual profits between 1909 and 1915 had "averaged close to 20 per cent."[41]

Miners responded by organizing a series of strikes, the largest of which took place in 1913. In turn, CF&I hired a small army of guards and engaged the services of the Baldwin Felts Detective Agency. CF&I guards used firearms freely and shot at anyone they suspected of supporting unionization.[42] The UMWA inaugurated a statewide organizing drive in response. In September, the union held a convention in Trinidad. While the convention was taking place, CF&I began evicting miners from company camps in Huerfano County in preparation for the strike; the company planned to bring in strike-breakers to occupy the miners' residences. Mother Jones spoke to the Colorado miners:

> We have waited a long time boys . . . and now I will tell the Baldwin-Felts guards I shall stay here and we will win just as we did in West Virginia . . . Stand together and don't surrender. . . . You will not be asked to do so by your offi-cers. They will sell the coats on their backs first. I know them. I never knew them to quit. They did a lot for the fight in West Virginia. They have never told me what to do except to say, "Mother, why don't you take a rest?" My answer is, "When I organize Colorado and Alabama, then you can tell me to rest if you want to, but not until."[43]

Miners answered Mother Jones's plea and called a strike for September 23.[44] The UMWA leased land and set up tent colonies for the strikers, who had been evicted from company housing. Nearly 98 percent of the coal miners in southern Colorado joined the strike.[45] Mother Jones visited the camps, and urged the striking miners and their families to persevere.

Helen Krmpotich and her family lived at the company camp of Hastings at the time of the strike and, when they were evicted, they gathered their belongings and walked to the Ludlow tent colony in the pouring rain. Miners and families established their own town council and did their best to regularize life in the colony. They designated a central meeting tent and elected governing officials. They assigned translators so that the 1,200 miners and their families who spoke twenty-four different languages and dialects could communicate. Their shared struggle tied them together, and helped them to accommodate their language and ethnic differences.[46]

Krmpotich's family had a double tent, with a kitchen where the children slept and a bedroom for the parents. Krmpotich's mother gave birth in their tent soon after they moved in. Krmpotich, who was eight at the time, remem-bered the daily activities as not that different from life in the coal camp: "We kids just played on the grounds there, you know, and just had fun and went to school. The mothers were always washing clothes and being busy. We . . . used to have parties together. You know where everybody would bring something." But that familiar round of activities was soon disrupted.

In addition to hiring guards and detectives, CF&I convinced the governor of Colorado to provide National Guard troops "to protect private property," even though that the UMWA had rented the land where the tent colony stood. The union and the National Guard skirmished repeatedly in the win-ter of 1913–1914, before the governor withdrew most of the troops. Some members of the National Guard remained as private employees of CF&I.[47]

On the morning of April 20, CF&I's private army attacked the miners at the Ludlow tent colony. Helen Krmpotich remembered the morning:

> They started shooting like crazy. . . . shells were flying all over . . . my dad said, "go on, you'd better go on with momma." And then my sister dragged me— I didn't want to go. I wanted to go with my dad, and he said, "No, you can't go. You gotta go with momma." So, my mother took all of us, and it was right after Easter, the next day . . . I still had my lace dress on. I didn't want to go and my sister grabbed me by the hair and pulled me, and we went in [and hid in] the water tank.

Other women and children hid with the Krmpotich family in the water tank: "we just huddled up all our families." A woman living near the tent colony learned that the militia knew where the women and children were hiding and planned to drown them. The woman found a way to warn those who were hiding in the water tank. Krmpotich recalled, "so we all got out of there, and we ran down this creek. And this here Italian man, the machine gun shot him. I stepped on him, and I ran, and got caught in the wire, the barbed wire, and I ran, and ran. We ran for miles and miles to a ranch some place." Later, Krmpotich and her family discovered that fire had engulfed the tent colony during the militia's attack: "When they burned all our tents down, we lost everything. All our certificates and our birth certificates—everything."

The attack on the 1,200 women, children, and men at Ludlow was brutal and bloody. Machine gun fire raked the colony for over twelve hours. Guardsmen, according to witnesses, shot at anything that moved and looted the possessions of the mining families. Miners fought back, using rifles that some of the Greek immigrant miners had hidden from the National Guard. It was a battle that ended in the massacre of eighteen people who had been living in the tent colony, five miners who died from gunshot wounds, and two women and eleven children who suffocated in a fire set by troops.[48] By 8:30 P.M. on April 20, the militia was in command of the community that was no more.[49]

When word spread of the massacre, mining families throughout Colorado rose up in armed protest. Support poured in from around the country, especially from miners in Appalachia. Union officials of UMWA District 15 (Colorado, Wyoming, Utah, and New Mexico) issued a "Call to Rebellion." The union directed miners to organize into military-like companies, because, as union officials reported to UMWA national headquarters, "all hell is loose in this state."[50] For ten days, miners throughout Colorado fought. They succeeded in taking control of a large region of the southern coalfields, an area eighteen miles long and five miles wide.[51] Both striking miners and CF&I guards acted as though they were engaged in war: planning long-range strategy, reporting casualties, and claiming territory. Newspapers spread the story of the massacre and of the miners' uprising, and declared that a revolution was taking place in Colorado's coalfields.[52] In response, the governor sent in the National Guard again and persuaded President Woodrow Wilson to send the U.S. army to help CF&I's private troops put down the rebellion. Within days the Coal War was over.

Sixty-six miners and their wives and children were killed during the 1913–1914 strike. The coal companies met none of the workers' demands and miners lost nearly everything they owned. Miners and their supporters, however, built strong alliances with members of the UMWA across the country. Some of the miners at Ludlow found work in West Virginia and Kentucky. Others joined the ranks of organizers. The massacre and Coal War that followed publicized the dangerous working conditions miners faced and the use of hired armies against working people. A congressional commission investigated the Coal War and found that the miners were justified in protesting their low wages and unsafe working conditions. This was small consolation for the miners.[53] Nonetheless, through the experiences of organizers like Mother Jones, community members like Helen Krmpotich, and countless other participants, both in Colorado and in other mining areas, a culture of solidarity took root.

CULTURES OF SOLIDARITY IN APPALACHIA, 1912–1932

The findings of the 1914–1915 congressional commission did little to dissuade mining companies from hiring private armies of strikebreakers.[54] Strikebreaking was big business by the early twentieth century, and the United States had the distinction of being the only industrial country that allowed private companies to hire armies of armed mercenaries.[55] A culture of intimidation and violence pervaded the mining industry. Between 1912 and 1932, battles erupted in coal-producing regions across the country. Some of the most violent clashes took place in the southern Colorado–northern New Mexico and Appalachian coalfields, where the Baldwin-Felts Detective Agency set out to destroy unions. The agency built a power base in these regions that equaled that of the state governments; it operated as a law unto itself. Baldwin-Felts agents infiltrated unions and spied on miners, their families, and other members of coal communities.[56] They kidnapped miners suspected of organizing strikes or having pro-union sentiments and beat them or escorted them out of coal camps. They used guns against miners with impunity.

The tactics agents used, of course, prompted miners and their supporters to develop countertactics of their own. In developing these tactics, members of coal communities created more elaborate cultures of solidarity, deepening their commitments to one another and often drawing on support from outsiders, including writers, intellectuals, and students. In sketching the contours of these newly expansive cultures in broad strokes, one can lose sight of the ways in which the multiple bonds of mining womanhood set the stage for novel expressions of solidarity. So it is crucial to remember that all the coalfield drama in this era was played out against a backdrop of tightly knit coal communities, where women's ties to both men and other women created collectivities that were worth defending.

One of the first reactions to Baldwin-Felts came in 1912 and 1913, when striking miners in Paint Creek and Cabin Creek, West Virginia, rose up against the agents. In response, Baldwin-Felts set up a machine gun on a company-owned building and threatened to mow the miners down.[57] In February 1913, late at night, Baldwin-Felts agents arrived at the striking miners' tent colony in a train fitted with an armored car they called the "Bull Moose Special." A large group had gathered in the mess tent at the center of the colony to listen to a concert by a group of miners. According to one historian, "Miners were enjoying violin, guitar, and banjo [music] when the death train crawled through the cut into [the camp]."[58] The agents opened machine gun and rifle fire on the residents, shooting from one end of the colony to the other, killing one miner and seriously wounding an elderly woman as she slept in her bed.[59]

Eight years later, in 1921, Baldwin-Felts agents hired by the Red Jacket Coal Company evicted miners from the company's coal camp at Stone Mountain, near Matewan, West Virginia.[60] The animosity between coal miners and Baldwin-Felts agents exploded at Matewan when agents tried to take Sheriff Sid Hatfield, who was sympathetic to the miners, into custody.[61] Miners opened fire on the agents and a gun battle ensued. The battle and Sid Hatfield's role in it were reported in newspapers around the nation, which publicized the Baldwin-Felts union-busting activities. The publicity brought new supporters to the coal miners' cause. In addition, the news coverage sparked a large-scale union drive in West Virginia and other mining regions.[62]

During World War I, coal production expanded dramatically, transforming the economy and workforce of coal producing regions in only a few years. In eastern Kentucky, for example, the majority of working people either mined coal or provided services for mining communities.[63] The UMWA responded to the rise in production, drawing strength from earlier struggles, from the publicity that violent labor conflicts elicited, and from a culture of solidarity that had developed among miners and supporters. Still, the UMWA was not always successful. The coal mines that proved to be the most difficult to organize were those in Harlan County, Kentucky. In 1931, the UMWA started a campaign to organize miners in the county. The union met with fierce resistance from coal companies, and it was not until 1937 that the UMWA succeeded in organizing the Harlan County coalfields.[64] In 1931, working conditions in Harlan County were among the worst in the nation. Miners faced low wages; unemployment and underemployment; the short-weighing of coal by companies, which allowed them to underpay miners for their work; lack of health benefits; and the almost complete control of every aspect of their lives by coal companies. When miners tried to organize among themselves or respond to union organizing drives, coal owners and operators brought in a private army to intimidate them.[65]

As the UMWA met one defeat after another in Harlan County, other unions began to make inroads there. Communist organizers were the most successful. They offered an alternative to the capitalist world that miners saw developing around them, which privileged business-government alliances and offered little, if any, protection of the rights of working people. Communism presented miners with a way to historicize and make sense of their experiences and to forge alliances with other miners around the world. In February 1931, the three-year-old National Miners' Union (NMU) called a strike in Harlan County after a successful organizing drive. This racially integrated union, founded under the auspices of the both the Trade Union Unity League and the Trade Union Education League of the Communist Party, was especially appealing to black and other non-white miners, including *hispanos* who had migrated from the Southwest. Its official newsletter, *The Coal Digger*, charged that "no discrimination against Negro or foreign-born miners shall be the policy of the National Miners' Union."[66] Many white workers, too, were drawn to the utopian, anticapitalist message of NMU organizers. The success of the union is remarkable, given that white men made up 90 percent of the mining workforce, and it demonstrates that miners could, in some circumstances, create a community based on interracial cooperation.[67]

The 1931 NMU strike was a bloody, brutal affair that was crushed by coal company thugs and deputized company guards. It drew the outrage of prominent writers and intellectuals, as well as students, from around the country, including Theodore Dreiser, Mary Heaton Vorse, W.E.B. DuBois, Muriel Draper, Arthur McDowell, Upton Sinclair, Edna St. Vincent Millay, Lester Cohen, Langston Hughes, Suzanne LaFollette, and John dos Passos.[68] After the strike, the NMU redoubled its efforts to organize miners throughout the state. In December, the union called for a convention to set a date for a statewide strike against coal operators. Then, in early 1932, the organizing efforts of the NMU inspired miners in Kentucky and Tennessee to go out on strike. In response, *New Republic* writer Waldo Frank and others, hearing reports of starvation in mining camps, joined the NMU and traveled to Kentucky with food.[69] Similarly, news reports of the miners' troubles prompted a Columbia University professor to organize a group of college students to travel to Harlan and Bell counties. A newspaper article reported:

> Two hundred students from Yale, Harvard, Princeton, Columbia, the College of the City of New York, New York University and Smith and Hunter colleges piled into buses and automobiles here today, planning an impartial "search for truth" in the coal-strike region of eastern Kentucky. Rob F. Hall, president of the Social Problems Club at Columbia University, who accompanied the party, warned the students before leaving that mine operators suspected they were Communists. To forestall attempted indictments on charges of criminal syndicalism each student was to carry full credentials. Mr. Hall also told the students, "above all, don't anybody wear leather jackets! They're the mark of a Communist!"[70]

In all, thirty colleges and universities sent faculty and student delegations to Kentucky to protest terrorism in mining communities and to distribute relief.[71] This heralded a dramatic change in the response of academics to labor unrest. Earlier, most college students and faculty members who became involved in labor conflicts were young men whose goal was to break strikes. Historian Stephen Norwood argues that strikebreaking gave these earlier students a way to demonstrate their masculinity. He contends that the decline of such behavior came with the radicalization of students during the Depression, when their own economic position was threatened.[72] Thus, this era saw cultures of solidarity expanding to create an ever-widening circle of "we."

The delegations of intellectuals, students, and activists who traveled to Kentucky in 1931–1932 encountered hostility, derision, and, in some cases, violence. The District Attorney of Bell County told reporters that if students caused trouble, "they would be presented with all-day suckers, lollipops and sprigs of mountain laurel and sent back to their schoolrooms."[73] He initially refused police protection for the delegations, writing to the National College Committee, "my advice to these rattle-brained college students is to stay out of Southeastern Kentucky."[74] More than snide remarks and veiled threats awaited other delegations of intellectuals and activists. Waldo Frank and the eleven writers who traveled with him to Kentucky were beaten by coal company guards shortly after their arrival. The twelve were then kidnapped and dumped across state lines and told not to return. Two members of the group, Doris Parks and the playwright Harold Hickerson, were jailed on charges of disorderly conduct for trying to prevent company guards from confiscating food they planned to distribute to striking miners.[75]

The violence against Frank and others in his delegation came on the heels of an attack on the reputation of another well-known writer. A few months earlier, when Theodore Dreiser held hearings to investigate what he called the "frightful reign of terror imposed by thugs and jailbirds in Harlan County," authorities in Bell County retaliated by charging Dreiser with adultery and immoral behavior and then convened a grand jury to review the case.[76] The charges were based on the testimony of two traveling salesmen who claimed they had propped a toothpick against Dreiser's hotel room door after his secretary, Marie Pergain, had entered his room one evening, and found it still in place the following morning. The only other evidence presented in the grand jury hearing was a hotel register indicating that Dreiser and Pergain had checked in at the same time. Dreiser, who had returned to New York, claimed that the charges were preposterous, because he was, in his own words, "impotent." He was, he told the jury, certain that the charges were made solely to divert attention from the "evil crimes that are being committed against the poorest and most underpaid and most long-suffering type of laborer, his wife, and child, that I have ever seen."[77]

In his instructions to the grand jury, the Bell County Circuit Court Judge revealed that Dreiser's infidelities were less a concern than his support of a radical union. The judge told the jury that Dreiser "got around him a crowd of Communists and radicals to come into Harlan and Bell Counties to conduct a pretended investigation of conditions in this country." He claimed that Dreiser and other outsiders "came here for no other purpose than to revive the trouble we previously had in Harlan County. . . . I just want to impress upon you, gentlemen of the jury, and the citizens with the hearing of my voice the reality of Communism here in America." The judge gave the jury ten pages of typed instructions—mostly warnings about the threat of communism. His concluding remarks sum up his position: "To hell with Russia and all the communists and Bolshevicks. . . . I intend to use the full power of my court to prevent these human rattlesnakes from injecting the virus of communism into the veins of the American workingman." He ended by saying that his remarks may have "somewhat transgressed on the construction of a technical instruction to a grand jury."[78]

Charges of communism dominated public and private discourse in Harlan County during the 1930s. Red baiting occurred in other coal regions as well, to counter miners' protests against wage cuts and job losses, as more and more mines slowed or shut down operations.[79] What is of particular interest to the expansion of a culture of solidarity that brought together striking miners, coal communities, and outsiders with no direct experience in the industry, is the slippage of language used to challenge such alliances. NMU opponents invoked "communism" and "the communist threat" to attack the union's multiracial membership and its call for racial equality.

Coal operators spread leaflets spread throughout the strike area, for example, that reprinted passages taken from court depositions made by miners opposed to the strike. These miners claimed to be "born again Americans"—former members of the NMU who had become disillusioned with the union's mission. One such miner wrote, "This is to certify that I do at this time denounce the NATIONAL MINERS UNION and its activities as the driving power is from Russia."[80] Another miner charged that the Communist Party and the NMU "teach that there is no God, that a white woman is equal to a colored woman, that a negro had a right to marry a white woman, that Christ is a myth and that there is nothing in the resurrection."[81] And a third described an NMU meeting in which union leaders told members that "they just as [soon] leave their girls to marry a negro as a white man."[82] Still another claimed that the Communist Party "believes in white and colored marrying each other and if you refuse for the negro men to keep company with your daughter you cannot be a friend to Soviet Russia." The union responded by issuing its own flyer, stating:

> The NMU does not hide the fact that it fights for complete equality for Negroes. . . . The NMU knows that no working class struggle can be won without the firmest solidarity of white and Negro. It realizes that white workers can never be free as long as workers in a black skin are in chains. . . . it calls on all miners, white and Negro, native and foreign born to unite in unshakeable solidarity for the fight against starvation wages and slave conditions in the mines.[83]

NMU insistence that blacks and "foreign" miners be treated as equals both on the job and in public places threatened a particular culture of solidarity that was based on white supremacy and embraced by many coal operators and their supporters in the Jim Crow South. NMU founding principles—that separate was *not* equal—challenged coal companies not only for control over the work place but also for control over the social world in which the companies operated. Appeals to patriotism and whiteness are scattered throughout flyers, editorials, court depositions, speeches, and letters from the Harlan County Coal Operators Association, denouncing the NMU and the interference of "outlanders," or outsiders, in the mountains of east Kentucky. This language of racial superiority united some white miners and mine owners across class lines. Mine owners sought to maintain racial segregation as a way of preserving a particular image of America, while miners in the NMU fought to break down cultural and racial divisions and create their own culture of solidarity. By holding up these mountain communities as both exemplars and symbols of white America, coal operators sketched out their own culture of solidarity, one based on exclusionary racial practices. They constructed NMU organizers and eastern intellectuals, both white and black, as outsiders bent on destroying American ideals: they were communists and integrationists, led by morally bankrupt men like Theodore Dreiser and by NMU organizers who plotted the end of religion, the end of white supremacy, the end of democracy, and the end of America. Or they were immature college students, dupes of their communist teachers.

Although the mine operators succeeded in breaking the 1931 strike, they failed in their efforts to divide miners. The reign of terror in Harlan County only increased miners' resolve and bound them more tightly together, despite their differences. The bloody battles in Colorado, Appalachia, and other mining regions made members of coal communities increasingly aware of their shared experiences. The intensity of the struggle in every coal region of the country, the habitual abuse of power by mine owners and operators, and the belief that coal companies' violation of workers' rights threatened the continued existence of their world—a world where hard work was honored and provided the foundation for all other rights and privileges—forged strong ties among miners and fellow travelers that continued in the decades to come.

REPRISE

These ties were still evident sixty years later at Camp Solidarity in Virginia. At rallies and around campfires, in the dining hall and on the picket line, miners and their supporters traded stories about Ludlow, Matewan, and "Bloody Harlan."[84] Singers gave renditions of coal mining songs that celebrated the long history of miners' struggles in the United States. A favorite was, "Which Side Are You On?" written by Florence Reese, the wife of an NMU miner recalling the 1931 Harlan County strike. The Camo Song Book, distributed to miners during the Christmas season, included a tribute to Mother Jones from the "Daughters of Mother Jones," the women of Camp Solidarity. It featured an illustration of two women wearing sweatshirts with Mother Jones's name and image emblazoned upon them (figure 15.1).[85] Miners from Colorado asked for support for a memorial for the victims of the Ludlow Massacre at the site of the tent colony. Residents of Camp Solidarity

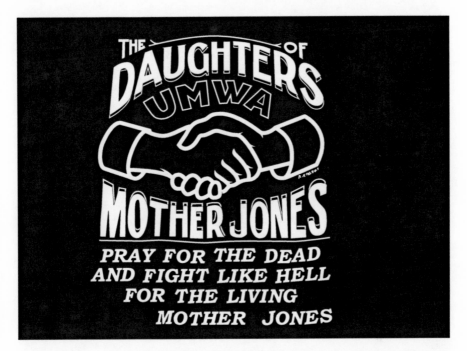

Figure 15.1 Image of Daughters of Mother Jones sweatshirt. Courtesy of Camille Guerin-Gonzales.

exchanged books and other reading materials that detailed past struggles in coal mining communities.

Thus the culture of solidarity that evolved in Virginia in 1989–1990 reflected the contemporary struggles of coal mining communities, as well as those of other working people caught in the throes of late industrial capitalism, but it also drew on deep historical roots. It stemmed from the peculiar place of women in twentieth-century coalfields, where masculinist rhetoric coexisted uneasily with the reality of women's work in both mines and households. It stemmed from the efforts of organizers and everyday members of besieged coal communities during Colorado's Coal War of 1913–1914. And it stemmed from the participation of miners, Communists, writers, and students who fought coal companies' insidious use of detective agencies, private armies, and the state to crush unions in Appalachia from 1912 to 1932.

Of course coal companies, too, could draw on a historical repertoire of tactics to achieve their goals. The Pittston Coal Group employed its own private army, Vance Security's "Asset Protection Team," to intimidate miners and their supporters.[86] In spite of such tactics, Pittston and its hired guns largely failed. The miners and their supporters who gathered at Camp Solidarity ultimately won their struggle, and the coal company acceded to the workers' key demands, which centered on benefits rather than wages. The victory was not permanent; ten years after the strike ended, Pittston closed many of the mines for good.[87] But the women and men of Camp Solidarity, mindful of the past and hopeful for the future, surely have left a priceless legacy for those of us who continue to dream and work toward a more just tomorrow.

NOTES

1. I extend my deepest appreciation to the Pittston miners and the Daughters of Mother Jones: Judy Chaffin, Cosby Ann Totten, Paul Dishman, Tommy "Tucker" Taylor, and Sam Hughes. I am very grateful to Marat Moore, Donnie Sams, David Phillips, and Debbie Baca of the United Mine Workers of America; and to Bruce Bostick, District 28, United Steelworkers of America. I also thank the courageous students in my labor history class who became part of Camp Solidarity in the fall and winter of 1989. This essay would not have come to fruition without the intellectual and editorial support of Susan Lee Johnson; conversations with Ralph Mann; and the research assistance provided by Kelly Caulkins, Erik Larson, and Tricia Price.

2. I am indebted to Rick Fantasia for this concept and for his insight that "solidarity is created *and* expressed by the process of mutual association." Fantasia argues that cultures of solidarity refer to "a cultural expression that arises within the wider culture, yet which is emergent in its embodiment of oppositional practices and meanings." See his *Cultures of Solidarity: Consciousness, Action, and Contemporary American Workers* (Berkeley: University of California Press, 1988), 17–22.

3. "U.S. and Soviet Miners Meet and Find Surprises," *New York Times*, January 22, 1990. Miners from the Kuznetsk coal region in Siberia made similar observations.

4. Many of these women were in the United States for the Eleventh National Conference of Women Miners held in late June 1989, in Springfield, Illinois.

5. Suranda Gonzalez describes one such community in "Talking Like My Grandmothers: Spanish Immigrant Women in Spelter, West Virginia" (MA thesis, University of West Virginia, 1991).

6. Here I draw on but do not entirely replicate Richard White's concept of the middle ground. White's middle ground is one where the competing interests of different cultural groups were negotiated through a complicated process of mutual misunderstanding that often masqueraded as cultural understanding. See *The Middle Ground: Indians, Empires, and Republics in the Great Lakes Region, 1650–1815* (Cambridge: Cambridge University Press, 1991).

7. Michael Forman, *Nationalism and the International Labor Movement: The Idea of the Nation in Socialist and Anarchist Theory* (University Park: Pennsylvania State University Press, 1998), 63.

8. See David Harvey, *Justice, Nature, and the Geography of Difference* (Cambridge, MA: Blackwell, 1996), 334–365. See also Fredric Jameson, "Utopianism and Anti-Utopianism," in *The Jameson Reader*, ed., Michael Hardt and Kathi Weeks (Cambridge, MA.: Blackwell, 2000), originally published in Jameson, "The Antimonies of Postmodernity," *The Seeds of Time* (New York: Columbia University Press, 1994); Jameson, "Utopia, Modernism, and Death," *The Seeds of Time*.

9. Letter from Michael E. Odom [1989]. Author's files. Emphasis in original.

10. Cover letter from Michael E. Odom, Chief Executive Officer of Pittston Coal Group, Inc., accompanying Pittston Coal Group information packet mailed November 1989. Author's files. Emphasis in original.
11. See Raymond Williams, *Politics and Letters: Interviews with the New Left Review* (London: New Left Books, 1979), 286. Williams first introduced the concept of a "structure of feeling" in 1954. See his novel *Border Country* (1960; London: Hogarth Press, 1988).
12. Patrick Joyce, "The Historical Meanings of Work: An Introduction," in *The Historical Meanings of Work*, ed. Patrick Joyce (Cambridge: Cambridge University Press, 1987).
13. Jameson, *The Seeds of Time*, 104.
14. Coal production, thus, was elastic in the upswing but inelastic in the downswing. For a clear, concise, and insightful analysis of this peculiarity of coal production and its implications for labor relations, see David Brody, "Market Unionism in America: The Case of Coal," in *In Labor's Cause: Main Themes on the History of the American Worker* (New York: Oxford University Press, 1993).
15. Barbara Freese, *Coal: A Human History* (Cambridge, MA: Perseus, 2003), 45.
16. Male gender ideals were changing in this era from an emphasis on "manliness" to one on "masculinity," but I use the term "masculinity" here in a more generic sense to denote constructions of male gender. See Gail Bederman, *Manliness and Civilization: A Cultural History of Gender and Race in the United States, 1880–1917* (Chicago: University of Chicago Press, 1995). On working-class masculinities in mining, see, e.g., Elizabeth Jameson, *All That Glitters: Class, Conflict, and Community in Cripple Creek* (Urbana: University of Illinois Press, 1998); and Gunther Peck, *Reinventing Free Labor: Padrones and Immigrant Workers in the North American West, 1880–1930* (Cambridge: Cambridge University Press, 2000).
17. Angela John, *By the Sweat of their Brow: Women Workers in Victorian Coal Mines* (London: Croom Helm, 1980), 20, 95 n. 60, 231.
18. Emil Zola, *Germinal* (New York: Oxford University Press, 1998).
19. John, *By the Sweat of their Brow*, 184–186. Women in these photographs were asked to pose and usually directed to wear specific pieces of clothing.
20. Audrey Smith Hawkins Interview, Marat Moore Collection, Series I, Box I, Folder 3, Archives of Appalachia, Archives and Special Collections, Sherrod Library, East Tennessee State University (hereafter cited as Marat Moore Collection).
21. Alice Elizabeth Crawford Interview, Marat Moore Collection, Series I, Box 1, Folder 1.
22. Billy Hepler Interview, Marat Moore Collection, Series I, Box 1, Folder 4.
23. Ethel Day Smith Interview, Marat Moore Collection, Series I, Box 1, Folder 10; and see Marat Moore, *Women in the Mines: Stories of Life and Work* (New York: Twayne, 1996), 27–31.
24. Ethel McCuiston Interview, Marat Moore Collection, Series I, Box 1, Folder 7; Moore, *Women in the Mines*, 39.
25. *McDowell County Record* (West Virginia), October 28, 1942, newsclipping, Marat Moore Collection, Series I, Box 1, Folder 2.
26. Alice Fulford Interview. See also Moore, *Women in the Mines*, 45–48.
27. Alice Fulford Interview. See also Moore, *Women in the Mines*, 45–48.
28. *Daily News* (Welch, West Virginia), November 19, 1942, newsclipping, Marat Moore Collection, Series I, Box 1, Folder 2.

29. Moore, *Women in the Mines*, 48.
30. Dominick Morelli Interview, Marat Moore Collection, Series I, Box 1, Folder 1.
31. Alice Crawford Interview.
32. Madge Kelly Interview, Marat Moore Collection, Series I, Box 1, Folder 5.
33. Alice Crawford Interview.
34. Audrey Smith Hawkins Interview.
35. Dominick Morelli Interview.
36. Ethel Day Smith Interview; see also Moore, *Women in the Mines*, 27–31.
37. Helen Krmpotich Interview, Rock Springs, Wyoming, November 4, 1989. Conducted by the author. All quotations from Krmpotich in the following paragraphs are from this interview.
38. Between 1887 and 1897, the national average was 2.56 deaths per thousand, while in Colorado the rate was 4.64 per thousand. Between 1884 and 1912, Colorado's rate jumped to 6.81, while the national average was 3.12. James Brian Whiteside, "Protecting the Life and Limb of our Workmen: Work, Death, and Regulation in the Rocky Mountain Coal Mining Industry" (PhD diss., University of Colorado, 1986), 134.
39. Priscilla Long, *Where the Sun Never Shines: A History of America's Bloody Coal Industry* (New York: Paragon, 1989), 243–245; H. Lee Scamehorn, *Pioneer Steelmaker in the West: The Colorado Fuel and Iron Company, 1872–1903* (Boulder, CO: Pruett, 1976), 169.
40. Quoted in Long, *Where the Sun Never Shines*, 245.
41. U.S. Commission on Industrial Relations, *Final Report and Testimony*, Vols. 7–9. Senate Doc. 415, 64th Cong., 2d Sess. Washington, DC, 1916, 7: 6554–6555.
42. Howard Zinn, "The Ludlow Massacre," in *The Politics of History* (Boston: Beacon, 1970), 83.
43. *Proceedings*, Special Convention of District Fifteen, United Mine Workers of America, Trinidad, Colorado, September 16, 1913, 16–21. Typewritten copy in Western History/Genealogy Department, Denver Public Library. Reprinted in Philip S. Foner, ed., *Mother Jones Speaks: Collected Speeches and Writings* (New York: Monad, 1983), 234–235. And see U.S. Congress, House Subcommittee on Mines and Mining, *Conditions in the Coal Mines of Colorado*, 2 vols. Pursuant to H.R. 387. 63d Cong., 2d Sess., Washington, DC, 1914, 2: 2633; Long, *Where the Sun Never Shines*, 269; Zinn, "Ludlow Massacre," 86.
44. Zinn, "Ludlow Massacre," 86.
45. Long, *Where the Sun Never Shines*, 273.
46. Helen Krmpotich Interview; Long, *Where the Sun Never Shines*, 274.
47. Sam Vigil Interview, Huerfano County History Project, Walsenburg Public Library, Walsenburg, Colorado, 1979; Sarah Deutsch, *No Separate Refuge: Culture, Class, and Gender on the Anglo-Hispanic Frontier in the American Southwest, 1880–1940* (New York: Oxford University Press, 1987), 104.
48. Zinn, "Ludlow Massacre," 92–94; McAlister Coleman, *Men and Coal* (1943; New York: Arno, 1969), 86–87. One of the women and four of the children were *hispanos* from southern Colorado and northern New Mexico.
49. Helen Krmpotich Interview; Long, *Where the Sun Never Shines*, 291–292; Zinn, "Ludlow Massacre," 93.
50. Long, *Where the Sun Never Shines*, 293; Coleman, *Men and Coal*, 86–87.

51. Graham Adams, Jr., *Age of Industrial Violence, 1910–1915: The Activities and Findings of the United States Commission on Industrial Relations* (New York: Columbia University Press, 1966), 160; Long, *Where the Sun Never Shines*, 294.

52. Adams, *Age of Industrial Violence*, 161.

53. U.S. Commission on Industrial Relations, *Final Report and Testimony*, 8: 7120–7121.

54. The publicity surrounding the hearings prompted Rockefeller and CF&I to establish a form of corporate welfare, dubbed the "Rockefeller Plan," but the goals of plan were to reduce criticism and co-opt unions. See Fantasia, *Cultures of Solidarity*, 30–31, 38.

55. Stephen H. Norwood, *Strikebreaking and Intimidation: Mercenaries and Masculinity in Twentieth-Century America* (Chapel Hill: University of North Carolina Press, 2002), 3–4.

56. Norwood, *Strikebreaking and Intimidation*, 128.

57. Robert Michael Smith, *From Blackjacks to Briefcases: A History of Commercialized Strikebreaking and Unionbusting in the United States* (Athens: Ohio University Press, 2003), 24.

58. Fred Mooney, *Struggle in the Coal Fields: The Autobiography of Fred Mooney*, ed., J.W.Hess (Morgantown: West Virginia University Library, 1967); Foner, ed., *Mother Jones Speaks*, 339.

59. Norwood, *Strikebreaking and Intimidation*, 128. Another vehicle in the Baldwin-Felts armory, a bullet-proof open car with a machine gun and search-light mounted on its body, was dubbed the "Death Special." During the 1914 CF&I strike, this vehicle terrorized Helen Krmpotich and the other residents of the Ludlow tent colony. One morning, Baldwin-Felts agents drove the Death Special alongside the tents and opened machine gun fire on the residents. They shot 600 rounds of ammunition, killing a miner and wounding a child. The agency operated with such impunity that it continued to use the Death Special to intimidate CF&I miners even after the strike ended. Agents drove the armored car through coal communities, with the Colorado State Attorney General along for the ride, thus offering state sanction to the agency's tactics. See Smith, *From Blackjacks to Briefcases*, 31, 138.

60. Smith, *From Blackjacks to Briefcases*, 32.

61. Matewan Collection, Eastern Regional Coal Archives, Craft Memorial Library, Bluefield, West Virginia; Lon Savage, *Thunder in the Mountains: The West Virginia Mine War, 1920–1921* (Pittsburgh: University of Pittsburgh Press, 1990), 20; David Alan Corbin, *Life, Work, and Rebellion in the Coal Fields: The Southern West Virginia Miners, 1880–1922* (Urbana: University of Illinois Press, 1981), 201; Coleman, *Men and Coal*, 99.

62. Matewan Collection; Corbin, *Life, Work, and Rebellion*, 202.

63. Crandell A. Shifflett, *Coal Towns: Life, Work, and Culture in Company Towns of Southern Appalachia, 1880–1960* (Knoxville: University of Tennessee Press, 1991), 119.

64. John W. Hevener, *Which Side Are You On: The Harlan County Coal Miners, 1931–1939* (Urbana: University of Illinois Press, 2002), xviii.

65. Hevener, *Which Side Are You On*, xvii.

66. Philip Foner, *Organized Labor and the Black Worker* (New York: International, 1974), 194–196.

67. Hevener, *Which Side Are You On*, 3.

68. Herndon Evans Papers, Special Collections and Archives, University of Kentucky, Lexington (hereafter cited as Herndon Evans Papers); Muriel Draper Papers, Beinecke Library, Yale University.
69. Herndon Evans Papers; Coleman, *Men and Coal*, 188.
70. "Students Off to Study Strike," n.p., newsclipping, Herndon Evans Papers.
71. *New York Times*, March 13, 1932, newsclipping, Herndon Evans Papers.
72. Norwood, *Strikebreaking and Intimidation*, 15–33.
73. Bell County District Attorney, Walter B. Smith, quoted in "Students Off to Study Strike," n.p., n.d., newsclipping, Herndon Evans Papers.
74. Bell County District Attorney, Walter B. Smith, quoted in "Collegians Leave for Mines Survey," n.p., n.d., Herndon Evans Papers. His comments were more moderate when he spoke later with the Knoxville *Journal* about the impending visit of college students and their professors, saying he "would welcome them if they come with a sincere purpose to learn the truth," Knoxville *Journal*, n.d. The governors of both Kentucky and Tennessee, too, warned "the group of eastern collegians to get out and stay out [of Appalachia]." "Get Out and Stay Out," Hamilton, Ohio *News*, April 21, 1932.
75. Articles reprinted from the Louisville *Times*, May 9–12, in "The Situation in Bell and Harlan Counties, Kentucky," A Survey Made for the Louisville *Times* and the North American Newspaper Alliance, c. 1932, 8, Herndon Evans Papers.
76. "Dreiser's Feud with Kentucky," *Literary Digest*, November 28, 1931; Louisville *Courier-Journal*, October 16, 1931, in Philip D. Supina, "Herndon J. Evans and the Harlan County Coal Strike," *Filson Club History Quarterly* 56, no. 3 (July 1982): 324, in Herndon Evans Collection.
77. Herndon J. Evans, "The Truth About the Dreiser Case," unpublished manuscript, Herndon Evans Papers; Norfolk, Virginia *Pilot*, November 12, 1931.
78. Herndon Evans Papers.
79. A number of historians have examined this strategy, as well as the role of the Communist Party in organizing Depression-era workers. See, e.g., Robin D.G. Kelley, *Hammer and Hoe: Communists During the Great Depression* (Chapel Hill: University of North Carolina Press, 1990); and Corbin, *Life, Work, and Rebellion*.
80. Testimony of Finley Donaldson to Bell Circuit Court, Kentucky, n.d., reproduced in leaflet, "Miners Expose Reds," Herndon Evans Papers.
81. Testimony of Harvey Collett to Bell Circuit Court, Kentucky, February 10, 1932, reproduced in leaflet, "Miners Expose Reds," Herndon Evans Papers.
82. Testimony of H.L. Doan to Bell Circuit Court, Kentucky, February 11, 1932, reproduced in leaflet, "Miners Expose Reds," Herndon Evans Papers.
83. "Expose the Lies of Our Enemies! Build the NMU!!" Flyer, Herndon Evans Papers.
84. This section is based on my visit to Camp Solidarity in 1989.
85. *Camo Carols*, adapted by Julie McCall, illustrated by Mike Konopacki (Washington, DC: Labor Heritage Foundation, 1989), 9.
86. Moe Seager, "One Day Longer Than Pittston," *Z Magazine*, October 1989, 13–24. According to Seager, Vance International was owned by Chuck Vance, son-in-law of former President Gerald Ford.
87. Richard A. Brisbin, Jr., *A Strike Like No Other Strike: Law & Resistance During the Pittston Coal Strike of 1989–1990* (Baltimore: Johns Hopkins University Press, 2002).

Mining Women Find a Voice: Working Class and Environmental Feminism in the Twenty-First Century

Jaclyn J. Gier

In the introduction to this volume, we have identified our subject as "mining and women," but as the title of the book suggests, there is an alternate agenda. For as labor historians and women's historians turned "global" historians, we have also been preoccupied with "mining women," a sort of double entendre which implies that we are also unearthing another aspect of a shared and gendered past—the role of women in mining and the roles of women in relation to the mining industry and to men. This journey through nearly three hundred years of mining history could not have been accomplished without the contributors to this volume, who give meaning and substance to our envisioned past(s). This history would not have been possible without the women and men whose stories people it.

But the past, as always, is *before* us. We walk through it each and every day in large and small ways to live in this reality we call the "present," and though its corridors still reverberate from the sound of voices already lost to history, we somehow reach the future. As historians we cannot predict the future from the past, but as human beings we live to envision and ultimately, to create it. So what does this history of mining women tell us about *their* past with its all too often silenced or disconnected voices? What future world have mining women begun to envision for themselves? And what may grow from the roots of this collected historical experience?

The title of this Epilogue hints that there is another chapter, perhaps not yet ready to be written in full, but already being lived by the mining women of the twenty-first century. While their story is deeply rooted in the previous century, it is also the product of new forces and influences that have emerged as a consequence of previous developments. These developments include the emergence of a global economy, the process of deindustrialization among the

older developed nations and the dissolution of many of the traditional institutions of labor, the destruction of the environment and with it the displacement of indigenous peoples and their ways of life, and the emergence of a
global feminism, to name only a few. All over the world, from Britain, to
India, to Bolivia, mining women have responded to some of these challenges
by organizing to voice their concerns about their communities, the environment, and social justice issues. The material that follows highlights some of
these recent developments.

As the first nation to experience an industrial revolution, Great Britain,
and some of the remnants of its once global empire, were among the first
nations to experience the economic dislocation of deindustrialization. The
response to this drastic change of fortune for mining communities in Britain,
which began shortly after World War I, was initially through the trade union
movement. Massive strikes, at first over hours and wages—as was the case
with the Miners' Lockout of 1926—and later over the closing of collieries,
which led to the Great Miners' Strike of 1984–1985, became the increasingly
prevalent tactic of the frustrated miners' unions and their members.

The first women's "auxiliary—the so-called Union of Miners' Wives—was
founded in 1927 as a response to the dire conditions experienced by the
women of mining communities of Britain during the post-strike period.
Although the women's section of the Labor Party had assisted miners' wives
all over the coalfields in 1926 with donations of food, money, and clothing,
many miners' wives felt that some more direct action and organization was
needed by them in the coalfield communities, and in the following year they
organized rallies and meetings all over the coalfields of northern England.
Their agenda was to make their voices heard by the union, which many
miners' wives felt had disregarded the concerns of women during 1926. In
the aftermath of the strike, many women believed their long suffering had
entitled them to express an opinion. As one oral history interviewee con-
fided, her father finished off the 1926 strike suntanned and fit from playing
football with his mates, while her mother had become pale and thin from the
stress of trying to feed a family on handouts.[1]

By the time the Great Depression hit, many mining families had already
departed for the United States, Australia, and Canada. In the Illawara region
of New South Wales, Australian miners' wives from Wales and Yorkshire
brought their radicalism with them; meetings of miners' wives began as early
as 1929, with the first formal organization, the Australian Miners' Wives
Auxiliary, formed in 1934.[2] In the still frontier atmosphere of Australian mining towns the auxiliaries were both social and political in nature, supporting
the men during stoppages, but also organizing activities for women. Some of
these miners' wives even became active members of the Australian Communist
Party, supporting radical causes that were beyond the scope of the union's
agenda, such as campaigning against the Vietnam War.[3]

Although auxiliary members sometimes recorded the visits of overseas
union presidents to Australia, such as that of Arthur Horner and his wife
from the Miners' Federation of Great Britain, the auxiliary groups remained

largely disconnected from contact with other miners' wives outside their home country. But this situation would change with the formation of Women Against Pit Closure, during the 1984–1985 Miners' Strike in Britain, a strike that began with the announcement that the National Coal Board would close twenty mines and cut twenty thousand jobs.[4]

The coal industry of Britain had already gone through huge cuts since the industry was nationalized in 1947, as alternate sources of fuel and cheaper sources of coal were made available after World War II. Between 1957 and 1970, more than 400,000 jobs had been lost. As the international oil crisis began to hit home, the National Union of Mine Workers brought strikes in 1972 and 1974 to a successful conclusion, with large salary increases for the miners and humiliating defeats for the government. By the early 1980s The Conservative Party and Prime Minister Thatcher were committed to privatization of the energy sector, citing the unprofitability and costliness of the coal industry. By 1984 the government was well prepared to begin the process of colliery closure under the directives of the new head of the National Coal Board, Ian MacGregor. The tensions that led to the strike were the result of an initial announcement to close five mines without complete and proper review.

Women Against Pit Closures (WAPC) started as a scattered group of regional organizations or "Support Groups", as they were often called in the early months of the strike, whose principle purpose was to collect funds for mining families that were being denied strike pay by the government and to distribute food parcels. Prime Minister Margaret Thatcher, with the support of the courts, had declared the strike illegal since the National Union of Mineworkers had begun the strike after a vote by its Executive, not a vote by members as a whole. There was concern by some in the union that a national vote would fail because the government had for the time being only announced colliery closures in certain areas, a strategy obviously designed to divide the union on the strike issue.[5]

But when the NUM called for a strike, the vast majority of miners rallied to the call. Throughout the strikes emotions ran high and groups far removed from the coalfields were drawn into the dramatic events. By the end of the strikes twenty thousand people had been injured, more than one thousand people fired for striking, two hundred taken into custody, and two persons were killed. For the elderly generation of the coalfield communities who could remember the 1926 strike, it seemed that this strike might herald the long awaited red dawn.[6]

All over Britain groups such as the Swansea, Neath, and Dulais Valley Miners' Wives Support Group, became offshoots of general community support groups. Eventually a network of these local groups led to the formation of what was to become Women Against Pit Closure, founded in Barnsley. This nationwide network was hailed by the British left as the first organization of working-class women and wives. Few people were old enough to remember that miners' wives nearly sixty years before had organized a similar group to make their voices heard in their communities and beyond.

Nevertheless, the organization drew a plethora of different groups into the cause, and for the first time many miners had social contact with people outside of their own communities and social milieu. Gays and lesbians of London hosted miners and their wives one weekend, and later visited them in their communities. In Wales, a gay support group donated a van so that miners' wives who did not have access to cars could get to meetings across the country. The women debated if they should put lettering on the van to identify where the donation had come from. Finally the discussion was settled when one miner's wife remarked that if anyone dare trash the vehicle because it was a gift from "the gays" they'd be found out and have hell to pay for it.[7] Another woman recalled that she'd never expected to have so much fun dancing with lesbians: the weekend in London with their new "friends" had been great; even if they'd had to eat greens the whole time because their hosts were vegans.[8]

Then, too, there had been plenty of support from overseas. French miners overturned railway cars with coal destined for Britain in solidarity and miners' children were offered holidays on the continent by European supporters of the strike. Academics, feminists, and rock stars (Elvis Costello and Billy Bragg donated their talents to a benefit concert at the University of London) all lined up to support the cause. And the miners' leader, Arthur Scargill, who was alternately demonized and canonized in the press, has lived long enough to see his reputation vindicated; twenty years later he has been catapulted to folk-hero status. All in all these were heady times for the British Left.

And yet Thatcher and the NCB remained firm: coal must go, the pits must close, and the pains of privatization in one form or another must be borne by all. Britain would be the only European country that would not subsidize its coal industry, no matter what. By March 1985 it was clear to many in the leadership of the National Union of Mineworkers and to the miners that this was a strike, not unlike 1926, that could not be won. While grassroots sympathy ran high, the strike was often portrayed in a negative light on the television and for the most part, the affluent "home counties" had little sympathy for coalfield people and their communities. The miners were increasingly portrayed as misguided, backward looking, and unwilling to accept that they, too, like the rest of the country, must accept the Thatcher program of privatization and the virtual dismantling of the British welfare state. The prime minister would fight the miners as she would fight the last chill of the cold war, with absolute tenacity and the conviction that she was right.

But when the strike ended in March 1985, what amounted to a practical defeat of the NUM was seen by many as a moral victory. Communities all across Britain had been united by the ordeal; new coalitions, such as The London-Wales Congress, had been formed; and a constituency that would support "new" labor in future elections had begun to take shape. The strike may have spelled the end of the miners as the most powerful union in Britain and ultimately the end of the coal industry, but it was the beginning of a turn away from Thatcherism, and a public expose of its excesses. But more than this, working-class housewives, especially miners' wives, were drawn into the vortex of history as never before.

Miners' wives who had little self-confidence and who had never before spoken in public learned to give speeches in front of huge crowds of supporters. Women who had never had so much as a parking ticket suddenly found themselves going to jail for their protests against colliery closure. On the picket lines women discovered the tactics of the Greenham Common women peace campers: resistance and civil disobedience. There were stories of Welsh women dressed in skirts, panty hose, and high heels, who laid down in front of lorries delivering coal from abroad to an electric power station and the police who could not believe what they were seeing (see figure E1 and E2).[9] The photos which follow show women on the picket lines in South Wales during the 1984–85 British Miners' Strike.

For the most part, miners' wives wondered about the words they heard thrown around by the media to describe them—"working-class feminists," wives turned warriors," and so on. For them, the movement had not started out as a protest for women's rights, but rather as an appeal to save mining communities and the right to work. It was spawned in the kitchen and the local pub; while packing food parcels and ironing clothes. To a lesser extent, the women's support groups were also about the situation of mining

Figure E.1 Two members of the South Wales Women's Support Group on the picket line during the 1984–1985 British Mines' Strike, behind them, bemused police officers.

Figure E.2 Police restrain miners' wife during picket line confrontation in while other Women's Support Group members look during on, 1984–1985 Miners' Strike, Great Britain. Permission: Original photographs by Abigail Porter taken during 1984–1985 Miners' Strike.

Figure E.3 Miners' wives of the South Wales Women's Support Group discuss their future at the end of the 1984–1985 Miners' Strike.

housewives, often isolated in their households and villages, rediscovering their neighbors and communities and the concerns they held in common. These women, whose lives and identities had long ago been defined by the first industrial revolution and the division of labor, whose existence revolved around the remains of a threadbare domestic ideology, were now being asked, *and by a woman*, to accept an end to their way of life. For many miners' wives (and for many miners) the prospect of a future without coal, without work, and without the living presence of an honored past, was not only unacceptable, it was inconceivable. Would they become like their ancestors, the first proletarians, caught up in the process of industrialization, a lost generation of men and women—only this time as the nameless victims of capitalist *de* industrialization and government privatization?

It may be one of the ironies of history that people become more of who they really are when history is on the verge of forgetting them. And in the Great Strike of 1984–1985, this was true of both the miners and their wives. History would not abandon them because they could not abandon their history. Instead, the women of coalfield society, admittedly under duress, forged for themselves an identity that would place them and their husbands and their communities at the center of historical narratives about the strike. This year 2004–2005, marks the twentieth anniversary of the Great Miners' Strike, and it is being remembered throughout Britain as an event that changed lives and galvanized a generation of working-class men and women to take action.

In October 2004, National Women Against Pit Closures hosted an International Celebration to commemorate the strike, enjoining women from all around the world to come and celebrate women's class struggles in the twentieth century. Their gala event was to be followed by special events hosted in mining districts for the duration of the 2004–2005 year, each one an historical epiphany for those who had lived through the strike. But beyond the celebrations, it is clear that the consequences of the strike have left bitter rifts in coalfield communities, and wounds that may never completely heal. Anger from miners' wives who remembered picking coal to heat their homes in freezing December weather, anger and regret from union officials who were denigrated for initiating the return back to work, and anger toward a government that many believed was out to get the working classes of Britain.

Yet for many women the strike was a time of intense creative activity and self-discovery. Some women decided to go back to school after the strike to broaden their horizons, others left unsatisfactory marriages in search of greater independence. There were those who thought feminism was rubbish at the start of the strike, only later to embrace it. But in general, women of WAPC have seen themselves as a movement in support of others, not as working-class feminists. For some women the strike was a consciousness-raising experience that drew them into the political arena for the first time. By all accounts, if we can measure the importance of an historical event in relation to the impact it has on people's lives, then the 1984–1985 Miners' Strike was a pivotal experience for many miners' wives and for those who supported them.

When the strike ended, many of the local WAPC groups became dormant in the months afterward. In some instances it was simply that the months of activity and the end result had taxed group membership too much. For some women, the need to return to "normal" life was uppermost in their minds, and not continue the struggle. Nevertheless, in 1992, when the government announced that British Coal would close thirty-one of its fifty remaining deep coal mines, with the loss of thirty thousand more jobs, and an additional loss of seventy thousand jobs related to the industry, there was a massive public outcry.[10]

The Lancashire branch of Women Against Pit Closures reorganized their group in response to this new crisis and decided to take action. They decided to model themselves after the women who had camped at Greeham Common and to set up a camp at a colliery called Parkside that was scheduled for closure. The pit became the site of their media campaign against colliery closure, which was operated out of several caravans. Most of the women involved were the daughters, wives, or mothers of miners. Both the National Coal Board and the local police were reluctant to interfere or attempt to remove the women, who effectively used their gender on behalf of the miners' campaign against colliery closure.[11]

As in the case of 1984–1985, the response of the union was sometimes ambivalent toward WAPC and ancillary groups. While the NUM was happy to endorse action directed by them, independent action by the women's groups, or any criticism of union conduct, was generally met with hostility. In the post-strike period of the 1984–1985 strike, some of the women's support groups convened to hold closed-door discussions about the unions' attitude toward them, such as the meeting of the South Wales Women's Support Group depicted in the photograph which follows. Many expressed anger at the "return to the kitchen, please, Ladies" treatment they had received, but being working-class women, their loyalty was often expressed by a willingness to keep quiet in public about their feelings.[12]

As important as the British Miners' strike and the formation of WAPC was, it is not the final word on mining women in a global context. From around the world "mining women," that is, those women who are miners' wives, women who mine for a living or simply live in mining areas, and more recently, some women who own mines, have come together in to discuss issues relevant to "mining women." In addition, a number of groups which include women's concerns have emerged to address the problems and issues created by extensive mining operations in lesser developed parts of the world. These include JATAM in Indonesia; Mines, Minerals and People (MMP) in India; Minewatch Asia-Pacific (MWAP, Philippines); Third World Network Africa (Ghana); People Against Rio Tinto and Subsidiaries (Partizans); Indigenous Peoples Links (PIPlinks); and the International Women and Mining Network (RIMM).

The most vocal and global of these groups is the International Women and Mining Network. The group was first established in 1993 through a pilot project of Minewatch, United Kingdom, called "Women and Mining," which solicited input and ideas from women affected by mining operations. By 1997, the first international conference for the group was organized in the Philippines by Minewatch and The Women Workers Program of the Philippines. Representatives at the convention included women miners, women trade unionists, NGOs, and women who lived in mining communities. Seventeen countries and five continents were included in the work of the conference.

The second conference was held in Iroco, Oruro, Bolivia in 2000, and at that meeting thirty-five delegates from twenty countries and five continents convened to create the International network, "Women and Mining." At these conferences, topics included making the invisible work of women miners visible: the effects of mining on the environment and on health, the impact of transnational companies on women and their families in mining areas, and the rights of indigenous peoples and women to land and natural resources. This past October 1st-9th, in Visakhapatnam, India, the Third International Women and Mining Conference was held, and a statement was issued by the group proclaiming that they consisted of women affected by and displaced by mining, women who worked in the mines, and human rights activists who sought "gender justice" in a statement issued for the conference, the group summarized their belief that mining has a serious and negative impact on women's lives and formally challenged the development myths generated by the mining industry. Moreover, the group went on to state that mining affected women's lives, their cultural status, sexual rights, ecological spaces, and their customary rights.[13] Unlike the mining women of WAPC, the women of the International Women and Mining Network have little interest in seeing the mining industry expand in their home countries and argue further that mining itself is an unsustainable industry, which over the long term does not lead to the social and economic well-being of people.[14]

While in some respects WAPC and IWMN share similar agendas as with regards to the mining families, communities, and the environment, philosophically the positions of the two organizations are at odds with each other. WAPC remains a group in support of male miners and their exclusively male union; IWMN counts among its constituency female miners and those who are in opposition to the mining industry itself. It is doubtful that any leader of the miners' in Britain who wished to sustain the industry would find the platform of IWMN acceptable. And few in IWMN would support the idea that the mining industry has been "good' for British miners, their wives, and children.

Indeed, the members of IWMN state that one of their goals is the creation of positive economic activities and sustainable livelihoods for women, and they argue that the mining industry has actually marginalized women and destroyed the possibility of diversity in work opportunities for females. And again, this situation is largely supported by the historical experience of women in British coalfield communities. The new generation of mining women in the twenty-first century as embodied by the membership of

IWMN is not interested in salvaging the inherently backward looking agenda of the NUM and WAPC, with its emphasis on sustaining class conflict and a gendered division of labor. Rather, they seek to restore a much older relationship between women and mining, one which emphasizes the role of women as caretakers of the environment and protectors of the earth and its natural resources for future generations.

NOTES

1. Angela John, "A Miner Struggle? Women's Protests in Welsh Mining History," *Llafur* 4, no. 1 (1984).
2. Winifred Mitchell, J. Gier personal interview, Australia, 1990.
3. Ibid.
4. William Schimdt, "Britain to Shut Most of Its Coal Mines," *New York Times*, October 14, 1992, C1.
5. Raphael Samuel et al., 5–8.
6. B. Davis, J. Gier Personal interview, Wales, UK 1992.
7. M. Donovan, personal interview with J. Gier, Wales, UK 1985.
8. S. Phillips, personal interview with J. Gier, Wales, UK.
9. Donovan 1985.
10. Karen Beckwith, "Struggle and Standing: Standing as Women in a Men's Movement," PONSACS Seminar Synopses, Weatherhead Center for International Affairs, Harvard University.
11. Ibid., 7.
12. Meeting of South Wales Women's Support Group, April 6, 1985, from personal notes of author.
13. Ibid.
14. Web site of Mines and Communities http://www.minesandcommunities. org/Action/press141.htm.

BIBLIOGRAPHY

Aiken, Katherine G. "'When I Realized How Close Communism Was to Kellogg, I Was Willing to Devote Day and Night': Anti-Communism, Women, Community Values, and the Bunker Hill Strike of 1960." *Labor History* 36 (Spring 1995): 165–86.

Alexander, Peter, and Rick Halperin, eds. *Racializing Class, Classifying Race: Labor and Difference in Britain, the U.S.A. and Africa.* New York: St. Martin's Press, 2000.

Allina-Pisano, Eric. "Resistance and the Social History of Africa." *Journal of Social History* 37, no. 1 (2003): 187.

Alsop, Rachel. *A Reversal of Fortunes? Women, Work and Change in East Germany.* New York: Berghahn Books, 2000.

Amanor, Kojo Sebastian. *Land, Labour and the Family in Southern Ghana: A Critique of Land Policy under Neo-Liberalisation.* Uppsala: Nordic African Institute, 2001.

Amutabi, Maurice, and Mary Lutta Mukhebi. "Women and Mining in Kenya: The Case of Mukibira Mines in Vihiga District." *Jenda: A Journal of Culture and African Women's Studies* 1, no. 2 (2000): 1–26.

Aulette, Judy, and Trudy Mills. "Something Old, Something New: Auxiliary Work in the 1983–1986 Copper Strike." *Feminist Studies* 14 (Summer 1988): 251–268.

Bacon, David. "World Labor Needs Independence and Solidarity." *Monthly Review* (July 2000): 84.

Bakewell, Peter. *Miners of the Red Mountain: Indian Labor in Potosí, 1545–1650.* Albuquerque: University of New Mexico Press, 1984.

Barrios de Chungara, Domitila. *Let Me Speak! Testimony of Domitila, a Woman of the Bolivian Mines.* New York: Monthly Review Press, 1978.

Basu, Amrita, ed. *The Challenge of Local Feminisms: Women's Movements in Global Perspective.* Boulder, CO: Westview Press, 1995.

Baylies, Carolyn, and Janet Bujra. *AIDS, Sexuality and Gender in Africa: Collective Strategies and Struggles in Tanzania and Zambia.* London: Routledge, 2000.

Beik, Mildred Allen. *The Miners of Windber: The Struggles of New Immigrants for Unionization, 1890s–1930s.* University Park, PN: The Pennsylvania State University Press, 1996.

Belshaw, John Douglas. *Colonization and Community: The Vancouver Island Coalfield and the Making of the British Columbian Working Class.* Montreal: McGill-Queen's University Press, 2002.

Benson, John. *British Coal-Miners in the Nineteenth Century: A Social History.* New York: Holmes & Meier, 1980.

Binns, Tony, and Etienne Nel. "The Village in a Game Park: Local Response to the Demise of Coal Mining in KwaZulu-Natal, South Africa." *Economic Geography* 79, no. 1 (2003): 41.

Boyle, Paul, and Keith Halfacree. *Migration and Gender in the Developed World.* London: Routledge, 1999.

Breitenbach, Esther, and Eleanor Gordon, eds. *Out of Bounds: Women in Scottish Society 1800–1945.* Edinburgh: University of Edinburgh Press, 1992.

Brown, Carolyn A. *"We Were All Slaves": African Miners, Culture and Resistance at the Enugu Government Colliery, Nigeria.* Portsmouth, NH: Heinemann, 2003.

Brown, Kathleen A. "The 'Savagely Fathered and Un-Mothered World' of the Communist Party, U.S.A.: Feminism, Maternalism, and 'Mother Bloor'." *Feminist Studies* 25, no. 3 (1999): 537–570.

Brown, W. Norman. *India, Pakistan, Ceylon.* Ithaca, NY: Cornell University, 1951.

Bury, Jeffrey. "Livelihoods in Transition: Transnational Gold Mining Operations and Local Change in Cajamarca, Peru." *The Geographical Journal* 170, no. 1 (2004): 78.

Cabrillo, Francisco. *The Economics of the Family and Family Policy.* Cheltenham, England: Edward Elgar, 1999.

Cain, P.J., and A.G. Hopkins. *British Imperialism: Innovation and Expansion, 1688–1914.* London: Longman, 1993.

Campbell, Bonnie, ed. *Regulating Mining in Africa: For Whose Benefit?* Uppsala: Nordic African Institute, 2004.

Cargill, Jack. "Empire and Opposition: The 'Salt of the Earth Strike.'" In *Labor in New Mexico: Unions, Strikes, and Social History since 1881,* ed. Robert Kern. Albuquerque: University of New Mexico Press, 1983, 183–267.

Chafetz, Janet Saltzman, and Anthony Gary Dworkin, *Female Revolt: Women's Movements in World and Historical Perspective.* Totowa, NJ: Rowman & Allanheld, 1986.

Chizuko, Ueno. "The Politics of Memory: Nation, Individual and Self." *History and Memory* 11, no. 2 (1999): 129–152.

"Great Britain." In *The Columbia Encyclopedia* 6th edn. edited by Paul Lagass. New York: Columbia University Press, 2004.

Conboy, Katie, Nadia Medina, and Sarah Stanbury, eds. *Writing on the Body: Female Embodiment and Feminist Theory.* New York: Columbia University Press, 1997.

Corbin, David Alan. *Life, Work, and Rebellion in the Coal Fields: The Southern West Virginia Miners 1880–1922.* Urbana: University of Illinois Press, 1981.

Crompton, Rosemary. *Women and Work in Modern Britain.* Oxford: Oxford University Press, 1997.

Denemark, Robert A., Jonathan Friedman, Barry K. Gills, and George Modelski, eds. *World System History: The Social Science of Long-Term Change.* London: Routledge, 2000.

Díaz, María Elena. *The Virgin, the King and the Royal Slaves of El Cobre: Negotiating Freedom in Colonial Cuba, 1670–1780.* Stanford: Stanford University Press, 2000.

Dixon, Ruth B. *Rural Women at Work: Strategies for Development in South Asia.* Baltimore: Resources for the Future, 1978.

Drew, Eileen, Ruth Emerek, and Evelyn Mahon, eds. *Women, Work, and the Family in Europe.* London: Routledge, 1998.

Dumett, Raymond E. *El Dorado in West Africa: The Gold-Mining Frontier, African Labor, and Colonial Capitalism in the Gold Coast, 1875–1900.* Athens, OH: Ohio University Press, 1998.

Eakin, Marshall C. *British Enterprise in Brazil: The St. John d'el Rey Mining Company and the Morro Velho Gold Mine, 1830–1960.* Durham: Duke University Press, 1989.

Edney, Matthew H. *Mapping an Empire: The Geographical Construction of British India, 1765–1843.* Chicago: University of Chicago Press, 1997.

Edwards, Louise P., and Mina Roces. *Tradition, Modernity and Globalisation*. St. Leonards, NSW: Allen & Unwin, 2000.

Emdad-Ul Haq, M. *Drugs in South Asia: From the Opium Trade to the Present Day*. Basingstoke: Macmillan, 2000.

Engel, Barbara Alpern, and Anastasia Posadskaya-Vanderbeck, eds. *A Revolution of Their Own: Voices of Women in Soviet History*. Boulder, CO: Westview Press, 1998.

Ewen, Lynda Ann. *Which Side Are You On? The Brookside Mine Strike in Harlan County, Kentucky, 1973–1974*. Chicago: Vanguard Books, 1979.

Farnsworth-Alvear, Ann. *Dulcinea in the Factory: Myths, Morals, Men and Women in Colombia's Industrial Experiment, 1905–1960*. Durham, NC: Duke University Press, 2000.

Fausto-Sterling, Anne. *Sexing the Body: Gender Politics and the Construction of Sexuality*. New York: Basic Books, 2000.

Fetherling, Douglas. *The Gold Crusades: A Social History of Gold Rushes, 1849–1929*. Toronto: University of Toronto Press, 1997.

Finn, Janet L. *Tracing the Veins: Of Copper, Culture, and Community from Butte to Chuquicamata*. Berkeley: University of California Press, 1998.

———. "Mining Men: Chile Exploration Company and the Politics of Copper, Culture, and Gender, 1921–1971." In *Gendered Modernities: Ethnographic Perspectives*, edited by Dorothy L. Hodgson. New York: Palgrave, 2001, 205–234.

Fleisher, Michael L. " 'War Is Good for Thieving!' The Symbiosis of Crime and Warfare among the Kuria of Tanzania." *Africa* 72, no. 1 (2002): 131.

Forestell, Nancy M. "The Miner's Wife: Working-Class Femininity in a Masculine Context, 1920–1950." In *Femininity and Masculinity in Canada*, edited by Kathryn McPherson, Cecilia Morgan, and Nancy M. Forestell. New York: Oxford, 1999, 139–157.

Foster, Gwendolyn Audrey. *Troping the Body: Gender, Etiquette, and Performance*. Carbondale, IL: Southern Illinois University Press, 2000.

Freese, Barbara. *Coal: A Human History*. New York: Penguin, 2003.

French, William E. *A Peaceful and Working People: Manners, Morals, and Class Formation in Northern Mexico*. Albuquerque: University of New Mexico Press, 1996.

Frey, Marsha, Joanne Schneider, Linda Frey, Marsha Frey, Joanne Schneider, and Linda Frey, eds. *Women in Western European History: A Select Chronological, Geographical, and Topical Bibliography, the Nineteenth and Twentieth Centuries*. Vol. 2. Westport, CT: Greenwood Press, 1984.

Ganguly, Šumit and Ted Greenwood, eds. *Mending Fences: Confidence- and Security-Building in South Asia*. Boulder, CO: Westview Press, 1996.

Garlick, Barbara, Suzanne Dixon, and Pauline Allen, eds. *Stereotypes of Women in Power: Historical Perspectives and Revisionist Views*. New York: Greenwood Press, 1992.

Geary, Dick. "Beer and Skittles? Workers and Culture in Early Twentieth-Century Germany." *The Australian Journal of Politics and History* 46, no. 3 (2000): 388.

Gezari, Janet. *Charlotte Bronte and Defensive Conduct: The Author and the Body at Risk*. Philadelphia: University of Pennsylvania Press, 1992.

Ghorayshi, Parvin and Claire Bélanger, eds. *Women, Work, and Gender Relations in Developing Countries: A Global Perspective*. Westport, CT: Greenwood Press, 1996.

Giesen, Carol A.B. *Coal Miners' Wives: Portraits of Endurance*. Lexington: University Press of Kentucky, 1995

Goldman, Minton F., and Karl W. Ryavec. *Revolution and Change in Central and Eastern Europe: Political, Economic, and Social Challenges*. Armonk, NY: M.E. Sharpe, 1997.

Gorn, Elliot J. *Mother Jones: The Most Dangerous Woman in America*. New York: Hill and Wang, 2001.

Goshal, Kumar. *The People of India*. New York: Sheridan House, 1944.

Gray, Marion W. *Productive Men, Reproductive Women: The Agrarian Household and the Emergence of Separate Spheres in the German Enlightenment*. New York: Berghahn Books, 2000.

Greaves, Thomas, and William Culver, eds. *Miners and Mining in the Americas*. Manchester, UK: Manchester University Press, 1985.

Green, Archie. *Only a Miner: Studies in Recorded Coal-Mining Songs*. Urbana: University of Illinois Press, 1972.

Green, Maia. "Trading on Inequality: Gender and the Drinks Trade in Southern Tanzania." *Africa* 69, no. 3 (1999): 404.

Griffiths, Percival. *The British Impact on India*. London: MacDonald, 1952.

Grusky, David B., ed. *Social Stratification: Class, Race, and Gender in Sociological Perspective*. Boulder, CO: Westview Press, 1994.

Hanawalt, Barbara A., Thomas Dublin, E. Patricia Tsurumi, and Louise A. Tilly. "Women's History in the New Millennium: Women, Work, and Family After Two Decades." *Journal of Women's History* 11, no. 3 (1999) (see entire volume).

Harper, Fowler V. *Problems of the Family*. Indianapolis: Bobbs-Merrill, 1952.

Hartley, Anthony. "O! What a Fall Was There: Reflections on the Decline of Britain." *The National Interest* (Spring 1994): 36.

Heineman, Elizabeth D. "Who's Mothers? Age and Generation in Women's History Generational Difference, War, and the Nazi Cult of Motherhood." *Journal of Women's History* 12, no. 4 (2001): 138–163.

Herbert, Eugenia W. *Red Gold of Africa: Copper in Precolonial History and Culture*. Madison: University of Wisconsin Press, 1984.

Higgins, Kathleen J. *"Licentious Liberty" in a Brazilian Gold-Mining Region: Slavery, Gender, and Social Control in Eighteenth-Century Sabara, Minas Gerais*. University Park, PN: Penn State University Press, 1999.

Hildebrand, George H., and Garth L. Mangum. *Capital and Labor in American Copper, 1845–1990: Linkages Between Product and Labor Markets*. Cambridge, MA: Harvard University Press, 1992.

Hilson, Gavin. "The Environmental Impact of Small-Scale Gold Mining in Ghana: Identifying Problems and Possible Solutions." *The Geographical Journal* 168, no. 1 (2002): 57.

Hinde, John R. " 'Stout Ladies and Amazons': Women in the British Columbia Coal-Mining Community of Ladysmith, 1912–14." *BC Studies* 114 (1997): 33–57.

Hoberman, Louisa Schell. *Mexico's Merchant Elite, 1590–1660*. Durham: Duke University Press, 1991.

Hobson, J.A. *Imperialism: A Study*. London: George Allen & Unwin, 1905.

Huginnie, A. Yvette. "A New Hero Comes to Town: The Anglo Mining Engineer and 'Mexican Labor' as Contested Terrain in Southeastern Arizona, 1880–1920." *New Mexico Historical Review* 69, no. 4 (1994): 323–344.

Hyde, Charles K. *Copper for America: The United States Copper Industry from Colonial Times to the 1990s*. Tucson: University of Arizona Press, 1998.

Hyndman, David. *Ancestral Rain Forests and the Mountain of Gold: Indigenous Peoples and Mining in New Guinea*. Boulder, CO: Westview Press, 1994.

Imam, Ayesha. "The Dynamics of WINning: An Analysis of Women in Nigeria (WIN)." In *Feminist Genealogies, Colonial Legacies, Democratic Futures*, edited by

M. Jacqui Alexander and Chandra Mohanty. New York: Routledge, 1997, 280–307.

Iwahori, Yoko. "Work and Life at a Coal Mine: the Life History of a Woman Miner." *Gender and Japanese History,* vol. 2. Osaka: Osaka University Press, 1999.

James, Ronald M. and C. Elizabeth Raymond, ed. *Comstock Women: The Making of a Mining Community.* Reno: University of Nevada Press, 1998.

Jameson, Elizabeth. *All That Glitters: Class, Conflict and Community in Cripple Creek.* Urbana: University of Illinois Press, 1998.

Jameson, Elizabeth. "Imperfect Unions: Class and Gender in Cripple Creek, 1894–1904." In *Class, Sex, and the Woman Worker,* edited by Milton Cantor and Bruce Laurie. Westport, CT: Greenwood, 1977, 245–63.

Johnson, Susan. *Roaring Camp: The Social World of the California Gold Rush.* New York: WW Norton & Co., 2000.

Kahne, Hilda and Janet Z. Giele, eds. *Women's Work and Women's Lives: The Continuing Struggle Worldwide.* Boulder, CO: Westview Press, 1992.

Keck, Jennifer and Mary Powell. "Working at Inco: Women in a Downsizing Male Industry." In *Changing Lives: Women in Northern Ontario,* edited by Marg Kechnie and Marge Reitsma-Street. Toronto: Dundurn Press, 1996, 147–161.

King, Al. *Red Bait! Struggles of a Mine Mill Local.* Vancouver: Kingbird Publishing, 1998.

Kingsolver, Barbara. *Holding the Line: Women in the Great Arizona Mine Strike of 1983.* Ithaca, NY: Cornell University Press, 1989 and 1996.

Klubock, Thomas Miller. *Contested Communities: Class, Gender, and Politics in Chile's El Teniente Copper Mine, 1904–1951.* Durham: Duke University Press, 1998.

Klubock, Thomas Miller. "Working-Class Masculinity, Middle-Class Morality and Labor Politics in the Chilean Copper Mines." *Journal of Social History* 30, no. 2 (1996): 435–463.

Kumar, Nagesh. *Multinational Enterprises in India: Technical Distribution, Characteristics and Performance.* London: Routledge, 1990.

Kuyek, Joan Newman. "Overburdened: Understanding the Impacts of Mineral Extraction on Women's Health in Mining Communities." *Canadian Woman Studies* 23, no. 1 (2003): 121–123.

Lapchick, Richard E., and Stephanie Urdang. *Oppression and Resistance: The Struggle of Women in Southern Africa.* Westport, CT: Greenwood Press, 1982.

Launius, Michael A. "The State and Industrial Labor in South Korea." *Bulletin of Concerned Asian Scholars* 16, no. 4 (1984): 2–11.

Lawrence, D.H. *Women in Love.* Edited by David Bradshaw. Oxford, England: Oxford University Press, 1998.

Letwin, Daniel. *The Challenge of Interracial Unionism: Alabama Coal Miners, 1878–1921.* Chapel Hill, NC: University of North Carolina Press, 1998.

Lingenfelter, Richard E., ed. *The Mining West: A Bibliography & Guide to the History & Literature of Mining in the American & Canadian West.* Vols. 1 and 2. Lanham, Maryland: Scarecrow Press, 2003.

Łobodzińska, Barbara, ed. *Family, Women, and Employment in Central-Eastern Europe,* Westport, CT: Greenwood Press, 1995.

Lockwood, Matthew. "Structure and Behavior in the Social Demography of Africa." *Population and Development Review* 21, no. 1 (1995): 32.

Lombardi, Marilyn May. *The Body and the Song: Elizabeth Bishop's Poetics.* Carbondale, IL: Southern Illinois University Press, 1995.

Long, Kristi S. *Women in Poland's Solidarity Movement Women in Poland's Solidarity Movement.* Boulder, CO: Westview Press, 1996.

Long, Priscilla. *Where the Sun Never Shines: A History of America's Bloody Coal Industry.* New York: Paragon House, 1989.

Longhurst, Robyn. *Geography and the Body: Exploring Fluid Boundaries.* London: Routledge, 2001.

Lynch, Martin. *Mining in World History.* London: Reaktion Books, 2002

Madhuku, Lovemore. "The Right to Strike in Southern Africa." *International Labour Review* 136, no. 4 (1997): 509.

Maggard, S.W. "Women's Participation in the Brookside Coal Strike: Militance, Class and Gender in Appalachia." *Frontiers* 9, no. 3 (1987): 16–21.

Magubane, Zine. "Mines, Minstrels, and Masculinity: Race, Class, Gender, and the Formation of the South African Working Class, 1870–1900." *The Journal of Men's Studies* 10, no. 3 (2002): 271.

Mallon, Florencia. *In Defense of Community in Peru's Central Highlands: Peasant Struggle and Capitalist Transition, 1860–1940.* Princeton: Princeton University Press, 1984.

Malos, Ellen, ed. *The Politics of Housework.* Cheltenham, England: New Clarion Press, 1995.

Mathias, Regine. "Female Labour in the Japanese Coal Mining Industry." In *Japanese Women Working*, edited by Janet Hunter. London: Routledge, 1993.

Maynes, Mary Jo, and Ann Waltner. "Childhood, Youth, and the Female Life Cycle Women's Life-Cycle Transitions in a World-Historical Perspective: Comparing Marriage in China and Europe." *Journal of Women's History* 12, no. 4 (2001): 11–21.

Mayo, John, Simon Collier, and Charles Lambert, eds. *Mining in Chile's Norte Chico: Journal of Charles Lambert, 1825–1830.* Boulder, CO: Perseus, 1998.

Mba, Nina. *Nigerian Women Mobilized: Women's Political Activity in Southern Nigeria 1900–1965*, vol. 48. Berkeley: Institution for International Studies, 1982.

McCann, Carole R., and Seung-Kyung Kim. *Feminist Theory Reader: Local and Global Perspectives.* New York: Routledge, 2003.

Mcleod, John. *The History of India.* Westport, CT: Greenwood Press, 2002.

Mercier, Laurie. *Anaconda: Labor, Culture, and Community in Montana's Smelter City.* Urbana: University of Illinois Press, 2001.

Misra, Maria. *Business, Race, and Politics in British India, C.1850–1960.* Oxford: Oxford University, 1999.

Moghadam, Valentine M. *Democratic Reform and the Position of Women in Transitional Economies.* Oxford: Oxford University, 1993.

Moore, Marat. *Mother Jones, Woman Organizer, and Her Relations with Miners' Wives, Working Women, and the Suffrage Movement.* Boston: South End Press, 1976.

———. *Women in the Mines: Stories of Life and Work.* New York: Twayne Publishers, 1996.

Mouat, Jeremy. *Metal Mining in Canada, 1840–1950.* Ottawa: National Museum of Science and Technology, 2000.

Mouat, Jeremy. *Roaring Days: Rossland's Mines and the History of British Columbia.* Vancouver: UBC Press, 1995.

Moynihan, Ruth B., Susan Armitage, and Christiane Fischer Dichamp. *So Much to Be Done: Women Settlers on the Mining and Ranching Frontier.* Lincoln: University of Nebraska Press, 1990.

Muise, Delphin A., and Robert G. McIntosh. *Coal Mining in Canada: A Historical and Comparative Overview.* Ottawa: National Museum of Science & Technology, 1996.

Murphy, Mary. *Mining Cultures: Men, Women, and Leisure in Butte, 1914–1941.* Urbana: University of Illinois Press, 1997.

Nash, June. *We Eat the Mines and the Mines Eat Us: Dependency and Exploitation in Bolivian Tin Mines.* New York: Columbia University Press, 1979.

Nevin, Tom. "South Africa's Booming Sex Industry." *African Business* (December 1998): 15.

O'Neal, Eugenia. *From the Field to the Legislature: A History of Women in the Virgin Islands.* Westport, CT: Greenwood Press, 2001.

O'Neill, Colleen. "Domesticity Deployed: Gender, Race, and the Construction of Class Struggle in the Bisbee Deportation," *Labor History* 34, nos. 2–3 (1993): 256–273.

Palladino, Grace. *Another Civil War: Labor, Capital, and the State in the Anthracite Regions of Pennsylvania 1840–1868.* Urbana: University of Illinois Press, 1990.

Papanikolas, Zeese. *Buried Unsung: Louis Tikas and the Ludlow Massacre.* Salt Lake: University of Utah Press, 1982.

Parkins, Wendy, ed. *Fashioning the Body Politic: Dress, Gender, Citizenship.* New York: Berg, 2002.

Parpart, Jane. *Labor and Capital on the African Copperbelt.* Philadelphia: Temple University Press, 1983.

Paster, Gail Kern. *The Body Embarrassed: Drama and the Disciplines of Shame in Early Modern England.* Ithaca, NY: Cornell University Press, 1993.

Paxton, Nancy L. *Writing under the Raj: Gender, Race, and Rape in the British Colonial Imagination, 1830–1947.* New Brunswick, NJ: Rutgers University Press, 1999.

Peck, Gunther. *Reinventing Free Labor: Padrones and Immigrant Workers in the North American West, 1880–1930.* Cambridge: Cambridge University Press, 2000.

Penfield, Steven. " 'Have You No Manhood in You?' Gender and Class in the Cape Breton Coal Towns, 1920–1926." In *Gender and History in Canada*, edited by Joy Parr and Mark Rosenfeld. Toronto: Copp Clark Ltd., 1996, 270–293.

Philip, Kavita. *Civilizing Natures: Race, Resources, and Modernity in Colonial South India.* New Brunswick, NJ: Rutgers University Press, 2004.

Porsild, Charlene. *Gamblers and Dreamers: Women, Men, and Community in the Klondike.* Vancouver: UBC Press, 1998.

Prieto, Carlos. *Mining in the New World.* New York: McGraw-Hill, 1973.

Reinharz, Shulamit, and Lynn Davidman. *Feminist Methods in Social Research.* New York: Oxford University Press, 1992.

Reinventing Revolution: New Social Movements and the Socialist Tradition in India. Armonk, NY: M.E. Sharpe, 1993.

Rhodes, Linda. "Partners on the Periphery: Personal Ambiguity and Unpaid Labour in the Australian Mining Industry." *Journal of Australian Studies*, no. 76 (2003): 149–158.

Richman, Barry M. *Industrial Society in Communist China: A Firsthand Study of Chinese Economic Development and Management, with Significant Comparisons with Industry in India, the U.S.S.R., Japan, and the United States.* New York: Random House, 1969.

Robertson, Claire C. "Contemporary Issues Age, Gender, and Knowledge Revolutions in Africa and the United States." *Journal of Women's History* 12, no. 4 (2001): 174–183.

Robinson, David, and Derek Wilkinson. "Sense of Community in a Remote Mining Town: Validating a Neighborhood Cohesion Scale." *American Journal of Community Psychology* 23, no. 1 (1995): 137.

Rustow, Dankwart A. *The Politics of Compromise: A Study of Parties and Cabinet Government in Sweden.* Princeton, NJ: Princeton University Press, 1955.

Sachs, Carolyn E. *Gendered Fields: Rural Women, Agriculture, and Environment.* Boulder, CO: Westview Press, 1996.

Salm, Steven J., and Toyin Falola. *Culture and Customs of Ghana.* Westport, CT: Greenwood Press, 2002.

Saul, John S., and Colin Leys. "Sub-Saharan Africa in Global Capitalism." *Monthly Review* (July/August 1999): 13.

Savage, Lon. *Thunder in the Mountains: The West Virginia Mine War, 1920–1921.* Pittsburgh: University of Pittsburgh Press, 1990.

Schofield, Ann. "An 'Army of Amazons': The Language of Protest in a Kansas Mining Community, 1921–1922." *American Quarterly* 37 (Winter 1985): 686–701.

Seager, Allen, and Adele Perry. "Mining the Connections: Class, Ethnicity, and Gender in Nanaimo, British Columbia, 1891." *Histoire Sociale/Social History* 30, no. 59 (1997): 55–76.

Selden, Mark. "An Interview with Dev Nathan: the Naxalite Legacy and the Political Economy of Contemporary India." *Bulletin of Concerned Asian Scholars* 20, no. 2 (1988): 24–41.

Sharma, Shailja. "Citizens of the Empire: Revisionist History and the Social Imaginary in Gandhi." *Velvet Light Trap,* no. 35 (1995): 61–68.

Shifflett, Crandell A. *Coal Towns: Life, Work, and Culture in Company Towns of Southern Appalachia, 1880–1960.* Knoxville: University of Tennessee Press, 1991.

Shin, Donggyun. "Gender and Industry Differences in Employment Cyclicality: Evidence Over the Postwar Period." *Economic Inquiry* 38, no. 4 (2000): 641–650.

Shogan, Robert. *The Battle of Blair Mountain: The Story of America's Largest Labor Uprising.* Boulder, Co: Westview Press, 2004.

Shubert, Adrian. *The Road to Revolution in Spain: The Coal Miners of Asturias, 1860–1934.* Urbana: University of Illinois Press, 1987.

Siegelbaum, Lewis H., and Daniel J. Walkowitz. *Workers of the Donbass Speak: Survival and Identity in the New Ukraine, 1989–1992.* Albany: State University of New York, 1995.

Silver, Andrew. " 'Unnatural Unions': Picturesque Travel, Sexual Politics, and Working-Class Representation in 'A Night under Ground' and 'Life in the Iron-Mills.' " *Legacy: A Journal of American Women Writers* 20, no. 1–2 (2003): 94.

Simonton, Deborah. *A History of European Women's Work: 1700 to the Present.* London: Routledge, 1998.

Smil, Vaclav. *Energy in World History.* Boulder, CO: Westview Press, 1994.

Smith, Bonnie G., ed. *Global Feminisms Since 1945.* London: Routledge, 2000.

Smith, W. Donald. "The 1932 Aso Coal Strike: Korean-Japanese Solidarity and Conflict." *Korean Studies* 20 (1996): 94–122.

Solski, Mike, and John Smaller. *Mine Mill: The History of the International Union of Mine, Mill and Smelter Workers in Canada since 1895.* Ottawa: Steelrail Publishing, 1984.

Spencer, Elaine Glovka. *Management and Labor in Imperial Germany: Ruhr Industrialists as Employers, 1896–1914.* New Brunswick, NJ: Rutgers University Press, 1984.

Steedman, Mercedes, Peter Suschnigg, and Dieter K. Buse, eds. *Hard Lessons: The Mine Mill Union in the Canadian Labour Movement.* Toronto: Dundurn Press, 1995.

Stichter, Sharon B., and Jane L. Parpart, eds. *Patriarchy and Class: African Women in the Home and the Workforce*. Boulder, CO: Westview Press, 1988.

Tandeter, Enrique. *Coercion & Market: Silver Mining in Colonial Potosí 1692–1826*. Albuquerque: University of New Mexico Press, 1993.

Temple, John. *Mining: An International History*. New York: Praeger Publishers, 1972.

Tooley, T. Hunt. *Upper Silesia and the Eastern Border, 1918–1922 Upper Silesia and the Eastern Border, 1918–1922*. Lincoln, NE: University of Nebraska Press, 1997.

Turner, Terisa, and M.O. Oshare. "Women's Uprisings Against the Nigerian Oil Industry." In *Arise! Ye Mighty People!: Gender, Class & Race in Popular Struggles*, edited by Terisa Turner with Bryan Ferguson. Trenton: Africa World, 1994.

Tsurumi, E. Patricia. "Feminism and Anarchism in Japan: Takamure Itsue, 1894–1964." *Bulletin of Concerned Asian Scholars* 17, no. 2 (1985): 2–19.

Uno, Kathleen S. *Passages to Modernity: Motherhood, Childhood, and Social Reform in Early Twentieth Century Japan*. Honolulu, HI: University of Hawaii Press, 1999.

Vakil, C.N. *Economic Consequences of Divided India: A Study of the Economy in India and Pakistan*. 1st edn. Bombay: Vora, 1950.

Varikas, Eleni. "Gender, Experience and Subjectivity: the Tilly—Scott Disagreement." *New Left Review*, no. 211 (1995): 89–104.

Vickery, Kenneth P. *Black and White in Southern Zambia: The Tonga Plateau Economy and British Imperialism, 1890–1939*. New York: Greenwood Press, 1986.

Weiner, Elaine. "Assessing the Implications of Political and Economic Reform in the Post-Socialist Era: The Case of Czech and Slovak Women." *East European Quarterly* 31, no. 4 (1998): 473–491.

Wesseling, H.L. *Imperialism and Colonialism Essays on the History of European Expansion*. Westport, CT: Greenwood Press, 1997.

Wieck, Edward A. *The American Miners' Association: A Record of the Origin of Coal Miners' Unions in the United States*. New York: Russell Sage Foundation, 1940.

Wierling, Dorothee. "On Historical and Historiographical Relationships." In *The History of Everyday Life: Reconstructing Historical Experiences and Ways of Life*, edited by Alf Ludtke. Princeton, NJ: Princeton University Press, 1995, 149–163.

Wilson, Francis. "Minerals and Migrants: How the Mining Industry Has Shaped South Africa." *Daedalus* 130, no. 1 (2001): 99.

Wilson, Michael, and Deborah Rosenfelt. *Salt of the Earth*. New York: The Feminist Press at the City University of New York, 1978.

Women in Western European History: A Select Chronological, Geographical, and Topical Bibliography. Vol. 1. Westport, CT: Greenwood Press, 1982.

Wright, Tim. *Coal Mining in China's Economy and Society 1895–1937*. Cambridge: Cambridge University Press, 1984.

Yarrow, Michael. "The Gender-Specific Consciousness of Appalachian Coal Miners: Structure and Change." In *Bringing Class Back In: Contemporary and Historical Perspectives*, edited by Scott G. McNall, Rhonda Levine, and Rick Fantasia. Boulder: Westview Press, 1991, 285–310.

Yutaka, Nishinarita. "The Coal Mining Industry." In *Technology, Change, and Female Labour in Japan*, edited by Nakamura Masanori. Tokyo: United Nations University Press, 1994, 59–96.

Zanjani, Sally. *A Mine of Her Own: Women Prospectors in the American West, 1850–1950*. Lincoln: University of Nebraska Press, 1997.

Zantop, Susanne. *Colonial Fantasies: Conquest, Family, and Nation in Precolonial Germany, 1770–1870*. Durham, NC: Duke University Press, 1997.

Zellner, Sara L. "Condom Use and the Accuracy of AIDS Knowledge in Cote d'Ivoire." *International Family Planning Perspectives* 29, no. 1 (2003): 41.

Zhu, Liping, and Rose Estep Fosha, eds. *Ethnic Oasis: The Chinese in the Black Hills.* Pierre: South Dakota State Historical Society Press, 2004.

Zhu, Liping. *A Chinaman's Chance: The Chinese on the Rocky Mountain Mining Frontier.* Niwot, CO: University Press of Colorado, 1997.

CONTRIBUTORS

PASCALE ABSI is an anthropologist and a researcher at L'Institut de Recherche pour le Développement in Paris, which focuses on the relationship between humans and the environment. She received her doctorate from the l'Ecole des Hautes Etudes en Sciences Sociales (Paris) and is the author of *Ministers for the Devil: The Work and its Representations in the Mines of Potosí, Bolivia* (Harmattan, 2003). She collaborated with Philippe Crnogorac on the film *The woman, the mine and the devil* (BFC Production, 1999).

KWABENA O. AKURANG-PARRY is Assistant Professor of African History and World History at Shippensburg University, Pennsylvania. His articles have appeared in *Slavery and Abolition, African Economic History, International Journal of African Historical Studies, History in Africa, Transactions of the Historical Society of Ghana, Left History, Ghana Studies,* and the *Journal of Cultural Studies.* He is currently completing a book on slavery and colonial rule in Ghana. His poems have appeared in *Okike* and *Ufahamu.*

ELLEN BAKER is Associate Professor of History at Columbia University, where she teaches courses on women's and gender history, labor, social movements, and the American West. Her book, *Salt of the Earth: Working-Class New Mexicans in the Cold War,* will be published in 2006 by the University of North Carolina Press.

EVA BLOMBERG is Senior Lecturer at the Department of Social and Behavioural Sciences, Mälardalen University. Her publications deal with issues of gender and masculinities in the mining industry, including *Samhällets fiende: Stripakonflikten 1925–27* (The Enemies of Society, Stockholm, 1993), and *Män i mörker. Arbetsgivare, reformister och syndikalister. Politik och identitet i svensk gruvindustri 1910–1940* (Men in Darkness. Employers, Reformists and Revolutionary Syndicalists. Politics and Identity in the Swedish Mining Industry 1910–1940, Stockholm, 1995).

ANTHONY DESTEFANIS studies the cultural politics of military strikebreaking. He defended his dissertation, "Guarding Capital: Soldier Strikebreakers on the Long Road to the Ludlow Massacre," in the history department at the College of William and Mary in October 2004. He currently lives in Florida.

MARÍA ELENA DÍAZ is Associate Professor of Colonial Latin American and Caribbean History at the University of California Santa Cruz. She is the author of *The Virgin, the King, and the Royal Slaves of El Cobre: Negotiating Freedom in Colonial Cuba, 1670–1780* (Stanford University Press, 2004), the first of a projected trilogy about the Cuban mining town of El Cobre. She is currently working on the second volume, which moves forward the story of this important community into the modern mining age. The third volume will explore issues of colonialism, slavery, gender and ethnicity in the seventeenth century.

JACLYN J. GIER is Associate Professor/Director of European Studies in the University of Pennsylvania State System of Higher Education, SRU. She received a Maria Sybilla Merian International Fellowship to the Universit Erfurt, 2001, and was named a DAAD Fellow in 2002. The British Council, the Australian Research Council, and the Woodrow Wilson Foundation have supported her scholarly work. She has published in *History Workshop Journal, Frontiers,, Antipode,* and in *Women and Oral History* (University of Nebraska Press, 2001) and is the author of the forthcoming "The Last Days of Remembering: Gender and Generation in the British Coalfields, 1890–2005."

CAMILLE GUERIN-GONZALES is Professor of History and Chair of Chican@ and Latin@ Studies at the University of Wisconsin-Madison. She is the author of the forthcoming *How Black is Coal?: Appalachia, South Wales, and the American Southwest, 1890–1947,* and, *Mexican Workers and American Dreams: Immigration, Repatriation, and California Farm Labor, 1900–1939* (Rutgers, 1994). She is a *manita* from northern New Mexico.

ROSEMARY JONES has been a Fellow at the Center for Celtic Studies, University of Wales, Abersytwyth and the National Historical Monuments Commission for Wales. She has written widely on women in Welsh mining areas, and has contributed to several volumes on European and Welsh women's history. She is currently completing a volume on the social history of women in eighteenth and nineteenth century British mining communities.

YONG-SOOK JUNG is a Ph.D. student in History at the Ruhr University Bochum in Germany. She is currently working on the social history of the working-class family in the Ruhr area since the fall of the German coal mining industry in the late twentieth century.

JENNIFER KECK was an Associate Professor of Social Work in Laurentian University of Sudbury, Ontario. She was a leading activist until her death from breast cancer in 2002, at the age of 48. Well-known in the women's community, Jennifer was asked by women miners to document their experience, which led to the study she and Mary Powell undertook of women who first entered mining in the 1970s.

KUNTALA LAHIRI-DUTT is a Research Fellow at the Resource Management in the Asia Pacific Program of the Research School of Pacific and Asian Studies, The Australian National University. She focuses on gender, marginal and ethnic identities, and gender issues in formal and informal mining as they are practiced in South Asian countries, particularly India. Her publications include *In Search of a Homeland: Anglo-Indians and McCluskiegunge* (Calcutta 1990) and "From Gin Girls to scavengers: Women in the Raniganj Coalbelt," *Economic and Political Weekly* (2000).

LAURIE MERCIER is Associate Professor of History at Washington State University, Vancouver. She is the author of *Anaconda: Labor, Community, and Culture in Montana's Smelter City* (University of Illinois Press 2001), which received the Clark Spence Mining History Award in 2004. She has published numerous articles about labor, women's and public history and is currently completing a book about women's oral narratives.

REIKO MIYAUCHI was Associate Professor of Sociology at Sapporo International University. As a photojournalist, she worked many years to document the lives of women and men miners in Hokkaido through oral history interviews and visual representations. Her published works include *Coal Mines—Memories of Their Rise and*

Fall (Hokkaido 2003), *Women in Hokkaido* (1986), and *Women of the Sapporo Merchant Class* (1982). She died of pancreatic cancer on November 9, 2004, in Sapporo, Japan. She was 59 years old.

MARY POWELL is Associate Professor of Political Science, Laurentian University, Sudbury, Ontario. She worked closely with Jennifer Keck on a study of women who first entered mining in the 1970s. Together, they have published book chapters and articles in women's studies journals, such as *Atlantis*.

SACHIKO SONE is a lecturer in the Japanese program in Asian Studies, University of Western Australia. Her academic interest is cross-cultural studies. Her recent articles include "Exploitation or Expectation? Child Labour in Japan's Coalmines before the World War II," *Critical Asian Studies* (2003).

MERCEDES STEEDMAN is Associate Professor in Sociology and Coordinator of the Labour and Trade Union Studies programme at Laurentian University, in Sudbury, Ontario. She is coeditor of *Whose National Security? The Canadian State and the Creation of Enemies* (Toronto, 2000) and *Hard Lessons of Labour: The Mine Mill Centennial Conference* (Dundurn Press, 1995). She is currently working with the Mine Mill union on a book about a recent Mine Mill/Canadian Autoworkers Union strike at Falconbridge Nickel in which she took an active role.

BONNIE STEPENOFF is Professor of History at Southeast Missouri State University in Cape Girardeau. She has published two books and numerous articles in labor history and environmental history. Her most recent book, *Thad Snow: A Life of Social Reform in the Missouri Bootheel* was published in 2003 by the University of Missouri Press.

KAYOKO YOSHIDA is Professor of English and Dean of Hokusei Gakuen University Junior College in Sapporo, Japan. Her article, "From Atomic Fragments to Memories of the Trinity Bomb: A Bridge of Oral History over the Pacific," published in *The Oral History Review* 30 (Fall 2003), received the Honorable Mention of the 2004 Oral History Association's Best Article Award.

INDEX

(Please note that a page number followed by *n* indicates an endnote; *t* indicates a table; and *f* indicates a figure.)